THE NEW WORLD OF TRAVEL 1988 BY ARTHUR FROMMER

The New World of Travel 1988 by Arthur Frommer

A FROMMER BOOK

PUBLISHED BY

PRENTICE HALL PRESS

NEW YORK

Published by Prentice Hall Press
A Division of Simon & Schuster, Inc.
Gulf + Western Building
One Gulf + Western Plaza
New York, NY 10023

Book Design by Claudia Lebenthal

ISBN 0-13-048886-0

Manufactured in the United States of America

Contents

An Introduction to Arthur
Frommer's New World of Travel 1988

Page
xiii

I What's Wrong with Travel—and What We Can Do About It

1. *The Scandal of American Vacation Time*   2
   While other developed nations provide their citizens with five weeks and more of paid leave, we squeeze out a meager two—or two-and-a-half

2. *Ethical Travel: Does Tourism Cause More Harm Than Good?*   6
   Rethinking the "rights" and "wrongs" of our vacation trips

3. *A Plea for "Social Tourism"*   10
   Isn't it time we brought the benefits of travel to *all* our citizens?

4. *Some Particular Gripes About U.S. Airports and Airlines*   14
   The trouble with travel: cafeterias, cancellations, and cabs

II Alternative Travel—a New Kind of Vacation That Improves Upon the Stale and Tired Variety

5. *Offbeat Vacations, I: People, Politics, and Personal Adventure*   18
   Thousands are turning to new varieties of travel that lend content and meaning to the standard, listless tour: people-to-people travel, political travel, integrated travel, adventure travel

6. *Offbeat Vacations, II: Beaches, Biology, and Brainwork*   22
   New modes of travel that differ sharply from the usual variety: beachfront travel, biological travel, study travel, congress travel

7. *Offbeat Vacations, III: Working, Riding, and Camping Together*   26
   Four more new modes of travel that differ from the tired variety: solidarity travel, bicycle travel, workcamp travel, cooperative camping

8. *Offbeat Vacations, IV: From the Farm to the Foam-rubber Bus*   30
   New and better forms of travel: farm/ranch travel, special-interest travel, homestays travel, foam-rubber bus travel

Contents

9. *Trekking as a Cheap and Fulfilling Mode of Travel*   34
   Organized walks along the lower slopes of the Himalayas, Andes, and Alps

10. *Tented Safaris: In the Footsteps of Meryl and Robert*   40
    African camping tours offer an improved, new approach to the world of wildlife

11. *Meet the Political Travel Agent, a New Breed*   44
    Their trips and tours are sharply different from the usual variety—profound and
    stimulating

12. *Cooperative Camping with 14 Others in a Fully Equipped Van*   48
    The valuable new travel mode that no one properly describes

13. *A Search for Reliable Sources of Bicycle Tours*   52
    A dozen companies that take you biking to all parts of the world

14. *The Bold New World of the Feminist Tour Operator*   56
    Organized travel for women only

15. *A Selfless Vacation, the Jimmy Carter Way*   60
    From two to four weeks with Habitat for Humanity or the Friendship Force

III Alternative "Resorts"—the Holiday Camps and Communities That Can Change Your Life

16. *On the Road to Utopia, I*   64
    At "intentional communities" across the U.S.A., short stays and visits are a
    mind-expanding experience

17. *On the Road to Utopia, II*   68
    The unique vacation: a weekend or weeklong stay on the grounds of a utopian
    community

18. *On the Trail of Eternal Youth, at a European Spa*   70
    Can 200 million Europeans be wrong? Or is there validity to the treatments at
    European health resorts?

19. *America on $25 a Day, Via the Yoga Route*   74
    Remarkable vacations, rewarding and cheap, at ashrams clustered near both coasts

20. *Vacationing, for a Change, at a Whole-Grain Resort*   78
    At macrobiotic centers clustered on both coasts, the cuisine is as soothing as the
    setting

Contents

21. *A Visit to the World of "Small Is Beautiful"*   80
    At the Centre for Alternative Technology in Wales, the most basic assumptions of the Industrial West are attacked and derided

22. *Vacationing at a "Personal Growth Center," I: Esalen*   84
    At Esalen near Big Sur, on the California coast, human transformation is the goal of a holiday stay

23. *Vacationing at a "Personal Growth Center," II: East Coast and West*   88
    The many offshoots of Esalen explore the human potential, in a thoroughly delightful way

IV Enlarging Your Mind by Using Vacations to Study: Short-Term Educational Trips

24. *A Yank at Oxford—or Cambridge (Summer-style)*   94
    Short summer study courses at the great British universities offer an unusual supplement to the standard English holiday

25. *Meet the Danish "Folk High School," and Never Be the Same Again*   98
    A winter week or two at a residential college for adults

26. *Low-Cost Language Schools Abroad*   102
    The careful use of travel to acquire fluency in a foreign tongue

27. *A Nonprofit Approach to the Group Study Tour*   106
    Germany's Organization for International Contacts has created an unusually rewarding form of purposive travel

28. *The Love Boat and the Learn Boat*   110
    Expedition cruising brings education to the high seas

V Bargain Air Fares: Does Only the Chump Pay Full Price?

29. *Meet the Air Fare "Bucket Shop"*   116
    They've moved here from Britain, a remarkable source of discount tickets

30. *More About Discount Travel Agencies ("Bucket Shops")*   120
    Some additional reflections and further specifics on travel's most significant recent development

31. *Unscrambling the Domestic Air Fares Mess*   124
    By following several little-known approaches to the purchase of air tickets, you can heighten the chances of paying a lower fare

32. *Unscrambling the Transatlantic Air Fares*   130
    A mystifying assortment of prices and possibilities now confronts the would-be traveller to Europe—and I'm gonna explain it all!

33. *Flying for Free (or for Peanuts) as an On-Board Air Courier*   134
    By permitting your baggage allowance to be used for freight, you fly at the cheapest rates in travel today

VI The Glut in Cruise Ships—Bargains and Values Afloat

34. *Under-the-Counter Discounts—the Latest Craze in Cruising*   140
    Does only a "chump" pay full price for a cruise? Yup

35. *Good News for Devotees of the Meandering Cruise by Freighter*   144
    After declining to a dangerous level of capacity, the passenger-carrying freighter is on the rise again

36. *Choosing the Right Cruise Ship for Your Sea-Going Vacation*   148
    Each of the great liners has a distinct personality—and if it doesn't match yours, watch out!

37. *The Trend to the Tiny Ship*   152
    Increasing numbers of vacationers are opting for intimate vessels able to take them to secluded places

VII The Cheapest of Everything: New Ways to Save Money While Travelling on Land

38. *The Travel "Cheapstakes"*   158
    Low-cost record holders among travel firms and travel products

39. *My Own "Little Black Book" of Cheap Destinations*   162
    Six holiday areas with prices in pennies and values galore

40. *America's Best-Kept Travel Secrets*   166
    Most of us are still unaware of "Entertainment Books," the "second night free," and "poor man's spas"

Contents

41. *Learn to Bargain in the Marketplace of Hotels* 170
    By ridding yourself of pompous dignity, you can save thousands of dollars in the years ahead

VIII Just-Plain Motoring Through the U.S.A.: The Way to Do It, and Some Recommended Itineraries

42. *In America, Motoring Vacations Are Better Than Ever!* 176
    This summer, we celebrate 25 years of remarkable improvements to our lives on the road

43. *Surviving the Summer Motoring Crush: New Mexico, Missouri, Minnesota, the Two Coasts of Florida* 180
    Four motoring itineraries that take you where the tourists aren't

44. *Weekends of History, by Self-Drive Car* 186
    Five American regions crammed with historic sights, all within an hour of a key hub city

IX Travel Opportunities for the Older American—What's Helpful, What Isn't

45. *Our Greatest Retirement Bargains—Extended-Stays Overseas* 194
    A month in Spain for $765, including air fare, and similar trips to Yugoslavia and Australia

46. *The Battle for the Older American Traveller, I* 198
    Five major travel firms are following a unique approach in their sale of vacations to seniors

47. *The Battle for the Older American Traveller, II* 202
    Appraising the five specialist firms and their five differing approaches

48. *A Guide to Mature Travel, I* 206
    At the age of 56, I follow 12 new approaches to vacations and tours that improve upon my travels of earlier years

49. *A Guide to Mature Travel, II* 210
    Rules 7 through 12 of painfully acquired vacation wisdom

Contents

50. *Travelling Alone in the Mature Years—Plight or Opportunity?*   214
    The problem is not confined to women; the question should be rephrased to ask: "Can a single woman, or a single man, travel enjoyably alone? And can this be done at a mature age?"

51. *Some Travel Options—Good, Bad, and Indifferent—for the Mature American*   220
    As the travel industry scrambles to win over the senior citizen, a mixed bag of programs emerges

52. *Removing the "Youth" from "Youth Hostels"*   224
    A revolution has altered the character of these inexpensive lodgings, making them available to mature adventurers of every age

53. *Vacations at Pritikin Centers Are High Priced But Healthy*   228
    Bland meals and mild exercise at Miami Beach, Santa Monica, and Downingtown, Pa.

54. *Vacationing with the Seventh Day Adventists*   232
    A less costly form of Pritikin-like treatments for mature Americans

X A Fresh Way to Visit Old Destinations

55. *Sweden: A Return to the World of Tomorrow*   238
    There's new ferment in the greatest social laboratory on earth—and special "institutes" can reveal it all to you

56. *"Home Stays" in the British Isles*   242
    A number of impressive organizations now permit Americans to visit with Britons of distinctive social viewpoints and achievements

57. *Seeing Britain Differently*   246
    On industrial visits made by appointment, the intelligent traveller can enter the dynamic world of British science and industry—and benefit greatly from it

58. *Viewing Their Cities vs. Our Cities*   252
    A new point of reference for your European tour

XI New Destinations

59. *"Frommer's Favorites"*   258
    The largely unvisited destinations that haven't yet been spoiled by mass tourism

60. *U.S. Winter Vacations—Mostly Odd and Unexpected*   264
    Domestic destinations for your December-through-March holiday

61. *A Pilgrimage to Arcosanti*   272
    Soleri's City of Tomorrow, on a barren desert floor

62. *A Memoir of Bruges*   276
    Arrested in time, a Pompeii or a Brigadoon

XII Thirty Largely Unknown Travel Organizations That Can Alter, Even Revolutionize, Your Vacation Trips—for the Better

63. *Companies That Make Travel as Broad as Life Itself*   282
    Their focus: on Nicaragua, psychology, world poverty, Helen Nearing

64. *Student Exchanges, Hospitality Stays, Volunteer Workcamps*   286
    Dig for a while on the nonprofit side of the U.S. travel industry, and you'll quickly discover nuggets of gold

65. *Cracking the Codes of the Travel Trade*   290
    Some highly technical travel organizations too important to be left to the "pros"

66. *Five Outstanding Travel Organizations Known to Very Few*   294
    Globetrotters, *TRANET*, Interhostel, Partners, and INNterlodging

67. *Travel "Davids" Against Travel "Goliaths"*   298
    Six small but emerging companies that enjoy a growing clientele

68. *Travel Oddities (But Maybe They're Just What You Need)*   302
    Soviet cruise ships, camping tours in deepest Alaska, and more

XIII Carefully Guarded Travel Tips, New Developments, and New Travel Products

69. *The World's 15 Finest Travel Products*   306
    Selecting the gadgets, totebags, and tools that make travel into a fine art

70. *Europe: Satisfying Champagne Tastes on a Beer Budget*   312
    Rules for spending a moderate sum on even the most luxurious of facilities

71. *The Industrial Revolution Comes to the Ski Slopes*   316
    Meet "superchair," the "rapid lift," the "express gondola," the "detachable quad"

XIV Careers in Travel

72. *Can You Really Become a Part-Time Travel Agent?*   322
    As many as 100,000 Americans earn income from the sale of travel while holding down full-time jobs in other fields

73. *The World of the One-Man (or One-Woman) Tour Operator*   324
    Specialty travel, exploring the narrowest interests or the oddest destinations

74. *Travelling for Free as a Tour Escort, I*   326
    Pursuing a dream job, a fantasy career: the companies that hire, the people they hire

75. *Travelling for Free as a Tour Escort, II*   330
    More than 450 companies are now making use of tour escorts

Appendix

Twenty-one of America's Foremost Discount Travel Agencies   336

Eleven Reliable "Distress Merchants" of Travel (Offering Last-Minute Discounts)   338

Six Leading "Rebators" (Discounting Every Trip)   341

Nineteen of the Nation's Leading Discount Cruise Agencies   343

The Four Leading "Hospitality Exchanges" Available to Americans   345

Five Major "Vacation Exchange Clubs"   347

Five "Homestay" Organizations for Americans Travelling Abroad   349

Forty Student Travel Agencies at Home and Abroad   351

Forty-two of America's Foremost Bed-and-Breakfast Reservations Organizations   353

Seven Major Transatlantic Charter Operators   359

Ten Best Travel Values of 1988   360

Photo Credits/Acknowledgments   361

Index   362

About the Author   367

An Introduction to Arthur Frommer's New World of Travel 1988

"*N*el mezzo del cammin di nostra vita"—At a midpoint in the path of my life, to crib from Dante, I felt a sharp malaise about the state of American travel, and with my own role in it.

After 30 years of writing standard guidebooks, I began to see that most of the vacation journeys undertaken by Americans were trivial and bland, devoid of important content, cheaply commercial, and unworthy of our better instincts and ideals.

And overpriced, even in the budget realm.

Those travels, for most Americans, consist almost entirely of "sight-seeing"—an activity as vapid as the words imply. We rove the world, in most cases, to look at lifeless physical structures of the sort already familiar from a thousand picture books and films. We gaze at the Eiffel Tower or the Golden Gate Bridge, enjoy a brief thrill of recognition, return home, and think we have travelled.

Only later do we ask: to what end did I travel? With what lasting rewards?

And these disappointments are not always reduced or affected by the decision to travel cheaply—as I once largely believed. Though the use of budget-priced facilities will *usually* result in a more meaningful trip—because they bring us closer to the realities of the countries through which we pass—they do not guarantee that condition. Even people staying in guesthouses and pensions can pass their days in senseless "sight-seeing," trudging like robots to Trafalgar Square and various Changings of the Guard.

No. To me today, travel in all price ranges is scarcely worth the effort unless it is associated with people, with learning and ideas. To have meaning at all, travel must involve an encounter with new and different outlooks and beliefs. It must broaden our horizons, provide comparative lessons, show us how those in other communities are responding to their social and industrial problems. At its best, travel should challenge our preconceptions and most cherished views, cause us to rethink our assumptions, shake us a bit, make us broader-minded and more understanding.

It is toward achieving that kind of travel—that infinitely more memorable form of travel—that this yearly book hopes to contribute. Its method is to turn a spotlight on a host of little-known travel programs and organizations that surface each year, usually to benefit only the smallest portion of our population.

All over the world, and at home as well, a tiny segment of the travel industry is laboring to add valuable content to the travel experience:

ALL OVER THE WORLD, A TINY SEGMENT OF THE TRAVEL INDUSTRY IS LABORING TO ADD VALUABLE CONTENT TO THE TRAVEL EXPERIENCE

• These are the people who operate ambitious study trips, and scientific tours; they offer challenging, politically oriented journeys, and excursions into the Third World.

• Their aim is to change your life. They experiment with new lifestyles and spiritual quests at yoga retreats and utopian communities, at tented Caribbean resorts and macrobiotic farms, at personal growth centers and adult summer camps.

• They sail the smallest of cruise ships into tiny ports and fishing villages unsullied by mass tourism.

• They practice "integrated tourism," using local facilities, and broadcast appeals for ethical tourism and tourism for the poor.

• They go on treks into the Himalayas or bicycle tours into the Dordogne.

• They enable Americans to study foreign languages at overseas schools, stay as guests in the homes of private families abroad, share the life and rhythm of Australian sheep farms, study 16th-century art with a connoisseur in the Belgian Ardennes.

• They promote homestays among people of accomplishment in Britain, or volunteer workcamps on the coasts of four continents.

But they are fledgling travel companies without funds to properly advertise their new approach; their trips, in consequence, are confined to the barest few.

In this book, hopefully, they will find their voice. Each new edition will attempt to introduce the best of them, and especially those with novel travel ideas: new themes of travel, new travel methods, new programs, new vacation possibilities, new and better ways of visiting old destinations, new destinations. Out of the welter of obscure new travel organizations emerging each year, surely one will lead to at least one new vacation activity for each of our readers.

One, did I say? Why not two or three? Travel should be no occasional fling, but a normal and frequent, integral part of one's life. To have that requires that you learn to cut transportation costs. And so the second theme of this yearly book will be the many new methods of traveling cheaply—from air fare bucket shops to travel rebators and distress merchants, from freighters, charters, and standby fares to air courier services and discount cruise agents—all the myriad travel bargains that surface each year to permit the most alert of our fellow citizens to travel frequently. All this will be discussed not as an end

TRAVEL, FOR TOO LONG, HAS BEEN TRIVIALIZED IN THE POPULAR PRESS AND BY THE PROMOTERS OF MASS-VOLUME TOURS; IT DESERVES BETTER

in itself, but simply as a means of reaping the pleasures and rewards of frequent, far-ranging foreign travels.

Our ability to engage in that sort of travel is nothing short of a miracle. We are the first generation in human history to fly to other continents as easily as people once boarded a train to the next town. We are the first generation in human history for whom travel is not restricted to an affluent few, but is available to many.

We should not squander our opportunity. Travel, for too long, has been trivialized in the popular press and by the promoters of popular tours; it deserves better. It is an enduring subject of human concern, the essential requisite for a civilized life, perhaps the most effective tool for reducing foolish national pride and promoting a world view.

It is too important a subject to be left to the commercial megaliths of the travel industry.

Hence, this book.

See you next year.

ARTHUR FROMMER

January 1988

A Request for Comments

The best of books is a collaboration between author and reader. In subsequent editions of this book, we hope to supplement our own recommendations with yours. If you know of additional travel organizations or programs of the sort we've cited, or if you have comments of any sort relating to our text, won't you let us know of them?

Send your comments and/or selections to Arthur Frommer, c/o Prentice Hall Press, One Gulf + Western Plaza, New York, NY 10023.

*To
Pauline
from
her proud father*

I

What's Wrong with Travel—and What We Can Do About It

The Scandal of American Vacation Time

houghtless, at the very least. Barbaric, at worst. Inhuman, certainly. Short-sighted and ill-advised. Miserly. Unhealthy.

Depending on the depths of your passion, those are the words you may want to use to describe employer attitudes toward vacation time in the United States.

We Americans put up with the shortest, most miserably limited vacations of any advanced, prosperous nation. The result is a stunted quality of life and (if that doesn't bother you) a stunted commercial travel industry.

To gauge how bad things are, place yourself, hypothetically, into one of four national contexts:

• Imagine, first, that you are "Wilhelm Preizendorff," a young Austrian, and that you have just gone to work as an office clerk for a Viennese stationers. From the moment you enter the mailroom door, you are entitled by law to five weeks per year of paid vacation.

• Or you are "Nigel Lawson," floor manager of a small Sydney, Australia, department store. Each year, by practice of your firm, common in Australia, you receive six weeks of paid vacation. Sometimes you store up three months of vacation and take the family on an around-the-world trip.

• Or you are "Chantal Lasserre," buyer for a Paris dress shop. You are this time

We Americans put up with the shortest, most miserably limited vacations of any advanced, prosperous nation.

entitled, by minimum guarantee of French law, to five weeks' paid vacation per year. You take a month off every summer, which you then supplement with a week in winter or spring.

• And now you are "Mary Jones" or "John Smith," an American. This year you have no vacation at all; you have recently changed jobs and lost the time accrued under your former employer. Next year: one week with pay. The year after that: two. After five years of consecutive employment with the same firm, you will have three weeks per year of paid vacation—but never more than that. All your working life: three weeks per year.

Is this an exaggerated comparison? I wish it were. In numerous studies of vacation time, only a single one shows the American public enjoying as many as two and a half weeks of vacation time.

WHILE OTHER DEVELOPED NATIONS PROVIDE THEIR CITIZENS WITH FIVE WEEKS AND MORE OF PAID LEAVE, WE SQUEEZE OUT A MEAGER TWO

Most other reports fix the average figure at two weeks—or even less.

Two weeks. Even two and a half weeks. Those compare with the five weeks enjoyed in numerous other advanced, industrialized nations, and with the remarkable six-week policy of Australia. Even in nations having nowhere near our own material prosperity or per-capita income —such as Britain—the average working person enjoys nearly four weeks per year of paid vacation. (My British statistics are from a 1985 survey by the respected *Economist* magazine of London.)

And it gets worse. Not only is the American average a paltry two or two and a half weeks, but even that brief interlude is enjoyed under the most fragile of circumstances. Leave your job and you lose your vacation time. Painfully, patiently, you must start all over, accruing new vacation privileges from a new employer. The past counts for nothing.

No law protects the vacation. Though the United States subscribes to the Universal Declaration of Human Rights— which prescribes "the right to rest and leisure, including . . . periodic holidays with pay" as a fundamental privilege of life—not a single federal or state law, to my knowledge, guarantees a single day of paid vacation to anyone.

Either we Americans are the workaholics of the world, or we are exploited in this regard, or in our drive for improved wages, we have simply neglected to secure the time in which to enjoy the fruits of our pay.

However the neglect came about, it contributes to a serious decline in the quality of our lives. A barrier to our cultural growth. Inadequate time for study or reflection, human relationships, the eternal verities. Burn-out. Even, perhaps, worsened health.

Shouldn't we all consider whether the time for leisure is fully as important as other aspects of material prosperity? Would it not be worth a trade-off to enjoy greater respite from constant labors? A life more dignified and fulfilling? When the political pendulum of the United States begins to shift from its present rightward course, as must inevitably happen; when labor again becomes aggressive in its collective bargaining; when ordinary people once more demand improvements to their lot—shouldn't the goal of increased vacation time be high on the national agenda?

And if these quality-of-life arguments don't suffice, shouldn't we at least consid-er the impact of increased vacation time on our commercial travel interests?

The U.S. travel industry is also a victim of limited vacation time: it is puny in comparison with its European counter-parts. Because of their enhanced vacation

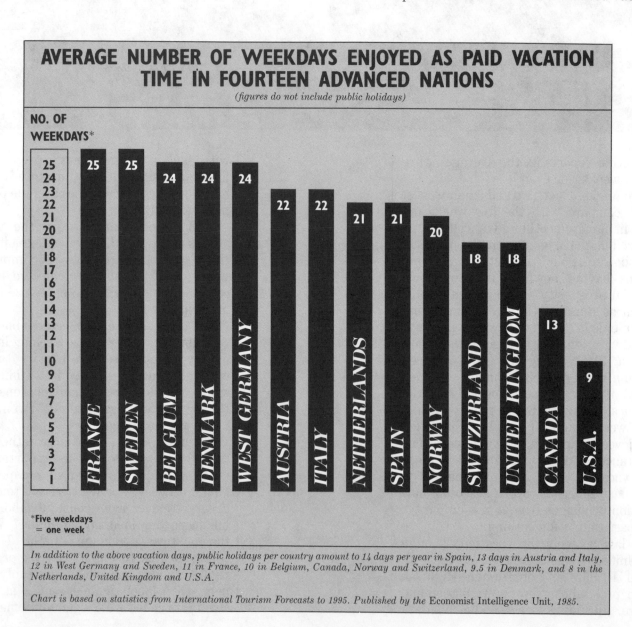

AVERAGE NUMBER OF WEEKDAYS ENJOYED AS PAID VACATION TIME IN FOURTEEN ADVANCED NATIONS
(figures do not include public holidays)

NO. OF WEEKDAYS*

FRANCE	SWEDEN	BELGIUM	DENMARK	WEST GERMANY	AUSTRIA	ITALY	NETHERLANDS	SPAIN	NORWAY	SWITZERLAND	UNITED KINGDOM	CANADA	U.S.A.
25	25	24	24	24	22	22	21	21	20	18	18	13	9

*Five weekdays = one week

In addition to the above vacation days, public holidays per country amount to 14 days per year in Spain, 13 days in Austria and Italy, 12 in West Germany and Sweden, 11 in France, 10 in Belgium, Canada, Norway and Switzerland, 9.5 in Denmark, and 8 in the Netherlands, United Kingdom and U.S.A.

Chart is based on statistics from International Tourism Forecasts to 1995. Published by the Economist Intelligence Unit, 1985.

HOWEVER THE NEGLECT CAME ABOUT, IT CONTRIBUTES TO A SERIOUS DECLINE IN THE QUALITY OF OUR LIVES

periods, tiny Benelux countries send as many people to winter vacation destinations in Spain and North Africa as the entire United States sends in that period to certain major islands of the Caribbean. With nearly four weeks of paid vacation available to their clientele, at least a dozen British tour operators each handle several hundreds of thousands of vacation arrangements each year, while here in the United States, with four times the population, the same companies are perhaps six in number.

Every day of vacation time added to the American average would create a need for hundreds of new hotels and resorts, tens of thousands of new jobs in leisure areas, additional airplanes, trains, and buses. The multiplier effects are dazzling.

And each such result comes about at lesser cost to employers than higher wages or other traditional fringe benefits. In service industries, and especially in those smaller economic units where vacation time is particularly meagre, people take on extra tasks—work harder and in broader functions, take up the slack—when their colleagues go on vacation. The common experience of all of us confirms that increased vacation time costs less to employers than other employment benefits.

Who ideally should agitate for increased vacation time? I suggest the more than 250,000 Americans who work as travel agents. No other social change could better secure their futures, add to their opportunities, expand their industry, while at the same time performing an act for the common good. One could even argue that only travel agents and other travel professionals possess the kind of direct, compelling self-interest in the

Either we are the workaholics of the world, or we are exploited in this regard, or have simply neglected to secure the time in which to enjoy the fruits of our pay.

matter, and the political numbers, capable of changing American vacation policies.

But is it likely that travel agents will head such a drive? Not under their present leadership. Notoriously short-sighted, almost automatically conservative, the male officials of the American Society of Travel Agents—a profession that is 70% female—recently battled congressional efforts to secure maternity leaves for working women (it would raise their payroll costs). Imagine their reactions to proposals for additional vacation time.

Someday this may change. Someday both the men and women of America's travel agencies will realize that though they work in small storefront locations, they need not possess the souls of shopkeepers. Someday the sophistication of their travel lives will lead to a corresponding sophistication in their social outlooks, and they will champion the fight for civilized standards in vacation policies.

The way to do it? A modest, one-sentence addition to the Federal Wages and Hours Act: "All persons engaged in interstate commerce shall receive a minimum of three weeks each year of paid vacation." By bringing along those persons enjoying less than three weeks, such legislation would surely add at least half a week to the national average, setting off an explosive increase in this nation's vacation facilities and travel-related industries. What more business-like way to improve the lives of all of us!

And then we ought to work for four or five weeks of yearly vacation time. Why should Americans enjoy less than the Scandinavians, Austrians, Germans, or French?

Ethical Travel: Does Tourism Cause More Harm Than Good?

At the bar of a tropical nightclub, on an island whose language is Dutch, two tipsy young tourists are exchanging loud comments on the "childish behavior" of the natives. "They haven't any concept of time." "They're so disorganized." "They move in slow motion." Nearby, overhearing each word, his English near perfect, a bartender stands seething with anger.

• In the marketplace of a Hindu village, a travelling couple bargain over the cost of a trinket. Though the price is that of an ice cream at home, they're determined to pick up "a steal." Resignedly, the shopkeeper reduces her quote to a marginal level, hardly enough to bring her a single rupee of real income.

• On the streets of a Mexican city, two confident visitors in costly tennis clothes go strolling in high spirits to a favorite bar. Unseeing, uncaring, they pass clusters of ragged children, who in turn stare at the elegant pair with envy and resentment.

• In the air-conditioned restaurant of a Nigerian hotel, owned by a multinational chain, guests dine on tournedos flown in from Argentina, and wash down the steak with a fine French wine. Of the monies charged for their meals, only the tiniest

The capacity for harm is deeply ingrained in the very practice of tourism, which often brings more injury than good to poor nations.

part remains in Nigeria.

• Onto the tarmac of the Bangkok airport steps a group of German tourists, all of them male. They have come for prostitution. Included in their "package," at no extra charge, is a young Thai farm girl for the entire week.

Does tourism involve ethics? Should tourists be trained to act responsibly? Are travel practices—and institutions—in need of reform? Each of these questions was studied last fall by a group of American church people at a conference in San Anselmo, California. Their gathering came several years after the organization of similar groups abroad.

In 1975 a conference of Asian church leaders in Penang, Malaysia, issued a broad condemnation of tourism as it was then practiced in their countries. They decried the boorish antics of tourists to Asia, the harmful role models offered to impressionable Asian children by foreign tourists, their patronizing attitudes and harsh demands, the pollution of authentic settings and communities by modern hotels, the disrespect for Asian cultures by numerous tourist groups, the heavy use of prostitution as an Asiatic tourist lure, the monetary inflation and social trauma caused by a sudden touristic influx.

But their criticism went deeper. In a dizzying outflow of bulletins, pamphlets, newsletters, and even a quarterly magazine (*Contours*, standing for "concern for tourism") occurring in the years since, the Ecumenical Coalition on Third World Tourism (ECTWT, the continuing organization) has appeared to argue that the capacity for harm is deeply ingrained in the very practice of tourism; that it brings more harm than good to poor nations; that

RETHINKING THE "RIGHTS" AND "WRONGS" OF OUR VACATION TRIPS

it is, in effect, a new form of economic colonialism; that all of us should step back and rethink the methods by which tourism is conducted; and that the problem is worldwide in scope, erupting wherever the Rich travel to visit lands of the Poor.

Think for a moment about the geographical directions of tourism. On an international level, most vacation travel consists of people from the "First World" (United States, Europe, Japan) travelling to visit islands, beaches, and picturesque towns of the "Third World" (Mexico, the Caribbean, Africa, Southeast Asia, India). Most of it occurs for the purpose of returning for a short time to a simpler way of life—to lost innocence, in settings old-fashioned and open-air.

But though we opt for the "tropical paradise," we demand that it come with all the comforts of home. So we drop glass-and-steel hotels next to peasant villages or fishermen's huts, creating luxuriant, forbidden facilities that no resident would dare enter, let alone use. We instantly separate *us* from *them*.

Within these bright new edifices, we staff all the servile posts—waiters, busboys, chambermaids—with native labor, but bring in executives from our own developed world to run the show (when, in the tropics, did you last see a native-born general manager?).

We then parade our wealth before people who can never enjoy our incomes. Though we ourselves may be only modestly well-off, we pay prices of a staggering size in local terms. Our very presence creates the most appalling contrasts.

In the course of our stays, we make no use at all of the lodgings that residents use, or of their transportation or dining spots. We create our own.

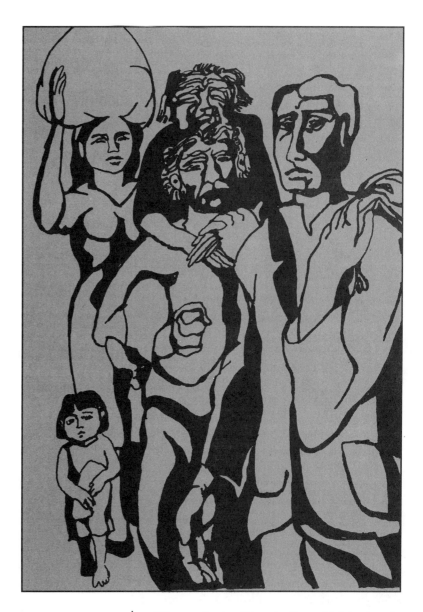

We arrive without the slightest advance knowledge of their ways of life, customs, or culture. We challenge them to quickly brief us on the spot ("orientation sightseeing tours"). We demand that they pose quaintly for our Kodaks and Minoltas, dance for our amusement ("Thursday night: native entertain-

THE SOLUTIONS INVOLVE ENCOURAGING THE GREATER USE OF SIMPLER, INDIGENOUS LODGINGS AND FACILITIES FOR VISITING TOURISTS

ment"), show us their funny clothes. We care not a fig for their politics, but expect them to admire our own. Unlike the great travellers of the past—Marco Polo, Rubens, Byron—we show no real regard for their achievements and discoveries, art and literature, but expect them, in essence, to have adopted our culture, at least a bit: to speak the same language we do ("luckily, they all speak . . ."), to stock our newspapers and our books in their newsstands and shops.

In short, we pay them massive disrespect. We assault their human dignity; we necessarily imply that they are inferior to us. Some—especially the young in Third World nations—begin to believe just that.

We injure them.

But if this is the situation, what is the solution? Having read my way through a stack of the literature on ethical tourism, I intend no slight of the various Ecumenical Coalitions when I state what they would readily admit: that their work to date has defined the problem but rendered less satisfactory solutions.

Still, some solutions have emerged. They begin with a frontal, public relations attack on the most blatant exploiters of Third World people for touristic purposes: in particular, the operators of sex tours using women coerced by poverty (or physical force) into a criminal world of prostitution; the decriminalization of that activity, eliminating the exploiters, is a goal of some of the ecumenical organizations.

The solutions include political opposition to the worst excesses of tourist development: the sprawling airports and monumental hotels plopped into the midst of small villages and rural beauty.

The solutions involve encouraging the greater use of simpler, indigenous lodg-

Though we opt for the "tropical paradise," we demand that it come with all the comforts of home. So we drop glass-and-steel hotels next to peasant villages or fishermen's huts.

ings and facilities for visiting tourists; supporting and even subsidizing the operation of small guesthouses and guest-accepting private homes, pensions, and farms; promoting the sale of purely local crafts to tourists and the consumption of local food products; arranging visits by tourists to meetings of local service organizations and, indeed, to people's homes.

The solution means marketing—giving badly needed publicity to—those underfinanced travel organizations that practice "integrated tourism," placing visitors into the facilities used by local people themselves.

Finally, and perhaps most important, the solution involves educating travellers to comport themselves properly in the Third World. A recent victory of the Ecumenical Coalition was to persuade Lufthansa to show a film of advance cultural preparation and ethical conduct on its holiday flights to certain Third World nations. Another has been the widespread dissemination and increasing acceptance of a code of ethics for tourists: "Travel in a spirit of humility. . . . Be sensitively aware of [their] feelings. . . . Cultivate the habit of listening and observing. . . . Realize [they] have time concepts and thought patterns different from your own. This does not make them inferior, only different. . . . Do not expect special privileges. . . . Do not make promises [you cannot] carry through. . . ."

Once the exclusive domain of Asian and European groups, the drive for ethical travel practices is now on the march in the United States. Its "general" is Virginia T. Hadsell, her recently formed organization is the **Center for Responsible Tourism, 2 Kensington Road, San Anselmo, CA**

94960 (phone 415/843-5506), and her initial conference took place in that city (near San Rafael) in November 1986. Send her a large, self-addressed, stamped envelope, and she'll send you literature, including the interesting Code of Ethics for tourists.

Or you may make a direct contact with the **Ecumenical Coalition on Third World Tourism, P.O. Box 9-25, Bangkhen, Bangkok 10900, Thailand,** requesting a copy of the fascinating *Contours*. They'll mail it to you free, but you're invited to send a small contribution —say, $3 or so—to defray the costs.

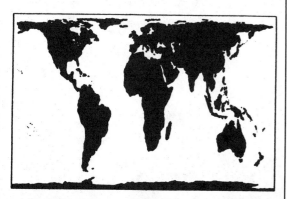

> We parade our wealth before people who can never enjoy our incomes. Our very presence creates the most appalling contrasts.

A CODE OF ETHICS FOR TOURISTS

1. Travel in a spirit of humility and with a genuine desire to learn more about the people of your host country. Be sensitively aware of the feelings of other people, thus preventing what might be offensive behavior on your part. This applies very much to photography.
2. Cultivate the habit of listening and observing, rather than merely hearing and seeing.
3. Realize that often the people in the country you visit have time concepts and thought patterns different from your own. This does not make them inferior, only different.
4. Instead of looking for that "beach paradise," discover the enrichment of seeing a different way of life, through other eyes.
5. Acquaint yourself with local customs. What is courteous in one country may be quite the reverse in another—people will be happy to help you.
6. Instead of the Western practice of "knowing all the answers," cultivate the habit of asking questions.
7. Remember that you are only one of thousands of tourists visiting this country and do not expect special privileges.
8. If you really want your experience to be a "home away from home," it is foolish to waste money on travelling.
9. When you are shopping, remember that that "bargain" you obtained was possible only because of the low wages paid to the maker.
10. Do not make promises to people in your host country unless you can carry them through.
11. Spend time reflecting on your daily experience in an attempt to deepen your understanding. It has been said that "what enriches you may rob and violate others."

—Issued by the Ecumenical Coalition on Third World Tourism

A Plea for "Social Tourism"

*I*n all the years you've read the Sunday travel sections, have you once observed a reference to "social tourism"?

Probably not. It is a concept known to every prosperous nation other than our own, to every rich continent other than North America, to every major language other than English.

"Social tourism" is tourism for the poor.

Here in America, we don't push it. Apart from various "fresh-air funds" sending underprivileged children to summer camp, not a single major program brings away-from-home vacations to low-income groups. While you and I enjoy all the widely recognized benefits of travel— the awesome beauties of an outside world, the broadening impact of foreign cultures, the mind-tingling sense of human possibilities—the same rewards are simply unavailable to persons of adult age who happen to be poor and living in the United States.

But should this be? If the ability to enjoy rest and leisure is a fundamental human right—and it certainly is— shouldn't we concern ourselves with travel opportunities for the poor? With "social tourism"?

In Europe as early as 1956, leading travel figures met to discuss the contradiction between low income and the right to travel. From those talks emerged, years later, the Bureau Internationale du Tourisme Sociale, headed today by 73-year-old Arthur Haulot of Belgium, a former chairman of the European Travel Commission.

Haulot presides over some 90-odd orga-

If the ability to enjoy rest and leisure is a fundamental human right—and it certainly is—shouldn't we concern ourselves with travel opportunities for the poor?

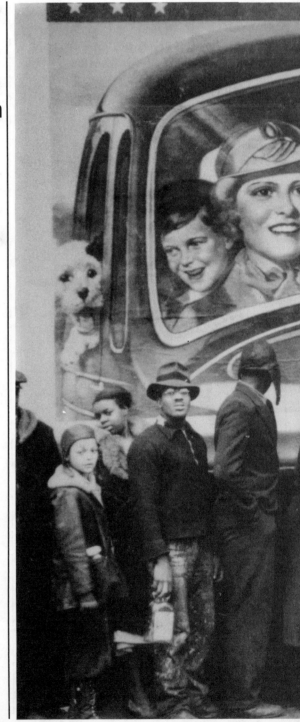

ISN'T IT TIME WE BROUGHT THE BENEFITS OF TRAVEL TO *ALL* OUR CITIZENS?

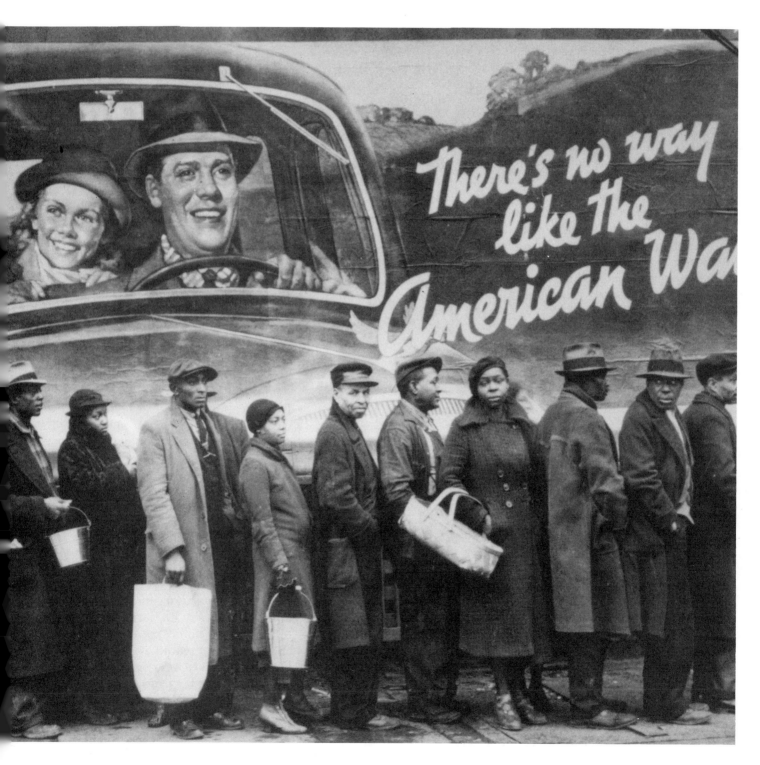

THE AMERICAN POOR HAVE BEEN ABANDONED ALMOST ENTIRELY BY THE COMMERCIAL TRAVEL INDUSTRY

nizations of "social tourism" in Europe and North Africa, in South America and the Pacific Rim—but not, astonishingly, in the United States. Though their work may seem utterly basic, even a bit simple, it is of remarkable importance.

The vacation itself. They agitate, first, for the fundamental right to a yearly paid vacation by people of all income strata. Sounds self-evident, right? Yet in an America that mandates (in effect) the 40-hour week and the eight-hour day, no law protects the right to a paid vacation, and numerous low-income persons fail to receive one. What maid, for instance, enjoys the security of an assured, paid period of rest?

> **No law protects the right to a paid vacation, and numerous low-income persons fail to receive one.**

Access to the vacation. They seek to persuade governments, owners of the railways, to provide poor persons with a free or drastically reduced round-trip rail ticket, once a year, to a vacation destination. By eliminating or lowering that transportation cost—as France, Portugal, and Switzerland have done—they bring proper vacations into the financial reach of a great many of the poor, yet at no cost at all to their railroad systems.

A fulfilling vacation. They attempt to eliminate the substandard, cinderblock motel and fast-food restaurant as the sole affordable facility for vacationing poor. They promote the construction and operation of dignified, low-cost "vacation villages" in seaside and mountain areas, by political parties of both the left and right, by labor unions and philanthropic societies, all receiving low-interest loans, grants, or tax rebates for the purpose, from local or national governments.

(I have visited several such "social resorts" in Europe. They permit the poor to experience nature and the finer aspects of culture, solitude, rebirth; they encourage the self-esteem of their guests; leave them replenished in energy and spirit for an assault on their own poverty. In short, they provide the poor with the same vacations that you and I enjoy—and isn't that an unarguable goal?)

Filling unused accommodations. They enroll farmers with large and partially underutilized homes, or educational institutions with vacated residence halls, to list those facilities for holiday use by the poor, at low rates, and then disseminate such availabilities to a low-income population, helping both the user and the provider.

A host of other measures. They work for the creation of "land banks" or additions to national parks, preventing the wholesale private purchase of scenic areas, which would block their use by persons of lesser means. They develop camping facilities—the cheapest form of meaningful travel—and caravaning; issue reduced-price travel vouchers and credit facilities for travel by the poor; advocate staggered vacation schedules as the most efficient means of reducing the cost of vacations for low-income persons; and perform a multitude of other needed functions.

But now you undoubtedly have questions.

First, isn't "social tourism" a form of subsidized tourism? Of course it is—but so is "commercial tourism." When the nonpoor travel, who pays for the highways on which they drive their cars? Who funds the aviation authorities that secure the safety of their flights? Who maintains the port facilities, docks, and marinas at which they park their boats and yachts? Because the taxpayer is already so heavily supporting travel by middle-income and high-income Americans, common justice demands that at least some resources be spent on travel for the poor.

Second, don't we provide any semblance of "social tourism" in this country? Not really. Some unions maintain holiday facilities for their members—but those are not the "poor." Several hundred companies belong to the National Industrial Recreation Association, operating travel programs for their employees—but neither are those the "poor." While state and national parks are "social" in their character, their long-stay facilities (lodging, restaurants) are notoriously unsuited to the

Apart from various "fresh-air funds" sending underprivileged children to summer camp, not a single major program brings away-from-home vacations to low-income groups.

needs of the truly poor.

The "poor" of which I speak are those 50 million Americans living either below the federal poverty line or perilously close to it. At their levels of income, almost absurdly low, the road to travel and tourism is effectively blocked.

How, then, do the "poor" vacation in the United States? The overwhelming number never leave their homes. Those who do, in my experience, squeeze out a stay of three-or-so days near theme parks or casino cities, whose attractions and activities are of the basest sort—dumb and contrived, consumerist. Just as low-income groups have failed to receive adequate low-income housing from private industry, so the American poor have been abandoned almost entirely by the commercial travel industry. They simply have no access to vacations of worth and meaning. Yet such interludes are surely the birthright of every American, the essential requisites for a civilized life.

Don't we need an Institute for Social Tourism in this country? A private body to devise, coordinate, and encourage efforts in this field? And shouldn't persons in the travel industry be the leaders of that movement?

Franklin Roosevelt said that "from those to whom much is given, much is expected." Those who earn handsome incomes from the commercial industry of travel should be the first to labor at extending the benefits of travel to those less favored.

I plan to write more on "social tourism." And I'd be grateful to have your comments and suggestions. Send them to the address listed in our introduction, and they will find their way into a subsequent edition of this book.

Some Particular Gripes About U.S. Airports and Airlines

Don't get me wrong, as we used to say: I love to travel, and admire most travel people, but still I find a great deal that's amiss with the current travel industry, starting with airports and airlines.

The unconscionable fleecing of air travellers by airport cafeterias and restaurants leads my list.

I

About to board a recent flight, and not feeling overly hungry, I decided to confine my airport meal to three vegetables: a scoop of mashed potatoes, a portion of creamed corn, a tiny pile of spinach. At the end of the serving line, I added a small carton of chocolate milk.

The bill came to $5.85.

This unconscionable fleecing of air travellers by airport cafeterias and restaurants leads my list of what I don't like about U.S. aviation.

An airport is a public institution, operated in most instances by public or quasi-public agencies. It is also a monopoly, conferring a near-immunity from competition upon the food concessions in it. In awarding those concessions, does any airport authority require assurance of moderate prices or reasonable markups? Or does the award simply go to the highest bidder, who then proceeds to fleece a captive audience?

Note that I'm not complaining here about the quality of airport food. Hardened by time, expecting little, I make no protest at all about those ubiquitous chili dogs found on every concourse, oozing with ulcer-creating lard ($1.95). I swallow in complete submission those rock-like slices of lemon meringue pie ($2.45). Those stale Danish pastries ($1.85). That acid coffee (95¢). I'm not asking for real reform.

But if we can't eat well at an airport location, can't we at least eat cheap? And is there no city politician looking for an issue, no airport official, no Lochinvar of the skies, who will come to our aid?

II

You appear on time for a 3 p.m. flight, at a gate surrounded by a suspiciously small handful of other travellers. Sure enough, as departure time approaches, the flight is cancelled. "There's a mechanical problem," mumbles the embarrassed airline attendant, his eyes averted from yours. "But we've protected everyone on the 6 p.m. flight." Comes 6 p.m. and in wondrous fashion, as with the loaves and fishes, more than enough seats materialize to accommodate both the earlier passengers and the later ones.

Is it just my imagination or are an unusual number of flights being cancelled nowadays that just happen to be lightly booked? And is it those light sales of a particular flight—not mechanical problems—that provide the real reason for the cancellation?

When I was young in travel, only charters were cancelled for "inadequate participation." The very essence, the core meaning, of scheduled transportation was that the plane flew regardless of the number of passengers aboard.

Now we fly in an era of deregulation. With all former rules erased (and as confirmed to me by the U.S. Department of Transportation), cancellation of a flight for economic reasons (too few passen-

THE TROUBLE WITH TRAVEL: CAFETERIAS, CANCELLATIONS, AND CABS

gers), even moments before departure, is perfectly legal. Only if the frequency of cancellations reaches the massive level of fraud or unfair competition will the D.O.T. step in.

And what protects the passenger from a moderately practiced policy of "economic cancellations"? Are you ready for this? "Market forces." "Word-of-mouth reports." "The airline's concern for its reputation." We are all supposed to know the identity of the frequent offenders, so that we may boycott the sinners and thus deter

If we can't eat well at an airport location, can't we at least eat cheap?

right to expect performance, except for reasons of weather, air-traffic delays, or mechanical misfunctions.

Is there a member of Congress listening to this screed? Ready to legislate? If so: reregulate! While few of us would advocate broader supervision of the airline industry, we have a right to enjoy this minimal protection of our travelling time.

III

Now it is 7 p.m. on still another travel day, and you sit fuming in the back of a taxi or motorcoach crawling to the airport at far too slow a pace to make your flight. You miss it, of course, and yet wearily pay out $31.75 to the cabbie, or an equally outrageous $8.75 to the bus driver.

The lack of modern rapid transit—a train—from downtown locations to most U.S. airports is an American scandal. The failure to plan for moving large numbers of people to air terminals has clogged our airport-bound highways with cars, buses, and taxis, raised the cost and inconvenience of air travel to unacceptable levels, and caused multitudes to miss their flights while stuck in traffic jams. How municipal officials can tolerate (or escape blame for) this near-total absence of rail transportation to a major public facility is an enduring wonder. And why have the rest of us remained so silent over the lack?

all airlines from cancelling too often. While economists of the 18th century might have expected those results of free enterprise, practical men and women don't and shouldn't.

Even one "economic cancellation" is too many! The last-minute cancellation of a flight for economic reasons is a fraud upon the passengers who appeared for that flight. When people respond to a printed, advertised schedule, disrupting their own schedules to make the flight, they have a

In Chicago and Cleveland, in a few other scattered towns, rail transportation has done wonders toward easing the burdens of air travel. Why not in all major cities? As we continue to spend billions on highway improvements, ugly cloverleaf transfers, additional lanes to already-broad motorways, can't we spare a few paltry millions for monorails or light trains to where planes depart?

II

Alternative Travel—a New Kind of Vacation That Improves Upon the Stale and Tired Variety

Off-Beat Vacations, I: People, Politics, and Personal Adventure

A re you a bit bothered, as I am, by the sameness of travel? In a world of accelerating change, does it seem that much of the current travel product is static and traditional, confined to mindless recreation or trivial sightseeing (the Eiffel Tower, the Golden Gate Bridge)? Unworthy of your own intelligence and curiosity?

A great many Americans believe just that. Though their numbers are still small, an increasing assortment of tourists and fledgling travel companies are turning to at least a dozen new and relatively unknown forms of travel meant to impart a greater meaning to their holidays and tours. From an ever-expanding list of choices, they're opting for people-to-people travel, political travel, integrated travel, study travel, adventure travel, biological and wilderness travel, work-camp travel, holistic-fitness travel, solidarity travel, bicycle travel, cooperative travel, Third World travel.

In each of the next four essays I'll review at least four of these new approaches to travel, hoping they can enhance your vacations (and thus enrich your life).

(1) People-to-People Travel. In place of lifeless statues, ancient battlefields, stately museums, you first substitute people. You make a particular effort to meet peo-

Thousands of hosts belonging to Servas will quite literally transform the quality of your vacation experience in their cities.

A "Friendship Force" encounter

ple from cultures very different from ours, conducting yourself with humility, listening and observing, asking questions rather than knowing all the answers, reflecting at the end of each day upon the hopes, aspirations, and outlooks of our fellow earth-dwellers—surely nothing in travel is more exciting or rewarding.

By writing well in advance of departure to the **International Visitors Information Service, 733 15th Street NW, Suite 300, Washington, DC 20005 (phone 202/783-6540)**, and enclosing $4.95, you obtain a booklet listing organizations in dozens of countries that arrange for you to meet their English-speaking citizens, at tea or at dinner, at cafés or in their homes. With that information, you supplement and vastly improve a standard vacation trip.

By writing even further in advance to

THOUSANDS ARE TURNING TO NEW VARIETIES OF TRAVEL THAT LEND CONTENT AND MEANING TO THE STANDARD, LISTLESS TOUR

the remarkable **Servas** (from the Esperanto, "to serve"), **11 John Street, Suite 706, New York, NY 10038 (phone 212/267-0252)**, requesting membership, you arrange free overnight stays of up to three nights apiece in the homes of persons in 85 nations who will also have you as a nonpaying guest at their breakfast and dinner tables, and invite you to share their daily activities, simply because they believe such contacts further the cause of world peace. (Servas will first screen you for membership to ascertain the seriousness of your intentions.) From Bangkok all the way to Bremen, from Manila and Sydney to Madrid and Siena, Servas's thousands of hosts will quite literally transform the quality of your vacation experience in their cities.

Finally, if you prefer group contacts to "one-on-ones," you write to the **Friendship Force, 575 S. Tower, 1 CNN Center, Atlanta, GA 30303 (phone 404/522-9490)**, and join the dynamic movement so closely associated with former President Jimmy Carter. At intervals throughout the year, Friendship Force assembles up to 80 people and flies them to one-week stays with foreign families (followed by a one-week organized tour) in 38 countries, Asian as well as European. (We've discussed the Friendship Force at greater length in a later chapter on new approaches to travel advocated by former President Jimmy Carter; see page 60.)

(2) Political Travel. You travel now to meet, question, and hear both government officials and dissidents, planners and activists, foreign journalists and teachers, in developing countries around the world. Here, the leading firm is **Schilling Travel Service, Inc., 722 Second Avenue South, Minneapolis, MN 55402 (phone**

> You travel to meet officials and dissidents, planners and activists, journalists and teachers, in developing countries all over the world.

612/332-1100), whose monthly newsletter, *Away to Discover*, is a riveting publication that makes a pioneering use of travel to provide tourists with a global perspective on the key issues of our time. You journey with Schilling for two weeks to visit political institutions of the Caribbean Basin (Jamaica, Barbados, Antigua), for three weeks to capitals and leaders of the Pacific Rim (Tokyo, Beijing, and Hong Kong), for two weeks to delve into the social and economic realities of Greece and Cyprus, for one week to the small-business developments and refugee settlements of Costa Rica. You are accompanied by experts; you meet influential people at each destination.

Managed by dedicated feminists determined to obtain their own database of political facts, Schilling is open-minded to a degree rarely found in similar firms; unlike the operators of "solidarity tours" discussed in a subsequent essay, it operates tours to Nicaragua without judgment. It arranges to meet not simply with Sandinistas but with Roman Catholic clergy and editors of opposition newspapers. Every tour there is like its first. Though mainly booked by Minnesotans (and by both sexes) on departures from Minneapolis/St. Paul, it accepts participants from every state, and can usually arrange to fly them from other departure cities. (For more on Schilling, see the full discussion of the political travel agent starting on page 44.)

(3) Integrated Travel. On the usual trip, the very character of your lodgings separates you from the indigenous life and culture of the destination, walls you off from the sounds, sights, smells—and attitudes—of each community. In low-income nations, you inhabit a splendid

ON AN ADVENTURE TOUR, YOU VACATION IN THE OPEN AIR, ACCEPTING VARIOUS FORMS OF PHYSICAL CHALLENGE

Nepalese trekking guides

high-rise called Hyatt or Hilton. In post-colonial settings seething with resentment, you dine each night on continental delicacies.

The wholly different activity known as "integrated travel" places you squarely in the villages of the Third World, or directly in the residential settings of the First World. You live as the locals live, using *their* transportation, *their* eating places, *their* lodgings.

In the more developed nations, you achieve such integration by using the **Experiment in International Living, Kipling Road, Brattleboro, VT 05301 (phone 802/257-7751)**, to place you with a foreign family for one to four weeks; or you join the **Vacation Exchange Club, 12006 111th Avenue, Unit 12, Youngtown, AZ 85363 (phone 602/972-2186)**, to swap your own home or apartment for the residence of a foreign family during the period of your respective vacations.

In the Third World, you discover—if you but make the effort—a surprising number of such programs. For example, the program known as GATE (Global Awareness Through Experience) brings you to low-income neighborhoods in Mexico, Nicaragua, Cuba, and Peru for a ten-day experience, often searing, of certain Latin American realities—the kind that eventually must be confronted and dealt with by all of us. Contact **Sister Patricia McNally, U.S. GATE Coordinator, P.O. Box 3042, Harlingen, TX 78551.**

(4) Adventure Travel. Perhaps the fastest growing of all the new holiday categories, this is a theme featured by several scores of new holiday companies that take us into the great outdoors, to exotic or remote locations both at home and abroad, on treks by van, canoe, or afoot involving varieties of physical challenge graded as to difficulty, from easy to arduous. Unhappily, too many center on the imagined fantasies of travel, turning us all into Indiana Jones, as if the world existed for our entertainment. A more serious adventure company, and one I very much like, is **Journeys International, 4011 Jackson Road, Ann Arbor, MI 48103 (phone 313/665-4407),** a specialist in Nepal (but which also goes to Africa, the Andes, Sri Lanka, and Costa Rica). It takes extraordinary steps to explain the finer nuances of the Nepalese culture, contributes a portion of each tour fee to the Earth Preservation Fund, enlists its tour members to carry down hundreds of

pounds of trash left by climbers on the slopes of Mount Everest or Annapurna, restores village prayer wheels, and engages in reforestation.

Cheapest of the adventure companies? That's **Adventure Center, 5540-TI College Avenue, Oakland, CA 94618 (phone 415/654-1879),** operating to all parts of the world. Slower paced and more basic in arrangements than the others, it nevertheless achieves considerable savings.

And don't forget the giants: **Overseas Adventure Travel, 6 Bigelow Street, Cambridge, MA 02139 (phone 617/876-0533, or toll free 800-221-0814 outside Massachusetts),** a specialist in Tanzania; and **Sobek Expeditions, P.O. Box 1089, Angel's Camp, CA 95222 (phone 209/736-4524),** a specialist in Peru—both discussed elsewhere in this book.

For several wholly different (and important) viewpoints on political and people-to-people travel, write to **Co-Op America, 2100 M Street NW, Suite 310, Washington, DC 20063 (phone 202/872-5307),** for their spring 1986 publication dealing with those and other topics of travel.

Off-Beat Vacations, II: Beaches, Biology, and Brainwork

A re you travelling more but enjoying it less? All over the world, growing numbers of people are reacting badly to the standard forms of commercial tourism.

Why? Because some of the standard trips are simply being booked by too many. Because tour buses, charter flights, and crowds of frantic, camera-toting visitors are spilling over from celebrated plazas, squares, beaches, and airports in the more popular, standard cities or islands. Because attractions like the Louvre and the Sistine Chapel, the Nikko Shrine and Waikiki, are often mob scenes. Because, in response to the numbers, multinational chains have thrown up massive, towering hotels that soon pre-empt the field, but only serve to separate their guests from the life and atmosphere surrounding them.

The solution, for the sensitive tourist, is a new type of travel, one that stretches the mind and involves active participation in the events and theme of the trip. In the immediately preceding essay I wrote about the strange but immensely satisfying new forms of (1) people-to-people travel, (2) political travel, (3) integrated travel, and (4) adventure travel. In the next three sections of this book I'll deal with 12 additional options, starting with:

(5) Open-Air Beachfront Travel. On vacation in a warm tropical area, why use a hotel at all? You've undoubtedly pondered that question, as I did on a first visit to the Caribbean. With nighttime tempera-

Increasing numbers are weary of high-rise hotels that only serve to separate their guests from the life and atmosphere around them.

Musicale at Maho Bay Camp

tures in the 80s, I reasoned, why shouldn't I be sleeping in a tent or on a canvas-topped platform erected by some shrewd entrepreneur on an isolated beach? Why not enjoy the very essence of the tropics, à la Gauguin, and save a great deal of money at the same time?

Like all good vacation ideas, this one has in fact occurred to a great many entrepreneurs, and several have brought it to fruition. The stunningly successful Maho Bay Camps, on St. John in the U.S. Virgin Islands, places you, at a fraction of normal hotel costs, in canvas-sided, tent-like "cottages" on wooden platforms canti-levered out from the foliage-covered slope of a hill overlooking sheer seaside enchantment. You live for a week or more in nothing but a bathing suit, cook your own meals (though communal eating facilities also exist), disport yourself in nature, far from the casinos, "barflies," tawdry shows, and plastic decor of so many West

NEW MODES OF TRAVEL THAT DIFFER SHARPLY FROM THE USUAL VARIETY

Indies resorts. Write for literature to **Maho Bay Camps, 17A East 73rd Street, New York, NY 10021 (phone 212/472-9453).**

Write at the same time to **Cinnamon Bay Campgrounds, c/o Rockresorts, 30 Rockefeller Plaza, Room 5400, New York, NY 10112 (phone 212/765-5950).** It's a similar, tented complex on the island of St. John, operated by the prestigious Rockefeller travel interests, but at low cost.

(6) Biological and Wilderness Travel. The setting now is the world's great wilderness areas; the theme is nature, the groups small and select, the guides all expert naturalists. In this field, **Biological Journeys, 1876F Ocean Drive, McKinleyville, CA 95521 (phone 707/839-0178, or toll free 800/548-7555),** is the behemoth, its specialties whales and birds, its preferred areas the Sea of Cortez along the coast of Baja California (using its own small cruise ships, with daily hikes ashore), the Galápagos Islands off Ecuador, and the "inside passage" of southeast Alaska. Though passengers are all amateurs, the quest is scientific, profound, thrilling. For the jungle-river equivalent of that saltwater emphasis (with shore excursions into matters anthropological), **Wilderness Expeditions, 310 Washington Avenue SW, Roanoke, VA 24016 (phone 703/342-5630),** is the key name: it explores the famous, fragile ecosystem of the Amazon River area of Peru, starting at Iquitos, then proceeding by lazy stages in chug-chugging motorboats to jungle game preserves. In Central America (the safe and secure part), **Wind**

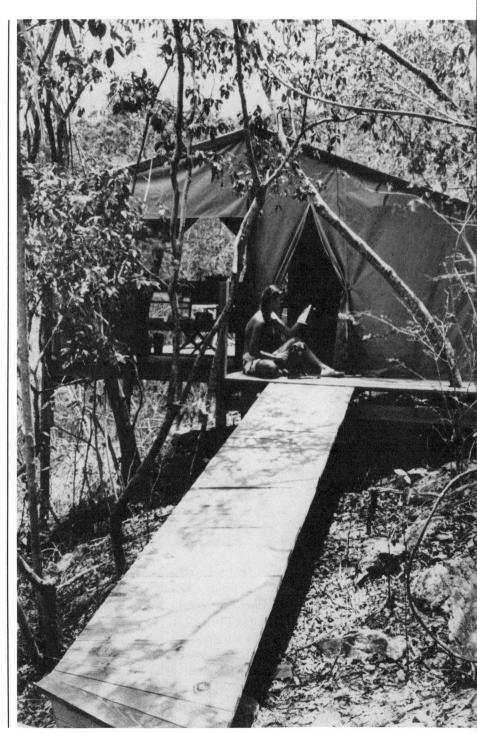

Tent-cottage at Maho Bay

COULD ANY BETTER WAY BE FOUND TO COMBINE THE STANDARD ADVENTURES OF TRAVEL WITH AN ADVENTURE OF THE MIND?

Over Mountain, c/o Larrabee, P.O. Box 7190, Boulder, CO 80306 (phone 303/444-8028), provides both short and protracted stays in the winter months at the Marine Biology Center of Belize. And you've

The concert pavilion at Maho Bay

heard, of course, about nonprofit **Earthwatch, P.O. Box 43, Watertown, MA 02171.** Known for its archeological expeditions on which participants work full-time at actual digs (and therefore receive tax deductions for their contributions to scientific research), it also sponsors similar ventures in biological or ecological research. Each is led by an eminent academic expert, whose assistant you become in the arduous work of collecting, classifying, and analyzing the raw data to which you're assigned (earning, once more, a valid deduction of your travel costs).

All four organizations under this heading produce mouthwatering literature, free on request.

(7) **Educational and Study Travel.** Using vacations to pursue short-term, but very formal, courses of instruction abroad, is sharply on the rise. Hundreds of Americans enroll in four-week summer courses at Oxford, Cambridge, or Trinity Colleges in England and Ireland (consult the British Travel Authority or Irish Tourist Board for details, or read the essay in Part IV of this book entitled "A Yank at Oxford—or Cambridge"). Thousands more study languages for a month or more at the Alliance Française or Eurocentre in Paris, the Goethe Institutes in Berlin, Munich, or Dusseldorf, the Instituto Dante Alighieri in Florence, the Colegio de Estudios Hispanicos in Salamanca, the several such schools in San Miguel de Allende, Mexico (contact the appropriate tourist offices for information; and see the essay on language study abroad in Part IV). In the course of a year hundreds are staying for as little as three weeks in one of the two English-language "folk high schools" (adult residential colleges) of Denmark, on an idealistic return to the liberal arts (I've discussed these remarkable schools in a separate essay in Part IV). Write to the **New Experimental College, Skyum Bjerge, Snedsted 7752, Thy, Denmark (phone 936-234)**, or the **International Peoples' College, 1 Montebelloalle, 3000 Elsinore, Denmark (phone 213-361).**

Persons aged 60 or older (and their spouses of any age) possess the most stunning of all the short-term study-tour opportunities in the remarkable Elderhostel program—a major success that accounted for nearly 180,000 travelling "students" in 1987. For as little as $215 a week (plus air fare), they receive room, board, and tuition for one to three weeks at one (or a combination of three) of 800 colleges and universities both at home and abroad, including 4½ hours of classroom instruction (on a wide range of subjects) each day. Consult the Elderhostel catalogue at your local library (most carry a copy), or write to **Elderhostel, 80 Boylston Street, Boston, MA 02116 (phone 617/426-7788).**

(8) International Congress Travel. Here, in the typical example, you stay in any of a number of small hotels near a rambling château meeting center on the shores of a lake in Switzerland. Each day for a week you join 200 to 300 others from around the world in English-language (or simultaneously translated) seminars, group discussions, meetings, and debates interspersed with formal speeches, panel presentations, lunchtime programs, social cocktail gatherings, evening parties in which the talk goes on and on. In the usual format, you have paid one registration fee that covers accommodations, all meals, all events, and even side excursions to nearby attractions.

What I have just described is an international congress, of which thousands—literally thousands—are held throughout the world each year. Unlike a convention, these are not limited to members of a single organization, but instead invite persons from widely varying backgrounds, places, and callings to discuss the subject matter for which they are held. And although many are devoted to intensely technical topics, others deal with issues so general as to be capable of comprehension by any reasonably well-informed person.

Could any activity lend greater interest to an overseas vacation trip? Could any better way be found to combine the standard adventures of travel with an adventure of the mind?

Among the congresses recently held, open to participation by any serious person, were the World Congress on the Year of Peace, in Copenhagen, Denmark (five days), organized by the Secretariat for the International Year of Peace, 34 Kompagniestraede, DK-1208 Copenhagen K., Denmark; the International Congress on Human Resources in Community Development, in Marcinelle, Belgium (six days), organized by the International Association for Community Development, 179 Rue du Débarcadère, 6001 Marcinelle, Belgium; the International Congress on Educational Facilities, in Jerusalem, Israel (six days), organized by the Secretariat, P.O. Box 3378, Tel Aviv 61033, Israel; the Congress on Strengthening the Family and the Community, in Tokyo, Japan (seven days), organized by the International Council on Social Welfare, General Secretariat, 1/29 Kestlergasse, A-1060, Vienna, Austria.

Although, to my knowledge, no central clearinghouse exists for disseminating schedules to the public of international congresses, it's been my experience that the quarterly *Journal of the Association for World Education* contains at least four listings per issue of excellent future congresses on general issues. Send $15 for a yearly subscription to **Association for World Education, c/o Nordenfjord University, Snedsted 7752, Thy, Denmark.**

Off-Beat Vacations, III: Working, Riding, and Camping Together

*W*hen we go on va-
cation, must we
leave our minds at
home?

*St. Benedict didn't think
so. In his rule for the gover-
nance of medieval monasteries, formulated in the 6th
century, he prescribed a
yearly period of rest for his
cloistered monks, but carefully stipulated that the time
be spent in studies and reflection. Rather than simply
vegetate in their respite from
manual labors, they were to
read and compose prayers.
The activity was to be a
"vacation"—from the Latin
verb "vacare," meaning to
relinquish one thing and replace it with another.*

In the last two essays I've tried "to
replace" ("vacare") the standard holiday
trip with eight new forms of modern and
more serious travel, ranging from political study tours to scientific expeditions
into the African bush. Here I continue
with another four examples of "alternative travel" differing from the familiar and
increasingly unsatisfactory brand.

(9) Solidarity Travel. You travel in this
fashion to express your commitment to a

**While blind-sided
"solidarity trips"
aren't to my own
personal taste, they
are a recognized
category of travel
offered by
substantial firms.**

beleaguered nation, by your presence and
expenditures there, or by your vocal ex-
pressions of support to an anxious host. If
you are a reader of right-wing *Commentary* or the *National Review*, you go with
like-minded souls to Chile or the Union of
South Africa. If you subscribe to *The
Nation* or *The Progressive*, you go nowadays to Nicaragua. While blind-sided
trips of this sort aren't to my own personal taste, they are a recognized category of
travel, operated on a full-time basis by
substantial travel firms. And though the
people travelling with you are of one view
only, these trips do supply the opportunity for independent investigations of otherwise hard-to-reach nations, inaccessible
to most of us.

Specialists in the operation of solidarity
tours to Nicaragua include **Nicaragua
Network, 2025 I Street NW, Suite 212,
Washington, DC 20006 (phone 202/223-
2328); NICA, P.O. Box 1409, Cambridge,
MA 02238 (phone 617/497-7142); and
Casa Nicaragüense de Español, 853
Broadway, Room 1105, New York, NY
10003 (phone 212/777-2297).** Specialists to
the Soviet Union and countries of Eastern
Europe include **Anniversary Tours, 250
West 57th Street, Suite 1428, New York,
NY 10107 (phone 212/245-7501).** For trav-
el in China, CET (China Educational
Tours) offers custom-designed tours and
study programs which have included fem-
inist solidarity tours; contact **CET, 1110
Washington Street, Lower Mills, Bos-
ton, MA 02124 (phone 617/296-0270).**

(10) Bicycle Travel. Your mode of transport, in this instance, transforms the nature of the travel experience, brings you
close to the country life, small villages,
and rural population of your own nation
and those abroad. Example: the vastly

Bicycle tours of China

FOUR MORE NEW MODES OF TRAVEL THAT DIFFER FROM THE TIRED VARIETY

popular bicycle tours of China operated by **China Passage, 168 State Street, Teaneck, NJ 07666 (phone 201/837-1400).** Dissatisfied with the standard, urban-oriented tours of China, its Sinologist president, Fredric Kaplan (author of the definitive guidebook to China), persuaded the Chinese sports organization to provide the facilities for this offbeat approach, which visits communes and country villages, shares roads with thousands of cycling Chinese, and directly relates to the rural life led by 80% of the Chinese population. A support van carrying your luggage follows the cyclers at a discreet distance.

Here at home, dozens of organizations operate group cycling tours, but several stand out among them. The 11-year-old **Country Cycling Tours, 140 West 83rd Street, New York, NY 10024 (phone 212/874-5151),** sends cyclists to New England, the Middle Atlantic states, and Florida, in particular; the pioneering **Vermont Bicycle Touring, P.O. Box 711, Bristol, VT 05443,** does the same for the enchanting cycling lanes of its state. In the West and in Hawaii, **Backroads, P.O. Box 1626, San Leandro, CA 94577,** is a leader, as is **Tailwind Outfitters, 4130 S.W. 117th Avenue, Beaverton, OR 97005,** the latter focused on the Pacific Northwest. To Europe, try **Europeds, 883 Sinex Avenue, Pacific Grove, CA 93950,** especially active to France and Switzerland; or contact Country Cycling Tours of New York, or Vermont Bicycle Touring, listed above. All will send their four-color literature on request. (For a fuller exposition of bicycle touring, see the separate essay on the subject appearing later in this book.)

(11) Workcamp Travel. Like a miniaturized version of the Peace Corps, the inter-

> The bike brings you close to the country life, small villages, and rural population of your own nation and those abroad.

national workcamps movement sends you to labor at one of 800 socially significant projects in 36 countries during the period of your two-week or three-week vacation. In England, you refurbish the homes of disabled persons, or accompany disadvantaged children to the seashore or mountains. In Ghana or West Germany, you cart away debris from parks and game reserves. On our own shores, you maintain hiking trails in the Appalachians, or help construct low-cost housing in the town of Cambridge, Massachusetts. Although you pay your own air fare to get there, your room and board are otherwise free, except for a small registration charge. Indeed, some projects provide you with pocket money in exchange for your exertions.

Funded by over 100 U.N.-affiliated organizations, workcamps are attended by people from all over the world (their chief attraction), of whom most are in their late 20s, but some are of an older age—all intense idealists. Foreign-language ability is not, repeat *not*, usually required. While most of the camps are operated only in summer (through September), some continue all year—and it's mainly the latter that attract the older adult participants.

If you send $10 ($7 for students) to **VFP International Workcamps, Tiffany Road, Belmont, VT 05730,** by check made payable to "VFP," you'll receive a copy of the current summer workcamp directory, and also a photocopy of workcamp opportunities for the coming off-season (November through April); and you'll be placed on the mailing list to receive the organization's 1989 newsletter in March. From that start, you peruse a fascinating array of compassionate or socially useful activities, and make your choice of a meaningful, working vacation.

(12) Cooperative Camping Travel. In this increasingly popular mode—to which I've devoted a separate essay later in this book—up to 14 people share a van that comes supplied with state-of-the-art camping equipment, cooking utensils, and one paid professional driver/guide. Thus supplied, you embark on a preplanned itinerary through colorful sections of the U.S. or Europe. But because you carry your own tented "accommodations," you can improvise on that itinerary en route, detouring to nearby villages or festivals, boarding ferries for side excursions to the Greek islands, heading off into the wilds of northern Montana.

At the start, you jointly fix the size of a "food kitty" to which all campers contribute—usually about $5 per person per day. Periodically, on a rotating basis, you do the shopping and cooking for the group. All other days, you relax in the van (although you also pitch your own tent each night—it's a modern, sealed-in, pop-up variety erected in a few seconds)

Like a truncated version of the Peace Corps, the workcamp movement sends you to labor at one of 800 socially significant projects in 36 countries during the period of your two- or three-week vacation.

"Young Pioneers" in the USSR

and enjoy the freedom, fun, and flexibility of small-group travel, at costs of (exclusive of food) about $35 a day in Europe, slightly more in the U.S. and Canada.

Cooperative camping has been offered for dozens of years (and still is) by cost-conscious organizations located up and down Earls Court Road in London. The notion came to our country slightly more than 15 years ago, and although highly successful, is still one of the best-kept secrets of travel. **TrekAmerica, P.O. Box 1338, Gardena, CA 90249 (phone 213/321-0734)**, outside Los Angeles, is the key domestic name, a British organization operating camping tours to both Europe and areas of North America, with 135 custom-built vehicles currently in use, and a program of 18 itineraries jauntily described in a 28-page catalogue available free on request. They run throughout the year (though mainly April through October), refer to single people 18 to 35 as their chief clientele (and are therefore a potent matchmaker), but designate numerous departures as open to campers of all ages. Trek America attracts a worldwide but English-speaking following from Australia, New Zealand, Scandinavia, and Singapore, in particular, in addition to their American and British campers.

Cooperative camping, it should be noted, rarely ever involves a physically challenging expedition into difficult jungles or mountains. Rather, it tends to tour a classic itinerary, but in small vans, and with camping gear supplied to the group by a sponsoring organization. Some call it "participatory travel," but I prefer the explicit quality of the term "cooperative camping travel."

Again, an entire essay on cooperative camping appears later in this book.

Off-Beat Vacations, IV: From the Farm to the Foam-rubber Bus

*I*n the gilt and red-plush setting of a Paris cabaret, I had occasion recently to reflect anew on the inane quality of a great many travel programs.

At ten minutes to curtain time, not a single seat was full, not a Frenchman was in sight. Then tour buses began arriving and soon the hall was awash with people carrying cameras and guidebooks. "It is strictly prohibited," said a loudspeaker voice in English (and only in English), "to take photographs while the show is in progress."

What happened next . . . well, you know the rest. Tired dance numbers slouched onto the stage, their music canned, their theme without the slightest reference to even the popular culture of France. Broadly exaggerated imitations of French music-hall variety ensued, done without finesse or talent—and hardly rehearsed. Totally contrived for foreign visitors. Simple-minded.

And infuriating! Faced with such distortions of the travel experience, more and more of us "are mad as hell and not taking it any longer." We're turning to alternative forms of travel, of which a dozen have now been described in the preceding three essays. Here I'll conclude with a final four, designed like the others to lend substance and meaning to a holiday trip.

(13) Farm and Ranch Travel. When it sometimes seems that half the world is covered with asphalt, and life beset by frantic schedules and lists, a holiday stay on a working farm or authentic ranch is

Cabin at Rimrock Ranch, Wyoming

just what mind and body need. You return to the age-old cycles of food production and animal husbandry. You spend two or more weeks in dirty jeans and grimy face. You avoid not only the high costs, but the renewed pressures and activities, of the average slick resort.

Though guest-accepting, working farms are found around the world, the home-grown variety—around 40 major ones, supplemented by an equal number of guest-accepting, working ranches—allow you to live without language difficulties in close concert with a farm or ranch family, sharing their chores, dining at their table. At the working farms, you pay an average (expect wide variances) of $40 per person per day for accommodations and all three meals, perhaps $60 at the working ranches (I am obviously excluding the far-costlier, nonworking dude ranches and farm inns). At some, you are expected to make your own bed and par-

NEW AND BETTER FORMS OF TRAVEL

ticipate in a few light chores, exactly as if you were a nonpaying relative or guest of the proprietors.

The classic source of farm and ranch information—addresses, descriptions, and photographs, nationwide in scope, grouped by state—is a 224-page guidebook written and published for nearly 40 years by the dedicated Patricia Dickerman of New York, and largely sold through the mails. Send $11 to **Farm & Ranch Vacations, 36 East 57th Street, New York, NY 10022.** For farm holidays in Europe, request the free literature issued by most European tourist offices; and for the equivalent in Australia, write

to **Host Farms Association, c/o Mrs. Cheryl Inglis, Fairview, Pollockford Road, Unarrwarre, Australia.**

(14) Special-Interest Travel. In this broad category of tourism, you journey abroad to acquire direct experience of a hobby, profession, or other narrow subject matter: horticulture, let's say, or osteopathic medicine, automobile production or labor relations. But this time you gain that knowledge not in a classroom ("study travel"), but through interviews and visits with experts abroad, all scheduled in advance by organizations dealing with this form of travel.

Since most of the latter firms work only

> Faced with distortions of the travel experience, more and more of us "are mad as hell and not taking it any longer."

Evening entertainment at Rimrock Ranch

with groups, you turn for assistance to a government "institute" if you are a mere individual or couple travelling alone. Such quasi-governmental agencies as the Swedish Institute in Stockholm, the Danish Institute in Copenhagen, the Spanish or Austrian Institutes operating from New York—none of them charging a fee—will prepare a tightly scheduled program of interviews and briefings for serious individual Americans delving into a special interest in those countries; contact the tourist offices or cultural attachés of each such nation for the addresses.

Groups of at least ten Americans pursuing a special interest may want to use the rather remarkable **Organization für Internationale Kontakte (Organization for International Contacts), #5 Kurfürstenallee, 5300 Bonn 2, Bad Godesberg, West Germany,** to which I've devoted a separate essay in Part IV. Claiming an ability to organize briefings on any subject matter whatever—even a request for a two-week group program on ergonomics didn't recently stump them—O.I.K. is a nonprofit foundation, but charges for its services, and performs anywhere in Europe. Doing the same for major nations of Asia, again on a group

A farm vacation

IN THE DAYTIME, PASSENGERS GO RIVER-RAFTING, EXPLORING, WANDERING

Horse-packing through the Rocky Mountains

basis only, are: **Life Travel Service Co. Ltd., P.O. Box 10-1014 Petchaburitadmai, Bangkok 10311, Thailand;** and **Inter Cultural Travel Services, 43 De Waas Lane, Grandpass, Colombo, Sri Lanka.**

(15) Homestays Travel. Though closely allied to the people-to-people travel discussed in an earlier essay, international homestays involve no casual contact but a full-scale sojourn as a paying guest in the residence—and amid the comings and goings—of a foreign family. Young people have for decades enjoyed that uniquely rewarding experience through various student-exchange programs, but today adults of any age can enjoy the very same "long stays" on at least three dozen programs operated in widely scattered countries and cultures.

The definitive source of information is a 72-page booklet called *Vacations with a*

Difference, published by **Pilot Books, 103 Cooper Street, Babylon, NY 11702,** and available through the mails for $4.95, plus $1 for postage and handling. It lists homestays in Canada, France, Australia, Tahiti, and Scandinavia; homestays with Unitarians, humanists, Mennonites, and Quakers; homestays with farmers and wine growers; homestays for as little as $85 a week, including all meals. What you yourself may have done as a teenager—a month and more abroad with a foreign family—is now available in your adult and mature years, and for reasons obvious and profound, no other travel experience quite compares to it.

(16) Foam-rubber Bus Travel. From the innards of a large motorcoach, all the seats have been removed and then replaced by a foam-rubber platform. Why? So that 35 adventurous souls can stretch out to sleep, their heads on knapsacks or rolled-up coats, while the bus hurtles through the night. Daytime, the same passengers recline in varying positions, while some strum guitars or play the classics on a reedy flute. In vehicles so oddly outfitted, enabling an obvious lowering of travel costs (and an obvious camaraderie), the most casual (but perhaps the most insightful) of American tourists are today exploring geographic wonders of the U.S.A., Mexico, and Canada.

Some use the foam-rubber method to cross the country. Once every two weeks or so, from each coast (New York and Boston in the East, Los Angeles and San Francisco in the West), buses of the celebrated Green Tortoise line embark for a ten-day transcontinental adventure traversing 5,000 miles each way, yet costing only $199 per person. The buses drive mainly at night. In the day, passengers go

> When it sometimes seems that half the world is covered with asphalt, a holiday stay on a working farm or authentic ranch is just what mind and body need.

river-rafting on the Colorado, explore major national parks (Bryce, Zion, Yellowstone, Badlands, Tetons, depending on itinerary), and go wandering about all over the continental states.

Shorter Green Tortoise trips go to Baja California and mainland Mexico in the winter, to Yosemite throughout the year, up and down the West Coast. Though singles predominate, Green Tortoise urges—and receives—patronage from families and senior citizens. On one four-week tour to Alaska, the average age aboard was 45.

On all trips, passengers contribute about $5 each per day to a food "kitty" used to purchase vittles for a twice-daily cooperative cookout. Breakfast is coffee, eggs, and rolls purchased at various truckers' stops.

One of the few survivors of a number of alternative bus companies established in the late 1960s—they included the Briar Rabbit and the American Gypsy—Green Tortoise is no Greyhound, but still a flourishing company that publishes an irresistible quarterly tabloid, *Tortoise Trails*, about its most recent tour successes. For detailed information, write to **Green Tortoise, P.O. Box 24459, San Francisco, CA 94124 (phone 415/821-0803, or toll free 800/227-4766 outside California).** An East Coast competitor, but much smaller, is **Rainbow Buses, P.O. Box 29, Wendell Depot, MA 01380.**

There you have it: 16 alternative forms of travel. Have I missed any? If you think I have, please write me at the address listed in the introduction and I'll include your nomination in next year's edition of this book. In the meantime, let's work for meaningful travel.

Trekking as a Cheap and Fulfilling Mode of Travel

Like the character from Molière who suddenly discovered that he'd been speaking "prose" all his life, a growing number of Americans have learned that "trekking" is the unfamiliar word for their favorite vacation activity. Though only the barest handful of travel agents understand the term—and some misuse it horribly—international trekking has become a substantial travel activity pursued by at least 20,000 Americans each year, and currently marketed by upward of five nationwide organizations.

Trekking is walking of a special nature, elevated to a high art and mental adventure.

A trek through the Cordillera Blanca, Peru

In oversimplified terms, trekking is walking—the healthiest sport on earth—but walking of a special nature, elevated to a high art and mental adventure.

Unlike the hiking and backpacking pursued by individuals, trekking is an intricate, organized, group activity in which porters or pack animals carry your camping gear, cooking utensils, and food from one overnight campsite to another. Relieved of that weight, you're able to go where roads and paths aren't, through the most exotic of nations, over breathtaking terrain, but without performing feats of endurance or possessing mountaineering skills. Persons in their middle age are a familiar sight on treks, as are families and even seniors into their 70s.

That's not to say that minimal vigor isn't required—it is. Yet hundreds of perfectly ordinary, normally sedentary (even chubby) Americans are today found in such unlikely locations as the historic, 18,000-foot-high base camp in Nepal used

ORGANIZED WALKS ALONG THE LOWER SLOPES OF THE HIMALAYAS, ANDES, AND ALPS

by intrepid climbers for the assault on Mount Everest. They get there by trekking—organized walking—without setting a single metal wedge into stone or tugging a single rope.

And they achieve that forever-memorable trip for total land costs of less than $70 a day (plus air fare to and from Nepal, in this instance); trekking is one of the cheapest of travel modes, considering the distance you've covered and the highly personal nature of your travel arrangements (groups are never more than 15

IT IS THE ULTIMATE TRIP, THE ANSWER TO THE VAPID VACATION

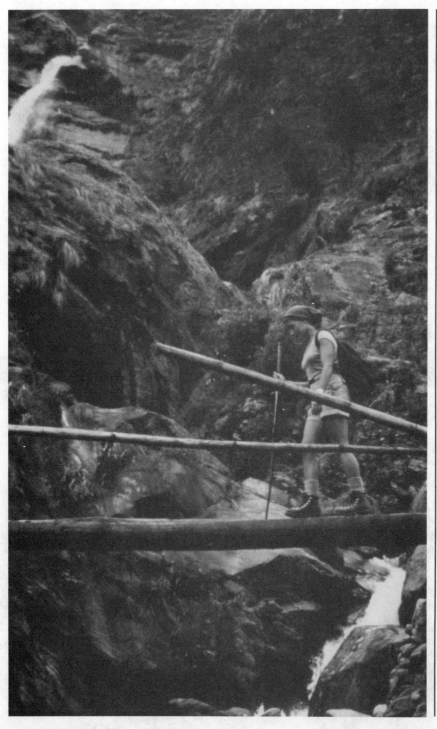

people in number). No money goes toward hotels or restaurants, because no such places exist in the areas for trekking. Apart from the one-time purchase of tents and gear by the trekking company, labor alone—the chief guide, the cook, the Nepali or Peruvian porters, let's say—are the only major expense of the venture.

I used the example of Nepal and Peru advisedly. For reasons not entirely clear to me, almost all international treks are operated to mountain areas of the world: the Himalayas, the Andes, the Swiss Alps in particular. (While you don't go atop them, you walk along their easy lower slopes, usually at elevations of 8,000 to 10,000 feet.) Though it is theoretically possible to trek through lowland valleys supplied with roads, it is apparently felt inappropriate and uninspiring to do so.

The mountain kingdom of Nepal, at the northern border of India, is the chief trekking destination, accounting for nearly 40% of all treks. The associated Indian states of Kashmir, Sikkim, and Ladakh, and portions of Bhutan, Pakistan, and Tibet, draw another 10% of all trekkers. Together these areas flank the full length of the most remarkable geographical feature on earth—the 1,500-mile-long chain of the Himalayas, the world's tallest mountains.

It was Nepal, almost entirely covered by mountains, that set off the trend to trekking. A country with scarcely any roads at all, isolated from the outside world until the 1950s, its widely scattered mountainside villages harbor 35 different ethnic groups whose ways of life have been scarcely touched by outside influences.

The people of Nepal have a particular

WHEN YOU HAVE TO WALK SIX DAYS TO A VILLAGE, YOU CAN BE PRETTY SURE IT IS UNSPOILED BY TOURISM

tradition of hospitality to strangers. As you trek the trails from village to village along the south slope of the Himalayas, you are invited to tea in small council chambers, sometimes to stay the night in the homes of villagers or in monasteries.

With unlimited access to the world's greatest mountains, in this peaceful Shangri-La whose half-Hindu, half-Buddhist population coexists without conflict, your own near-spiritual reactions are almost too intimate to describe. You awake at 6:30 a.m., when a cup of steaming tea or coffee is thrust through the flaps of your tent by a member of the cooking staff. Accompanied by experienced Sherpa guides, you take to the trails, trekking four to seven miles a day at your own pace. The trip starts and ends in the other-worldly capital of Katmandu, reached by air via New Delhi or Bangkok.

The Peruvian Andes, and that section of it known as the Cordillera Blanca, is next in popularity, accounting for perhaps 30% of all treks. From Lima you fly to Cuzco and there, your gear stowed atop a mountain burro, you embark on a 5-day, 35-mile walk along the ancient Inca Trail to the lost city of Machú Picchú, passing awesome Incan ruins unseen by conventional tourists. Again from Lima, you go by train to Huaraz to embark on an 8-day trek through the heart of Peru's highest mountain area. For an enhanced 11-day (Inca Trail) or 21-day (Inca Trail and Cordillera Blanca) trip of this nature, as packaged by some of the trekking companies, you pay $695 and $1,345, respectively (plus air fare to Peru)—an average of $68 a day for your all-inclusive needs in Peru.

In the Swiss Alps (a 10% share of the

The trekking company provides the tents, foam sleeping pads, and cooking gear; you provide the sleeping bag.

In the Himalayas

trekking industry), hut-to-hut trekking replaces the traditional variety, with vans bringing your food, clothing, and bedding to austere and unattended mountain lodges scattered among the mountain trails, a day's march from each other. The classic trip is of the Mount Blanc massif, on a trail dominated by the tallest of Europe's mountain peaks. Trips cost as little as $750 for 15 days (plus air fare to Switzerland), including lodging, meals, and the services of a support vehicle that moves camp each day.

The major trekking specialists are five in number:

Himalayan Travel, Inc., of Greenwich, Connecticut, proudly occupies the low end of the trekking industry in price: its consistently low rates for land arrangements ($60 and $70 a day, all inclusive) are matched by similar marvels in air fares, bringing you round trip between New York and Katmandu for $1,285 plus $13 tax (compared with the $1,600 from East Coast cities and $1,400 to $1,500 from West Coast cities charged by most other companies). How that fare is achieved is shrouded in secrecy and the subject of controversy. Its specialty, naturally, is Nepal (40 different treks there, 200 yearly departures), but all other mountain areas are also offered; and through its representation of a leading British trekking company, Sherpa, an extensive program of low-cost treks in the Swiss Alps, the Pyrénées, the Tyrol and Tuscany, is also available. Ask for the Sherpa catalogue when requesting other literature from: **Himalayan Travel, Inc., P.O. Box 481, Greenwich, CT 06836 (phone 203/622-6777, or toll free 800/225-2380 outside Connecticut).**

Wilderness Travel, of Berkeley, Cali-

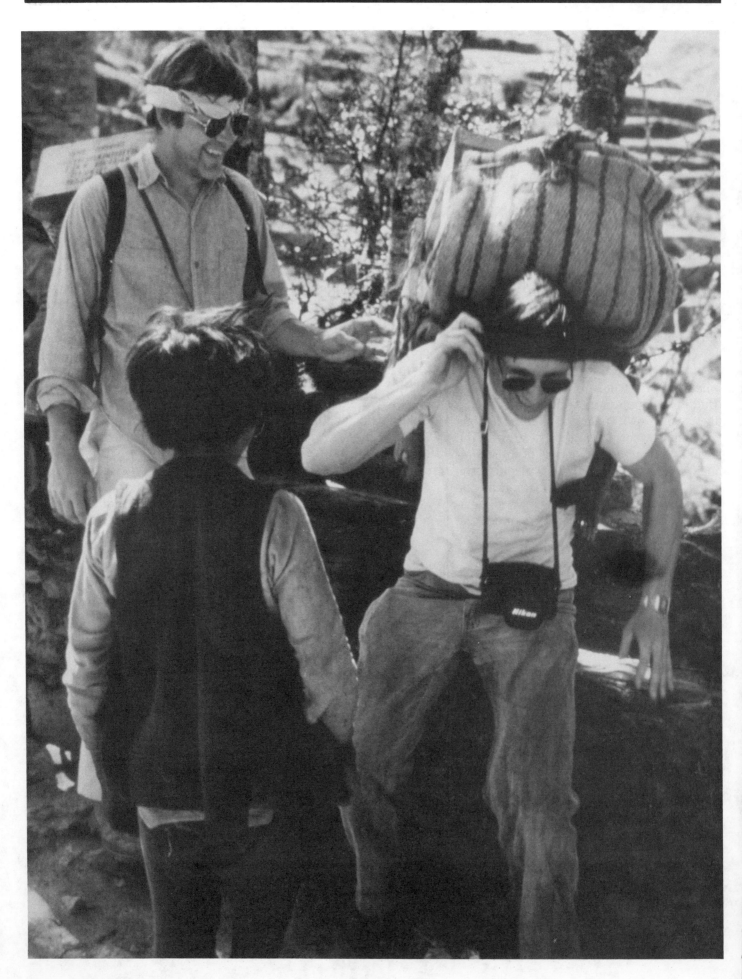

fornia, is the price competitor to Himalayan Travel, offering similar treks (including those to Nepal) but with a much greater emphasis on the mountain areas of South America, to which nearly half its passengers go. Both founders of Wilderness Travel have spent considerable time in Peru and the Patagonian region of Argentina and Chile; fittingly, the company's 24-day Patagonia Expedition is a highlight of all trekking programs. Impressive, too, is the expertise and experience of Wilderness's tour leaders, many with Peace Corps backgrounds or graduate degrees in the destinations of the treks. For interesting literature, write to **Wilderness Travel, 801 Allston Way, Berkeley, CA 94710 (phone 415/548-0420, or toll free 800/247-6700 outside California).**

Mountain Travel, of Albany, California, is the largest and oldest of the companies, operating an extraordinary variety of treks on at least five continents. Called "de luxe" by its competitors, its rates—in my reading of them—are only slightly above the industry level: an average of $80 a day in Nepal, from $80 to $150 a day in other mountain regions (plus air fare, of course). Those other areas include India, Peru, Bolivia, Turkey, and Tibet. Like all trekking companies, Mountain Travel provides the tents, foam sleeping pads, and cooking gear; you provide the sleeping bag. For free, four-color literature, write to **Mountain Travel, 1398 Solano Avenue, Albany, CA 94706 (phone 415/ 527-8100, or toll free 800/227-2384 outside California),** but for the fully unabridged, 90-page-plus Mountain Travel catalogue, add $5 (which includes postage and handling).

Journeys, of Ann Arbor, Michigan,

Relieved of your backpacks, you're able to go where roads and paths aren't, but without performing feats of endurance or possessing mountaineering skills.

Trying on the Sherpas' load

stresses the cross-cultural aspects of a trek to a far greater extent than the adventure-oriented others. It makes an intense effort to bring about meetings between trekkers and the hill people of each area. Even prior to departure, it involves its trekkers in cultural training for the trip, then delivers daily briefings en route and along the trail by speakers ranging from Buddhist monks to ordinary villagers (through interpreters). Specialists to Asia, especially Tibet and Ladakh, since 1978, and highly regarded, even by its competitors, Journeys also offers some departures to Central and South America, and charges the "going rate." Contact **Journeys, 4011 Jackson Road (P.O. Box 7545), Ann Arbor, MI 48107 (phone 313/ 665-4407, or toll free 800/255-8735 outside Michigan).**

Above the Clouds Trekking, of Worcester, Massachusetts, is still another small company whose strong suit is Nepal, with Europe (Transylvanian Alps, Yugoslavia) a strong second. "Everest from the East," using the less-traveled route there, is among its innovative, $70-a-day offerings in Nepal; the "Mountains, Monasteries, and Markets" trek its most popular tour. Like Journeys, the company stresses cross-cultural lessons, and designs its treks to maximize contacts with local residents. For brochures, write: **Above the Clouds Trekking, P.O. Box 398, Worcester, MA 01602 (phone 617/799-4499, or toll free 800/233-4499 outside Massachusetts).**

Trekking! Is this not the ultimate trip, the answer to the vapid vacation, the plastic "package," the madding throng? "When you have to walk six days to a village," a trekker once told me, "you can be pretty sure it is unspoiled by tourism."

Tented Safaris: In the Footsteps of Meryl and Robert

"We must be up early," he said, as the African moon glinted off a set of perfect teeth. "The lions tend to stalk their prey at dawn."

And she, in loving awe, stared back at the slim white hunter across a fold-up table littered with the orange peels of their dessert, the dregs of a distinguished wine. America's reigning movie queen, Meryl Streep, as the Baroness Blixen, soon to be Isak Dinesen, said little on these magical nights in the bush, but briefly dropped her hand upon his shoulder as she glided to her tent, setting the stage for a memorable movie tryst.

You have just emerged from the Academy Award–winning *Out of Africa*, and every fiber of your being yearns to go on safari into the Serengeti plains.

So you visit your travel agent and are quickly taught the facts of life.

The affordable safari

The classic African safari—the kind enjoyed by Meryl and Robert, on which native bearers cater to every need, and chill the wine for gourmet-level meals taken in the open air—well, that sort of safari costs from $600 to $700 per person per day, plus air fare to Africa. It can be had from the distinguished firm of Ker and Downey, "outfitters" of London and Nairobi, and it is not in the cards for most of us.

The more affordable safari—the so-called camera safari widely available through travel agents—transports you in

ZEBRA
(4–4 1/2 ft.
high at
shoulder)

ANTELOPE
(to 70 in. high
at shoulder)

GORILLA
(50–70 in. high)

RHINOCEROS
(3–6 1/2 ft. high at
shoulder)

On the Serengeti plain

a 12-person minibus carrying that number of mostly middle-aged Americans, on a well-travelled route through the game parks of Kenya. It costs (on the average) between $2,500 and $3,500 per person for 17 days, this time including round-trip air fare from New York, and all three meals daily while on safari.

Here, you stay each night in first-class hotels or lodges, and are served by waiters in black tie, in the dining room of each lodge, even on your memorable midtrip sojourn in a "treetops lodge." On that latter occasion, you hang a notice on the doorknob to your room, indicating which animals coming to the waterhole below are worth disturbing your sleep. "Wake me for a rhinoceros, but for nothing less," you write.

It's all so comfortable, but not quite what Ernest Hemingway—or Isak Dinesen, for that matter—had in mind.

The camping alternative

Where, then, do you secure an affordable safari closer to the classic vision of one? How do you court adventure (without risk), experience nature (without discomfort), travel through deepest Africa (without bankruptcy)? Only in the most recent years have Americans been able to do just that, by booking into group departures of a cooperative camping safari, as operated most prominently by **Overseas Adventure Travel, 6 Bigelow Street, Cambridge, MA 02139 (phone 617/876-0533, or toll free 800/221-0814 outside Massachusetts); by Sobek Expeditions, Inc., P.O. Box 1089, Angels Camp, CA 95222 (phone 209/736-4524); and by one or two other American specialists in adventure travel.

While not always cheaper than the

FOR ADVENTURE WITHOUT RISK, NATURE WITHOUT DISCOMFORT, THE CAMPING SAFARI IS THE AFFORDABLE ALTERNATIVE

others—$3,500 is the average for a 17-day trip, including round-trip air to Africa, and all-inclusive arrangements once there —these tours house you in two-person tents and on air mattresses, close to animals and nature (but without danger or discomfort); feed you out-of-doors from the bubbling pot atop a campfire; place you among high-spirited, life-challenging, intellectually curious Americans of all ages, from a tender 18 to a senior 72.

And they send you not to well-developed Kenya and its skyscraper-bestrewn capital of Nairobi, but to undeveloped, neighboring Tanzania, starting from the small city of Arusha and its transport facility with the spine-tingling name of Mount Kilimanjaro International Airport.

Why Tanzania? Because it harbors Africa's largest concentration of wildlife and outstanding natural sights. The great Serengeti plains are wholly within Tanzania. The "Rift Valley"—that seemingly endless expanse of lowlands between cliffs, pictured often in *Out of Africa*—is found from border to border in Tanzania.

In civilized Kenya, Masai warriors are frequently seen arriving at hotels to dance for tourists, but only after first changing in a back room from their jeans and T-shirts. In Tanzania, Masai are the real thing, nomadic herdsmen untouched by the modern West, running and chanting in unison to their elaborate rites of passage in the concealing hills—that scene that proved so initially frightening in *Out of Africa*.

Listen as Judy Wineland, founder and president of Overseas Adventure Tours,

> In Tanzania, Masai are the real thing, nomadic herdsmen untouched by the modern West, running and chanting in unison to their elaborate rites of passage in the concealing hills.

describes the camping safaris operated by her company with increasing frequency to Tanzania:

"We want our travelers to be active participants, not passive spectators. After a first night in a lodge in Arusha, we go as a group to the native market-place to buy our vegetables for the two weeks ahead. Meat has already been purchased and placed in freezers aboard our open-sided Bedfords, a hardy, British-made truck.

"Our groups consist of 15 Americans accompanied by three Tanzanians: a driver-guide, a cook, and a camp hand. But everyone helps to pitch the tents and cook the meals, as we drive from one game area to another."

Within those nature reserves, they quickly proceed to devour the most spectacular scenes of wildlife on earth. "We spend our first nights," she relates, "encamped on the floor of the 100-square-mile Ngorongoro Crater, surrounded by every species of animal, hearing them breathe, feeling goose pimples from the faraway roar of lions. We are at one with nature, fulfilling our internal wonders, living our dreams, experiencing unforgettable adventure but without risk.

"We get up at 7, are in the Bedford from 8 to 11 for game-viewing, drive again from 1 to 4, through such areas as the approach to Lake Manyara, with the world's largest density of elephants. We climb 5,000 feet to the Serengeti, a golden-green sweep of grass plains stretching for a hundred miles, passing for four days through herds of wildebeest numbered in the tens of thousands, seeing

several thousand zebras and giraffes in a single hour."

Masai domain

"In Tanzania," Wineland says, "we ride across eight vegetation zones, through places where no human being lives or has ever lived, except for the nomadic Masai. We have left civilization and coexist as equals with animals that have never seen a human being or truck, and have no fear of us."

One night on a recent camping safari, as Wineland tells it, a young man from Boston crept with his tape recorder outside the camp area to capture the nighttime sounds of owls. A passing Masai stumbled upon him, swore in Swahili, and was amazed to hear his words played back to him. He quickly ran away. Two hours later, as the safari group were about to enter their tents for the night, he returned with 19 other Masai, aroused from their own campsite miles away, to see the little black box that captured their speech. Until 2 a.m. they delighted in the miraculous machine and marveled at hearing their ancient chants played back to them in alternation with rounds of "Row, Row, Row Your Boat" sung by the safari campers.

That, dear readers, is travel adventure. If you're willing to be tempted beyond endurance, you can write to the above addresses for a copy of the colorful Overseas Adventure Travel catalogue, or for the thick Sobek Expeditions catalogue ($7.95 through the mails) listing adventure tours to exotic destinations all over the world, but especially to Tanzania.

Meet the Political Travel Agent, a New Breed

They are fed up and furious with the Changing of the Guard, the beach at Copacabana, the Golden Gate Bridge.

Though they are travel professionals, they are grieved by the often-trivial content of their profession. Unlike the usual travel agent—who tends to be a rather conservative retail merchant, glued to the bottom line—they are passionate idealists out to change the world.

Travel, they believe—properly conducted and serious in content—can change the consciousness of the traveller, and thereby alter the United States. Whether to the right, left, or center, and

Trips are preceded by predeparture seminars; resource people are contacted in advance to schedule interviews and lectures at the site of travel.

in however small a way, they feel they can make a difference.

Meet five examples of the "political travel agent" or "public affairs travel agent":

Schilling Travel Service, of Minneapolis/St. Paul: Open-minded, inquisitive, idealistic, and a little left of center is this increasingly well-known agency of four female partners (all unsalaried) and 12 hired hands. They emerged in unlikely fashion from the liberal wing of the Republican Party in Minnesota (now extinct), and once staged a counter-rally to the pro–Vietnam War appearance in Minneapolis of then-Gov. Ronald Reagan of California. Pushed from Republican ranks by these and other stands, they purchased an old-line travel agency and quickly proceeded to make Schilling Travel into a major source of public-interest tours booked by people from all over the country.

Though Schilling occasionally favors its middle-income clientele with the chic and

THEIR TRIPS AND TOURS ARE SHARPLY DIFFERENT FROM THE USUAL VARIETY—PROFOUND AND STIMULATING

glittering trip—accompanying the Minneapolis Symphony Orchestra to Hong Kong, or traipsing through vineyards and wineries in Australia—those are atypical lapses from a preoccupation with serious, contemporary issues. Almost monthly they send groups to Central America (Costa Rica or Nicaragua), or to compare Third World problems in Jamaica and the Dominican Republic (where they eschew the beaches and meet with activists of all views), or to visit the turbulent Philippines. Trips are preceded by predeparture seminars; groups are led by acknowledged experts in the destination; resource people are contacted in advance to schedule interviews and lectures at the site of travel.

Efficient to a fault, adept at modern marketing, the Schilling staff never forgets its larger goal. "If we could only persuade our senior senator to join our Nicaraguan tour," one Schilling partner wished aloud, "if he would go, as we go, to visit that nine-year-old crippled by a Contra landmine, and look into her eyes,

Post-revolutionary Managua

Grenadan official

he'd change his vote." For literature, write to **Schilling Travel Service, Inc., 722 Second Avenue South, Minneapolis, MN 55402 (phone 612/332-1100).**

GATE (Global Awareness Through Experience), of Harlingen, Texas: Here is the reflection in travel of the surging "Liberation Theology" movement in the Catholic Church. Determined to expose a wider public to the realities and sufferings of Third World nations, nuns of the Sisters of Charity founded the odd travel agency called GATE in Mount St. Joseph, Ohio, six years ago, then moved its offices in 1986 to Harlingen, Texas, near Brownsville and the Mexican border, to be closer to their population of concern. From Harlingen each month, photocopies of typewritten travel brochures—like none you've ever seen—go cascading forth to every part of the country, advertising GATE-led tours to Nicaragua and the barrios of Peru, or to "base communities" in Mexico. In place of "today we journey to the famous waterfall," GATE's literature talks of "dialogues with ministers, professors, and the poor," attendance at

HERE IS THE REFLECTION IN TRAVEL OF THE SURGING "LIBERATION THEOLOGY" MOVEMENT IN THE CATHOLIC CHURCH

"meetings of popular movements . . . supporting their search and struggle for freedom in their country." Tour rates (and amenities) are moderate in level; participation is ecumenical and increasingly promoted also by Protestant groups; tour leaders and destination representatives (some of them on-the-spot missionaries) are opinionated but noncontrolling.

But the emphasis is nonetheless on themes of Liberation Theology. As defined by Sister Patricia McNally, the U.S. GATE coordinator—it is "a theology in which we are all brothers and sisters, achieving equality, freeing and then empowering the oppressed to achieve their full dignity, enabling them not always to be dominated by some white-faced person . . . ." For literature, send a stamped, self-addressed envelope to **GATE, P.O. Box 3042, Harlingen, TX 78551.**

People to People International, of Kansas City, Missouri: This is the "centrist" of the political travel agencies, more heavily involved in broad public affairs than in special-interest advocacy or politics, and so prestigious as to be frequently mistaken for a U.S. government agency.

It once was. President Dwight D. Eisenhower founded it in 1956 out of a belief that people-to-people contacts across national boundaries were as vital as government efforts to maintain world peace. He initially made the organization a part of the U.S. Information Agency, then in 1961 persuaded his friend, Joyce Hall, of Hallmark Cards in Kansas City, to fund

Some believe that people-to-people contacts across national boundaries are as vital as government efforts to maintain world peace.

the transition to a private, nonprofit corporation for which the then-former President Eisenhower was the first chairman of the board. Today, in addition to its several Student Ambassador Programs sending teenagers abroad, and American-homestay plans for foreign visitors to the U.S., PTP organizes trips by several thousands of adult Americans each year to visit with their counterparts abroad: lawyers with lawyers, teachers with teachers, scientists with other scientists in their field. The goal: to "unleash the common interests among citizens of all countries and avoid the difference of national self-interest." More than 180 overseas chapters in 34 countries make the arrangements for personal contacts; several prestigious U.S. tour operators handle the technical arrangements. Because itineraries involve an intricate schedule of meetings, briefings, speeches, and seminars, the trips aren't cheap. Write: **People to People International, 501 East Armour Boulevard, Kansas City, MO 64109 (phone 816/531-4701).**

Friendship Tours, of Modesto, California: Another "centrist" approach to political touring, non-ideological but people-to-people in its orientation. To a broad variety of standard trips (China, Russia, Africa), Friendship Tours attaches university lecturers or noted journalists, then works to schedule meetings and interviews with relevant individuals at the destination. For information, write to: **Jo Taylor, Friendship Tours, 1508 Coffee Road, Suite H, Modesto, CA 95355 (phone 209/576-7775).**

Anniversary Tours, of New York City: The most leftward-leaning of all the groups, Anniversary Tours is almost in the category of a solidarity tour operator bringing preconvinced people to express their support of the Eastern European countries, to which its trips primarily go. Yet, surprisingly, some participants have reported open-minded exchanges of views and searching inquiries, even on the "Marxist Scholar Tour" to the Soviet Union, the "Friendship May Day Tour" to

factory workers, and officials of the Foreign Trade Ministry in Budapest, Tashkent, and Moscow. On a "Moscow Marathon Tour," you visit an Olympics training camp, speak with athletes, participate in an easy, ten-kilometer race. For the rest of your life, when friends boast of having traveled "off the beaten track," you can

Feminist conference, Nairobi

Russia and Prague, the "Bulgarian Youth Folk Dance Tour," the "Parents & Children's Tour to the German Democratic Republic." Tours cover a multitude of special interests, and are carefully designed to go leagues beyond the standard sights. On a "Comparative Economics Tour," you visit with noted academicians,

respond with the broadest of arrogant grins. For literature, write to: **Anniversary Tours, 250 West 57th Street, Suite 1428, New York, NY 10107 (phone 212/ 245-7501).**

Cooperative Camping with 14 Others in a Fully Equipped Van

" **W** *hen I use a word, it means just what I choose it to mean—neither more nor less."*

Those were the sentiments of Humpty Dumpty in Lewis Carroll's *Through the Looking Glass.* They could have applied to the antics of travel brochure writers in describing the activity of cooperative camping. By refusing to use the term—substituting instead a dozen or so contrived titles which only they understand—the pamphlet authors have so confused matters as to conceal this marvelous trav-

el mode from 80% of the people who could have benefited from it.

Cooperative camping (the name they won't use) is a cheap and sensible travel method for people who haven't the energy, funds, or commitment to buy and then

The vehicle is already supplied with up to 15 state-of-the-art tents and elaborate camping gear.

Camping destinations: exotic Nepal and the American West

transport their own camping equipment and/or camping vehicle to regions overseas or far away.

The operators of cooperative camping tours print literature in which they describe dozens of potential itineraries throughout the United States, Mexico, and Europe. They schedule departures for each itinerary, take bookings from widely scattered individuals, and ultimately assemble a group of about 14 for each departure.

When the group of 14 reaches the jumping-off point (London, Mexico City, Los Angeles, or New York), they board a 15-person van furnished by the operator and driven by a professional guide—the only paid employee on the trip. The vehicle is already supplied with up to 15 state-of-the-art tents, elaborate camping utensils, and (sometimes) sleeping bags—although most companies require that you provide the latter. Except for that last item, passengers avoid all the expense and burden of outfitting themselves for camping.

On the first day of the trip, participants vote to establish a "food kitty," fixing the sum they will collectively spend each day for campfire meals. Members of the group, in rotation, shop for groceries along the way, and then rotate the cooking and cleaning chores. They each pitch their own tent each night and pack it away in the morning. The driver drives. Since the group carries its own accommodations (the tents) and needn't adhere to hotel reservations, they are able either to follow the preplanned itinerary or make broad deviations from it. They are also able to travel through areas where standard hotels aren't found.

The entire trip is unstructured and fun,

THE VALUABLE NEW TRAVEL MODE THAT NO ONE PROPERLY DESCRIBES

close to nature and informal, adventurous, instructive—and cheap. The average cooperative camping tour costs around $35 a day, plus air fare, and plus about $4 per person per day in contributions to the food kitty.

So why haven't you heard of it? Blame the following:

TrekAmerica, of Gardena, California, is the largest U.S. operator of cooperative camping tours, but ought to be spanked for semantic inexactness. A "trek" isn't what they do; in holiday travel, a "trek" is an organized walk along the lower slopes of the Himalayas, Andes, or Swiss Alps, in which porters or pack animals carry your gear. Such adventure travel companies as Himalayan Travel, Mountain Travel, and Journeys, operate treks. Cooperative camping tours of the sort organized by TrekAmerica are often to distinctly unadventurous places—Yellowstone, Salt Lake City, Yosemite—but are accomplished through the delightful, semi-adventurous mode of camping.

Despite my quibbles, the company is a superb source of cooperative camping: 18 itineraries through North America, from two to nine weeks in length, with up to two dozen yearly departures per itinerary, at daily costs of $30 to $45, plus air fare, and plus a food kitty of about $30 a week. But passengers are limited to the age group of 18 to 35. Write for colorful catalogues to: **TrekAmerica, P.O. Box 1338, Gardena, CA 90249 (phone 213/321-0734).**

Toucan Adventure Tours, of Manhattan Beach, California, offers cooperative camping to offbeat locations in Mexico, and makes them available to people of all ages, encouraging even oldsters to come along. But how does their literature de-

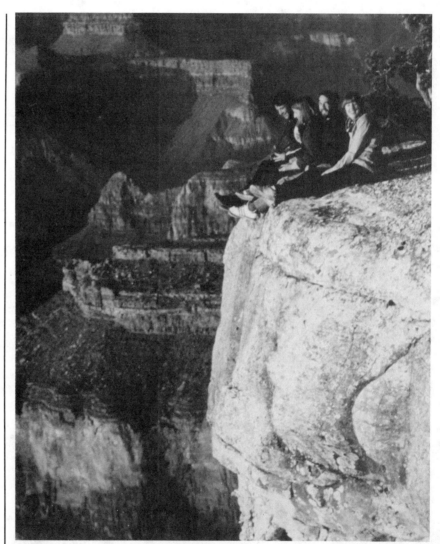

scribe the tours? As a "Mexico Toucan Adventure." Only within the text do you occasionally learn that "many nights we will camp along secluded beaches where we only have to step from our tents to reach the sea . . . We'll take time to climb a volcano, camp along beautiful mountain lakes, and visit villages where artisans craft fine works."

Toucan studiously avoids "tourist Mexico." Acapulco appears on no itinerary.

IT IS A SENSIBLE TRAVEL METHOD FOR PEOPLE RELUCTANT TO TRANSPORT CAMPING EQUIPMENT AND VEHICLE TO AREAS OVERSEAS OR FAR AWAY

Rather, from Mexico City you head south into the highlands, to Oaxaca and Tuxtla Gutierrez, or to enchanting San Cristobal de las Casas and Palenque. Or else you travel the length of Baja California, to Santa Inez and Guerrero Negro, to La Paz and Cabo San Lucas.

Itineraries are three weeks in length, cost as little as $670 (plus air fare and food kitty), and are mainly scheduled from fall through spring. Phone or write: **Toucan Adventure Tours, Inc., 1142 Manhattan Avenue, CP #416, Manhattan Beach, CA 90266 (phone 213/546-1196).**

Tracks, of London, England (now there's a trendy name describing nothing), raises the formal age limit to 38, but also explains that "travellers who are not in this age range are welcome, so long as they understand that our tours are designed for the 18–38's." Its vehicles (all supplied with camping equipment) traverse every standard European itinerary ("Ten Countries in 23 Days," "Eighteen Countries in 70 Days"), and even branch out to Eastern Europe and Russia, where it warns that "campsites . . . and camping conditions are not equal to those of Central Europe." Unlike the other companies I've surveyed, it frequently assembles larger groups than the standard 14 or so, and reserves the right to use 40-passenger motorcoaches for transportation between camping sites. But the gathering of larger groups makes for generally lower prices than the others: as little as $26 and $28 a day on the longer itineraries. To confuse matters even more, its U.S. representative is a "trekking" organization: **Himalayan Travel, Inc., P.O. Box 481, Greenwich, CT 06830 (phone 203/622-6777, or toll free**

Participants vote to establish a food kitty, fixing the sum they will spend each day for campfire meals.

800/225-2380 outside Connecticut), from which four-color brochures are available.

Finally, American Adventures, of Cambridge, Massachusetts, operates camping tours along nine far-ranging itineraries within the United States and Canada, for up to 13 passengers apiece, most for ages 18 to 38 but some for all ages also, travelling cooperatively. Trips are two to six weeks in length, average $35 a day (plus $5 daily for the food kitty), but require that you make your own way to the starting points, either New York or Los Angeles. Wonder of wonders, the company places the words "Camping Trips" (in small type) on the front cover of their catalogue, and may even go to the title "Tenting Trips" in 1988. Progress! Write to: **American Adventures, Inc., 650 Cambridge Street, Cambridge, MA 02141 (phone 617/499-2730).**

A Search for Reliable Sources of Bicycle Tours

Franklin Roosevelt did it in his youth, gliding for weeks along the country roads of Switzerland and Germany in the course of an enchanted summer.

John F. Kennedy, Jr., did it more recently, on vacation from prep school. And so have many more from other wealthy, or at least moderately well-off, families.

On the lanes and roads of rural France, on the always-level pavements of cycle-loving Holland, over the softly rolling hills of Vermont, in Oregon, and even in Hawaii, increasing numbers of Americans—of ever-increasing age—are flocking to the group bicycle tour.

But why is the activity so expensive—often $100 a day? Why are bicycle tours more costly, on occasion, than tours by escorted motorcoach? After all, it is you and your two legs that provide the transportation, eliminating a costly vehicle.

Or is that the case?

What most of us fail to consider, in scanning the bicycle brochures, is that a vehicle almost always does accompany the group to carry luggage. Unless you've opted for the most rugged form of tour, carrying nothing but your cycling costume, a van or truck and a paid driver follow the bicycling tour at a discreet distance.

> What most of us fail to consider is that a vehicle almost always does accompany the group to carry luggage.

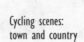
Cycling scenes: town and country

Because that group is usually limited to 20-or-so people, the cost of the vehicle and driver is also divided among fewer persons than on a 45-seat motorcoach trip. And because this mode of travel appeals to a more limited audience, all other costs —marketing of the tour, scouting the itinerary, escorting the group—are also proportionately higher per person.

Thus bicycle tours, except in rare instances (see below), will continue to cost a hefty sum—but one that's justified by advantages aplenty: the best sort of exercise in the open air, the closeness to nature and contact with rural people, the scenery, and the relief from urban pres-

A DOZEN COMPANIES THAT TAKE YOU BIKING TO ALL PARTS OF THE WORLD

sures.

But there are pitfalls; they mainly stem from the ease with which underfinanced or inexperienced people can schedule a bicycle tour. Because so many shaky operators flood the mails each year with ill-conceived programs, destined to cause trouble, I've sought to ferret out the firms that have made a substantial, long-term commitment to this travel sport. The list is by no means complete; if you know of others, please write me at the address given in the introduction.

Unless otherwise stated, all tours accept members of any age, provide a supply van, and will rent you a bike (for an extra charge) if you haven't brought your own.

Vermont Bicycle Touring, of Bristol, Vermont: The pioneer in country inn cycling, 15 years old, it operates almost wholly in the unspoiled state of Vermont, with its well-maintained and relatively traffic-free roads. The tours of interest to most are five days long, cost an average of $95 a day, and include two high-quality meals daily and lodging in charming country inns, some of luxury standard. A mouthwatering, four-color, 32-page catalogue is had by writing **Vermont Bicycle Touring, P.O. Box 711, Bristol, VT 05443 (phone 802/453-4811).**

Vermont Country Cyclers, of Waterbury Center, Vermont: The chief competitor to Vermont Bicycle Touring, with similar tour features, prices, and policies, and an excellent catalogue. Its five-day tour of the coast of Maine ($100 a day) is a popular addition to its Vermont repertoire. Write **Vermont Country Cyclers, P.O. Box 145, Waterbury Center, VT 05677 (phone 802/244-5215).**

Country Cycling Tours, of New York City: A well-established (11 years) operator of bicycle tours through the eastern United States and to Europe. Domestic itineraries are particularly novel, and go "island-hopping" in New England (Martha's Vineyard, Nantucket, Newport), to the horse-and-wine country of northern Virginia, along the eastern shores of Maryland; they also include the unique feature of transportation from Manhattan to the place where tours start. To Europe, tours go (for two weeks) to the Cotswolds of England, County Donegal in

ONE ELEGANT BIKE TOUR USES HIGH-QUALITY VILLAS, CASTLES, COUNTRY
HOMES, AND CHÂTEAUX FOR ITS OVERNIGHT LODGINGS

Ireland, the Loire and elsewhere in France. Lodgings are comfortable country inns in the U.S., two-star or three-star hotels in Europe; two meals a day are always included; and tours average $100 a day in both the U.S. and Europe ($92 a day in Ireland), plus air fare. Write **Country Cycling Tours, 140 West 83rd Street, New York, NY 10024 (phone 212/874-5151).**

Euro-Bike Tours, of DeKalb, Illinois: Well-priced tours of Europe (by the pricey standards of bike touring; about $90 a day, plus air fare), almost all of two weeks' duration. Interesting itineraries (the Dordogne of France, the islands of Scandinavia, the "Romantic Road" of Germany), operated June through early October, on which you receive room, breakfast, and 30% of your dinners, in lodgings ranging from first-class hotels down to intimate inns without private bath. Write **Euro-Bike Tours, P.O. Box 40, DeKalb, IL 60115 (phone 815/758-8851).**

International Bicycle Tours, of Chappaqua, New York: Primarily Holland (though elsewhere in Europe too), for one or two weeks, as organized by a native Amsterdammer, now a longtime resident of the U.S. Tours to Holland include high-quality hotels with breakfast, and three dinners, and cost $850 for one week tours and $1,200 for two week tours (not including air fare)—the latter tour works out to about $80 a day, a value. Because the flat terrain of Holland makes cycling easy for even older Americans, some departures are designated for persons over the age of 50 only. Contact **International Bicycle Tours, 12 Mid Place, Chappaqua, NY 10514 (phone 914/238-4576).**

Butterfield & Robinson, of Toronto: A highly elegant (and expensive) Canadian

Some novel bike tours go island-hopping in New England (Martha's Vineyard, Nantucket, Newport), to the horse-and-wine country of northern Virginia, or along the eastern shores of Maryland.

company active as well in the United States. Its major bike program is to Europe (France, Italy, England, especially); uses high-quality villas, castles, country homes, and châteaux; includes two meals a day (with minor exceptions) at top restaurants; throws in "wine tastings"; and averages $200 (some tours more, some less) per person per day, not including air fare to Europe. Special student departures cost considerably less. Write for an 86-page catalogue, like a costly picture book, to **Butterfield & Robinson, 70 Bond Street, Toronto, Ontario, Canada M5B 1X3 (phone 416/864-1354, or toll free 800/268-8415 outside Ontario), or 11 Pourtales Road, Colorado Springs, CO 80906 (phone toll free 800/387-1147).**

Far West Tours International, of Los Angeles: Offers an unusually broad array of European itineraries, on which it uses good, middle-class hotels; supplies two meals a day; and (unlike the practice of most companies) includes use of a seven-speed Swiss bike for free. Prices average $100 to $125 a day, plus air fare. Write **Far West Tours International, 4551 Glencoe Avenue, Suite 205, Marina del Rey, Los Angeles, CA 90292 (phone 213/827-8181, or toll free 800/533-1016, 800/648-8827 in California).**

Gerhard's Bicycle Odysseys, of Portland, Oregon: In February and March of each year: 20-day bike tours of New Zealand, costing $90 a day, plus air fare. From June through September: two-week tours to Germany and Austria, at $120 a day, plus air; all are personally led by German-born Gerhard Meng, now in his 15th year of bicycle-tour operation. Fine country hotels are used; cyclists receive daily breakfast and almost all dinners. Write **Gerhard's Bicycle Odysseys, 4949**

S.W. Macadam, Portland, OR 97201 (phone 503/223-2402).

Backroads Bicycle Touring, of San Leandro, California: All-year-round tours of the western states, Baja California, Hawaii, New Zealand, Tasmania, Bali, and, new in 1988, France—all well described in a slick, 32-page free catalogue. Groups are of all ages; if seniors find some itineraries overly taxing, they can ride in the support van (the aptly named "sagwagon") for part of each day. Tours include all three meals daily, plus accommodations in fine inns, and average $120 a day, though some are cheaper. Write **Backroads Bicycle Tours, P.O. Box 1626-Q355, San Leandro, CA 94577 (phone 415/895-1783)**.

Paradise Peddalers, of Charlotte, North Carolina: Three-week tours to New Zealand and Australia, every January through March, at the remarkable price of $50 a day (plus round-trip air fare) for inns or motels and two meals a day; but no support van accompanies the group, and members place their clothing and equipment into bicycle "panniers." Two experienced guides cycle with each group. Write **Paradise Peddalers, P.O. Box 32352, Charlotte, NC 28232**.

Arrow to the Sun, of Taylorsville, California: Energetic, exotic tours of Baja California, the Canary Islands, the Yucatán, and Costa del Sol (in addition to weekend trips through the West), camping out each night in tents carried in a support van and supplied by the tour operator, and including three meals a day. Prices average $40 a day, plus air fare. Write **Arrow to the Sun, P.O. Box 115, Taylorsville, CA 95983**.

China Passage/Asia Passage, of Teaneck, New Jersey: Bicycle tours of China,

The cost is offset by advantages aplenty: the best sort of exercise in the open air, the closeness to nature and contact with rural people, the relief from urban pressures.

Bali, and Mongolia, 16 to 22 nights in duration, all inclusive except for breakfast in Hong Kong and bicycle rentals. Because of the high air fares, included in tour prices, total charges range from $2,225 to $3,650, but actual land costs average about $100 a day. Write **China Passage/Asia Passage, 168 State Street, Teaneck, NJ 07666 (phone 201/837-1400)**.

Forum Travel International, of Pleasant Hill, California: In business for 22 years, it claims to be the oldest and largest of America's bicycle operators, but achieves that status in part by representing a number of foreign operators, for which it accepts bookings. Aside from going to all the standard places (it has particularly cheap tours to France), it operates where the others don't: Peru, Kenya, Madagascar, Czechoslovakia, Rumania, Hungary, Sweden, Norway, North Africa, China, Australia, the Caribbean. Almost all tours use quality hotels and provide two meals a day and a support van, and average $80 to $100 a day, plus air. Write **Forum Travel International, 91 Gregory Lane, Suite 21, Pleasant Hill, CA 94523 (phone 415/671-2900)**.

American Youth Hostels, of Washington, D.C.: The price champion of all the bicycle operators, for people of all ages, its trips average $25 a day in the U.S., $65 a day in Europe, including all three meals (cooperatively prepared by the group) daily, but plus air fare to the jumping-off point. That's because spartan hostels are used for lodgings, and no van accompanies the group; rather, you balance a knapsack over the rear wheel. Write **American Youth Hostels, P.O. Box 37613, Washington, DC 20013**.

The Bold, New World of the Feminist Tour Operator

Should women travel only with other women? Should they do so on occasion?

If the trip is one of outdoor adventure, involving physical challenge, should they travel only with other women? Should they agree to accompany men on a group tour only if the group is led by a woman?

Because so many women are responding to one or more of the above questions with a resounding "Yes," a sizable new segment of the travel industry has emerged to serve their wants. As surprising as it may seem, more than 50 tour companies in a dozen major states are now openly feminist in their orientation, and limit their clients or leadership to women only.

The reason is unrelated to sexual proclivities or the lack of them. From a review of their literature, not one of the 50 new firms seems operated for homosexuals, and most stand carefully apart from a wholly separate group of tour companies openly appealing to gay men or gay women.

Rather, the move to feminist travel seems motivated by a combined goal of consciousness-raising and female solidarity, and by the belief that women enjoy a holiday change of pace, stress-free, relaxing, when they travel only with other women. Though the philosophy is rarely

A sizable, new segment of the travel industry has emerged to serve the feminist cause.

articulated in the feminists' tour brochures, and is obtained with difficulty even in conversations with feminist tour operators (I've now spoken with several), the gist of it seems as follows:

When women travel with men, and especially on outdoor trips, both they and the men, say the feminists, tend to fall into predetermined gender roles: the men do the heavy work, the women putter about and cook. Travelling only with other women, women accept greater challenges, court greater responsibility, acquire new skills, gain confidence and a heightened sense of worth.

Male travelers are conditioned by society to be excessively goal-oriented: they must conquer this or that mountain, show prowess and strength, domineer. Most

ORGANIZED TRAVEL FOR WOMEN ONLY

women, by contrast, enjoy the mere experience of travel, the joy of encountering nature, all without stressful competition or expectations. They have less need to

boast and strut; they lack the male's inner urge (from early upbringing) to seem always skillful, strong, serene, and protecting. "I don't want to be protected on vacation," say many women; "I want to be myself."

In the presence of the other sex, so goes the argument, both sexes find it difficult to "let down their hair." On a tour limited to women, say the feminists, these tensions subside. Women spend less time on personal appearance and grooming, dispense with sexual role-playing, care only for themselves.

"And why should men feel threatened by that need?" asks one prominent female tour operator. "Why should an all-female tour be the subject of sneers? Men have been going off to hike or fish 'with the boys' for centuries."

Practical considerations: Since everyone on a woman-only trip is "single," participants pay no single supplement, but instead share rooms and costs. Since some male spouses don't care for outdoor trips, feminist tours often provide the only vacation outlet for women who genuinely enjoy the attractions of nature. Then, too, women who are recently widowed or divorced are enabled by such tours to meet others in the same situation; the experience is healing, restorative. But mainly, the women "take charge" of their holiday, free from the customary domination of men.

The largest (65 departures a year) and oldest (11 years) of the feminist tour operators, and a clearinghouse for all the rest, is Woodswoman, of Minneapolis. Nonprofit, and eager to promote the offerings even of its competitors, its twice-yearly publication, *Woodswoman News*, is replete with the ads of dozens of widely scattered feminist travel firms. Most of the latter are engaged in purely local operations.

While Woodswoman is also heavily ori-

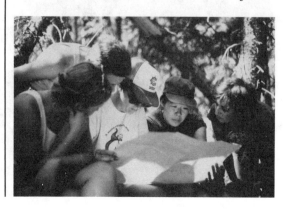

TRAVEL AS A FORM OF CONSCIOUSNESS-RAISING

ented toward its own state of Minnesota (and the nearby Northwest), it supplements that emphasis with expeditions to California, Alaska, Ireland (for biking), the Swiss Alps (for hiking), and Nepal (for trekking, an organized walk along the lower slopes of the Himalayas). Send either $2 (for postage and handling) for a copy of the organization's 20-page *Woodswoman News*, or else $15 for a year's membership (including all publications and related services) to: **Woodswoman, 2550 Pillsbury Avenue South, Minneapolis, MN 55404 (phone 612/870-8291).**

Runners-up to the leader? Marian Stoddart's Outdoor Vacations for Women Over 40, of Groton, Massachusetts, and Bonnie Bordas's Womantrek, of Seattle, Washington, vie for the No. 2 spot. The first is active mainly in the northeastern states; the second (Womantrek) ranges far afield to New Zealand and China (on bicycle

Swiss Alps

Nepal

tours), Peru, Nepal, and northern India (for trekking), Egypt, Africa, and Baja California (the latter for sea kayaking, open to "absolute beginners"). Write **Outdoor Vacations, P.O. Box 200, Groton, MA 01450 (phone 617/448-3331,** or **Womantrek, 1411 East Olive Way (P.O. Box 20643), Seattle, WA 98102 (phone 206/325-4772)**, requesting literature on the areas that interest you.

Still another relatively large firm is Womanship, of Annapolis, Maryland, offering a learn-to-sail program in a field of sport heavily dominated by men. Because (according to founder Suzanne Pogell) men tend to handle the main tasks on sailing expeditions, women are rarely able to do more than prepare the sandwiches; certainly they never "take charge" of the vessel. With Womanship, they do, gaining confidence, achieving independence. Weekend, weekday, and weeklong cruises are offered for beginners ages 20 to 70, in locations ranging from Chesapeake Bay, Long Island

> Traveling only with other women, they believe, women gain confidence and a heightened sense of worth.

Sound, the west coast of Florida, and the Pacific Northwest (San Juan and the Gulf Islands) to the U.S. Virgin Islands. Write **Womanship, Inc., 137 Conduit Street, Annapolis, MD 21401 (phone 301/269-0784 or 301/267-6661).**

Other major feminist tour operators include **New Dawn Adventures, 518 Washington Street, Gloucester, MA 01930 (phone 617/283-8717)**, heavily emphasizing camping retreats on the island of Vieques, Puerto Rico; **Mariah Wilderness Expeditions, P.O. Box 248, Point Richmond, CA 94807 (phone 415/233-2303); Adventures for Women, P.O. Box 515, Montvale, NJ 06745 (phone 201/930-0557)**, centering on New Jersey and New York; **Alaska Women of the Wilderness, P.O. Box 775226, Eagle River, AK 99577 (phone 907/688-2226); Earthwise, 2F Brookside Condominiums, Brattleboro, VT 05301 (phone 802/254-2522);** and **New Routes, Inc., R.F.D. 2, Box 2030, Brunswick, ME 04011 (phone 207/729-7900).**

A Selfless Vacation, the Jimmy Carter Way

H *is life—comparatively speaking—was in ruins. He had been defeated for reelection to the presidency. His family business was in debt. Prematurely retired, shaken and adrift, he faced a mid-life crisis more intense than most, but similar in essence to that confronting millions of middle-aged Americans.*

And so he and his wife travelled. But in a different way. What restored the spirits of Jimmy and Rosalynn Carter, among several major steps, was an uncommon series of selfless, "outer-directed" trips. For them, travel was undertaken to discover new world issues and social needs, and—equally important—to be involved in curing the ills that travel revealed.

The vacation challenge, writes the former president, "lies in figuring out how to combine further education with the pleasures of traveling in distant places, and, on occasion, helping to make the lives of the people you visit a little better." Having done both, the Carters leave little doubt that the activity has launched them on a second, rewarding phase of life.

In a remarkable book recently published by Random House—*Everything to Gain: Making the Most of the Rest of Your Life*—Jimmy and Rosalynn Carter tell, among other things, of the several life-enhancing travel or travel-related organi-

The vacation challenge, writes the former President, "lies in [combining] further education with the pleasures of traveling."

zations with which they have associated their names, or which they recommend to others. These are: the Friendship Force, Habitat for Humanity, GATE (Global Awareness Through Experience), the Citizen Exchange Council, and International Executive Service Corps.

The Friendship Force is already known to many Americans. It is the 10-year-old, nonprofit, Atlanta-based organization founded by the Carters and the Rev. Wayne Smith, which each year sends thousands of adult travellers ("citizen ambassadors") to live for one or two weeks in foreign homes found in 45 countries, including the Soviet Union. Subsequently, the foreign hosts come here to live in American homes. Since the stay in each case is basically without charge (except for transportation and administration), the cost of a Friendship Force holiday is considerably less than for standard trips to the same destination, and upward of 400,000 people have thus far participated. Upon returning, they continue to exchange correspondence or privately arranged visits with the families they have met. In this way, writes Rosalynn Carter, "friendships are . . . made that can only lead to a more peaceful world."

For information on membership in the Friendship Force, and on the 1988–1989 exchanges planned from dozens of U.S. cities, write: **Friendship Force, Suite 575, South Tower, One CNN Center, Atlanta, GA 30303 (phone 404/522-9490).**

Habitat for Humanity is a less obvious travel resource. Based in Americus, Georgia, near the Carter household in Plains, it was created 11 years ago (before the Carters' involvement in it) to work for the elimination of poverty housing (namely, shacks) from the U.S. and the world.

THE REWARDS OF UNDERTAKING AN UNCOMMON SERIES OF "OUTER-DIRECTED" TRIPS

Its founder, a fierce Christian crusader named Millard Fuller, enlisted the assistance of Jimmy Carter in the period immediately following Carter's defeat for reelection.

At Fuller's urging, the Carters travelled by bus to Manhattan, lived in a spartan, church-operated hostel, and worked each day for a week as carpenters in the rehabilitation of a 19-unit slum tenement in New York's poverty-ridden Lower East Side. The worldwide publicity from that volunteer effort made Habitat into a powerful organization that built more than 1,000 houses in 1987 (and a projected 2,000 homes in 1988) in 205 locations in the United States and Canada, and in 19 Third World nations overseas.

Jimmy and Rosalynn Carter continue to travel periodically to workcamps at these locations.

Though others may recoil from the suggestion that arduous, physical labor on a construction site can be a "vacation" activity, hundreds of Habitat volunteers disagree. To cast their lot with the poor is, for them, many times more refreshing than lazing at a tropical resort. If they have one to three weeks off, they travel to work at more than 40 Habitat locations in the U.S., paying for their own transportation and food, and often receiving accommodations—rather basic—at the site. No prior construction experience is required; almost anyone can be taught to perform a useful building function.

When volunteers do possess special qualifications, and have at least a month to give, they can occasionally go to the overseas projects of Habitat (managed by three-year volunteers), again paying their own way. There, they work side by side

The traveller, he believes, should be involved in curing the ills that travel reveals.

with the very Zaireans, Ugandans, Peruvians, and South Sea islanders who will eventually occupy the homes under construction.

For information on how you can devote your vacations to building a "habitat for humanity," or for application forms, contact **Habitat for Humanity, Habitat and Church Streets, Americus, GA 31709 (phone 912/924-6935)**.

Other Carter-approved travel programs include the **International Executive Service Corps, Eight Stamford Forum (P.O. Box 10005), Stamford, CT 06904 (phone 203/967-6000)**, arranging trips by retired business executives to lend their expertise to would-be entrepreneurs in developing nations; **Citizen Exchange Council, 18 East 41st Street, New York, NY 10017 (phone 212/889-7960)**, offering group trips to engage in exchange of views with counterpart organizations in the Soviet Union; and **GATE (Global Awareness Through Experience), P.O. Box 3042, Harlingen, TX 78551**, with tours to experience the realities of Third World life, operated by a Catholic order, the Sisters of Charity.

For the Carters, as for so many Americans, simply to lie on a beach, or otherwise turn off the mind, is no longer the sole—or even the wisest—approach to vacationing. Using the mind is a far happier leisure activity. Seeking challenge and new ideas is the way to travel pleasure. A change can help us, in Allan Fromme's words, "become more alive again."

And when the changes achieved through travel are combined with selfless activity—work designed to help others or advance world understanding—then what results is not a mere vacation, but some of the most rewarding interludes of life.

III

Alternative "Resorts"—the Holiday Camps and Communities That Can Change Your Life

On the Road to Utopia, I

S̲how me a utopian community, and I'm soon walking on air. The very thought of people uprooting themselves and reassembling to lead a rational life brings goosepimples to my flesh, awakens youthful dreams of a better world.

Well, wonder of wonders, our nation harbors a hundred and more utopian communities, and some of them accept short-term visitors. Can you think of a more rewarding weekend or weeklong stay than at a modern Walden, an Erewhon, a Shangri-La?

None of them, of course, would be so bold as to style themselves by those long-hallowed names. Rather, they are simply "intentional communities" or "New Age communities"—modern terms for those who have gathered onto a rural or small-town site to pursue a carefully planned life of cooperation and sharing.

Some are simply working farms occupied by three or four families, and obviously unsuitable for visiting tourists. Others, a growing number, are elaborate villages, with 60 to 100 residents, that encourage visitors and maintain overnight lodgings for them. From there they take you to classrooms, tour you through the site, lecture and prod you to reexamine your own harshly competitive life.

If all this seems threatening, or against your political grain, you might pause to consider that throughout history, similar intentional communities—both here and abroad—have introduced approaches to

Can you think of a more rewarding weekend or weeklong stay than at a modern Walden, an Erewhon, a Shangri-La?

life, and forms of social organization, that later became commonplace.

The communal homes of a Denver or Washington, D.C., in which young single people share costs, are outgrowths of the experience of intentional communities. So are the ever-more-frequent platonic households of two singles of the opposite sex sharing an apartment.

The very same intentional communities first launched to a broader audience the current, widespread consumption of health foods, the growing practice of holistic medicine, protection of the natural environment, energy conservation and the use of renewable, nonfossil fuels, the soaring interest in Eastern philosophies and religions (zen, tao, yoga), humane attitudes toward animals.

"We are like laboratories for research into the future," said a member of one community in the course of my own visit. "We are testing the methods that people a hundred years from now will use to improve their lives."

Among the communities that take visitors are these prominent examples (rich opportunities for your next holiday trip):

Twin Oaks, near Louisa, Virginia: Nearly 100 people live in this 20-year-old collection of farm buildings on 400 acres of woods, creeks, hilly pastures, and meadows—their goal an eventual community of 200 to 300. To promote both membership and viewpoints, visits are permitted, but only on most (not all) Saturday afternoons from 1 to 4 p.m. (no food is served), for $3 per adult, and only through prior arrangement by phone. Those more seriously

AT "INTENTIONAL COMMUNITIES" ACROSS THE U.S.A., SHORT STAYS AND VISITS ARE A MIND-EXPANDING EXPERIENCE

interested in joining are then allowed to make a three-week visit, for $2 a day, using self-supplied sleeping bags on the floor of several visitors' rooms.

Heavily influenced by the utopian novel of the Harvard psychologist B. F. Skinner *(Walden Two)*, the community attempts to be a "model social system" through rational approaches to life that avoid the spiritual emphasis of several other communities. Political solutions are stressed, logic is the tool, and all forms of modern media—books, records, tapes, and magazines, everything except television (because it promotes "those values and products that we are trying to avoid")—are amply available on site.

At Twin Oaks, all labor, property, and resources are held in common, but personal privacy is fiercely protected. Children are raised as in an Israeli kibbutz, occupying their own residence and raised by all adult members. Supervision of economic life is by numerous planner-managers elected to short terms, and the community is self-sufficient through the manufacture of handcrafted hammocks and chairs, other small industries, the cultivation of extensive organic gardens serving a mostly vegetarian table.

Twin Oaks is easily reached by bus or car from Washington, D.C., but is even closer to Richmond, Charlottesville, or Culpeper. For literature, or to schedule a visit (even the afternoon visit must be booked in advance), contact **Visitor Program, Twin Oaks Community, Louisa, VA 23093 (phone 703/894-5126).**

East Wind, near Tecumseh, Missouri, in the Ozark hills, is another, kibbutz-

Some are elaborate villages, with 60 to 100 residents, that encourage visitors and maintain overnight lodgings for them.

like, B. F. Skinner–influenced community of 70-or-so members pursuing a "peaceful, cooperative, and egalitarian" life free of "racist, sexist, and competitive behavior." Constantly experimental, open-minded, and diverse, it places a music practice space next to a dairy barn, a trailer-library alongside the inevitable shops for producing hammocks, sandals, and—a proud specialty—"nut butter." Members, each with a full vote, have substantial labor or production quotas, but enjoy weekend rest, plus three weeks of vacation a year, and can earn additional vaca-

tion by producing "overquota." Children are raised by "metas"—members who have chosen childcare as their work—but have at least three other "primary people" in their lives: their parents, and one or two others chosen by the parents.

Because East Wind is anxious to expand, it encourages free visits for up to three weeks by people who then work the same number of hours as members and spend only the amount of money on site as would equal a member's allowance. Any fears of a spartan life that these rules may evoke are soon overcome by the idyllic natural setting of the site, an area re-

"WE ARE LIKE LABORATORIES FOR RESEARCH INTO THE FUTURE," SAID A MEMBER OF ONE COMMUNITY IN THE COURSE OF MY VISIT

nowned for its swimming, canoeing, hiking, and other outdoor recreation.

Write ahead for reservations (and don't simply drop in) to **East Wind Community, P.O. Box FB5, Tecumseh, MO 65760 (phone 417/679-4682).**

Sirius, near Amherst, Massachusetts, emphasizes spirituality to the same or even greater extent than its political notions of cooperation and sharing; indeed, it differs from numerous other communities by encouraging members to earn their own incomes, sometimes at jobs in neighboring towns. But members purchase food jointly, take most meals communally, own the 86 acres of their site jointly, reach community decisions by consensus—and meditate until all members acquiesce in the "rightness" of the decisions taken.

Like Thoreau, the Sirius participants have built their homes "in the woods," and there they engage in organic gardening, holistic health practices, and solar

building. But it is personal growth to which most attention is paid. Though members are free to pursue varying spiritual disciplines, they believe in the God within each human being and the "interconnectedness" of all nature (animals, plants, humans). Several prominent members are alumni of the famous Findhorn Community in Scotland (we'll be visiting that magical place in a subsequent essay) and apply the same loving care to gardens and forests that Findhorn regards as a moral imperative.

Personal growth, so claims the Sirius

Throughout history, similar "intentional communities" have introduced approaches to life, and forms of social organization, that later became commonplace.

group, results from the demands of harmonious group living. Members rid themselves of old patterns, become "agents of change," build for themselves and others "a more peaceful, loving world."

Visits by outsiders can be made for several days or up to several weeks. Less intensive, free open houses are held on the first and third Sundays of every month, starting with a tour at 11 a.m., a meditation at 12:30 p.m., and ending with a "potluck lunch" (meaning, bring your own food) from 1 to 3 p.m. On overnight stays of any duration, guests either join in community work or spend the time in quiet contemplation; accommodations fees are on a sliding scale according to the guest's income, include all three meals daily, and range from $15 to $30 a day. Guests are always asked (even for attendance at a free Sunday open house) to phone first for instructions

and to let Sirius members know that they are coming.

Though Sirius is located on Baker Road in Shutesbury, its mailing address is: **Sirius Community, P.O. Box 388, Amherst, MA 01004 (phone 413/259-1251).**

Sunrise Ranch, near Loveland, Colorado: One of the oldest (1940s) and most successful (140 residents) of the alternative communities, its emphasis is almost entirely on personal, spiritual growth, and not on communal, social, or economic practices. Still, the major activity is organic gardening (supplying most of the ranch's foodstuffs), followed closely in the use of personnel by clerical functions supporting the worldwide activities of the Society of Emissaries, the sponsoring organization. The latter's doctrines are a mild, broad, and initially hard-to-comprehend philosophy of "quality living" through "alignment with the rhythms and cycles of life." "Manipulation," says Sunrise teacher Nick Giglio, "as well as hidden agendas and tools of persuasion are unnecessary excess baggage."

Visiting facilities are extensive, cost only $20 a day, including all three meals, and should be reserved in advance by writing to **Sunrise Ranch, 5569 No. County Road 29, Loveland, CO 80537 (phone 303/667-4675).** Loveland is 50 miles north of Denver, and the ranch is seven miles from Loveland.

Stelle, 90 miles south of Chicago: At the opposite political spectrum from the communal societies described above, Stelle is a small, planned village (like a miniature Columbia, Md., or Reston, Va.) in which homes are privately owned and incomes privately earned. But various cooperative (not communal) institutions bind the residents together, including bulk purchases

> Personal growth, they claim, results from the demands of harmonious group living. Members rid themselves of "old patterns," become "agents of change," build for themselves and others "a more peaceful, loving world."

of food, joint operation of a local telephone exchange, periodic "celebrations," and a town hall form of pure democratic government. Residents consider themselves an extended family.

The village is most productively visited not for contacts with its residents (here, occasionally difficult to arrange), but for exposure to the library, publications, and audio-visual presentations of its quarterly, *Communities Magazine*, dealing with subjects that affect the operation of intentional communities. You do this either on

a day trip, or overnight for $20 single, $25 double, including breakfast, at any of about 20 bed-and-breakfast houses. Write or phone in advance to **Communities, 105 Sun Street, Stelle, IL 60919 (phone 815/256-2252).**

On the Road to Utopia, II

"*T* *he mass of men lead lives of quiet desperation." So said Henry David Thoreau, and pained by the thought, he took to the woods to start a new and better life.*

At least 200,000 modern Americans have done much the same. In hundreds of small farm settlements or tiny villages, or more frequently in thousands of urban communal households, they have rejected the current forms of society and sought Utopia: a life of cooperation not competition, of sharing not owning, of full equality and democracy, without direction or domination from above.

Care to observe? The most rewarding vacations I know are spent as a guest (or working guest) on the grounds of a hundred "intentional communities" that avidly encourage visitors as a means of spreading their utopian views. They house and feed you for the most nominal charge, because their goal (to put it bluntly) is to change your life—and the life of this planet.

Yet though they proselytize, they do not brainwash. The mildest of people, they fully expect you to recoil initially from such New Age community concepts as "trans-species interaction" (communication with animals, insects, and plants) —and they take no offense at your own disbelief. They are just as accustomed to resistance when first they introduce you to "communal childcare," "planetary citizenship," or "extended families." Instead of arguing, they return calmly to work

In hundreds of small farm settlements or tiny villages, they have rejected society as we know it and sought a life of cooperation not competition, of sharing not owning, of full equality and democracy.

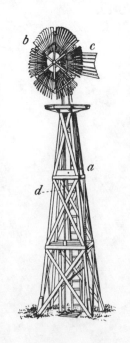

while you, in dazed confusion, ponder upon an unsettling eruption of new ideas.

And ponder them you will. Just wait until you encounter "variable labor credits" or "flexible work weeks"! Your mind will almost audibly stretch as you learn, at some communities, that members performing desirable work  (like childcare) receive fewer hours of credit than members performing undesirable work (like cleaning latrines). By opting for the latter, aspiring artists and writers can reduce their communal labors to two or three days a week—and isn't that sensible?

In the previous essay I wrote about five relatively large intentional communities that accept visitors from the outside world. Now, for readers preferring the intimacy of a lesser size, I'll quickly suggest another five of the smaller variety:

Appletree, near Eugene, Oregon: A tiny, farm commune of rational, egalitarian practices. Members can work or not, as they wish (receiving food and lodging regardless of whether or not they do), but spending money is distributed only to those who do work. Overnight or week-long visitors pay $4 and three hours of work a day, and are asked to apply by writing at least two weeks in advance. Persons staying in nearby towns can visit for part of a day by simply phoning at least a day ahead. Write **Appletree, P.O. Box 5, Cottage Grove, OR 97424 (phone 503/942-4372).**

Mettanokit, in southern New Hampshire: An income-sharing, decision-sharing group of 20 individuals seeking to create a society (in their words) of "loving, cooperative, zestful, intelligent, cre-

THE UNIQUE VACATION: A WEEKEND OR WEEKLONG STAY ON THE GROUNDS OF A UTOPIAN COMMUNITY

ative human beings." They work by consensus, apportion all household and cleaning tasks equally, and enjoy receiving a constant flow of prenotified visitors who pay $10 a day for room and board on visits of several days (visitors share in the work and social activities of the community). Write **Mettanokit, Another Place, Route 123, Greenville, NH 03048 (phone 603/878-9883 or 878-3117).**

The Foundation for Feedback Learning, on Staten Island, New York: Minutes from the towers of downtown Manhattan, a 35-member group inhabits five large houses in which they pursue researches so eclectic as to defy generalization: language training, psychodrama, biofeedback, dance therapy, and furniture repair. Visitors to New York may stay with them for one-month periods, for $350 per person in double rooms, including all meals. Write **Foundation for Feedback Learning, 139 Corson Ave., Staten Island, NY 10301 (phone 718/720-5378).**

Breitenbush Community, 60 miles from Salem, Oregon: Here are 30 adults (with 9 children) of widely divergent political and spiritual views, but all with a fierce urge to enjoy a life in nature, and warm, caring relationships. At a 3,000-foot elevation in the Cascade Mountains, they found and restored this isolated warm-springs resort, where they provide guests with vegetarian meals, holistic health care, meditation, and other New Age "therapies" for only $30 a night, with full board. Those more seriously interested in the communal practices of Breitenbush may stay for a week entirely free on a Volunteer Work Program involving moderate duties and full opportunity to attend all meetings and discussions. Write **Breitenbush Community, P.O. Box 578, Detroit, OR 97342 (phone 503/854-3501 or 854-3314).**

> They house and feed you for the most nominal charge, because their goal (to put it bluntly) is to change your life—and the life of this planet.

Green Pastures Estates, in Epping, New Hampshire: A spiritual community in a small New England village; the 75-or-so members aged 10 to 84 occupy a compound of period structures clustered around a central dining room where meals (nonvegetarian) are taken communally. Some members "live in" but "work out" at jobs in neighboring towns, and then pay Green Pastures for their room and board. Others work the adjoining 235-acre farm. All pursue a goal of spiritual growth or maturity that stress-  es the responsibility of each individual for his/her own emotional state. By attaining that growth (taught, among other topics, at four evening "services" each week), members aid the community to become a joyful, creative, smoothly interacting group. Visitors wishing to participate for a short stay will receive room and board for only $25 a day by writing in advance to **Green Pastures Estates, Route 3, Box 80, Epping, NH 03043 (phone 603/679-8149).** Epping is between Portsmouth and Manchester, about seven miles from Exeter.

Since most intentional communities receive frequent visits by like-minded members of other such communities, members are usually aware of the distinctive features, pros and cons, of several. They share this knowledge with visitors, networking in open, unabashed fashion. Soon you become aware of both the nationwide and international ramifications of the New Age movement, enriching your knowledge of the contemporary world, and perhaps learning of how people will live in future years.

On the Trail of Eternal Youth, at a European Spa

*A*s *I lowered my limbs into that unheated tub of carbonated water, piped in from peat bogs of the Belgian Ardennes, I felt slightly chilly, faintly embarrassed, and more than a bit dubious about the whole thing.*

Yet in 20 minutes my arms and legs were as heavy as lead, my head drooped to my chest, and I could barely stagger to a nearby cot before falling asleep. Hours later I awoke vigorous and refreshed.

I was at a "baths establishment" in the Belgian city of Spa, taking a cure of the sort pursued each year by hundreds of thousands of Europeans.

American doctors think "water cures" are unscientific garbage. European doctors think American doctors, on this point, are boobs.

For centuries, physicians overseas have been sending their patients to spas chosen as carefully as specific medicines for particular ailments—this spa for arthritis, that spa for asthma, still another for neuritis or gallstones or worse. And today so many thousands of Americans are following their lead that a small but thriving segment of the travel industry—close to a dozen U.S. tour operators—has emerged to package the transatlantic health vacation as its sole activity.

Beauty vs. health

Why the trend to foreign spas? Let me suggest a reason or two.

The Europeans practice a form of "alternative medicine," stressing natural, health-giving substances in the earth, waters, and minerals around us, or biological substances taken from our fellow animals.

Compared to a European spa, the average American spa is like an elementary school next to Harvard, like a pickup softball team next to the New York Mets. Such dazzling resorts as The Golden Door, La Costa, The Palms, and Rancho La Puerta are almost wholly concerned with diet, exercise, and massage. Their aim is cosmetic; their methods are hardly the stuff of medical journals.

European spas pursue therapy, the prevention of illness. They operate under strict medical supervision and are recognized by national health plans, which reimburse their costs (if a doctor has prescribed the treatment) to residents of all E.E.C. countries. They screen patients and turn away those for whom their particular treatments are inappropriate. In short, they practice a form of "alternative medicine," stressing natural, health-giving substances in the earth, waters, and minerals around us, or biological substances taken from our fellow animals.

Though none of this has impressed the American medical profession, neither did acupuncture years ago, or the Lamaze method for natural childbirth, or numerous other overseas-originating practices until they were forced upon our M.D.s by popular insistence. That thousands of distinguished European doctors opt for spa therapy is unsettling at the very least, and indicates the wisdom of keeping an open mind.

Certainly no such doubts are harbored by the tour operator specialists in the health-and-fitness field. "Have you ever noticed," says Gerrie Tully of Santé International, "that many Europeans are far less prone to winter colds and other common ailments than we are here? They visit a spa once a year, for two weeks or

CAN 200 MILLION EUROPEANS BE WRONG? OR IS THERE VALIDITY TO THE TREATMENTS AT EUROPEAN HEALTH RESORTS?

so, and renew themselves for the next 12 months." "While the statistics are difficult to verify," says Willy Maurer of HBF Resorts, "there is simply no denying the effectiveness of spa therapy. Too many centuries have proven it, too many case studies, too many strong reactions. And remember: this is the chosen course of highly intelligent people, in mature, sophisticated nations."

Though overseas spas are frequently identified with mineral waters and hot mud—"thermal cures," "balneotherapy," "taking the waters"—their concerns extend to three other significant treatments: live-cell injections (heavily done in Switzerland), procaine-based cures (Romania), and anti-psoriasis regimens (Israel, in resorts along the Dead Sea). For each there's a tour operator (or several), and each has a "package" for every purse.

Live-cell therapy

Not the dream of Faust, or eternal youth, but at least a slowing of the aging process is the aim of this radical treatment created by the legendary Paul Niehans in the early 1930s, at his Clinic La Prairie near Montreux. Niehans, who remained active until the age of 89, administered the therapy to thousands of rather affluent persons (including Pope Pius XII, Winston Churchill, and Joan Crawford), and his clinic has since given it to a total of 50,000 seekers from around the world. Fetal cells from an unborn lamb are injected into the muscles; because the embryo has not yet developed the properties that would normally cause it to be rejected by other human tissues, it remains in the body, causing other cells to stay active

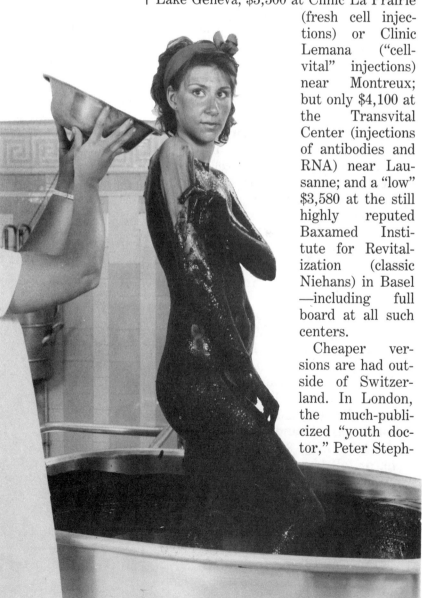

and dynamic (so goes the theory).

As you'd expect, the treatment is fiendishly expensive in the main Swiss clinics: as much as $7,000 plus air fare at the ultra-deluxe Biotonus Bon Port Clinic (classic Niehans injections) overlooking Lake Geneva; $5,500 at Clinic La Prairie (fresh cell injections) or Clinic Lemana ("cell-vital" injections) near Montreux; but only $4,100 at the Transvital Center (injections of antibodies and RNA) near Lausanne; and a "low" $3,580 at the still highly reputed Baxamed Institute for Revitalization (classic Niehans) in Basel —including full board at all such centers.

Cheaper versions are had outside of Switzerland. In London, the much-publicized "youth doctor," Peter Steph-

OUR AMERICAN HEALTH RESORTS ARE ALMOST WHOLLY CONCERNED WITH DIET, EXERCISE, AND MASSAGE. THEIR AIM IS COSMETIC. EUROPEAN SPAS PURSUE THERAPY, THE PREVENTION OF ILLNESS

ans, injects a serum of cells and placenta, at fees including examination and post-injection care of about $1,750 (but without room and board, for which patients make independent arrangements). In Montecatini, Italy, Dr. Antonio Caporale charges $2,700 (including room and board) for injections of a carefully prepared "biological cocktail" (and also provides a nine-week supply of suppositories containing such cells for continuing treatment). And in Paris, the president of the International Association of Physicians for Age Retardation, the English-speaking Dr. André Rouveix, charges approximately $1,200 (without room and board) for his own approaches to cell therapy (which include placenta "implants") at his heavily visited Clinique Nicolo.

For one-week packages using the services of the above three physicians, or for a stay at the Transvital Center in Switzerland, contact **Santé International, 850 Seventh Avenue, New York, NY 10019 (phone 212/247-3830);** its president, Gerrie Tully, a former patient of Dr. Stephans and recipient of such therapy, is a stunning blonde looking 15 years younger than her true age. For one-week packages to La Prairie, Lemana, or the Baxamed Institute in Switzerland, contact **HBF Resorts** (formerly Health and Fitness Vacations), **2911 Grand Avenue, Coconut Grove/Miami, FL 33133 (phone 305/445-3876, or toll free 800/FITNESS outside Florida).** And for the costly Biotonus Clinic, contact **Biotonus, 135 West 50th Street, Suite 1105, New York, NY 10020 (phone 212/541-8291 or toll free 800/437-7200 outside New York).**

Procaine-based therapies

One of the rare chemicals used at European spas, Procaine is a derivative of

American doctors think "water cures" are unscientific garbage. European doctors think American doctors, on this point, are boobs.

Novocaine, widely reputed to dilate the blood vessels and thereby bring greater oxygen to tissues and cells from increased blood circulation. Mixed with other substances into a serum known as Gerovital H3 and Aslavital (both denied admission into the U.S. by the F.D.A.), it is administered to many thousands of elderly Europeans each year as a treatment for diseases and declines of the aged. But though the substance is found in every spa (and in unauthorized forms, highly controversial and of disputed effectiveness, in European pharmacies), the cognoscenti get their Procaine in Bucharest at the clinics and resorts supervised by the celebrated Prof. Dr. Ana Aslan, who created Gerovital and Aslavital in the mid-1950s, and is still active in her own mid-80s.

The key Procaine clinics are at the modern Flora Hotel in the parks district of Bucharest, and the more traditional Otopeni Sanatorium on the outskirts of the city, about eight miles away; both provide the classic Gerovital H3 and Aslavital treatments. The key tour operator is **Litoral Travel, 249 East 77th Street, New York, NY 10021 (phone 212/535-7746, or toll free 800/445-1514 outside New York),** charging a winter-season (November through March) price, at either establishment, of $1,314 for two weeks, $1,575 for three weeks, including round-trip air from New York on Pan Am or Tarom Romanian Airlines. Since full board, laboratory tests, and daily treatments are also included, the value is considerable. For comparisons, you might also request the Romanian brochures of **Health & Pleasure Tours, 165 West 46th Street, New York, NY 10036 (phone 212/586-1775, or toll free 800/443-0365 outside New York).**

Anti-psoriasis treatments

Called "climatotherapy"—climate therapy—it consists of only sea and sun. But it's pursued in the briny sea and ultraviolet sun found only at the lowest point on earth, along the shores of the Dead Sea in Israel, 1,300 feet below sea level. There, in waters with the world's highest concentration of salts, whose constant evaporation produces a mist that prevents sunburning rays from reaching the earth, victims of skin-blemishing psoriasis lie safely under the burning sun for hours on end, and bathe for half an hour daily in the jelly-like sea.

What results from all this is like a biblical miracle: remission of psoriasis for substantial periods in a remarkable percentage of cases. The subject of weighty medical studies for more than 20 years, the benefits of these Israeli spas are today confirmed by exact clinical data of which other therapies can only dream; many physicians regard them as no longer open to doubt—and one weeps for psoriasis sufferers who are unaware of the healing Dead Sea.

Along the Dead Sea, the specialist spas for psoriasis are the Moriah Gardens (not to be confused with the Moriah Dead Sea Spa), Galei Zohar, the Hotel Lot, and Ein Bokek. The major U.S. tour operator for them is **Jericho Spa Tours Co., 555 Fifth Avenue, New York, NY 10017 (phone 212/286-9291).** And the rates are unusually cheap: in a seven-month, split off-season (June through August and November through February) prices average $650 for two weeks (the suggested bare minimum), $1,250 for four weeks (the recommended stay), including two meals a day and all treatment.

Water cures

And finally you have the classic treatments—"carbogaseous baths," "fango mud," "vapour inhalations," underwater massage, saunas, "Kneipp foot baths," "thalassotherapy," "algae baths" and repeated draughts of mineral water—as practiced with exquisite deliberation (different treatments, different spas, for different ailments) at quite literally hundreds of spas in Italy, Austria, Yugoslavia, France, Belgium, Germany, and Switzerland. While your average, celebrated U.S. spa charges $1,800 a week and up (to as much as $3,000 a week at The Golden Door) for its "beauty care" and "weight loss," a European spa can be had for as little as $600 a week in the Yugoslavian locations, for an average of $1,200 a week (depending on spa) in Italy (where Abano, Montecatini, and Ischia are the key names), and for $1,250 and up per winter week in Switzerland. The properties and programs are all lavishly described in glossy catalogues mailed free by Santé International and HBF Resorts from the addresses set forth for them, above.

The ultimate question

Is there anything to it? I tend to think there is; but whether or not, it is surely the worst smugness, a form of jingoism, to dismiss the claims of European spas out-of-hand and without investigation, as so many do.

Shakespeare warned that "there are more things in heaven and earth, Horatio, than are dreamt of in your philosophy." Perhaps there is more to medicine than the chemical-based prescriptions of U.S. doctors.

America on $25 a Day, Via the Yoga Route

I *am not a yogi. And considering my feverish lifestyle, horrendous eating habits, and stubborn rationalism, that's the understatement of the year.*

But yogi or not, some of my happiest holidays have been spent at yoga retreats. When it comes to inducing sheer serenity, restoring vigor, flushing toxins from both mind and body, nothing beats these mystical *ashrams* (schools, places of learning) with their vegetarian meals and quiet hillside settings, their twice-daily *asanas* (languid stretching exercises) and moments of meditation, their gentle people.

And when it comes to cost, nothing else in the vacation field even remotely compares. At a score of residential, countryside ashrams clustered near both coasts, the charge for room and all three meals amounts—if you can believe it—to $25, $35, and $40 a day.

Why so cheap? Because the meals are vegetarian, the sites are often donated,

A philosophy of life, not a religion; a questing science, not a dogma—yoga is the most tolerant of creeds, its practitioners good-humored, broad-minded, and modest.

Ananda Ashram

Yogi Amrit Desai of Kripalu

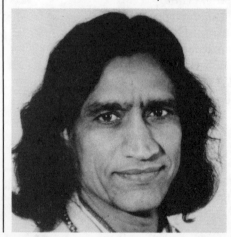

and the staff works for free, performing karma yoga (selfless service).

Why, then, aren't they inundated with guests? Because the public, in general, recoils from Eastern thought, equating all such teachings with those of Sun Myung Moon, assuming dreadful acts of brainwashing or abandoned conduct, as at the turbulent Rajneeshpuram in Oregon or the doomed Guyanese community of mad Jim Jones.

As applied to the yoga movement, nothing could be further from the truth. A philosophy of life, not a religion; a questing science, not a dogma—yoga is the most tolerant of creeds, its practitioners good-humored, broad-minded, and modest, non-authoritarian. At the U.S. ashrams, nothing is mandatory other than attendance at the asanas (physical exercises or postures) and silent meditations —and that, only to screen out persons who are simply seeking a cheap crashpad for their vacations.

Apart from those two limited daily sessions, no one cares about what you do or where you go, or whether you even attend lectures of the guru. He or she is regarded with affection, called *guruji* or *swamiji* (dear little guru, dear little swami), but treated as fallible, and certainly not as a Godhead. Some instructors at the ashrams—even a director or two—will stress their distance from Hindu theology and their pursuit of yoga primarily for its physical and calming benefits.

Though the residential ashrams in North America number far more than a score, not all have guaranteed staying-

REMARKABLE VACATIONS, REWARDING AND CHEAP, AT ASHRAMS CLUSTERED NEAR BOTH COASTS

power. Those that do, include:

The Yoga Retreat, on Paradise Island, the Bahamas: You've heard of Club Med; now meet Club Meditation (at a fifth the price). The ashram that's a 150-bed tropical resort, it sits next to sugary-white sands, across the bay from Nassau on four beachfront acres donated to the Sivananda Vedanta movement by an admirer; the popular, other-worldly complex is now in its 21st year. You arise at dawn to meditate on the beach, proceed immediately (and before breakfast) to a 1½-hour exercise class (asana), partake at last of a mammoth vegetarian brunch, and are then allowed to do nothing at all (except swim, snorkel, and sun) until 4 p.m., when a second

round of asanas is followed by supper at 6 p.m., meditation at sunset, and bed. Accommodations range from airy dorms in a colonial building ($40 per person per night, including meals and exercise classes) to double rooms in modern cabins ($45) to "meditation huts" ($50) overlooking the sea. Contact **Sivananda Ashram Yoga Retreat, P.O. Box N7550, Nassau, Bahamas (phone 809/326-2902)**, for reservations or literature.

The Kripalu Center, near Lenox, Massachusetts: In the many wings and 400 rooms of a former Jesuit monastery, on a hillside overlooking Lake Mahkeenac in the Berkshire Mountains of western Massachusetts, Kripalu is one of the largest of all ashrams, with one of the most varied programs—its brochure resembles a col-

lege catalogue crammed with courses and options. Soothed by the ministrations of a largely unpaid staff of volunteers, you exercise, meditate, wander, and soak, attend lively seminars and yet dine in complete silence at thrice-daily vegetarian buffets, hear lectures by the impressive Yogi Amrit Desai (*gurudev*—beloved teacher). Accommodations are comfortable, in spacious dorms (8 to 18 people) of wide-frame, wooden double-deckers, or in pleasant private rooms, and yet the all-inclusive charge—for housing and all three meals, exercise classes, and most other activities—is only $45 per person in the dormitories, $55 per person in a standard double room. Write or phone

Kripalu Center, P.O. Box 793, Lenox, MA 01240 (phone 413/637-3280). A smaller branch pursuing similar policies is maintained on a wooded site outside Philadelphia: **Kripalu Yoga Ashram, 7 Walters Road, Sumneytown, PA 18084 (phone 215/234-4568)**.

The Yoga Ranch, at Woodbourne, New York: About two hours by bus from New York City, it occupies a stunning setting atop a wooded hill, looking down into a

I PRESS MY HANDS BENEATH MY LIPS, AND INTONE: "JAI BHAGWAN" ("I HONOR THE SPIRIT WITHIN YOU")

valley and up onto another hill, the mountains of the Catskills receding into the distance. Dotted about are open areas devoted to organic farming or used by grazing deer. On the extensive grounds, a one-acre pond is deep enough for swimming, while nearby stands a stone-faced sauna, wood-fired, rock-heated, and steamed by pure, mountain spring water —one-of-a-kind. "You'll be doing good for a lot of people if you recommend us," said the co-director at the end of our talk. "They come here with jangled nerves, and then leave completely restored." The charge for that revival is an astonishing $25 per person per day (half price for children under 15), including yoga asanas (exercises), meditation, accommodation in twin or triple rooms, and two vegetarian meals. Write or phone **Sivananda Ashram Yoga Ranch, P.O. Box 195, Woodbourne, NY 12788 (phone 914/434-9242).**

Ananda Ashram, near Monroe, New York: Despite its resident guru (a softspoken, self-effacing, former physician, now Shri Sarasvati) and classic activities (which include lessons in the muchstressed science of pranayama—breath control), this 24-year-old yoga retreat has a far-less-pronounced Eastern orientation than some others: it schedules meditation for as late as 9 a.m. on weekends, invites guest teachers from all religious disciplines, and presents classes in creative music, drama, dance, and visual arts. Less than 90 minutes by bus from New York City, at the base of the Catskill Mountains, it occupies 100 wooded acres, including a large private lake, and houses 60 visitors in several guesthouses, for an all-inclusive, room-and-meals charge (on seven-night stays) of $175 per week. Contact the **Ananda Yoga Retreat, R.D. 3,**

You've heard of Club Med; now meet Club Meditation (at a fifth the price).

Box 141, Monroe, NY 10950 (phone 914/782-5575).

The Yoga Farm, at Grass Valley, California: Cheapest of the residential ashrams ($25 a night, including meals), but the smallest also, with space for just 30 guests, the Farm is the personal favorite of the eminent Swami Vishnu Devananda, head of the Sivananda movement. Like thousands of others over the years who have driven up the 50-or-so miles from Sacramento and then followed dirt roads to the isolated setting, he values the special simplicity and quiet of this rustic, two-building resort, with its changeless routine of meditation/exercises/free time. In the latter period, as you hike to the top of an adjoining hill and lie daydreaming on its crest, you see the majestic Sierras

spread out before you. A very special place. Write or phone **Sivananda Ashrama Vrindavan Yoga Farm, 14651 Ballantree Lane, Grass Valley, CA 95949 (phone 916/272-9322).**

Alive Polarity, at Murrieta Hot Springs, California: In a low coastal valley near San Diego, peaceful and smog-free, this is a marginal choice because it really isn't a Hindu-based yoga resort (but teaches, at best, a form of "Western yoga") and is also considerably more costly than the others: $63 a day per person. But for that, you receive three gourmet-level vegetarian buffets daily, enjoy three mineral-water pools, free exercise classes designed to shift energy currents of the body, and a private room, not a dorm. For residents of southern California unwilling to travel 400 miles north, it is a trendy substitute for the yoga retreats near Sacramento. Write or phone **Alive Polarity, Murrieta Hot Springs, CA 92362 (phone 714/677-7451).**

The Expanding Light, near Nevada City, California: A strange amalgam of faiths, this is the yoga ashram located on the grounds of a larger utopian Christian community known as the Ananda World Brotherhood Village. The "town," 1,000 acres in size, was formed in 1967 by 250 devout people who are also practitioners of yoga, and regard it as complementary to the other faith. Today, at the Brotherhood Inn and other scattered structures and (in summer) tents, 125 visitors can engage in a retreat of classic yoga practices—early-morning and late-afternoon asanas and meditations—supplemented by classes and workshops on both Christian and yogic themes. For weeklong stays, the daily charge is $35 in a dorm, $45 in a shared room, $55 in a private cabin, including all three vegetarian meals and classes. Ananda is 12 miles from Nevada City; the latter is 60 miles north of Sacramento. Contact **The Expanding Light, c/o Ananda World**

> When it comes to inducing sheer serenity, nothing beats these mystical retreats with their vegetarian meals and quiet hillside settings, their twice-daily *asanas* (languid stretching exercises) and moments of meditation.

Brotherhood Village, 14618 Tyler Foote, Nevada City, CA 95959 (phone 916/292-3494).

I have not described the important 2,000-bed Muktananda Center in South

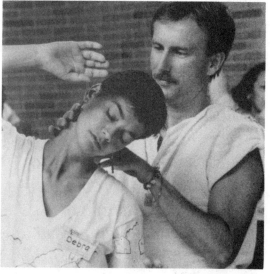

Fallsburg, New York, because of its heavy (and somewhat atypical) theological emphasis, which stresses chanting and meditation to a far greater extent than hatha (physical) yoga and exercises. But you should know that Muktananda charges only $25 a night for bed and all three meals in its dormitory rooms.

Nor have I mentioned large retreats in Canada and Baja California.

To find other residential ashrams, phone the in-city centers listed under "Yoga Instruction" in the *Yellow Pages*, and ask the personnel to name the countryside location, if any, to which they go for an occasional retreat. I'd be grateful if you'd also send the information to me, at the address listed in the introduction; and in gratitude, I press my hands together beneath my lips, and intone: "Jai Bhagwan" ("I honor the spirit within you").

Vacationing, for a Change, at a Whole-Grain Resort

Just as you occasionally need a vacation (which is presumably why you are reading this book, so does your stomach occasionally need a vacation. Both can achieve that restful interlude at a macrobiotic center, of which our nation has a dozen. Without necessarily subscribing to the tenets of macrobiotics—a diet of cooked whole grains and vegetables—you can turn for a time to a gentler form of life, lacking in stress, free of fats, and full of companionship among the most amiable people.

Many thousands of Americans make an exclusive use of the macrobiotic cuisine, which they often first encounter and learn to prepare at residential centers clustered on the two coasts.

Contrary to a popular misconception, macrobiotics has no necessary connection to Zen, Zen Buddhism, or even Bud-

Grains, they believe, should make up 50% to 60% of the diet, supplemented by vegetables, beans, an occasional bit of fish.

dhism, although a great many of the latter persuasion adhere to the theory. It is a purely secular approach to nutrition based on the teachings of the late George Ohsawa, born in Japan, who believed in essence that people should live in harmony with what he perceived as natural cycles and elements of the physical universe. Thus they should eat only those foods that had grown for centuries in the places where those people lived. They should, in the United States, emphasize grains, the staff of life, supplemented by vegetables, beans, vegetarian soups—on occasion a bit of fish.

Translating those ingredients into tasty meals takes skill. Accordingly, all macrobiotic centers include cooking courses, taught to all guests. Yet even at the hands of a gourmet cook, the subtly flavored macrobiotic dishes are bland compared with the steak and potatoes of the average American diet, and thus offer a radical change of pace—a soothing one—to the average American.

You pursue that relaxing course in centers operated by disciples of Ohsawa, of whom Japanese-born Michio Kushi on the East Coast and Herman Aihara on the West Coast are certainly the most prominent. Try, for example:

Vega Study Center, of Oroville, California: Ninety minutes north of Sacramento, in an old and sleepy town of Victorian homes and later shops and stores of the 1920s, is this large, residential, teaching base of Herman and Cornellia Aihara. Their courses (including "hands-on" cooking classes) run for one to three weeks throughout the year, and cost $450 for one week, $850 for two weeks, with full board. Guests live in shared rooms with pine beds and wonderfully firm futon mat-

AT MACROBIOTIC CENTERS CLUSTERED ON BOTH COASTS, THE CUISINE IS AS SOOTHING AS THE SETTING

tresses; wake at 7 a.m. for meditation, Eastern-style exercises, and tea; attend lectures delivered by the charming Aihara himself; and eat classic macrobiotic meals often prepared by Cornellia. Contact **Vega Study Center, 1511 Robinson Street, Oroville, CA 95965 (phone 916/533-7702)**, for an interesting catalogue.

The Kushi Foundation, in the Berkshires of western Massachusetts: Placid and still, on 600 mountain acres, its main building is an old mansion with spiralling wooden staircases and stone fireplaces for cool evenings. It is an appropriate setting for the calm and gentle lectures of Michio Kushi and his wife, Aveline. Seven-day residential seminars on emotional harmony and healthy food preparation cost $800 for a shared room and all meals. A unique opportunity to study with the "master." Write or phone **Kushi Foundation, Berkshire Center Program, P.O. Box 7, Becket, MA 01223 (phone 413/623-5742)**.

Lady Diane's, on the island of Jamaica: A lavishly decorated macrobiotic hotel near the airport of Montego Bay, with superb views of the bay. There's no classroom instruction, but an imaginative macrobiotic cuisine enhanced with Jamaican touches for holiday purposes: breakfast might consist of hot grits, turnips, miso soup, and whole-wheat biscuits. Rates for room and full board at the charming seafront resort, for a full seven-

Students live in tastefully decorated rooms and pursue classes in cooking, philosophy, shiatsu massage, natural-food shopping, and the effects of macrobiotics on serious health problems.

night week, average $600 per person (double occupancy), and include shiatsu massage. Contact **Lady Diane's, 5 Kent Avenue, Montego Bay, Jamaica (phone 809/952-4415)**.

And then there are the macrobiotic summer camps, for a cheap, refreshing, and restorative holiday in the open air. Try the Mid-Atlantic Summer Camp, from June 15 to June 20 in the Pocono Mountains of Pennsylvania ($495 for all meals and dorm accommodations in rustic cabins)—write **Macrobiotic Center of Baltimore, 604 East Joppa Road, Towson, MD 21204 (phone 301/321-4474)**; the 800-guest Kushi Institute Summer Camp, from July 5 to July 12 in a comfortable Swiss army base in the Swiss Alps, near Lenk ($595 per person)—contact **Jan Call, 41 Sylvia Street, Pittsburgh, PA 15214 (phone 412/734-2082)**; the Macrobiotic Summer Conference, in August at Simon's Rock of Bard College in the Berkshires of Massachusetts near Great Barrington ($595 per person)—write the **Kushi Foundation, P.O. Box 1100, Brookline, MA 02147 (phone 617/738-0045)**.

I have, in my description of macrobiotics at the beginning of this essay, compressed a complex subject into a simplistic and inadequate paragraph. I have failed, in particular, to explore the emphasis of the theory on the need to properly balance the expansive (*yin*) and contractive (*yang*) varieties of food, and their counterparts in other areas, or the claims that a macrobiotic way of life can prevent or cure serious illness.

All this you'll hear—and more—in one of the most restful interludes of your life, as you grant time off to your overworked and suffering stomach.

A Visit to the World of "Small Is Beautiful"

What do we really seek on a holiday abroad? Should we travel simply to feel pleasure? Or should we travel sometimes to get mad? I opt for the brand of travel that disturbs mental calm, compels you to think, challenges your most cherished beliefs, supplies new ideas and comparative lessons, leaves you a bit different from when you began.

In the alpine-like center of Wales, near the dreamy little town of Machynlleth (pronounced "mah-hun-lith"), Britain's Centre for Alternative Technology does just that. It disputes the very need for industrial development, rejects all arguments for large-scale commercial growth, condemns the activities to which the greater number of Americans have devoted their lives. In so doing, it acts as the

It is a working city meant to be visited and observed by a steady stream of tourists, a teaching device as much as a laboratory.

cutting edge for an ideological movement that has won the loyalty of millions of Europeans, and even achieved a semblance of political power in Germany. To the "Greens" of Europe, the extreme ecologists, the fierce, anti-nuclear-power activists, the advocates of "Small Is Beautiful," to similar groups in 21 European nations, the Centre has become a secular Mecca to which more than 60,000 people make visits each year. No one understands contemporary Europe who does not understand the movement it represents.

You reach Machynlleth by British Rail in four comfortable hours from London's Euston Station, changing at Shrewsbury (pronounced "shroze-berry") and proceeding from there through the "harp-shaped hills" of Wales (Dylan Thomas's phrase) into one of the least populated areas of the British Isles—a scene of rocky heights dotted with patches of dark-green outcroppings. At Machynlleth, a three-mile ride by taxi or bus takes you to the bottom of a soaring but thoroughly exhausted slate quarry where signs advise you, in Danteesque fashion, to

The Centre for Alternative Technology, in Wales, offers options to high technology, from solar houses to hands-on brickmaking and organic farming.

AT THE CENTRE FOR ALTERNATIVE TECHNOLOGY IN WALES, THE MOST BASIC ASSUMPTIONS OF THE INDUSTRIAL WEST ARE ATTACKED AND DERIDED

abandon your car and ascend the steep hill on foot.

You are leaving behind civilization as we know it. The Centre—a tiny, working village—is unconnected to the electric grid of Britain, or to water mains. It provides its own power from wind, solar, or hydro sources, is virtually self-sufficient from its own organic gardens, fish ponds, and poultry yards (and striving to be entirely so), replaces worn-out machinery with parts forged by its own blacksmith. Within its bounds, nothing is wasted: organic refuse is recycled into compost-created fertilizers; metal is fired down and reused; sludge is collected from septic tanks and placed into methane digesters for the production of combustible gas and fertilizer by-products; homes are insulated to an extraordinary degree; even human urine is preserved for soil fertilization via amusing, odorless "pee collectors" discreetly placed at convenience stops. On the grounds, past a forest of solar panels, near a grove of modern metal windmills of every shape and size, runs an electric truck recharged by on-site water turbines powered by rushing streams. Using and displaying such "alternative technology," a utopian community enters its 14th year in mid-1988, locked in combat with the enemies that its chief theorist, the late E. F. Schumacher, succinctly ticked off as "urbanization, industrialization, centralization, efficiency, quantity, speed."

The combatants in this awesome battle, permanent residents of the Centre, are a slowly changing group of 32 young Britons whose average tenure here is about four years. A highly attractive lot, neatly if simply dressed in work clothes, well educated and articulate, they defy the

> The Centre disputes the very need for industrial development, rejects all arguments for large-scale commercial growth, condemns the activities to which the greater number of Americans have devoted their lives.

stereotyped image of the "eco-freak," and emerge from a broad mix of schools and skills. Two are Ph.D.s in electrical and mechanical engineering, one is a registered architect. All receive the same, subsistence-level salary, except those with dependent children, to whom a "need-related" supplement is given. They eat communally (of a largely vegetarian diet), govern themselves by consensus reached at fortnightly meetings, confront daily decisions in 15-or-so, four-member "topic groups" each dealing with specialized work areas. They receive no major government support, and are a nonprofit organization subsisting almost entirely on admission and study-course fees paid by members of the public.

Why have they come together at the Centre to lead lives that, to the outsider, seem so harsh and confined? It is because they share a common vision that goes far beyond the well-publicized conservation-

ist goals of preserving natural beauty and reducing harmful pollution. To the European ecological movement, simple technology and decentralized economic orga-

IT IS MORALLY INDEFENSIBLE, THEY BELIEVE, THAT THE WEST SHOULD MAKE SUCH A DISPROPORTIONATE USE OF THE WORLD'S RESOURCES

nization are part of a happier, healthier approach to life, as well as a moral imperative. By using renewable sources of energy present in nature, by keeping technology simple and small, one preserves meaningful work opportunities for more and more people, they argue; one spreads the activity of production over broad rural areas, slows the movement to cities and the creation of inhumanly large industrial complexes, keeps nations democratic and people healthy, promotes nonviolence in all spheres of life, teaches personal responsibility, and—most important—

shares the dwindling supply of finite fossil resources more equitably among all the people of the earth.

To these ends, all 32 of "The People," as the Centre styles its staff, are researchers relying for their daily existence almost entirely on small machines and devices which make use of wind, sun, water, and biomass for their energizing forces. Though the technology itself emerges from universities and laboratories around the world, it is the Centre's task, they believe, to "live with" the machines, discovering the necessary modifications and

A highly attractive lot, they defy the stereotyped image of the "eco-freak" and emerge from a broad mix of schools and skills.

improvements that only actual experience can provide.

Are they, then, simply a test-tube community? They are more. Though officials of the Walt Disney organization would blanch at the comparison, they are perhaps a tiny version of what the late Walt Disney once envisioned as his EPCOT Center in Orlando, Florida: an actual working city that would, at the same time, be visited and observed by a steady stream of tourists—a teaching device as much as a laboratory. While Disney obviously failed to pull off the feat of combining two such antagonistic functions, the Centre quite demonstrably does.

It teaches. Its staff supplies a running commentary as they go about their tasks. You compliment a chef on the bean-sprout salad served in the Centre's superb vegetarian restaurant and he runs into the kitchen to extract a large bell jar in which the sprouts are grown, explaining how you, too, can enjoy such daily treats from the moistened seeds of simple alfalfa. You gaze over the shoulder of an engineer adjusting a "biomass gasifier" and she hastily explains how a renewable supply of wood, burned in a near-vacuum, will result in a combustible gas capable of powering an electric generator. Everywhere are colorful, cartoon-illustrated explanations and exhortations: "Use Less/ Build to Last/Reuse/Repair/Recycle." "What good is efficiency if it puts people out of work and uses up resources?" "Gross product per head measures only the quantity of our wealth, not the quality of our lives. Are we happier?"

The Centre's staff heatedly deny that their work is of exclusive relevance to the Third World, responding to a frequent comment. It is morally and politically

You are leaving behind civilization as we know it.

indefensible, they affirm, that the advanced West should make such a lavish disproportionate use of the world's resources, especially fossil fuels (America, with 6% of the earth's population, uses 40% of the world's primary resources). And there are insufficient such resources for the entire world to follow the wasteful, indulgent course of the West; consequently, that course must change—in all areas.

They also deny that the current glut in oil is at all significant; it is a brief lull in the crisis, a fool's paradise. Even were those supplies sufficient, their use exacts too high a human toll in acid rain, pollution, industrial blight, ruined lives; and fossil sources can, in any event, be put to better use than as energy. So goes the argument of Wales's Centre for Alternative Technology, in seminar presentations, group discussions, courses, gardenside chats, quiet admonitions from engineers tinkering with a biomass gasifier, a solar roof, a waterless toilet, a compost heap, or an "aerogenerator" manufactured at the Centre and sent around the world.

Two days set aside from the normal routines of a British vacation, or added to it, suffice for a thorough visit to the Centre. After travelling there by train

from London (£27.50, approximately $44, round trip), most visitors base themselves in Machynlleth (where the Wynnstay Hotel, phone 2941, is your best bet, followed in distant second place by the Glyndwr, phone 2082) or in Corris, two miles from the Centre (Hotel Braich Goch, phone 73/229), or in several guesthouses in the area.

The Centre is open to visitors every day of the year except Christmas, for an admission charge of £2.20 ($3.50). Two weekends a month from October to June it offers two-day courses in which you pursue one topic per weekend: blacksmithing, low-energy buildings, solar collectors and systems, organic gardening, wind power, etc. Free time involves explorations of Machynlleth, mid-Wales, and the Cambrian Coast. For specific dates, subjects, and application forms, write to the **Courses Coordinator, Centre for Alternative Technology, Machynlleth, Powys, Wales, U.K.**

Visits of lesser duration are best followed by self-drive tours through awesome Wales, perhaps starting at the nearby small (but active) seaside town of Aberystwyth, heading north from there to Snowdon, highest mountain in Britain, visiting abandoned lead mines en route. Richard Llewellyn's Welsh classic, *How Green Was My Valley*, is your best preparatory reading.

But now it is dusk, at the end of a day of "alternative technology," and you are coming down from the mountain, perhaps jarred and disquieted, perhaps exhilarated, always alive with new ideas. This new approach—this confrontational approach —to travel has converted a routine British vacation into a memorable one, of lasting value.

Vacationing at a "Personal Growth Center," I: Esalen

On a broad lawn leading to a steep cliff, above the rocky surf and sea lions of the Pacific Ocean, couples hugged or stroked each other's arms. Occasionally they reached out to pat the cheek of a passing stranger.

Others raged in response to a trivial slight. Some of them arm-wrestled, grimly, to settle a dispute.

In scenes such as this, flung across the covers of *Life* and *Look*, the Esalen Institute of Big Sur, California, introduced America in the 1960s to "encounter therapy" and related offshoots of the "human potential movement." Drunk with the vision that they could lead humankind into a

Though no longer in the news, it perseveres, even thrives, but at a more measured pace.

The view from Esalen

new era of heightened insight, sensitivity, and understanding, the personalities associated with Esalen—Michael Murphy, Fritz Perls, Ida Rolf, Abraham Maslow, Will Shutz, Virginia Satir, Rollo May, Gregory Bateson—converted that isolated stretch of seafront heights into a place of unfettered experimentation in psychology, and fired the thought of millions, while offending or frightening legions of others.

What has happened to Esalen in the ensuing years? Though no longer in the news, it perseveres, even thrives, but at a more measured pace, thoughtful and cautious. And it has spawned over a dozen imitators: residential retreats where hundreds of Americans devote their vacations to exploring a range of psychological subjects so broad as to require college-like catalogues to list them all. Encounter therapy—that almost-instant process of shedding inhibitions and responding to every repressed emotion—is now only one of numerous treatments under study at America's personal growth centers.

For one thing, the early leader of the encounter movement—Michael Murphy, co-founder of Esalen—is no longer certain of the long-term benefits of the art. It is, he believes, only a start—this stripping away of defenses through encounter techniques—which must be succeeded by longer-lasting and less dramatic work. Others have concluded that encounter therapy can be positively dangerous, exposing serious underlying pathologies without providing a trained therapist to deal with what's exposed.

And so the core curriculum of the centers is currently devoted to such multiple emerging sciences as gestalt therapy, psychosynthesis, Ericksonian hypnosis,

AT ESALEN, NEAR BIG SUR, ON THE CALIFORNIA COAST, HUMAN TRANSFORMATION IS THE GOAL OF A HOLIDAY STAY

shamanic healing, neurolinguistics, Feldenkrais, and Rolfing. From these basic inquiries emerge, at some centers, more popular discussions: "Intimate Relationships: Keeping the Spark Alive," "Burnout: Causes and Cures," "Letting Go—Moving On," "Building Community: A Learning Circle," "Agenda for the 21st Century." All are aimed at expanding human potential, tapping into energies and abilities as yet unknown.

At Esalen, instruction is through seminars or workshops extending over a weekend ($270, including room and board) or five-day midweek ($530). Many first-timers select the orientation workshop

In the 1960s, that isolated stretch of seafront heights became a place of unfettered experimentation in psychology.

simply known as "Experiencing Esalen" (sensory awareness, group process, guided fantasy, meditation, massage), or the somewhat similar "Gestalt Practice"; others choose from more than 100 other widely varied subjects taught throughout the year.

Studies are combined with exquisite relaxation, in a lush oasis of gardens, birds, and natural hot springs; the latter bring 110° sulfurous water into bathhouses where residents can soak for hours while watching the sun or moon set into the ocean below. Rooms are comfortable and pleasantly decorated, but must be shared with others (usually), and lack

telephones, TV sets, or radios; a retreat atmosphere is maintained. Meals are served in a dining hall where dress and decor are casual but the cuisine is gourmet. The Esalen gardens and nearby farm supply the majority of the many options in the daily salad and vegetables bar.

When the 100 guest beds are not fully booked (which is common during the winter season and sometimes happens during midweek in summer), it is possible simply to stay at Esalen without enrolling in a seminar. The cost of this varies, but falls into the $50 to $75 range for a night and a day, including dinner, breakfast, and

> Studies are combined with exquisite relaxation, in a lush oasis of gardens, birds, and natural hot springs.

lunch. Often people come to Esalen simply for a bout of quiet writing, or during a time of life transition. As workshops and bed spaces fill up early (especially in summer), it is important to plan a trip to Esalen well in advance. You may either phone for a catalogue or to reserve a workshop on your credit card (call 408/ 667-3000), but the preferred method is to write c/o **Reservations, Esalen Institute, Big Sur, CA 93920.** The location is 300 miles north of Los Angeles, 175 miles south of San Francisco, between the spectacular coastal highway and the 100-foot cliffs overlooking crashing waves below.

The approximate East Coast counterpart to Esalen is the somewhat less intense, summer-only (early June to September) Omega Institute at Rhinebeck, New York, on 80 acres of lakefront woodlands and rolling hills in the Hudson River Valley. Here, dozens of workshops are led by celebrated names in psychology and related fields, ranging from the profound and abstruse ("Touching the Core of Healing: Introduction to Craniosacral Therapy") to what might appear only warm-weather frivolity ("Vocal Joy: Letting the Secret Out"). For a full description of Omega, including rates and policies, see the next essay.

Meanwhile, having visited Esalen, I can best report the reaction of a middle-aged couple from Santa Barbara who come here for a semi-annual "fix," to "feel alive and revitalized." Apart from their interest in Aikido movement/meditation (subject of their workshop), they feel Esalen "has the nicest piece of real estate in the world—beach, rocks, surf, sea, air, mountains, hot tubs, good food, and loving people—who could ask for anything more?"

The beach at Esalen

Vacationing at a "Personal Growth Center," II: East Coast and West

*I*t all began at Esalen, near Big Sur, on the California coast. There, in the 1960s, heralds of the "New Age" gathered to pursue daring new studies of human psychology.

Their goal? To fulfill the "human potential," to expand consciousness and improve personal relationships, to tap the same mysterious sources of energy and spirit that enable mystics in other lands and on other levels to enjoy trances and visions, to walk on nails or fast for days.

Their method? Workshops of a week's or a weekend's duration, attended by vacationing members of the public, who offered up their own psyches to these new therapies or to classroom training. And thus began the first holiday facility known as a "personal growth center," of which our nation now possesses more than a dozen major examples.

Unlisted in any directory of which I am aware, and marketed through severely limited mailings or classified ads in magazines of small circulation, they are nonetheless open to all and worthy of far broader dissemination.

East coast

Omega Institute, R.D. 2, Box 377-AF, Rhinebeck, NY 12572 (phone 914/338-6030 from September 15 to early June and 914/266-4301 from early June to September 15), is—apart from Esalen—the lodestone; it attracts up to 500 people a

> Their method? Workshops of a week's or a weekend's duration, attended by vacationing members of the public.

Instruction at Omega Institute

week during its summer operating period from mid-June to mid-September. On a broad lake flanked by extensive, hilly grounds of forest and clearings, in a joyful atmosphere of kindness and smiles, it presents weekend and weeklong workshops ranging from the clearly lighthearted ("Vocal Joy," "Delicious Movement") to the softly therapeutic ("Working with Dreams," "The Fear of Losing Control," "Choosing to Connect") to the arcane and abstruse ("Oriental Diagnosis," "Interfacing Psychology and Spirituality," "The Tibetan Path of Love and Compassion"); many of the most famous figures in the human potential movement—Ram Dass and Ashley Montagu, Ilana Rubenfeld and Per Vilayat Inayat Khan—make an appearance. Tuition averages $50 a day; housing and meals (vegetarian) add $27 or $35 in campsites or dorms, up to $50 in private cabins. You can contact Omega directly

THE MANY OFFSHOOTS OF ESALEN EXPLORE THE HUMAN POTENTIAL, IN A THOROUGHLY DELIGHTFUL WAY

mountain in the Berkshires with a permanent community of "Sufis"—the gentlest of people who have made an eclectic choice from the prophetic messages of all religions, both Western and Eastern. Faculty includes a Benedictine monk, a rabbi, an American Indian. Sample workshops: "Optimal Functioning in Daily Life," "Healing and Wholeness in Psychotherapy," "The Shared Heart," "Buddhist Meditation," "Homeopathic Medicine"; there is much meditation. To weekend tuition costs averaging $100, add room and board charges of about $30 a day in a

for a copy of their 72-page catalogue.

Camp Lenox, Route 8, Lee, MA 01238 (phone 413/243-2223): In the southern Berkshires, on 250 hillside acres overlooking a lake, it accepts adults in June and September only, in facilities otherwise operated as a children's summer camp in July and August. Seminars are on weekends only, cost $140 to $215 per person including full board (gourmet vegetarian), and pursue such themes as "Living in the Spirit," "An Invitation to Radical Aliveness," and "The New Sacred Psychology."

Aegis, The Abode, R.D. 1, Box 1030D, New Lebanon, NY 12125 (phone 518/794-8095): On three-day weekends from June through September, supplemented by five-day midweek sessions in June and July, and occasional workshops in other seasons, outsiders come to study on this

private cabin, $25 in a dorm.

Wainwright House, 260 Stuyvesant Avenue, Rye, NY 10580 (phone 914/967-6080): A stately mansion on elegant

grounds, just north of New York City, it offers year-round daily workshops—some for only a day in duration—in Jungian studies, spiritual disciplines, "health and wholeness," other topics of psychology. Themes are far-ranging—"Exorcising Violence," "Psychic Awareness," "Sonic Meditation," "The Psychology of Illness" —but from a relatively traditional, even Christian, viewpoint. One-day tuition ranges from free to $50, and overnight accommodations run from $20 (dorm) to $30 (per person, double room). Meals are offered in the dining room at additional cost.

West coast

Naropa Institute, 2130 Arapahoe, Boulder, CO 80302 (phone 303/444-0202): Summer only. In a partly urban setting, but on the slopes of the Rockies, it is serious and intellectual, but with a heavy

emphasis on innovative, psychological approaches to music, theatre, dance, and creative writing. Nevertheless, workshops also include "The Intimate Relationship as a Practice and Path," "Nurturing," "Contemplative Psychotherapy," "Christian or Buddhist Meditation." Most short-term guests (less than a month) use nearby University of Colorado housing for room and board costs of about $150 a week, to which tuition fees of about $240 should be added.

Feathered Pipe Ranch, P.O. Box 1682, Helena, MT 59624 (phone 406/442-8196): Open in spring and summer only, using log-and-stone ranchhouse accommodations in a stunning Rocky Mountain location bordered by a national forest. The program consists of "holistic life seminars," heavily spiritual, but also including standard yoga workshops, studies in holistic health, male/female relationships. Ilana Rubenfeld presented her widely acclaimed five-day "synergy" workshop (gestalt therapy combined with Feldenkrais and other forms of "body work") at Feathered Pipe last August. Charges average $650 a week for instruction, meals, and dorm-style lodging.

A STAY WILL CAUSE YOU TO DISCOVER, AT THE VERY LEAST, IMPORTANT NEW ASPECTS OF YOUR INNER LIFE

Ojai Foundation, P.O. Box 1620, Ojai, CA 93023 (phone 805/646-8343): Workshops with intensely spiritual themes are conducted throughout much of the year on these 40 acres of semi-wilderness land two hours north of Los Angeles. "Ritual Geomancy and Celebration," "Engaged Buddhism," "The I-Ching," and "Taoist Yoga" are among the studies pursued.

> Their goal? To expand consciousness and improve personal relationships.

One hundred miles north of Vancouver, in the Strait of Georgia, this is a summer-only (June through September) facility on an expanse of beach and 23 acres of gardens, orchards, and forest. Workshops are generally five days in duration, average $475 (and less) for tuition, room, and board, and explore such subjects as "Tibetan Buddhism," "Exploring the World of Alternative Medicine," "Vipassana Meditation," and "The Tao of Movement."

Each center issues catalogues or other descriptive literature, to be carefully perused before enrolling. From personal experience, I can assure that a stay will

Tuition (including lunch) is $120 for a weekend, $175 for four days, $275 for a week; campsite use, breakfast, and dinner are $15 a day more.

Hollyhock Farm, P.O. Box 127, Manson's Landing, Cortes Island, B.C., Canada V0P 1K0 (phone 604/935-6465):

cause you to discover, at the very least, important new aspects of your inner life and relations with others.

IV

Enlarging Your Mind by Using Vacations to Study: Short-Term Educational Trips

A Yank at Oxford —or Cambridge (Summer-style)

They are known as "Quads" because they spread between the enclosing wings of a quadrangular building, and they are magical beyond compare—other-worldly and still, their silence challenged only by the chirpings of a thrush, yet the very air within seems to pulse with the joy of human achievement, 800 years of learning. They are the "quads" of the colleges at Oxford and Cambridge, some so old that one built in the 1300s is still known as New College.

Who among us hasn't dreamed of studying there? How many of the most eminent Americans still harbor a secret disappointment over having failed to win a Rhodes Scholarship or some other form of admission to the ancient universities of Britain?

Well, life in this instance affords a second chance (for a week to a month, at least). From late June through early September, most of the major British universities—Oxford and Cambridge among them—offer study courses of one, two, three, four, and six weeks' duration, to overseas visitors of any age, with adults quite definitely preferred. While a sum-

> While a summer week or more in the quiet, near-deserted quads isn't quite the opportunity you craved in younger days, it provides a memorable communion with these awesome institutions.

mer week or more in the quiet, near-deserted quads isn't quite the opportunity you may have craved in younger days, it provides a memorable communion with these awesome institutions, and a learning experience that has edified and enchanted a great many discerning visitors before you.

By the end of spring, the undergrads of Oxford and Cambridge, in their abbreviated black cloaks flung over tweedy suits and dresses (you won't be wearing one), have all departed for the beaches and hills; but instruction in summer is by the unvarnished "real thing": eminent dons (teaching masters) who pursue a clipped and no-nonsense approach to learning that contrasts quite refreshingly with some American pedagogy. The mind responds—stretching to accommodate difficult concepts and queries, directly and sometimes brutally put. At night you join your instructors in the always-active pubs of the university towns, enjoying conversation as heady as a glass of good brandy. Though individual tutorials aren't provided to summer students, opportunities abound to continue classroom discussion in less formal settings.

In all other respects the experience is reasonably akin to that of British university life. You live in the temporarily vacated quarters of an Oxford or Cambridge student. You dine at the long, wooden, refectory tables of an Oxford or Cambridge dining hall—though "high table," the elevated realm from which faculty members take their wine-accompanied meals, is normally vacant at these times. You roam the stacks of the historic Bodleian Library of Oxford, browse among ancient tomes in the hush of Cambridge's Pepysian Library, lie on the sunlight-

SHORT SUMMER STUDY COURSES AT THE GREAT BRITISH UNIVERSITIES OFFER AN UNUSUAL SUPPLEMENT TO THE STANDARD ENGLISH HOLIDAY

flecked grass as you cope with the heavy reading load that most courses entail.

What courses do you pursue? While Shakespeare and other giants of English literature dominate the lists—and attract the greater number of international students—most remaining studies deal with contemporary aspects of British life and institutions: "Political Thought in England," "The English Educational System," "The United Kingdom Economy," "History of English Painting," among a wide selection of others.

The top summer programs are those

St. John's College, Oxford

WHO AMONG US HASN'T DREAMED OF STUDYING THERE?

offered by departments of the two great universities that concern themselves with extension or continuing education. Cambridge's "official" program, the International Summer School, offers the broadest choice of courses and, unlike Oxford, makes no great point of imposing deadlines for application. It operates a first "term" of four weeks in July, a second "term" of two weeks in early August, permits you to take either or both, and charges upward of £665 ($1,074) for the first term and £390 ($624) for the second. Charges include all tuition, a single room in a university residence, the services of a "scout" to clean your room (but not otherwise to wait upon you), and two meals a day (breakfast and dinner) in a soaring Gothic hall of ancient stone. For catalogue and application forms, write to: **The Director, Board of Extra-Mural Studies, Madingley Hall, Madingley, Cambridge CB3 8AQ (phone 0954-210636).**

Oxford's "official" summer course is a six-week session from July to mid-August, for which three-week enrollments are also permitted. Here, all students pursue the single theme of "Britain: Literature, History, and Society from 1870 to the Present Day," vividly presented in an integrated series of more than 50 lectures by noted Oxford academics (including such major "names" as Professors Richard Ellman, A. H. Halsey, F. S. Northedge, Christopher Ricks). Tuition for the entire six-week term is £1,180 ($1,888) and about half that for three-week sessions, which includes your room (in Exeter College, founded in 1314) and all three meals daily—as well as the occasional invitation to dine at "High Table" with tutors and lecturers. For further information, write to: **Deputy Director,**

> You roam the stacks of the historic Bodleian Library of Oxford, browse among ancient tomes in the hush of Cambridge's Pepysian Library, lie on the sunlight-flecked grass as you cope with the heavy reading load that most courses entail.

The view from Magdalen College, Oxford

Department for External Studies, Rewley House, 1 Wellington Square, Oxford OX1 2JA (phone 0865-270360). For applications, contact the: **Study Abroad Programs Division, Institute of International Education, 809 United Nations Plaza, New York, NY 10017 (phone 212/883-8200).**

If the "official" programs are full, or you have only two weeks available for study, you can opt for a number of "unofficial" courses organized by various Oxford and Cambridge dons on a purely private, entrepreneurial basis; the latter simply rent the use of classrooms and lodgings, and announce their own programs, some for durations of as little as two weeks. Typical are the courses offered at Oxford in "Modern British History and Politics" by the so-called Institute for British and Irish Studies; these are given in July and early August, for either one, two, or three weeks, intensively from 9 a.m. to 6 p.m. Contact the Institute c/o its U.S. representative, **Dr. E.C. Johnson, IBIS, Camford House, Almont, CO 81210 (phone 303/920-3770).** Or, for studies slower paced (lectures are confined to the mornings, afternoons are devoted to excursions), contact **British Summer Courses, 15 Bootham Terrace, York, England YO3 7DH (phone 0904-32081).**

No one suggests that courses such as these should be the sole activity of a British vacation; they can be combined, instead, with the most standard sightseeing and recreation. But what an opportunity awaits! The smart traveller seizes the chance, if the chance exists, to experience these hallowed institutions of learning in the manner they deserve: not as casual tourists, but as students, in the endless quest for light.

Meet the Danish "Folk High School," and Never Be the Same Again

*W*e began the day singing. From our places at a table of polished light pine, drenched in the sunlight reflected from a silver fjord, we sang a secular hymn to life and brotherhood, to goodness and sharing. "Would you care to attend my seminar this morning?" asked a young Danish beauty as she passed me a breakfast bowl of peaches and yogurt. "I shall be inviting people from other disciplines to help me over a rough spot in my paper on producer cooperatives."

I was at a Danish folk high school (folkehøjshole), more properly translated as a "people's college," one of 108 such residential centers of adult education in Denmark, of which two are conducted in English. They represent a massive contribution by Denmark to educational policies emulated all over the world, and they can be visited this coming fall and winter, for stays of as little as one and two weeks, by "intelligent travellers" from the United States and Canada.

Without Tests or Admissions

A "folk high school." The basic characteristics are easy to describe, but infinitely more complex in their application.

They are a massive contribution by Denmark to educational policies all over the world, and can be visited for periods of as little as one or two weeks by travellers of all ages.

There are no entrance requirements or admission exams; hence "folk" (meaning open to all). Students are adults, of post-school age (hence "high school," the term used sensibly, without the unfortunate meanings we Americans ascribe to the words). The schools are residential, and thus radically different from those attended on adult education programs in other lands. Folk high school theorists believe that adults, throughout their lives, should periodically wrench themselves from familiar routines and accustomed settings to go live in a rural residential college with their fellow citizens of all income classes, in a spirit of equality. In Denmark a full 20% of the current population has passed through a folk high school at least once.

Within the schools there are no tests, no final examinations, no certificates or degrees awarded. Learning is for the sheer love of learning. Students and teachers are equals. They are collaborators in the quest for learning. Though teachers initiate some discussions, they quickly cede to their students, and allow inquiries to develop as they naturally do. "It is not the teachers who ask their students questions," explains one folk high school principal, "but the students who interrogate their teachers."

The focus is always on discussions, oral presentations, lively seminars in which students confront their preconceptions and prejudices, their inner and often unexamined beliefs. A goal is to achieve democratic communication between persons of widely divergent backgrounds. Another goal is to tap creative talents lying hidden or subordinated to the harsh realities of earning a living. A Danish farmer with gnarled hands checks into a

The New Experimental College,
Snedsted, Denmark

folk high school near Aalborg, for one month; there he applies himself to easel and canvas, determined to give vent to a hitherto-submerged artistic urge. An operating-room nurse positions herself at a desk near a window looking out onto vistas such as Ibsen might have seen and patiently begins writing a play. While pursuing a thousand different educative tasks, students rediscover their better selves, delight in their nationhood, experience maturation. They study not a single practical subject, but return instead to the liberal arts: poetry, philosophy, history, music. "What did you get out of it?" was the challenge posed to an American businessman completing a two-week stint at one of the two English-language folk high schools. "I got absolutely nothing out of it," he replied, "but I left with my spiritual batteries recharged."

Some observers credit the high Scandinavian regard for law and various forms of community cooperation—including the vaunted Scandinavian cooperative movement itself—to the 140-year-old tradition of the folk high school.

Of the two English-language folk high schools in Denmark, one is very much in that tradition, while the other has passed light-years beyond even the radical formlessness of most schools. The "traditional" establishment is the International People's College (Den Internationale

A WINTER WEEK OR TWO AT A RESIDENTIAL COLLEGE FOR ADULTS

Højshole) at Elsinore, an hour by train from Copenhagen, in a Scandinavian-modern complex of low, glass-sided buildings on expansive grounds. Recognized (and subsidized) by the Danish government, it earns that support by officially offering 26 one-hour classes a week and by publishing a printed, purported curriculum of subjects ("alternative societies," "comparative religion," "life in the Third World"), but there all resemblance to the usual college ends. New subjects spring spontaneously to life, wholly unplanned subject matter grips the imagination of a particular term, while students rush to complete projects and papers that they themselves have conceived. Drawing its student body half from English-speaking Danes, half from other widely scattered nations; employing as "faculty" (read: fellow students) a Greek sociologist, a Ugandan lawyer in exile from successive regimes, an Australian poet, an Indian playwright—some without actual aca-

Folk high school theorists believe that adults, throughout their lives, should periodically wrench themselves from familiar routines to go live in a rural residential college.

The NEC, Snedsted, Denmark

demic credentials—the school shimmers with international vitality, excites even the casual visitor. Tuition, reduced by government grants, runs to all of $140 per week, including all three meals each day and lodging in single rooms.

While most students attend the International People's College for periods of four months and more in the fall/winter season, reserving short courses for the summer, the school will occasionally accept two-week and three-week students in winter, if space exists, and particularly if they start near the January 27 opening of a winter term. Address your applications to the white-bearded, cigar-smoking, prominent Danish educator, Eric Hojsbro-Holm, who heads the school. He's a notorious "softie" about making a place available for American adults anxious to attend, if only for a fortnight or so. Contact **Den Internationale Højshole, Montebello Alle 1, Elsinore, Denmark (phone 45-02-213-361).**

The competing, English-language folk high school has no problem at all in accepting short-term students. The New Experimental College (NEC) will eagerly clasp you to its side at any time of the winter, for as little as one, two, or three weeks, and regardless of whether it has on-premises sleeping space still available for you; if it doesn't, it will board you at nearby, comfortable farmhouses or at modern hotels less than ten kilometers away.

So radical in approach as to lack recognition and subsidy from even the permissive Danish government, NEC is still a highly regarded institution lauded by such celebrated educators as Harold Taylor and Paul Goodman. The late John Lennon and Yoko Ono are among its

"graduates." Located at the crest of a gentle hill overlooking a Danish fjord at the northern tip of the Jutland peninsula, it enjoys an enthralling setting supplemented by the comforts of a sprawling Danish farmhouse capable of housing about 50 students. Because of its lack of subsidy, it charges $160 a week for those able to pay, for tuition, room, board, evening sauna, and assignment to a sleep-inducing, over-stuffed leather chair in an extensive, quiet library sprinkled with U.N. publications, among its other resources.

At NEC there are no regular or recurring classes at all, not even an initial published curriculum. There are, in fact, no paid faculty members, no "teachers" at all. Every individual pursues his or her study interests, without interference or outside influence, the only element of discipline being the requirement to report, at a Saturday morning meeting, on what they have done the preceding week. If students should feel an earlier need for reporting their results to others, or obtaining comments from them, they "announce" a class or seminar, which they then present, and which others are free to attend or not, as they see fit. They select their own educational goals, define their own education, conduct a raging inner battle, award their own "certificate of completion" to themselves. In effect, they

commence a lifelong process of continually discovering what it is they wish to learn and how to go about doing so. They learn best, according to NEC, when that discovery is their own.

Throughout this process of self-realization, akin almost to a self-analysis, NEC remains almost coldly neutral. When outsiders "ask the question but what do you do there—what do people learn?" writes founder Aage Rosendal-Nielsen, 64, "we take our stand and . . . simply refuse to answer the question."

There is still social interaction. You, as a scholar/student, attend the seminars so continually announced by others. You participate in the *ting*—a Scandinavian-style town hall frequently invoked to pose a general question to the assemblage; anyone can call a ting. At a Friday-evening "celebration meal," you dress for a special candlelight meal at which volunteers deliver speeches on their work or thoughts. You converse on walks into the heather-covered hills. And occasionally at night you relax within a sometimes-coed sauna so hot as if almost symbolically to burn away the inhibitions, unthinking patterns, communications barriers, or narrow provincial attitudes with which you entered NEC.

To attend the NEC at any time of the year, but especially in winter, and for as little as a week or two, write to **New Experimental College, Skyum Bjerge, Thy, 7752 Snedsted, Denmark (phone 45-7-936234).** The school is reached from the airports of either Thisted or Ålborg, 50-or-so minutes by S.A.S. jet from Copenhagen, or 6½ hours by train from Copenhagen's central station. You will never be the same again—and isn't that the hallmark of intelligent travel?

Low-Cost Language Schools Abroad

"O *f course you don't get our business! Of course we don't send you our orders! You don't speak our language!"*

Such words of reproach from a normally courteous European surprised even the speaker, stirred some long-smouldering resentment, led to further indictment.

"It isn't that we're asking you to engage in technical discussions with us. But at a simple dinner party you can't carry on the most routine conversation with the lady on your left. You Americans take the cake!"

Why, among all the achievers of the world, do the overwhelming number of Americans fail to possess a second language? Or a third?

Sheer indolence is a first explanation. Torpor. Thoughtless indifference, largely stemming from unpleasant, subconscious memories of uninspiring language courses at ol' State U. Mistaken smugness ("they all speak English"). And failure to make the proper use of travel opportunities. Since languages can be acquired with surprising ease in situations where you are "immersed" in them, the mere decision to travel *solo*, unaccompanied by English-speaking spouse or companion, can yield the most remarkable results. When that vacation trip is further pursued at a European language school, in an

The brightest of travellers achieve fluency, or near-fluency, in one of the four major European languages at schools whose glorious traditions, settings, and remarkably low costs provide the greatest of travel pleasures in addition to instruction.

off-season period when tourists have fled and all you hear is one foreign language, at breakfast and in classes, on television and at the movies, in restaurants and bars, one language unendingly—the results are astonishing. You speak!

This fall and winter a great many bright Americans will enhance their cultural perspectives, careers, and lives by pursuing short language courses overseas, partially funded by European governments. They will achieve fluency, or near-fluency, in one of the four major European tongues—French, Spanish, German, or Italian—at schools whose glorious traditions, European settings, and remarkably low costs provide the greatest of travel pleasures in addition to instruction.

Most of the schools share common features, of which the most important is the timing of one-month classes to begin near the first of each month; schedule your applications and arrivals accordingly. Most will provide you with lodgings in the homes of private families, where you'll again be immersed in the local language. State-operated schools are usually considerably cheaper than private ones, without a loss of quality or intensity. Schools in secondary cities will send you to cheaper accommodations than those in famous ones: thus the families with whom you'll stay in Perugia will charge a third of what you'll pay in Florence.

You choose from the following:

For French: Ancestor to all the great European language schools, founded in 1883 to advance French culture and the French language to all the world, is the powerful Alliance Française. Directly funded by the French Foreign Ministry, it operates low-cost French-language

THE CAREFUL USE OF TRAVEL TO ACQUIRE FLUENCY IN A FOREIGN TONGUE

schools in more than 100 nations, but its soul remains in a great gray building on Paris's Left Bank, at 101 Boulevard Raspail, steps away from the trendy cafés, art galleries, and way-out boutiques of the busier Boulevard St. Germain.

In the large stone courtyard of the giant school, teeming with Egyptian caftans, African turbans, Canadian blue jeans, the atmosphere may be international but only one language is spoken: French. And French is spoken at every moment and exclusively throughout the day, in the very first class you attend, in the on-premises cafeteria where you take your meals, at theatrical performances and lectures in the school's auditorium. You are in class at least 3½ hours a day, then in earphone-equipped language laboratories for supplemental practice, then at near-mandatory social events—yet you pay only 400 francs ($61) a week, quite obviously subsidized, for all tuition—and house yourself in any of dozens of inexpensive Left Bank hotels clustered in this section of the Latin Quarter; there, too, you hear and speak French exclusively.

Alliance Française classes must be taken for a minimum of four weeks, start-

ing at the beginning of each month, and application should be made at least a month in advance. For further information and forms, write: **Alliance Française de Paris, 101 Boulevard Raspail, 75270 Paris CEDEX 06, France.**

For Italian: Choosing from a score of major, Italy-based, Italian-language schools, the clear consensus of the experts (I've spoken with three) favors the state-operated University for Foreigners of Perugia (Università Italiana per Stranieri) and the Cultural Center for Foreigners of Florence (Centro Culturale per Stranieri). Both are in that broad region

BECAUSE STUDENTS ARE FROM DOZENS OF COUNTRIES SCATTERED FROM JAPAN TO YEMEN, THE ONLY COMMON LANGUAGE AMONG THEM IS THAT OF THE HOST NATION

of Italy (Tuscany and Umbria) where the purest form of Italian is said to be spoken.

At Perugia, an Intensive Preparatory Course (5½ hours of classroom instruction a day, of which two hours are devoted to conversation and language laboratories) is priced at only 350,000 lire ($245) for a month—$60 a week. A normal beginner's course (4 hours a day), for either one, two, or three months, costs only 180,000 lire ($125) per month. Compare those rates to what you'd pay to a private language school at home!

Non-intensive courses start every two weeks, and may be taken for as little as a month. Students attend classes in a vast, baroque-style palazzo, stay with Italian families in private homes ($150 a month), and take their meals ($1 apiece) in one of two University of Perugia canteens. Weekends, they journey for culture and conversation to nearby Assisi, Orvieto, Spoleto.

At the more leisurely Florence school, where classroom time occupies only 2½ hours a day, but is supplemented with homework and language labs, courses run for ten weeks, start at regular quarterly intervals, and cost 310,000 lire ($220) for the entire term, independent of room-and-board costs. If you're fixed on Florence but can't stay ten weeks, or can't get into the official school, try the one-month, four-hour-a-day sessions of the prestigious-but-private (and costlier) Dante Alighieri Society ($360 a month, not including room and board).

Write for information and/or application forms to: **Università Italiana per Stranieri, Palazzo Gallenga, 4 Piazza Fortebraccio, 06100 Perugia, Italy; Centro Culturale per Stranieri, Università degli Studi, 64 Via Vittorio Emanuele,**

The mere decision to travel solo, unaccompanied by English-speaking spouse or companion, can yield the most remarkable results.

50134 Florence, Italy; or **Società Dante Alighieri, 12 Via di Bardi, 50125 Florence, Italy.**

And for a list of additional language schools in other Italian cities, contact the **Italian Cultural Institute, 686 Park Avenue, New York, NY 10021 (phone 212/879-4242).**

For German: The influential world role of German commerce and culture (one out of every ten books on earth is published in German) lends continuing importance to German language study. West Germany's own government provides heavily subsidized instruction via its Goethe Institutes, of which more than 100 are found in 60 countries, and 13 are maintained in Germany itself. The latter are marvelously diverse, in both large cities (Munich, Berlin), university towns (Göttingen, Mannheim), and idyllic countryside locations (Prien and Murnau in rural Bavaria).

If you've the time for an eight-week course, you can make your own selection of a Goethe Institute (and city) from the 13 available. Busier people able to devote only four weeks to it are confined to two locations: Rothenburg-ob-der-Tauber (that perfectly preserved medieval village on the "Romantic Road" near Nuremberg, from June through January), and Boppard (in the Valley of the Lorelei, along the Rhine, from February through May).

In each you are given 24 hours a week of classroom instruction, supplemented by at least 10 hours a week of private study, and additional sessions of conversation with German residents dragooned in for the purpose. Each institute makes all the arrangements for your room and board with a private family, and charges a total

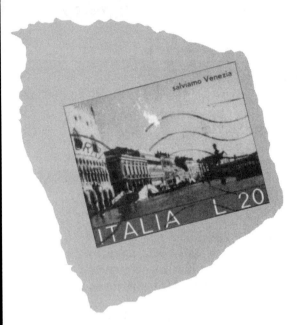

Most schools will provide you with lodgings in the homes of private families, where you'll again be immersed in the local language.

for the entire month—tuition, materials, room, and board—of 1,950 marks (approximately $1,083).

For further information and application forms contact **Goethe House, 1014 Fifth Avenue, New York, NY 10028 (phone 212/744-8310).** The U.S.-based branch will then forward your completed form to the Goethe Institute you've selected.

For Spanish: Salamanca is the place. Emphatically. Without a second thought. It is the heart of Old Castile, where Spanish is noble and pure, untainted by the Gallego accents of the northwest, the Catalán of the east, the assorted dialects of the south:

Its monumental University of Salamanca (dating from 1226) is one of the world's oldest. Together with similar medieval academies in Padua and Bologna, it developed an early tradition for attracting international students, and that reputation —even stronger today—has a wholesome impact on language studies there. Because students are from dozens of countries scattered from Japan to Yemen, the only common language among them is Spanish. You either speak it or suffer muteness.

Though Salamanca is only 2½ hours from Madrid, it is no Madrid in cost: $12 a day is more than enough for room and all three meals at scores of guest-accepting private homes. And tuition at the private language schools is as low as the Universi-

ty of Salamanca's, enabling you to study one-on-one with your teacher, or in small groups of seven or eight, for as little as you'd pay elsewhere in a class of 20. I like, for that reason, an intensely personal school called Salminter (Escuela Salmantina de Estudios Internacionales), which charges only $200 per month for four hours of instruction, five days a week.

Dominant among the other, all-year-round, private schools is the Colegio de España, whose intensive four-week course starting at the beginning of every month (four hours daily, in classes limited to 15 students) costs a remarkable 18,000 pesetas ($140) a month, to which you add about $70 a week for room and board. Weekends, its students travel by short bus rides to Ávila, Segovia, and Valladolid, though the older adults among them (like me on previous trips) scarcely budge from a sidewalk café seat on the historic Plaza Mayor—barred to traffic, and like a baroque drawing room, except out-of-doors. Churches and museums with Goyas, Velázquezes, and El Grecos are short steps away.

When people ask why I don't prefer the more accessible Spanish-language schools of Mexico to those of Spain, I answer diplomatically that Mexico is Mexico, but Spain is . . . well, Spain.

For applications or further information on the Salminter school, write to its U.S. representative, **Elisabeth Nebehay, 251 East 32nd Street, New York, NY 10016 (phone 212/689-2636),** or directly to **Salminter, Apartado de Correo 575, Salamanca, Spain (phone 211-808).** For the larger Colegio, write to: **Colegio de España, 65 Calle Compañía, 37008 Salamanca, Spain (phone 214-788).**

A Nonprofit Approach to the Group Study Tour

" ***B****ut how can you countenance the power and influence of Franz-Josef Strauss?"*

The interlocutor was a young American social worker, directing her remarks accusingly to an important columnist for the right-wing Bonn newspaper *Die Welt*. Earlier that day she and her nine travelling companions had received a three-

Travel catalogues list dozens of study tours, one usually worse than the next.

Beethoven's birthplace, Bonn

hour briefing on the German social welfare system from a junior official of the federal government's Ministry of Labor. Later they would visit, again in Bonn, a state-operated institute for the rehabilitation of criminals. After dinner in a leading restaurant of nearby Cologne, capped by a glass of fine cognac, members of the tiny group would each repair for overnight to the home of an English-speaking German family.

The events described are all part of a two-week "study tour," but one that relates to most other "study tours" as Tiffany's compares with the five-and-dime. It is planned and operated by Germany's prestigious Organization for International Contacts (O.I.K.) from the baroque rooms in a Bonn suburb of an 18th-century town house once belonging to the prince-elector of Schleswig-Holstein. The nonprofit O.I.K., almost a quasi-official arm of the German government, is the first in an emerging group of new, noncommercial European organizations dedicated to organizing meaningful study visits to Europe for groups from abroad.

The travel catalogues issued by foreign governments list hundreds of purported "study tours." One is usually worse than the next. Sold by commercial travel agents, operated for them by other commercial travel agents at the destination, they invariably turn out to be standard group visits of castles and cabarets, supplemented by a few perfunctory tours of factories and farms. Because their organizers have profit as their major aim, they are rarely able to enlist the cooperation of companies other than those wishing to sell their own wares to visitors from abroad (breweries, diamond cutters, cheesemakers). Why else should a serious

GERMANY'S ORGANIZATION FOR INTERNATIONAL CONTACTS HAS CREATED AN UNUSUALLY REWARDING FORM OF PURPOSIVE TRAVEL

Rheinische-Friedrich-Wilhelm University, Bonn

firm cooperate with a commercial tour operator? Nor is the income-producing study tour able easily to tap the knowledge of the public sector abroad. "They have no access at all to the government ministries or the universities," said one caustic observer.

How, then, can a serious group of Americans gain assistance in viewing the activities of their European counterparts? If ten-or-so of your colleagues in ecosys-tems, education, or electrodes want to meet this coming winter with European specialists in ecosystems, education, or electrodes, who is there to make the arrangements for transportation, housing, meetings, lectures, inspections, and cocktail gatherings—the essentials of a good study tour? Though European government "institutes" will assist in scheduling

COMMERCIAL FIRMS OPERATING STUDY TOURS HAVE ONLY SLIGHT ACCESS TO THE GOVERNMENT MINISTRIES OR UNIVERSITIES

interviews for individuals (but not in making arrangements for lodging and transportation), and though cultural attachés of foreign embassies will act to aid visits of major public importance, there was until recently no outstanding European organization able to handle both the practical and educational aspects of a profoundly serious study tour, yet one designed for ordinary Americans.

Enter, now, the Bonn-based Organization for International Contacts. Formed as a nonprofit foundation about ten years ago, its organizers emerged from the idealistic world of student travel determined to operate visits of unaffected, people-to-people understanding: first within Germany, more recently in other European nations as well, increasingly to countries of the Third World (India, Indonesia, Tanzania, Senegal).

"Our only limitation is that our clients must be a group of eight to ten persons," says founder Dr. Joachim Müller. "Beyond that, we impose no bounds at all. You can be robot-makers, torts lawyers, endive growers, hydraulics engineers—or pursue interests of which we've never heard. We will engage in whatever research is required, for months if necessary, to place you in contact with your European counterparts, on an intensive, well-planned program."

Ergonomics provides the most recent example. Anxious to view the work of their European colleagues in the increasingly important science of biotechnology, a group of American ergonomists sought the aid of O.I.K. Though the latter's research staff of several studious young German women had never heard the term, they combed the university faculties from Düsseldorf to Heidelberg and

Organizers of O.I.K. emerged from the idealistic world of student travel, determined to operate visits of unaffected, people-to-people understanding.

succeeded, after several weeks, in scheduling an early- morning - till - night, 14-day tour of every significant German effort in the field. Then, because the Americans were travelling under severe budgetary constraints, they arranged to house the visitors in homes of German ergonomists on nearly half the nights of their stay.

"Actually, we always make the offer of home stays," says Britta von Manteuffel, head of O.I.K.'s tour department. "It is a form of 'integrated tourism.' What could be better for a doctor on a medical tour than to stay with a doctor's family overnight, and then to accompany that doctor to his office the next day, viewing his methods and approaches, his problems?" On tours of the Third World, O.I.K. urges its clients to live in the villages they visit, or at least in small pensions, inns, local teachers' colleges, all institutions affording a close-up experience of the indigenous existence of the communities under study.

In Europe, the typical O.I.K. study tour is normally a more luxurious affair, of banquet dinners and speeches by distinguished figures, but always descends —at some point—to the gritty core of the subject under study: visits to drug-treatment centers in the case of social-welfare tours, close inspection of the most experimental of schools on tours for educators. O.I.K. has recently organized the tours to Europe of American research administrators (persons who seek public funds for research), computer scientists, social workers, town planners, architects, deep-sea divers—and railroad officials from Japan. Three to four months' advance notice is needed in summer, far less than that for fall/winter tours, plus a 20%

Market Square, Bonn

deposit against anticipated costs.

The rewards of well-planned travel! If you can persuade eight to ten of your colleagues (in whatever field you pursue) to devote a week or two to a European study tour, you can endow that tour with remarkable substance and content by con-tacting the **Organisation für Internationale Kontakte, 5 Kurfurstenallee, 5300 Bonn 2, Bad Godesberg, West Germany** (**phone 0228-357015**).

The Love Boat and the Learn Boat

*Y*ou step aboard to the *strains of Vivaldi and search in vain for a single casino. At night you amuse yourself not in a seagoing cabaret, but in that long-forgotten art of serious conversation with fellow passengers, over a brandy in a relaxing lounge. If a film is shown, it's of exotic tribespeople in an actual setting or of hump-backed whales off the Patagonian fjords.*

And when you retire to cabin or bunk, you're first handed a half-hour's reading for the day ahead.

You've heard of the "Love Boat." Now meet the "Learn Boat." Though it may seem like a contradiction in terms, the combination of cruising and education is creating a potent new vacation lure for thousands of intellectually curious Americans.

Every week nearly a dozen small ships —and their number seems to be growing —depart from Mediterranean, Central and South American, and South Pacific ports on so-called expedition cruises staffed by naturalists, anthropologists, and cultural historians.

The major programs are three in number:

Swan Hellenic Cruises: Cheapest of the lot—a remarkable value—are two-week cruises of the eastern Mediterranean aboard the 300-passenger M.T.S. *Orphe-*

They depart from Mediterranean, South American, and South Pacific ports, staffed by naturalists, anthropologists, and cultural historians.

us, operated continuously from mid-March to late September each year by the distinguished Swan Hellenic organization of the venerable P & O Lines of Britain.

Here you look in depth at the origins of the Greco-Christian-Judaic civilization, accompanied at all times by a minimum of four—often as many as five—British university lecturers, museum people, clergy, and authors. The dean of Merton College, Oxford, frequently lectures on board and ashore. So do several professors of ancient history at Cambridge, the archaeology editor of *The Illustrated London News,* a former dean of Salisbury Cathedral, a director of the Imperial War Museum.

"I so treasured our afternoon at Ephesus," wrote one passenger, "because as we sat in the theatre, the guest lecturer read to us from Acts 19 and instantly brought alive the story of the silversmiths who demonstrated against St. Paul in defense of their livelihood— the making of idols to the goddess Diana."

For such a profound combination of cultural discovery and water-borne pleasures, 16 days in length, you pay a total of $3,600 (in the bulk of cabins), which includes round-trip air fare between several U.S. East Coast cities and London ($190 more from the West Coast), and round-trip air between London and either Athens, Thessaloniki, Venice, or Dubrovnik, from which the ship departs. You're put up for two nights at a first-class hotel in London (one night before the cruise, one night after), and then cruise for a full 14 nights to the "isles of

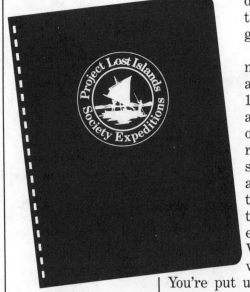

EXPEDITION CRUISING BRINGS EDUCATION TO THE HIGH SEAS

Greece," the coasts of Turkey, Yugoslavia, Bulgaria. The trip is so very all-inclusive—such a splended example of the refreshing British insistence on moderate travel costs—that even the daily shore excursions (with their eminent lecturers) are thrown in at no extra charge.

Swan Hellenic Cruises are represented in the U.S. by **Esplanade Tours, 581 Boylston Street, Boston, MA 02116 (phone 617/266-7465).** Contact them for a fascinating catalogue.

Society Expeditions: Now you're on voyages of daring (but deluxe) exploration and discovery, into the most mysterious and remote regions of the earth: the islands of Micronesia, Borneo and the Northwest Passage, the Antarctic, the Amazon and the Aleutians, the shores of Indonesia.

On a Society Expedition, the bent is distinctly naturalistic or anthropological, far less historical or archaeological than the themes of Swan Hellenic. You visit untouristed shores, not ports, making landfall on motorized rubber landing boats called "Zodiacs."

Thus conveyed, you go to otherwise inaccessible villages or riverbanks, where at night the beat of a shaman's drum raises appeals to ancestral spirits. You walk among upright penguins gathered by the hundreds on a shore of the Falklands. You meet and interact with Amazonian natives. To avoid "polluting" their natural or cultural life, your visits are scheduled for widely scattered dates.

The trips are realized aboard two luxuriously fitted ships: the 140-passenger *World Discoverer* and the 100-passenger *Society Explorer*, both with shallow drafts, specially hardened hulls, and bow-thrusters required for expedition cruising.

Each voyage is accompanied by a team of naturalists, marine biologists, and (sometimes) anthropologists. You sail with the likes of Dr. George Llano, chief polar scientist for the National Science Foundation; Prof. Lloyd Smith, noted Darwinian; or Bengt Danielsson, a member of Thor Heyerdahl's *Kon-Tiki* adventure.

Both ships go circumnavigating the globe, on different itineraries, throughout the year. Passengers, essentially, book segments of the voyage—usually from two to several weeks—and are flown to and from ports at both ends of the segment. Costs average slightly under $300 a day for the bulk of cabins and trips.

For a set of mouthwatering, award-winning, large, glossy brochures, contact

YOU GO TO OTHERWISE INACCESSIBLE VILLAGES OR RIVERBANKS WHERE AT NIGHT THE BEAT OF A SHAMAN'S DRUM RAISES APPEALS TO ANCESTRAL SPIRITS

Society Expeditions, 3131 Elliott Avenue, Suite 700, Seattle, WA 98121 (phone 206/285-9400, or toll free 800/426-7794 outside Washington).

Salen-Lindblad Cruising, Inc.: This final firm operates the smallest of expedition ships, some carrying as few as 36 passengers. An example, and its major pride, is the twin-hulled *Kimberley Explorer*, with an astonishing draft of only five feet, enabling it to cruise inlets of the world's last frontier: the virtually unsettled Kimberley Coast of Australia. A trip lasts 17 or 21 days, of which 13 are spent on ship and the remainder in various major Australian cities; departs once a month from January through December; and is led by naturalist Tom Richie, aided by an expert on Australia's aborigine population, who precedes your party ashore, equipped with walkie-talkie, to arrange meetings with these proud and capable people. Cost, including round-trip air from Los Angeles, meals, shore excursions, and all else, averages $4,800 for 17-day trips, $5,400 for 21 days.

Other year-round programs of Salen-Lindblad: to Indonesian waters, embarking from Djakarta on a 36-passenger, luxury catamaran yacht (world-renowned divers and naturalists accompany you); and to the Galápagos Islands (a specialty). Seasonal programs: along the Volga River of the USSR, and to the North Cape of Norway. For brochures, contact **Salen-Lindblad Cruising, Inc., 133 East 55th Street, New York, NY 10022 (phone 212/751-2300 or toll free 800/223-5688).**

So what will it be, the "Love Boat" or the "Learn Boat," the libido or learning? Some say that expedition cruising allows the best of both.

V

Bargain Air Fares: Does Only the Chump Pay Full Price?

Meet the Air Fare "Bucket Shop"

You've seen the ads a hundred times, and probably they confused you.

Two starkly simple, vertical columns: a list of cities, a list of prices. Nothing more.

From the East Coast: "London, $159." "Paris, $179." From the West Coast: "Singapore, $319." "Tokyo, $329." All manner of miracle air fares at nearly half the normal level. For scheduled flights.

But without a single airline name. Without, for that matter, a single recognizable name. A telephone number, of course. And a company title leaving naught to the imagination: "Travel for Peanuts, Inc." "Why Pay More, Ltd." "Don't-Be-A-Chump & Associates".

Meet the American "bucket shop"! A "discount travel agency" in more polite parlance, its counterpart has flourished in London for 20 years, but only recently taken root in the United States. Today nearly 200 are scrambling for business in big cities across the land—mainly New York, Philadelphia, Boston, Chicago, Los Angeles, San Francisco—where they are used by thousands, but shunned by tens of thousands more who feel somehow queasy, unsettled, about buying an international air ticket for less than list.

Their counterparts have flourished in London for nearly 20 years, but only recently taken root in the U.S. Today nearly 200 are scrambling for business in big cities across the land.

By negotiating directly with a score of major airlines, the "buckets" obtain those tickets for 35% to 50% below the normal price, and sell them to the public at discounts of 25% to 40%.

Why the term "bucket shop"? Because most are in shabby, upstairs offices crammed with ancient desks and telephones—the kind of setting remembered from stock market swindles of the 1920s. Owned very often by undercapitalized young people, they lack the colorful cardboard airline displays and racks of glossy brochures found in the traditional travel agencies. Physically, they fill you with dread.

But are they reputable? In my experience, yes. Though one of the leading New York firms was threatened with ruin only recently, it managed to squeak through; and I for one am unaware of any major scandal among them, or of any substantial number of purchasers who have failed to receive a valid ticket for money spent.

This is not to say that the "buckets" are to be trusted sight unseen. They should be visited, not simply phoned; scrutinized for proof of minimal financial resources: a typewriter or two, a desk, a junior employee. You might even protect yourself by a bit of choreography: you hold and hand over payment with your right hand while simultaneously picking up the ticket with your left. Once that's done, you'll immediately see (and sigh with relief) that you've received a totally valid ticket, issued by a real-life airline, but a ticket that's been drastically reduced in price through hard, selective bargaining by the bucket shop.

The industry response

Why don't traditional travel agencies

THEY'VE MOVED HERE FROM BRITAIN, A REMARKABLE SOURCE OF DISCOUNT TICKETS

engage in the same bargaining for bucket shop–type prices? Some do—but then don't advertise the fact. Eminent trade publications carry ads of "consolidators" (national bucket shops) in New York and St. Louis, offering dramatically reduced air fares to standard travel agencies (who presumably pass on the savings to their clients).

That more travel agents don't seek out these prices is, from my observations, either the result of torpor, inertia, or dullness, or of the inability of some to break away from the mind patterns formed during the recently ended era of airline regulation. Some of the agents are a stubbornly conservative lot.

Others refuse to sell at lower rates because of the claim by their trade association—the American Society of Travel Agents (A.S.T.A.)—that the practice is illegal. A number of half-forgotten treaties and long-ago laws make it arguable that certain forms of rebating in the international field are improper (although rebating of domestic air fares is clearly legal).

But even if that is the law, it is clearly, undeniably, not being enforced. In the face of the most urgent public entreaties by the chairman of A.S.T.A., the Department of Transportation has responded with massive inaction or carefully ambiguous pronouncements; its obvious refusal to turn back the clock and move against the "buckets" has led the rebate-hating *Travel Agent* magazine to write as recently as August 14 of last year: "While rebating on international airfare tickets may have once been illegal, in the real world it no longer is. . . . This country has decided to let 'em rebate."

> That more travel agents don't seek out the same prices is, from my observation, either the result of torpor, inertia, or dullness, or of mind patterns formed during the era of regulation.

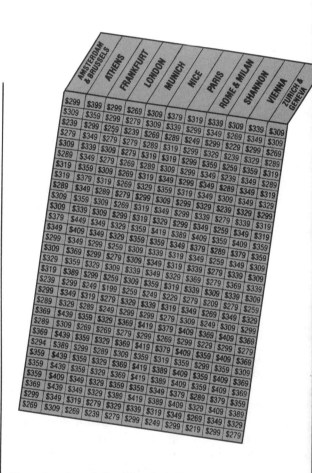

Drawbacks of the "buckets"

So the practice is unrestrained; the bargains are there. Why, then, don't more members of the public patronize the bucket shops? Why don't the customers of discount pharmacies and grocery stores, discount record shops and bookstores, flock in the same numbers and with the same eagerness to the travel bucket shops?

The reason is, in all fairness, that the contexts aren't identical, the products aren't similar. In many instances (not all, but many), the bucket shops do not provide you with quite the same air tickets or perform other highly desirable functions of a travel agent:

• First, the "buckets" provide no travel counseling. Ask one to recommend a

IN EVERY OTHER ECONOMIC AREA WE BENEFIT FROM TWO TIERS OF RETAIL SELLING: FULL-PRICE OUTLETS AND DISCOUNT OUTLETS. WHY SHOULD TRAVEL BE ANY DIFFERENT?

hotel, let alone book one, and they will fix you with a glassy stare. Theirs is a staff of order-takers selling air tickets only, and not even all tickets but only certain ones. Full-service travel agents they're not.

• They keep you guessing about the airline you've booked. Unless it is a Third World or Middle East carrier, they won't divulge its identity until you've paid in full. (The reason for the Third World and Middle East exception is that large numbers of the public are unwilling to fly on Bedouin Air or Air Village, and demand to know before they commit.) Bucket shop staff will be fired for divulging the name of any other sort of airline over the phone, thus protecting the "holier-than-thou" reputations of the more prestigious lines.

• Their tickets aren't really the full equivalent of normal ones. They are restricted tickets: nontransferable, nonendorseable, nonchangeable, noncancellable (without hefty penalties), and nonrefundable except from the bucket

> By negotiating directly with major carriers, the "buckets" obtain tickets for 35% to 50% below the normal price, and sell them to the public at discounts of 25% to 40%.

World carriers, whose route structures require them to fly first to their home cities before proceeding to where most people are going, they sometimes make you do silly things: traveling to Rome or Athens, you first fly all the way to Belgrade or Bucharest, for instance, change planes, and then "backtrack" for several hundred miles to Rome or Athens. Or you fly first to Toronto, change planes, and then use a Canadian carrier to Australia or Europe. Or you go first to Casablanca, change planes, and then fly on to Lisbon or Madrid. You inconvenience yourself and add several hours to the trip, but save hundreds and hundreds of dollars. (And in that Canadian example, the airline absorbs the cost of a flight from the U.S. to Toronto.)

• They make a heavy use of underbooked Middle East carriers to Europe (if

CAIRO $699 .... PARIS $27 99 .... ROME $378 .... AUSTRALIA $787 . SAN FRANCISCO $99

shop, never from the airline. And rumors persist that if a flight is overbooked, it is "you know who" that gets "bumped" the first.

• They send you, in perhaps a fifth the cases, on distorted routings. Because the buckets rely in part on underbooked Communist-bloc, Canadian, and Third

that should bother you—and it shouldn't). Even when the itinerary is a reasonably straight line, you frequently fly on carriers you would not ordinarily select, because those carriers make European stops (at heavy discounts) on the way to their capital cities. Thus, from the U.S., Royal Jordanian Airlines (Alia) flies to Vienna, Amsterdam, or Frankfurt on its way to Amman; Egyptair stops in Paris on its way to Cairo; Kuwait Airways stops in London or Frankfurt on the way to Kuwait. While some of these and other Middle East carriers refuse to deal with the buckets, the majority do, and a great many of the cut-rate fares to Europe result from that willingness.

But you needn't be overly edgy. In the great majority of instances, bucket shops are today using seats on the most celebrated of U.S., European, and Asian carriers. I know of only two European airlines that do *not* work on occasion with the buckets. I know of only a single U.S. carrier flying major international routes that definitely doesn't work with the buckets. Multitudes of Americans making payments to bucket shops have been pleasantly surprised to receive tickets on the most blue-blooded of airlines bearing household names.

> Physically, they fill you with dread. But are they reputable? In my experience, yes.

And isn't that all to the good? In every other economic area Americans benefit from two tiers of retail selling: full-price outlets and discount outlets. Why should travel be any different? Given a choice, numerous Americans will continue to use the full-service travel agencies, who will continue to charge full price (and perhaps an extra fee) for the wisdom of their advice, the beauty of their settings, and the ease of their itineraries. Others will opt for the buckets—the discount agencies offering no advice at all, greeting their customers in squalid lofts, sending them to adventures-in-the-air, via exotic cities and strange airlines.

As for me, I'll be with the bucket

In one particular area of air transportation—flights across the Pacific—discounting of air fares by virtually every airline has reached such epic proportions that only the most ill-informed traveller any longer pays list price.

Travel agents to the contrary, therefore, rebating seems here to stay. Like the ancient guilds seeking to halt the Industrial Revolution, like Canute vainly holding back the sea, the efforts of A.S.T.A. to thwart the travel bucket shops are clearly foredoomed.

shops—travelling to Belgrade to go to Rome, changing planes at Casablanca to go to Lisbon. Just as I find it unnatural, even antisocial, to pay hundreds of dollars extra for a few hours in a first-class seat, so I find it impossible to pass up a saving of several hundreds of dollars gained simply by adding three-or-so hours to an overnight flight. If you're of a similar mind, you'll join me in a hastily composed ballad, delivered in the tempo, let's say, of Aretha Franklin:

"Singin' the air fare blues? Prices got you down? Worried 'bout the tab? Try a bucket shop!"

More About Discount Travel Agencies ("Bucket Shops")

*I*n appearance, certainly, it's an odd "travel agency," without a poster or brochure in sight, without adornment of any sort. But high on the wall, two large blackboards catch the eye. On them are chalked, each day, the latest discount rates for international air tickets—like the quotes for pork-belly futures on the Chicago Commodities Exchange. And down below, staring up at the changing rates, are clamorous New Yorkers buying tickets there at the rate of 3,000 a week in high season.

What I've just described are the Manhattan offices of **Access International, Ltd., 250 West 57th Street, New York, NY 10107 (phone 212/333-7280),** which claims to be the nation's largest retail discount travel agency—a "bucket shop" in the slang of the trade. Access is a leading player in a highly significant recent development in travel: the emergence of price competition at the retail level.

The counterpart to Access on the West Coast is **Express Discount Travel, 5945 Mission Gorge Road #2, San Diego, CA 92120 (phone 619/283-6324).** Though only

> Their tickets are restricted, their itineraries often complex, and they provide no travel counseling. Yet for all of that, thousands sing their praises.

recently opened, Express Discount Travel's proprietors have for years been the largest wholesale source of discount tickets to more than a score of retail bucket shops in southern California, and are now marketing their low-cost ducats for Europe, South America, Japan and Australia directly to the public. In the Midwest no firm matches Access in volume, but **People's Air Tours, Inc., 2536 West Peterson, Chicago, IL 60659 (phone 312/761-7500),** is representative of perhaps a dozen, similarly sized "buckets."

In the previous essay I wrote about the often odd products and practices of these retail samaritans, whose tiny ads, causing rampant confusion, are scattered throughout the Sunday travel sections of big-city newspapers. I took pains to stress that their tickets are restricted: nonchangeable and refunded only with penalties; that their itineraries are often complex; and that they provide no travel counseling at all. Yet for all of that, thousands sing their praises.

Because the activity is such a major dividend of deregulation, and bound to increase in size, it's important to devote additional space to still other items of clarification—and warning.

• Don't mistake them for "distress merchants." Note, first, that the buckets are wholly different from those celebrated clubs and firms that market unsold seats on cruises, charter flights, and tours. The latter (names like Stand-Buys, Ltd., Moment's Notice, Vacations to Go, Discount Travel International, Last Minute Cruises—bless 'em all) are known in the trade as "distress merchants," and their savings are normally greater than the buckets'. That's because the distress mer-

SOME ADDITIONAL REFLECTIONS AND FURTHER SPECIFICS ON TRAVEL'S MOST SIGNIFICANT RECENT DEVELOPMENT

chants are frantically rushing to sell products about to perish: unfilled seats and cabins on departures scheduled in the immediate days and weeks ahead. By contrast, the buckets will sell you seats many months ahead—in fact they like to do that—and obviously they're able to discount those to a lesser extent than a last-minute emergency sale would warrant.

• Beware the imitators. Recall, next, that almost all the bucket shops employ a classic and unvarying format in their ads (that's how you spot them): two vertical columns with a list of cities and a list of prices—nothing more. So successful is this approach that many standard and even stodgy retail travel agencies have taken to "aping" it, but with normal, published, nondiscounted fares appearing in their vertical column of prices. The public, thinking they've discovered a bucket shop, rushes to respond—and walks away with no bargain at all. Therefore, in using the Sunday travel sections, look first at all the air-fare ads and compare. Jot down the various prices listed to your desired destination; the cheaper offerings are those of the bucket shops.

• Cull the good from the bad. In addition to studying multiple ads, make multiple phone calls to ascertain how much the ticket really will cost—and from whom. Some bucket shops (the bad ones) will instantly disavow their printed prices in the opening moments of your phone call. "Those are for departures in January," they'll say, or "Those must be booked more than 60 days ahead." Others (the good ones) will stand behind their claims —at least to a certain extent (nearly all of them fudge a bit). I recently made four test calls to bucket shops in Chicago that

They are wholly distinct from the companies selling tickets at the last moment, known as "distress merchants"; the buckets sell their tickets many weeks ahead.

had all advertised, in late summer, a round-trip fare to Rome of $499. The first three found various excuses (I had phoned too late, I was leaving too soon, I was travelling in peak season) for offering me a far higher fare of $768; only the fourth confirmed a price as low as $599, on a routing of Chicago–Toronto–Rome. While even the $768 fare would have been a major bargain (because, on an imminent departure, the alternative would have been a much higher standard fare), the advertised rate of $499 carried no mention of advance-purchase requirements. To come as close as $599, as the last one quite definitely did, is the mark of a "good" bucket shop.

• To the Far East, every travel agency should be a bucket shop. Though many of the buckets include flights to Tokyo, Hong Kong, Bangkok, Seoul, Taipei, and Manila in their Sunday ads, such tickets should be available at nearly the same

VERACITY, OPENNESS, AND INTEGRITY VARY WIDELY FROM SHOP TO SHOP

price from your own local travel agency. Nearly every such agency has access to nationwide ticket wholesalers who will pay commissions of 35% and up on flights to the hotly competitive Orient operated by nearly every major carrier. Those astonishing figures are set forth on openly circulated computer printouts mailed to thousands of agents—I'm looking at one as I write this—and obviously, when commissions are that high, they would normally be rebated to the customer, not retained as a windfall by the agent. *Warning:* The same high commissions are not widely available on flights to Australia or New Zealand, and must be sought from a limited number of bucket shops specializing in those and other locations in the South Pacific.

• Beware the expensive nationwide bucket shops. In part the bucket shops achieve their bargains by frugal operations: plain offices in low-rent districts, tiny ads, limited products leaving mainly from their own home cities, local phone calls for which the customer pays. Persons who have responded to nationally advertised toll-free "800" numbers have frequently been quoted prices higher than they could have obtained from a purely local bucket shop. While there are exceptions to this rule (especially among the national wholesalers heavily engaged in selling discount tickets to travel agents and only incidentally to the public), one normally can't have it both ways. If a bucket adopts the expensive practices of the traditional retail seller, its prices must go up.

• Current market prices. It remains to be noted that with so many airlines flying the long-haul routes, the bucket shops are generally glutted with available seats and

Discount travel agencies now join discount brokerages, discount pharmacies, discount record stores in bringing the benefits of free competition to the travelling public.

prices are low indeed. Bucket-shop proprietors with whom I've spoken are currently predicting that their transatlantic air fares for the coming winter of 1988 will drop to a one-way level of $210 or $230 from New York to London, $220–$230 to Paris, the same to Amsterdam, $260–$270 to Rome or Milan; and to a round-trip fare of only $610 to Athens. For equivalent fares from the Midwest, add about $50 each way; from the West Coast, add $85 each way. From New York to Singapore or Kuala Lumpur, some of the buckets will be charging a remarkable $850 round trip, $1,100 round trip from New York to Sydney or Melbourne in the peak-season month (to Australia) of February. To Hawaii from the West Coast, rates show signs of dropping to $275 round trip; to Mexico City, the same West Coast bucket shops will be charging only $265 round trip from Los Angeles, $293 to Acapulco. Except to Hawaii, the buckets will not be offering more than an occasional domestic seat, as winter air fares within the United States are already too low to permit further discounting.

And thus we enter a new era of travel pricing. Thanks to an unruly slew of scrambling entrepreneurs working out of shabby lofts—who rushed in where travel agents feared to tread—air fares now cost differing amounts depending on the retail outlets from which they are bought. Discount travel agencies now join discount brokerages, discount pharmacies, discount record stores, discount everything, in bringing the benefits of free competition to the travelling public. And soon you'll see the more "respectable" travel firms making a belated appearance onto the same discount scene. All hail the bucket shops for leading the way!

Unscrambling the Domestic Air Fares Mess

*T*hough cholesterol and high triglycerides are often blamed for heart attacks, I believe that domestic air fares are far more frequently the culprit.

Picture this. You have just been told that the cheapest rate by air from Pittsburgh to Portland, Oregon, is a whopping $505, one way. "$505!" you shout, as veins contract and pulses quicken. "That's right," says the airline reservationist. "You didn't call us far enough in advance."

And, resignedly, you board the flight, troubled and a bit unhinged, but willing to accept that dozens aboard have paid only $144 for tickets purchased seven days in advance. Yet as the plane takes off, you discover that the business traveller in the next seat has paid only $280 for a ticket purchased two days later than you did. And that the matron in the seat ahead has been charged only $320 for a ticket purchased that morning. What's more, she advises, a friend travelling to Portland on a later flight that day, on a different but equally prestigious airline, will be paying only $249 for the very same journey.

And suddenly, vision blurs, the chest constricts, small stabbing pains arrive to . . . .

Who's to blame for this unsettling condition? The airlines? The now-defunct Civil Aeronautics Board (which deregulated the airlines in 1978)? Your travel agent? While deregulation is the basic cause, it is often a less-than-comprehensive computer, a less-than-diligent retail travel agent or airline reservations

The eagerness, inventiveness, competence, and vigor of your travel agent can make a substantial difference.

clerk, who can cause you to overlook the cheapest fare for your flight. As maddening as it may seem, securing advantageous air fares is frequently an art, not a science, requiring that you master a code of musical-like notes and notations—in the form of an awesome, illogical alphabet soup.

Your airline ABCs

When deregulation occurred, a once-

BY FOLLOWING SEVERAL LITTLE-KNOWN APPROACHES TO THE PURCHASE OF AIR TICKETS, YOU CAN HEIGHTEN THE CHANCES OF PAYING A LOWER FARE

simple division of most domestic air fares into three basic categories—first class, coach, and "excursion"—exploded into a proliferation of fares, as many as a dozen per flight, each designated by a letter of the alphabet. When your travel agent "pulls up" an air-fare screen on a computer terminal, what comes to light is a forest of alphabetical letters next to prices. Though some letters are uniform

It is often a less-than-comprehensive computer, a less-than-diligent airline reservations clerk who can cause you to overlook the cheapest fare.

throughout the travel industry, others are arbitrarily chosen by individual airlines. A "K"-class fare on TWA can approximate a "Q"-class fare on Eastern airlines or a "B"-class fare on United.

The *top-priced fares* are easy to understand, but irrelevant to most travellers. "P" is preferred class, for deluxe sleeperettes costing $781 from Los Angeles to New York. "F" is first class ($735 for the same), "C" and "J" are business class (on Pan Am and TWA only, transcontinental), and "Y" is that old standard, an unrestricted economy-class seat costing $545 for the one-way transcontinental flight in daytime, $438 at night ("YN"), to use a single example.

Then come the reduced-price *advance-purchase fares*, available for the most part on a round-trip basis only, to people purchasing them several to many days ahead of departure—either 7 days in advance ("Q" class on most airlines), 14 days in advance ("M" class), 2 days in advance ("B" class on some, "H" class on others), or even 3 days in advance to a handful of cities ("K" class on several airlines). Advance-purchase fares also require, in all but isolated cases, that your stay at the destination extend over a Saturday night, but for no more than a maximum number of days; that the tickets be paid in full within 24 hours after the reservation has been made; and that you assume a penalty exposure (25% to 100% of the fare) for cancelling the transaction. By securing an advance-purchase fare, you save as much as 45% off for purchases made 14 days in advance, 25% off for those made 7 days in advance.

Next come the discount fares restricted to *Saturday* flights or other slow days of the week ("KL" class on TWA, "Q" or "B"

THE EAGERNESS, INVENTIVENESS, COMPETENCE, AND VIGOR OF YOUR TRAVEL AGENT CAN MAKE A SUBSTANTIAL DIFFERENCE TO YOUR AIRLINE COSTS

on others). And finally, certain *unrestricted discount fares* ("B" class or "M" class, or even "K" class, according to airline) are offered to a scattered few cities—these being ultra-cheap tickets available in small quantities per flight, and sold down to the very day of departure on flights to, say, Miami or Denver or Atlanta, where heavy airline competition reigns.

"Capacity Controls"—the "Catch-22" of aviation

To each of these alphabetical designations (and the discount fares they represent), the airlines allot a limited number of seats ("capacity controls"). To some popular flights they allot no discount fares whatever, regardless of whether would-be passengers have booked 30 or 14 days in advance. To others they allot a few, to some a great many. And therein lies the rub. Not only can the number of discount seats be set at a low figure, but that figure can periodically be raised or lowered, removed or reinstated, revised on even an hourly basis by the sophisticated computers programmed to maximize the airline's revenue from a particular flight. Thus a passenger seeking on June 1 to purchase a 30-day "super-saver" leaving on October 1 can be told that no seats remain to be sold at that price. Yet a similarly situated passenger phoning the very next day may obtain a seat at super-saver levels, either because another super-saver passenger has cancelled or, infuriatingly, because the airline has simply decided to make additional super-saver seats available on a slow-selling flight. (It's as if the airline prices were written in water, or projected by flickering candlelight on the walls of a cave, as

> As maddening as it may seem, securing advantageous air fares is frequently an art, not a science, requiring that you master an awesome, illogical alphabet soup.

banks of ominous, faintly humming computers go about tampering with our budgets and expectations.)

In a similar fashion, the number of so-called unrestricted "M"-class or "B"-class fares for particular flights may be initially set at a fairly low level, but then raised in quantity as the departure date approaches. Which means that business traveller Richard Smith phoning on Tuesday may be unable to fly cheaply on that Thursday, but business traveller Robert Smith phoning on Wednesday gets the cut-rate Thursday seat! Or else a high level of discount seats for a particular departure may suddenly be reduced. Does any other retail industry in America experience such rapid fluctuations in price?

The rewards of diligence

But the system isn't perfect, and the public can fight back. The smart traveller, after purchasing a higher-priced ticket, makes a daily phone call to the airline to determine whether a discount opportunity has surfaced at a later time. You make these calls down to the last date of advance purchase (for "Q" or "M" supersavers) or down to the very day of departure (for unrestricted "B"- or "K"-class fares). While, given the low state of travel-agency commissions on domestic air fares, it probably isn't fair to ask your travel agent to make those daily calls, it pays for you to make them, and then to demand that your fare be replaced by a cheaper one when discounts materialize.

You can even attempt to "override" the computer when the airline announces that all advance-purchase seats or unrestricted "B"-class fares are gone. While a great many travel-industry professionals will vehemently deny that this can be done, I can cite occasion after occasion when determined travel agents have successfully asked to "speak with a supervisor" in the wake of a discount turndown. By then using their own special "clout" with the airline, by implying a loss of that sale to the airline, by threatening to remonstrate to a "district manager" (and sometimes doing so), by citing a particular emergency need of the passenger, they have been able to persuade an airline official in "Inventory Control" to add a discount seat or two to a flight where none is shown. To claim, as some do, that airlines will not (supposedly on principle) perform such a favor for a favored, hard-hitting travel agent is to believe in fairy tales, goblins, and sleeping princesses. Smart travellers make their choice of travel agents with just this in mind.

"Cutting up" the trip

Diligence also pays off in utilizing discount fares on individual segments of your journey to undercut the "through" or direct fares to your destination. As noted earlier, the airlines often offer "unrestricted" (in the sense that they need no advance purchase) but "capacity-controlled" discount fares to cities where heavy airline competition warrants it, or to cities where they are seeking to develop an efficient "hub" operation. TWA does that to St. Louis, others to Miami or Denver. Yet although such fares appear on computer screens, their use in constructing longer flights is not always apparent to the travel agent or airline reservations clerk. Thus in the example that began this essay, a travel agent inquiring of a computer as to the cheapest last-

> **The smart traveller, after purchasing a higher-priced ticket, makes a daily phone call to the airline to determine whether a discount opportunity has surfaced at a later time.**

minute seat from Pittsburgh to Portland, Oregon, may see only an American Airlines flight costing $505 each way. It is only when that agent "digs" and experiments with various possible segments for such a trip—say, Pittsburgh to Denver, then Denver to Portland—that he or she discovers the chance to combine two United Airlines flights, Pittsburgh to Denver to Portland, for a total of only $320. That's because United Airlines offers unrestricted "B"-class fares on those heavily competitive segments. Yet, surprisingly, fares for the two "B"-class segments— Pittsburgh to Denver and Denver to Portland—fail to appear on the computer screen for flights from Pittsburgh to Portland, but only on screens specifically requesting those segments.

In other words, the eagerness, inventiveness, competence, and vigor of your travel agent can make a substantial difference to your airline costs. For the airline computers are not infallible; they do not always reveal the full range of pricing possibilities—they must be jolted or caressed, pressed or pestered by human hands. The same approach can also enable not simply a travel agent but an airline reservationist to achieve an extra result for you. By testing various trip segments, by trying flights via different cities, by adding the segments into a lesser total, they can achieve savings. If you do phone the airlines directly, it's important to stress to such personnel that you may not book on their airline unless they fly you at a discount rate. "Isn't there anything cheaper?" "Isn't there anything cheaper?" should be your irksome refrain. And then: "Can you check with a supervisor?" More frequently than you'd expect, an initial turndown can then become a "Yes."

SO LOW HAVE THE AIRLINES PRICED THEIR ROUND-TRIP "ULTIMATE SUPER SAVERS" THAT THEY HAVE INADVERTENTLY NULLIFIED SEVERAL OF THEIR HIGH-PRICED ONE-WAY FARES

Those short-term price wars

You'll note that I have not referred to the periodic airline "price wars" that blossom in newspaper ads, announcing almost-absurdly-low fares for short, intensive periods of time—like the three days commencing on Thanksgiving, or in the midweeks of January—to Miami. Under deregulation, airlines can slash their prices for even a single day, and no one—not even the airline executives—can now predict whether such "seat sales" will be repeated at the same time next year. Nor have I dealt with the wonderfully low-priced, but nonrefundable, "MaxSaver" fares, whose continued existence is very much in doubt (expect them to resurface only in slow winter periods of the year). In this essay I have dealt only with the fares available throughout the year, every year.

. . . And those "cheap airlines"

Nor have I written, yet, about those "cheap airlines" that price every one of their seats on every flight at low rates, without requiring advance purchase and without imposing pesky "capacity controls." Such names as Southwest Airlines, Challenge Airlines, Continental, Braniff, and (to a lesser extent) Midway are among those following a firm policy of always undercutting the standard "Y"-class fares of such longer-established airlines as American, United, Delta, TWA, and Northwest. But though they offer savings, and should be mentioned in our prayers each night, the "cheap airlines" do not always provide the least expensive means of flying from city to city. Rather, a limited number of standard discount air fares are lower than even those of Conti-

> Though they offer savings, and should be mentioned in our prayers each night, the "cheap airlines" don't always provide the least expensive fares.

nental and Braniff, although heavily ringed with restrictions on their use.

The cheapest air fares going

Currently, the cheapest air fares in all the land are those for advance-purchase seats sold more than 30 or 21 days ahead of departure (and called "Ultimate Super-Savers" or "Ultra Savers" by leading airlines). Provided only that you can make such flight decisions as far in advance as that, and then adhere to those plans, you should be paying as little as $149 from New York to Los Angeles in autumn months, and a remarkably low $59 or $79 from the East Coast to Cleveland or Milwaukee on several distinguished airlines. Those rates are cheaper than the probable Continental or Braniff fares for the months ahead, and cheaper than those of any other "cheap airline," but available, again, only to those few prudent travellers who can make their fixed-in-concrete appointments so long in advance.

If you can't, then your next-cheapest level of fares is on the "cheap airlines" of the Challenge Air or Southwest Air ilk. Long may they survive! Thanks to these philanthropists of the air, cardio-fitness and stress-free longevity are on the rise again among America's air travellers. And let's hope that some of the approaches advised in this essay will also stave off the day when your gorge rises, and temples pound, and veins constrict . . . at the thought of a one-way domestic air fare costing $505!

Some air fare tricks the airlines wish you didn't know

Shakespeare would have said they were "hoist by their own petard." So low have the airlines priced their round-trip "ultimate super-savers" that they have inadvertently nullified several of their high-priced one-way fares.

Let's assume that you, a New Yorker, are moving to California on a permanent basis. The airlines say you'll need to pay a one-way coach fare of $490. So what do you do? You buy a round-trip "super-saver" for $298 and then throw away, give away, or even sell the return ticket; if you can find a purchaser willing to fly under your name, you've made the trip to California free!

The same airlines have inadvertently nullified requirements that you stay for no more than 30 days at the destination when using a super-saver. Let's say you wish to fly from New York to California on June 1 and return on October 1. Because your stay there is for more than 30 days, the airlines refuse to sell you an ultimate super-saver, and require instead that you buy two one-way $490 coach tickets for a total of $980. So what do you do? You buy two round-trip ultimate super-savers. One is from New York to California on June 1, returning on the arbitrarily chosen date of June 8. The other, from California to New York on October 1, is to return on the equally fake date of October 8. You then proceed to throw away (or give away) the unnecessary halves of both tickets and fly to-and-fro for a total of $498 (two times $249) instead of $980. And if you can sell the two unused halves, you have flown free.

Other such anomalies abound. On one domestic airline, at the time of writing it costs less to fly from New York City to Muskegon, Michigan, via Chicago ($135), than simply to fly to Chicago alone ($270). At one time it cost less to fly to Austin, Texas, via Dallas than simply to fly to

Not only can the number of discount seats be set at a low figure, but that figure can periodically be raised or lowered, removed or reinstated, revised on even an hourly basis by sophisticated computers.

Dallas. Consequently, many Chicago- and Dallas-bound passengers have saved by purchasing tickets to Muskegon or Austin but walking off the plane at Chicago or Dallas. If they had luggage other than carry-ons, they checked the bags to Chicago or Dallas at curbside, where the redcaps aren't nearly as concerned as the counter personnel would be with the fact that the passenger is "underflying."

Choosing the right travel agent

Though most travel agents will make reasonable efforts to find you a better fare (by testing various flight segments; often two segments cost less than the whole), there's a limit to what can be expected of them. Twenty minutes of computer time can easily be expended in searching out all the possibilities, and how much, after all, is the agent earning for "marching that extra step"? Indeed, when the agent reduces your air fare, his or her commission income is reduced.

Be frank with your agent. If the lowest fare is always your chief consideration, it may sometimes be advisable to offer an extra fee for the extra time required to find it. With bargain fares proliferating, a fee-based system of compensation may ultimately prove far more productive and beneficial, to all concerned, than the current practice of allowing the agent a percentage of the ticket price.

Finally, take steps to ensure that your agent is competent to handle your needs. Attempt a mild form of cross-examination. Ask whether he or she is familiar with several of the air-fare "devices" described in this essay. If not, drop that agent forthwith and find another. The right one can save you a great deal of money.

Unscrambling the Transatlantic Air Fares

*O**nce it was as simple as choosing champagne or beer, caviar or marmalade. You either flew to Europe on a scheduled flight or you went there by charter. If you opted for the latter, you saved $200. Period.*

Now it's . . . uh, it's . . . uh, well, it's not that easy at all. It is, in fact, an unholy mess. A plot devised by the Marx Brothers. The charter is no longer the cheapest means of crossing the Atlantic. And at least five entirely new travel-industry concepts—"bucket shops," "distress merchants," "cheap airlines," "back-hauls," and "periodic standbys"—have made an all-but-incomprehensible hash out of the normal calculation of air fares to Europe. With heart in mouth, PC Jr. at hand, I'll try to impose a bit of order—but only a bit—on the single most confusing subject in travel today.

Introducing: the "cheap airlines"

If there is any constant at all on the trans-Atlantic scene, it is that three feisty carriers flying from Newark (New Jersey) International Airport—Virgin Atlantic, Continental and Highland Express—provide not necessarily the cheapest, but the most consistently-available, all-year-round "cheap" fares to Europe. **Virgin Atlantic (phone 212-242-1330)** charges a maximum of $289 each way, between Newark and London's Gatwick Airport, for a midweek

Where there is merchandise there are merchants, and at least a dozen "distress merchandise" companies provide their subscribers with listings of last-minute discounts on imminent departures.

crossing at the peak of the summer season, on a ticket purchased at least 21 days in advance (it charges considerably less in "shoulder" and "low" seasons). On tickets purchased within two days of departure, it reduces the rate to $259 each way (and to less in off-season). On tickets purchased on the very day of departure (a true stand-by), the Virgin price plummets to $225.

The new (autumn, 1987) **Highland Express,** flying from Newark to Prestwick, Scotland, and on from there to London's Stansted Airport, is cheaper still: $250 to London for midweek departures in summer, with no advance purchase necessary; $209 each way in shoulder season (September 15 to October 31); and probably much less than that in winter (as yet unannounced as this book goes to press). Highland currently lowers its stand-by fare to a remarkable $179 each way to London, and permits you to book and confirm the seat (the "last minute thrifty fare") within 48 hours of departure. **Phone 212/983-6760 (from New York State) or 800/533-7737 (from outside New York)** to snare that amazing bargain.

Continental Airlines (phone 800/231-0856) has no stand-by fare, and requires 21 days' advance booking for its lowest fare, but charges only $585 round-

A MYSTIFYING ASSORTMENT OF PRICES AND POSSIBILITIES NOW CONFRONTS THE WOULD-BE TRAVELLER TO EUROPE—AND I'M GONNA EXPLAIN IT ALL!

trip between Newark and London's Gatwick Airport, at the very peak of the summer season (the rate is less in other months).

A lesser-known but thoroughly reliable "cheap airline" known as **Tower Air (phone 718/917-8500)** flies a sleek 747 jumbo jet from JFK Airport New York to Copenhagen, Oslo and Stockholm, at round-trip rates to Copenhagen of $630 in peak summer, for only $599 starting August 15, and thereafter (in winter) for $515. Those rates are not much more than you'd pay for a charter flight to Scandinavia, and they position the "cheap airlines" as potent rivals of the charter, to which we now turn.

Those newly dependable charters

Heirs to a checkered past, survivors of a cut-throat competition that has by now eliminated the thinly financed firms, closely regulated by the Department of Transportation, and often owned by celebrated international airlines, today's charter-tour operators and charter airlines are a largely respectable lot whose record of financial responsibility, physical safety, and on-time performance compares quite well with that of the scheduled carriers. Their rates are also refreshingly cheap: an average of $229–$239 one way from New York to London in summer, $229 to $249 to Paris in the same season, $229 and up to Zurich and Munich, with proportionately higher levels from inland U.S. cities ($80-or-so more each way from Los Angeles). But are these the second-cheapest levels to Europe? Fairly comparable to Continental, Highland Express, Virgin Atlantic, and Tower? Not always, because of—

> Use a "bucket shop"—and you can improve on the published prices of the charters, while sometimes using a scheduled flight all the while.

The rapidly emerging "bucket shops"

Use a "bucket shop" and you can improve on the published prices of the charters, while sometimes using a scheduled flight all the while! And what are "the buckets"? Well (as earlier noted in this book), despite the unfortunate name, these are perfectly respectable, distressingly normal retail travel agencies scattered about the country who simply happen to enjoy a favored relationship with one or more charter-tour operators or international airlines; the latter use the bucket shops to dispose of a percentage of their seats at cut-rate prices—and not merely for last-minute availabilities, either. In the summer of 1987 you could, by visiting a bucket shop in Chicago, for instance, purchase scheduled seats for departures many weeks ahead at the remarkable round-trip rates of $699 between Chicago and Rome or Athens, only $599 between Chicago and London—

HEIRS TO A CHECKERED PAST, TODAY'S CHARTER TOUR OPERATORS AND CHARTER AIRLINES ARE A LARGELY RESPECTABLE LOT

better than most charter prices from the same city. While some traditional travel agents have angrily questioned the legality of selling international tickets through bucket shops, no official entity has yet moved against them or seems likely to do so; and if they should, it will be the bucket that's in trouble, not you the customer.

Where do you find the bucket shops? You look in the Sunday newspaper travel sections for small, one-column, two-inch ads consisting exclusively of a vertical column of European and Asian cities set next to a vertical column of round-trip prices—nothing more. The airline offering each fare is never listed, and can be ascertained only when you actually purchase your ticket. Nor is any other explanatory material included, not even a claim that these fares are, in fact, lower than official levels. Yet when you check the rates with others of which you've heard, you'll immediately notice a sharp reduction.

Warning: Some non–bucket shops have taken to imitating the classic format of the bucket shop ads, but with ordinary, non-discounted prices appearing in them. It is important to compare the rates to similar cities in the various ads in order to pluck out the advantageous bucket shops from the ordinary offers surrounding them.

How do the airlines justify their use of bucket shops? Some claim that these discounts result from commitments made by the shops to purchase tickets in bulk. Others insist that these are "introductory fares" (whatever those may be) made available through special outlets; or else they profess ignorance that their fares are being discounted, or retort that you should "Mind your own business." However they operate, the bucket shops seem a

Though many traditional travel agents haven't the foggiest notion of how to accomplish a "back-haul" flight with major savings, most bucket shops do.

now-permanent fixture on the travel scene, and are increasingly used by the most cost-conscious of travellers. But do they provide the cheapest of transatlantic crossings? No, that honor goes to the—

Increasingly prosperous "distress merchants"

For years, charter operators, cruise-ship companies, hotel chains, and resorts have made quiet, last-minute sales of their unsold seats, berths, and rooms at discounts of as much as 50% off published rates. In the week-or-so before sailings or air departures, amazing reductions are available, and the smartest of travellers actually go to the docks on the day of departure, or to the airport counters, and there bargain for that unsold berth or charter seat—the "distress merchandise" of travel.

Where there is merchandise, there are merchants, and at least a dozen "distress merchandise" companies now provide their subscribers with recorded listings of last-minute discounts on imminent travel departures, all via toll-free "800" numbers to be phoned on the Wednesday evening before a weekend of departures. By thus calling just a few days ahead, thousands of travellers crossed the Atlantic for as little as $179, one way, in the summer of 1987. They occupied seats on charter flights drastically reduced in price as a means of filling a few unsold places.

Bear in mind that radically discounted, eve-of-departure fares of this sort are regularly offered on charters and cruises, but only occasionally on the flights of scheduled airlines; the latter have thus far stayed aloof from the "distress merchants" (but not from the bucket shops offering lesser discounts). And distress merchandise is, of course, useful only to people with flexible work schedules, able to travel on a "moment's notice." The same brand of individual is able to take advantage of yet another low-cost device for crossing the Atlantic—

On-again, off-again standby fares

Though low-cost standby air fares to London have been available for several years, the concept was only recently extended to Brussels, Amsterdam, and Vienna, though not for every month of the year. A "now-you-see-it, now-you-don't" device, valid only during certain periods, withdrawn at other times, the very existence of standby privileges must always be constantly checked in advance by phoning the various airlines. Still, for a great many months of the year, virtually all airlines flying to London offer standby fares of $219, one way from New York, a bit more from other cities. In several months of the year TWA offers a $169 standby youth fare for ages 12 to 25 to Amsterdam or Brussels from New York (higher from other cities). And Tarom Romanian Airlines, of all unlikely candidates, offers a $225 one-way standby fare from New York to Vienna on Tuesday and Friday evenings in most months.

But what can you use if your plans are to fly to the more remote European cities, for which no standby, charter flight, bucket shop, or distress merchant may be available? Ready, now, for a "weirdy"? You book the "back-haul" flights of Communist-bloc or Canadian airlines:

"Back-hauls"

I'll assume (with little chance of contradiction) that you have no interest in flying to Belgrade, Bucharest, Moscow, or To-

> The occasional offer of standby air fares must constantly be checked by calling the airlines; it is an "on again, off again" device.

ronto, but that you'd be more than willing to pass through these cities on the way to your desired destination if the price were right. That, in essence, is the appeal of "back-haul" business. A great many Americans currently fly to Athens via Belgrade (though it's an awkward routing), or to Israel via Bucharest, or to Rome via Toronto (though this requires backtracking several hundred miles from New York or Boston first) because of the considerable price advantages offered to such passengers by airlines serving Belgrade, Bucharest, or Toronto. It is even possible to cut the London–Nairobi air fare considerably by flying there on Aeroflot, via Moscow! Though many traditional travel agents haven't the foggiest notion of how to accomplish these "back-haul" reductions, most bucket shops do, and a number of their most appealing values are based on these out-of-the-way routings that add several hours to the flight but save several hundreds of dollars.

Why do we go to such lengths to ferret out ever-cheaper means of crossing the Atlantic? It is because a yearly trip to Europe, for many Americans, has become the almost essential requisite of a civilized life. Europe—the repository of our heritage, the mature corrective for our less-polished ways, the sophisticated teacher of arts, fashion, and cuisine—is regarded by many as too important a pleasure to be thwarted by high air costs. "Europe is worth the effort," say more than six million yearly travellers to Europe from U.S. cities, and as long as that mighty an urge exists, then bucket shops and other exotic merchandisers of travel will continue to delight us with their artful schemes and devices.

Flying for Free (or for Peanuts) as an On-Board Courier

*I*n the novels of an Ian Fleming or a John le Carré, full of spies and foreign intrigue, the "courier" is typically seen sitting uneasily in an airplane seat, a black leather briefcase chained to his sweating wrist. In the somewhat less-pressured world of holiday travel, the "courier" wears no chain at all, carries no briefcase, and simply relaxes en route with a tall iced drink. Occasionally he breaks into a grin, or chuckles aloud over having won the air-fare game.

Doing nothing shady, and without assuming the slightest risk or major responsibility, an increasing number of Americans are acting as occasional "couriers," hired a trip at a time by overnight air-freight companies anxious to avoid the normal long delays in clearing goods through Customs or cargo sheds. Through the use of air "couriers" and the baggage checked by them, freight clears Customs or cargo as fast as baggage does —in a half hour or so. And the "couriers" receive either free or sharply reduced air fares for accomplishing that feat.

Though it's a rather weird way of going on vacation, you may want to consider doing exactly the same.

> Though it's a rather weird method of earning your trip, it's easily accomplished.

Anyone can become a courier. Most are ordinary working people who love to travel and act as couriers to take advantage of super-low air fares for vacations.

"It's absolutely wonderful," says Sylvia Roberts, who has flown to Europe 20 times in the last three years. "How else could you fly to London for $250 round trip, which includes flying on the Concorde on the return trip. I recommend it to all my friends."

The main drawback to flying as a courier is that you give up your baggage allowance. Couriers are permitted to take only one piece of carry-on luggage, because the courier company uses their baggage allowance to ship its clients' packages, which are mostly documents.

"People worry that we'll have them transporting drugs or guns, but in fact most of our packages are from stock market firms or advertising agencies— anybody who's willing to pay a premium to ensure that a document gets to Europe the next day or to Japan in two days," says Barry Pearlstein of Airsystems Courier in New York.

One courier firm charges $35 to transport an envelope weighing less than a pound from New York to London for next-day delivery, so it's easy to see how the courier companies use a passenger's 44-pound luggage allowance to make a profit.

Duties of the courier

People travelling as couriers are asked to carry a sealed envelope which contains a "manifest"—a list of items, usually mail in sacks, which travels with them—but the sacks are handled entirely by employees of the courier company. "You never touch anything at all," says Carl Rade-

BY PERMITTING YOUR BAGGAGE ALLOWANCE TO BE USED FOR FREIGHT, YOU FLY AT THE CHEAPEST RATES IN TRAVEL TODAY

bush. "When you get to the airport, they unload the van and put everything through the baggage check-in. Then they give you your ticket and a yellow envelope (the manifest) and off you go.

"At the other end, somebody from the courier company is waiting to meet you. You wait while the stuff clears Customs, which can take anywhere from 15 minutes

the manifest, but the accuracy of the manifest is solely the responsibility of the courier company.

Drawbacks of the courier life

Flying as a courier involves several distinct disadvantages, although most

to an hour, then off you go on holiday. You do the same thing coming back."

In international travel, the courier must declare to Customs the contents of the bags accompanying him as shown in

people feel these are outweighed by the savings. The first, mentioned earlier, is that you're limited to travelling with just one in-flight bag. One employee of a courier company who was interviewed for this article said, "Personally, I can't even con-

NOW VOYAGER REPRESENTS ALL THE COURIER SERVICES

ceive of going to Europe with one piece of carry-on. I would be a mental case."

Sylvia Roberts, on the other hand, says the baggage limitation taught her to travel light, whereas she used to lug three big suitcases.

A potentially more serious limitation is that, in an emergency, a courier can be bumped from a flight, although the companies make every effort to see that this doesn't happen often. The fee a courier pays for his passage is usually referred to as an "administrative charge" or some

such, and the company makes it clear that they are not in the business of selling airline tickets. In practical terms, this means that if your flight is cancelled, or if you are bumped by the courier company, you may not have the same rights as a regular passenger.

For two or more persons travelling together, special arrangements are necessary. TNT Skypak, the company Sylvia Roberts flies for, will make arrangements for two travelling companions to fly on consecutive days. Sylvia took advantage of this to arrange a ski trip to Europe for herself and three friends. Sylvia flew to Geneva on a Monday and her friends followed on Tuesday, Wednesday, and Thursday. They came back on a similarly staggered schedule. Was it worth the hassle? "It cost us $150 each for the air fare, and the hotel was $100 each for the week. That's skiing in Europe for a week for $250. You bet it was worth it!"

Another TNT Skypak courier is Frank Sansone. "I'm not a wealthy man," he says. "But how many people have been to three continents and the West Coast in two years?" As a present, he gave his mother a trip to Europe. "To be able to do that, it's great," he says. "It's like being a Rockefeller."

Where, when, and how much?

Courier companies operate from major U.S. cities, like Los Angeles, San Francisco, New York, Chicago, Miami, and San Juan, flying overseas to Rio de Janeiro, Tokyo, Hong Kong, London, Brussels, Amsterdam, Geneva, Milan, Madrid, Sydney, and Auckland.

Fares vary according to season and the popularity of the run. The least expensive flights seem to be those to Europe in the winter months and unpopular runs, like New York to Hong Kong, which is such a long trip that most people paying the full fare would prefer not to fly straight through.

The length of your stay abroad is determined before you go. To Europe it's usually a week; to the Far East, two weeks; to Frankfurt, Geneva, Amsterdam, and Brussels, the return date is often open.

To become a courier

Though your *Yellow Pages* phone directory may list a local firm using on-board couriers, under the heading "Air Courier Services," your best bet is to write to the "biggies," all but one of which urge you not to use the phone (see below). Rather, at least eight weeks in advance of departure, write a letter describing yourself and your travel desires, include a phone number where you may be reached during the day, enclose a stamped, self-addressed, #10 envelope (for application forms), and send the lot to:

TNT Skypak, 400 Post Avenue, Westbury, NY 11590 or **845 Cowan Road, Burlingame, CA 94010** (flights from New York to Rio, London, Frankfurt; from San Francisco to London, Sydney, and Hong Kong).

World Courier, Attention: Barbara Whitting, 137-42 Guy R. Brewer Boulevard, Jamaica, NY 11434 (currently has on-board couriers flying to London, Amsterdam, Frankfurt; personal interviews at the address listed above are a must).

A-1 International Courier, 1401 N.W. 78th Avenue, Miami, FL 33126 (Miami to Caracas, especially, with "open return" dates).

Now Voyager Freelance Courier, 74 Varick Street, Mezzanine B, New York,

Couriers take "carry-ons" only, because the courier company uses their baggage allowance for the shipment of small parcels and documents.

NY 10013 (represents a number of the smaller courier companies flying to all points, and charges a fee of $45 a year for its own services as a broker; it also encourages calls to a "hot line" recording at 212/431-1616 from 9 a.m. to 1 p.m. on weekdays, using the same number that afternoon to book).

Halbart Express, 147-05 17th Street, Jamaica, NY 11434 (phone 718/656-8189), flies from New York to Milan, Amsterdam, Madrid, Mexico City, Frankfurt, Paris and Brussels at fares ranging from $150 to $300. Call at least six to eight weeks ahead.

Rush Couriers, Inc., 481 49th Street, Brooklyn, NY 11220 (phone 718/439-8181), flies to San Juan, Puerto Rico; fares range from $75 to $100, depending on the season. There's no time limit on your return and you can even check one bag in addition to the carry-on.

Air Facilities (phone 305/477-8300) flies from Miami to Buenos Aires and Montevideo, or from New York to Rio, and from Miami to New York (New York to Miami is only booked as a return portion of a Miami-New York trip). You can expect to pay around $400 for a round trip between Miami and Buenos Aires. Call at least one month in advance.

Graf Airfreight, 5811 Willoughby Avenue, Hollywood CA, 90038, Attention: Ernie Kiefer (phone 213/461-1547), has flights to Chicago and New York's JFK Airport and expects to go to Dallas-Fort Worth by the summer of 1988. There's no limit to your stay and costs are $50 one way. Reservations are accepted by mail or phone—beginning on the first working day of a month for flights the following month (i.e., the first working day in December for January flights).

VI

The Glut in Cruise Ships—Bargains and Values Afloat

Under-the-Counter Discounts—the Latest Craze in Cruising

Six happy passengers at a festive table on a Caribbean cruise. *Four have paid $1,500 per person. Two have paid $1,100 per person. All six have purchased—and occupy —the very same category of cabin.*

If the four knew about the good fortune of the two, they would flog the first officer, keelhaul the captain, string the purser to a yardarm, commit mayhem and mutiny. They'd be livid.

And yet the scene I've described is not the exception but the current rule in cruising. According to people who know —eager, tattle-tale "deep throats" among former cruise-line executives—fully a third of all cruise-ship passengers are currently sailing at substantial discounts.

The reason, as you've guessed, is a glut—an extraordinary, undeniable glut. With more than 60,000 cruise-ship berths currently marketed to the U.S. public— double the number of less than ten years ago—the industry suffers from an overcapacity of 15% to 20% at profitable price levels, or so claim my sources.

And yet there's more such capacity on the way—at least 25,000 additional berths by the start of 1990. One emerging behemoth—the 2,284-passenger *Sovereign of the Seas*, largest cruise-ship afloat —goes into service in January 1988. Another, the faintly ominous *Phoenix Project* of the Norwegian Caribbean Line, carrying a near-inconceivable 5,000 passengers (the *QE2* hauls 1,850), is current-

> Perhaps as many as a third of all cruise-ship passengers are currently sailing at substantial discounts.

ly in the planning stages.

Why the frenzied construction? Not one of my confidants can point to a rational cause. Rather, in a purely defensive and Darwinian struggle for market share, lines scramble to match the modern new ships and equipment of their competitors. Others respond to irresistible prices from desperate (and often subsidized) foreign shipyards, whose building of oil tankers has virtually ceased. Some projects have been spurred (until recently) by tax advantages promised to syndicates of investors. In this bout to the death, ultimately bound to result in economic casualties, the gap between supply and demand makes airline struggles seem like a children's game.

The desperate response

To beat the glut, some cruise-ship lines have thrashed about experimenting in novel marketing approaches of the most specialized sort. Some offer music cruises, investment cruises, even slimming cruises with staff of the Golden Door resort. One recently proposed the operation of Club Med–style cruises, on which unlimited drinks, beauty treatments, and daily massage would all be included in the basic charge (reportedly, to attract the younger set). From the flashy Carnival Cruise Lines we have virtual bacchanals at sea, with eight meals a day (their most recent claim) and not one, but two postmidnight buffets. We have cruises, too, of brainy content, addressed by university lecturers and operated by the distinguished Swan Hellenic organization (moderately priced) or Society Expeditions (expensive).

But mainly we have under-the-counter discounts—the classic response to oversupply—in a staggering number of instances (though not on every departure), and even on the stuffy, top-of-the-line ships. Having scanned the discount lists, I find no prominent or consistent exception to the policy of quietly releasing a portion of each ship's capacity for sale at cut-rate levels by select, discreet discounters.

The discounts themselves

How and from whom do you get them? The major sources are two dozen in number, widely scattered. They rely heavily on direct mail, on word-of-mouth referrals, and occasionally on ads in limited-circulation cruise magazines in which they hint at their ability to produce the "best prices," but never quite say so. If they do advertise, they rarely list the exact ships or departures for which discounts are to be had.

For public consumption, the majority will explain these pricing feats by referring with studied vagueness to "group arrangements." One discounter caused considerable hilarity among her competitors by recently referring in a major newspaper interview to "commitments for blocs of cabins" (I'm paraphrasing) that result in discounted prices. "If I don't sell them all," she proclaimed, "I take a bath."

Another prominent firm, Cruises of Distinction, in White Plains, New York, is willing to speak with greater candor—to "go public," in a sense, with what every insider already knows. "How we get these rates is a combination of several factors," explains Michael Grossman, a former marketing vice-president of the important Norwegian American Cruises. "It depends on your contacts within the industry, their confidence in you, your rep-

> Cruise-ship tickets from discounters are indistinguishable from the full-priced variety.

DOES ONLY A "CHUMP" PAY FULL PRICE FOR A CRUISE? YUP

utation for successfully selling the cabins for the dates they need, the effort and money you'll spend on special, discreet marketing. When all the factors are right, you receive a continuing supply of cabins for sale at substantial discounts."

That supply is especially plentiful for the coming winter season, says Grossman. "I can't remember a year when we had Thanksgiving departures, Christmas departures, Valentine's Day departures, available at discounts. But we do this year, and the situation is deteriorating rapidly."

A former director of sales for Cunard and Norwegian American explains that he left the cruise-ship lines out of a belief that "for the next six years at least, the chief opportunity is to serve as a broker for distressed inventory." He cites impressive statistics on the growing discrepancy between cruise-ship capacity and the available market for cabins.

In the East, the two most prominent sources of cruise discounts known to me are the earlier-mentioned **Cruises of Distinction, Inc., 188 East Post Road, White Plains, NY 10601 (phone 914/682-9414)**, which markets its wares all over the nation, and receives most of its calls from California (its tickets are then delivered by overnight courier service); and **White Travel Service, 342 North Main Street, West Hartford, CT 06117 (phone 203/233-2648)**. The latter is headed by the effervescent Edie White and her son, Rick, who have themselves sampled virtually every cruise ship they sell.

In the South, **Esther Grossberg Travel, Inc., 6300 West Loop South, Bellair, TX 77401 (phone 713/666-1761)**, long a major sunbelt retailer, seems to have the same broad inventory of heavily discount-

With more than 60,000 cruise-ship berths currently marketed to the U.S. public, the industry suffers from undoubted overcapacity. In a purely defensive and Darwinian struggle for market share, lines scramble to match the modern new ships and equipment of their competitors.

ed departures on nearly all the major lines.

In the West, two active firms offering sharply reduced rates for cabins other people are buying at list price are: **Cruise Pro, Inc., 2900 Townsgate Road, Westlake Village, CA 91361 (phone 818/707-0667, or toll free 800/222-SHIP, 800/258-SHIP in California)**; and **Just Cruises and Tours, Inc., 801 Portola Drive, San Francisco, CA 94127 (phone 415/661-SHIP, or toll free 800/331-SHIP, 800/551-SHIP in California)**.

In the Southeast, **Cruise Reservations, Inc., 8975 N.E. Sixth Avenue, Miami, FL 33138 (phone 305/759-8922, or toll free 800/892-9929)**, does a great deal of discount advertising in cruise-ship publications, but is otherwise unknown to me.

A bit about their product: Unlike the tickets issued by airline "bucket shops," which are restricted ones, hard to change or cancel, the cruise-ship tickets obtained from discounters are indistinguishable from the full-priced variety. Because of that, a great many traditional retail travel agencies deal with the major discount firms, and you might very well ask your own preferred retailer whether they have a favorite among the group to which I've referred. Discounts are primarily available for those categories of cabins in greatest supply—those of the medium variety. (Top-priced cabins and lowest-priced cabins are usually the most heavily demanded, and therefore are less frequently discounted.)

The discounts average 20% and more—and that's no small sum. Since the great majority of cabins on most one-week cruises sell for at least $1,500 (including air fare to and from the embarkation port), the saving amounts to a hefty $300

Traversing the Corinth Canal

per person, and often to considerably more than that. Currently, some knowledgeable customers of the discounters are flying to the Caribbean from as far as Los Angeles or San Francisco, enjoying an all-inclusive seven-day cruise to and among several glamorous islands, and then flying back, for a spectacular $895 per person, including both the cruise and the air fare. Even at those bargain rates, some cabins go begging—as hard as that may be to believe.

"Why," asks a vicious joke, "did God create the upper middle class?" "So that somebody would buy at retail," goes the answer. Let's hope readers of this book will "go with the market" and thus avoid that wholly unnecessary fate.

Good News for Devotees of the Meandering Cruise by Freighter

*W*hat's up with pas-senger-carrying freighters? Are they still around? Still a viable vacation possibility for retired Americans with lots of time?

Had those questions been put a year ago, the answer to them might have been a shaky "No." Capping a ten-year decline, the number of such ships sailing from U.S. ports fell to a paltry 45-or-so in 1986. The departure from the field of two major cargo lines, Moore McCormack and Delta; the replacement of several older passenger-freighters with newer, all-freight vessels; a spasmodic reluctance by younger

Waitlists are back to a normal few weeks. Last-minute cabins and berths are increasingly available. Freighter fans are once again full of expectations and plans.

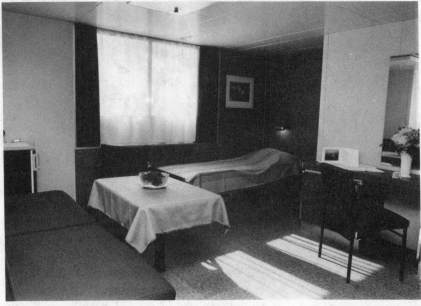

Freighter cabin

cargo executives to bother with passengers—all threatened to end the activity.

Since freighters are limited to a passenger complement of only 12 persons (otherwise they'd be required by law to carry an expensive doctor), the 1986 decline reduced the U.S. openings to fewer than 400 berths a month.

Gradually, you heard less—saw fewer ads and newsletter mentions—about those long, leisurely sails to Durban and Dar es Salaam, to Mombasa and Yokohama. Die-hards fretted and festered on waiting lists for a year and more; others, more desperate, flew to Hamburg, or Gdynia, Poland, to board the few Europe-originating passenger freighters.

Yet suddenly—in 1987—the picture changed. As with a pendulum, a Hegelian counter-reaction, 1987 saw a sharp, upward swing to more than 60 passenger freighters. And 1988 still more. A recent, radical mechanization of ship functions has reduced the need for crew, freeing additional cabin space for passengers. A cyclical glut in cargo capacity has forced lines to search for new revenue sources, which can only come from passengers.

Thus the German-owned Columbus Line has reentered the field with eight new passenger freighters sailing from both coasts to Australia and New Zealand; the British-owned Pace Line plies the same route with several passenger-adapted ships in 1988.

The Cast Line now carries passengers on a number of vessels from Montreal to Antwerp. Mineral Shipping has assigned additional ships to the classic task of "tramp steaming"—wandering the seas like a driven Ahab, dashing here and there as radio messages direct, changing course in mid-Atlantic to pick up containers from South America, diverting them to the west coast of Africa, and providing

AFTER DECLINING TO A DANGEROUS LEVEL OF CAPACITY, THE PASSENGER-CARRYING FREIGHTER IS ON THE RISE AGAIN

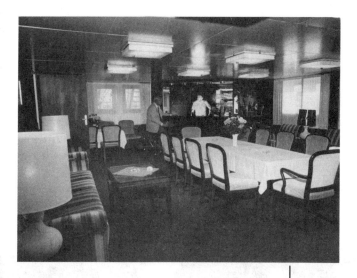

Freighter dining room

12 lucky passengers with the cruise of their lives.

(By freighter tradition, passengers pay for a fixed number of days; if the trip comes in early, they receive a refund; if it takes longer—as it often does—they receive the extra days free.)

Come 1988, we also see the return of the "cargo liner"—freighters deliberately built to carry 90-and-more passengers. The Norwegian-owned Navaran Line will provide us with one such vessel, sailing from the East Coast to South America on a near-regular schedule.

Waiting lists are thus back to a normal six weeks to four and five months. Last-minute berths are increasingly available. Freighter fans are once again full of expectations and plans.

Why such eagerness? Because the activity is incomparable.

You visit exotic, untouristed ports. Time stretches before you, unlimited, unpressured. You dine with ships' officers, have the run of the ship, attend periodic barbecues on deck and biweekly parties, dart into the galley to fix your own sand-

wich or pour a beer, as the mood hits. You delight in the intimacy of a lengthy, shared, unstructured experience, gathering at night around the VCR and its extensive library of tapes that all the ships now carry.

You incur half the daily cost of the average passenger liner. While benchmark rates are an average of $90 a day, some budget-style ships charge as little as $70 or $80 a day, some overseas-originating freighters as little as $50 or $60 a day.

What is asked of you is flexibility (you rarely know exact sailing dates until a week-or-so ahead) and time: voyages last for 30 days, 45 days, even 70 and 90 days.

Because of that, passengers are invariably in their 60s and early 70s and retired (unless they're professors on sabbatical or writers seeking seclusion—author Alex Haley sails on three or four freighter cruises each year). Interestingly, most freighter lines have recently raised their maximum age limits from 69 to 79 (and occasionally higher)—a tribute to the increasing vigor of today's senior citizens.

The largest of the passenger/freight companies is the Lykes Line, with upward of 25 ships in service; Columbus Lines is the next most numerous, with 10

PASSENGERS ARE INVARIABLY IN THEIR 60s AND MORE; AND INTERESTINGLY, MOST FREIGHTER LINES HAVE RECENTLY RAISED THEIR MAXIMUM AGE LIMITS TO 79

ships. American President Line, with its around-the-world freighter itineraries, is a popular company; while Polish Ocean Lines is among the cheapest ($60 to $85 a day), occasionally sailing from Port Newark.

The major current sources of freighter information (and/or reservations) are these:

Freighter World Cruises, Inc., of Pasadena, California, is the base of 59-year-old George Henck, an industry pioneer who has personally propelled a number of major freighter companies into the pas-

senger-carrying business.

He derides the widely held notion that freighter capacity is incapable of meeting the demand. "There is always space around if you don't care where you go," he says. "We can move a person in two weeks. Only when you insist on, say, New Zealand, or hot-weather ports in winter, must you wait three or four months for a ship."

To prove the point, Henck's 26-times-a-year "Freighter Space Advisory," a smartly edited six-page newsletter, devotes itself to photos and descriptions of

ships leaving in the next month or two from both U.S. and foreign ports.

The recent show-stopper: a late-December departure of a two-month sail from Hamburg to and along the east coast of South America for $3,000 ($50 a day), or an end-of-year sailing from Savannah, Georgia, going first to ports on the Amazon, then through the South Atlantic to Gibraltar, and on to four harbors in Italy and Greece before returning to Savannah (60 days for $4,500, $70 a day).

Write **Freighter World Cruises, Inc., 180 South Lake Avenue, Suite 335, Pas-**

You visit exotic, untouristed ports. Time stretches before you, unlimited, unpressured. You have the run of the ship, dine with the ship's officers. You delight in the intimacy of a lengthy, shared experience.

adena, CA 91101, and enclose $27 for a one-year subscription to the "Freighter Space Advisory"; the same firm then makes the reservations and handles all details.

Trav L Tips, of Flushing, New York, is the other combination freighter-travel agency/newsletter company, except that its publication, a bimonthly, is a slick and elaborate 32-page magazine (*TravLtips*), devoted not only to "freightering" (through first-person accounts by subscribers of their own recent trips), but to exotic or long-term sailings by ordinary passenger ships—the kind that would appeal to the heavily travelled, sophisticated devotees of freighters.

Currently edited and administered by the 33-year-old son of its founder, the late Ed Kirk, the publication/organization is staffed by several experienced reservationists and other cruise experts.

Send $15 for a one-year subscription (and membership) to **Trav L Tips, 163-07 Depot Road (P.O. Box 188), Flushing, NY 11358.**

Unlike the first two organizations, the 30-year-old Freighter Travel Club, of Salem, Oregon, makes no reservations, sells no trips or tickets, and simply confines itself to publication of a monthly eight-page (and rather crudely typewritten) newsletter. Send $16 (for a one-year subscription) or $28 (for two years) to **Freighter Travel Club of America, P.O. Box 12693, Salem, OR 97309.**

The larger companies are supplemented by a handful of smaller travel-agency specialists on freighters—usually a single individual—of which **Pearl's Travel Tips, 175 Great Neck Road, Great Neck, NY 11201,** is perhaps best known for long expertise.

Choosing the Right Cruise Ship for Your Sea-Going Vacation

With visions of "Love Boat" dancing in her head, the lithe young schoolteacher from Pittsburgh all but ran with excitement up the gangplank of a cruise ship anchored at the Port of Miami. And what did she see?

Corpulent old gentlemen in fire-red jackets covered with garish buttons, their faces aflush from the greetings shouted to members of their sea-going reunion. A separate group of determined evangelists standing in wait at the purser's counter, their hands clutching the pamphlets they'd soon be distributing in the course of the cruise. The freshman class—at least a part of it—of a small southern college, tossing Frisbees about on the crowded deck of the check-in area.

Too late to make a change, our eager young educator saw with dismay that she had booked the wrong sort of ship. Seven days of closely confined cruising lay ahead, among people she'd never remotely want to meet at home!

How real are the possibilities of being stuck with obnoxious companions on a vacation cruise? They are slight—and slighter still during the "high season" (January through April), when scenes of the sort described above are far less likely to occur.

But they are real nonetheless. While no one can guarantee the passenger composition of any cruise sailing, some of the ships tend to attract boisterous, beer-swilling groups (or other unpleasant types) to a greater extent than others.

While no one can guarantee the passenger composition of any cruise sailing, some of the ships tend to attract boisterous, beer-swilling groups (or other unpleasant sorts) to a greater extent than others.

For every cruise ship possesses a distinct "personality"; its strong, subjective characteristics attract a particular following. Some are graciously elegant, some even overly formal and stuffy. Some are aglitter with the flashy attitudes and big-name entertainment of Las Vegas. Some are throbbing with activities and special events, almost in the style of Club Med. Some are slower paced, a bit intellectual. Some, unfortunately, are downright vulgar, simply floating casinos, emphasizing that latter activity to the exclusion of physical recreation or adventures of the mind.

How can you heighten the chances that your own cruise will find you among a reasonably tasteful cross section of intelligent Americans? You can, of course, book one of the top-of-the-line ships—such super-luxurious vessels as the *Royal Viking Sky* or *Royal Viking Star*, the *Queen Elizabeth 2 (QE2)*, the *Sagafjord* or *Vistafjord*—but that may involve too high a price to pay, in more than one sense. The rates of the latter for the bulk of their cabins average $270 per person per day for winter/spring sailings, attracting an affluent but often elderly following, especially on the lengthier cruises. Although the magnificent *QE2*, with its immense capacity and wide variety of cabins, gets a great deal livelier and more youthful on its shorter excursions, there's no escaping the fact that the super-luxury ships are used in high season by a disproportionate number of elderly and extremely rich single ladies, and by equally wealthy couples well beyond their middle age. The resulting atmosphere on peak-season cruises tends to be formal, elegant, and occasionally a bit too staid for some tastes.

The price category just a tiny bit below that of the most expensive ships runs about $250 per person per day in most of

EACH OF THE GREAT LINERS HAS A DISTINCT PERSONALITY—AND IF IT DOESN'T MATCH YOURS, WATCH OUT!

the medium-range, double-occupancy cabins for a winter/spring sailing. This is the price range most p r o m i n e n t l y occupied by the actual "Love Boats" pictured on the popular TV sitcom: the *Pacific Princess, Island Princess, Sun Princess,* and *Royal Princess*. But although these are almost as costly as the top rank, they appear to attract (in the recollection of some observers) a somewhat greater percentage of trendy sophisticates, successful professionals, and active travellers, all mixed with the more familiar well-to-do retired passengers who account

for so much of the cruise clientele in these higher price ranges. This sort of group dresses up for evening dinner, affects dinner jackets and cummerbunds, would never dream of participating in loony games or potato-sack races, or in the noisy amateur shows and audience-participation nights that some cruise ships offer to lower the expense of hiring professional entertainers.

In the medium range of ships—$220 per person per day, double occupancy, for a medium-rated cabin in high season—several other ships stand out in attracting an intelligent, well-mannered clientele. Among these, the French-owned Paquet Lines—operating the *Mermoz*, in particular—is an interesting choice. With its French officers and French cuisine, its occasional music cruises featuring noted vocal and instrumental artists, its language lectures and cooking classes, and especially its free French wine served with every lunch and dinner (Paquet is among the few lines to practice a wine-is-free policy), it attracts a great many people of highly refined tastes and cultural aspirations. It is largely avoided by the eternally clamorous collegians, the feverish party-till-dawn set, or the gambling addicts whose idea of fun is to sit for 12 hours at a green baize table.

Other medium-priced lines also attract the more thoughtful brand of vacationer.

SELECT YOUR SHIP WITH PARTICULAR CARE AND DELIGHT IN THE SATISFACTION OF TRAVELLING WITH LIKE-MINDED PEOPLE

They include the ships of Sitmar Cruises (the *Fairwind*, the *Fairsea*, and the new *Fairsky*), staffed almost entirely by Italian crews. Though the evening entertainment and casinos aboard these ships are as slick and contemporary as any, they're conducted with exquisite good taste—and passengers react accordingly. Similarly priced ($220 per person per day through the end of April), extremely active, but with a marvelously light touch and witty humor throughout, are the celebrated members of the Royal Caribbean lines (*Song of Norway, Song of America, Nordic Prince, Sun Viking*), where scarcely a single offensively raucous group ever forms.

If you will now descend one further tiny price notch, into the lower bracket of the medium category, you'll encounter the long-established attractions of Holland America Line's *Rotterdam*, accompanied nowadays by the newer and more expensive *Noordam* and *Nieuw Amsterdam* of the same line. Though an older ship, the *Rotterdam* is beautifully maintained, a place of grand old-world elegance. And though its officers are open, friendly Dutchmen and Dutchwomen, they've been known to caution chronic noisemakers and tipsy imbibers about the ship's right to put them ashore. Here, men wear jackets and ties to dinner, and a sense of decorum underlies a rich program of sports, entertainment, and conviviality. In terms of value for price, yet in a cultivated atmosphere, the *Rotterdam* is another stand-out.

I've discussed barely 20 of the more than 70 major ships cruising from East Coast and West Coast U.S. ports, and from points in the Caribbean, to all the sunny regions of the world's seas. And although I'm enthusiastic about the ships

You can, of course, book one of the top-of-the-line ships, but that may involve too high a price to pay, in more than one sense.

I've cited, I've included them only as examples, and not as part of a ranking. Among the remaining 50 or so are numerous vessels of similar or even greater desirability in their respective price ranges.

Here, it's vital that you consult with people who have firsthand knowledge of the ships you're considering and who have sailed with sufficient frequency to have developed standards for comparison. This means travel agents who have sailed on or inspected a goodly number of ships, or well-travelled friends with tastes similar to yours.

And don't think I'm looking down my nose at the all-night gamblers, the beer guzzlers, barbershop quartets, and potato-sack racers—if that's your brand of fun, then pursue it with gusto! Nearly every travel agent can instantly name the several ships that are just for you. But if, like me, you crave the classic pleasures of a cruise—the enjoyment of a good book in the brisk sea air from a quiet spot and on a soft chaise lounge, the murmur of happy conversation and the heady aromas of a ship's restaurant, the slow and dreamy fox-trots on a moonlit deck to the hokey strains of a tuxedo-clad band, then you'll choose your ship with particular care and delight in the satisfaction of travelling with like-minded people.

Are Cruises Still a Value?

When compared with the costs of a resort holiday, the answer is, resoundingly, "yes." Though cruise-ship prices have risen considerably in recent years, so have the rates of Caribbean hotels and other land-based resorts. If a cruise ticket costing, say, $220 per person per day (for a ship of the medium category) seems high, then consider this:

• Nowadays, almost all cruise-ship prices include free or sharply reduced air transportation from the passengers' home city to the ports at which they board the ship. Since round-trip winter fares to the Caribbean or Mexico now average (except on charters) at least $400, the inclusion of air transportation in the features of the cruise results in a saving of as much as $60 per person per day.

• Good-quality Caribbean or Hawaiian hotels now routinely charge as much as $120 to $140 per room per day in season, when taxes and service charges are added in. Top-quality hotels in Bermuda charge $200 to even $250 a night in peak season. Thus the accommodations element of a land-based holiday can alone account (in hotels of a standard equivalent to that of a ship) for $60 to $100 or so per person per day, not including meals.

• Meals in most high-quality winter resorts cost at least $7.50 for breakfast, $15 for lunch, $30 and more for dinner (a total of $52.50 per person per day), and do not offer nearly the quality, the variety, or the number of courses one receives at sea. Some ships serve (with their midnight buffets, their mid-morning bouillon, their afternoon tea) the equivalent of five meals a day!

• After dinner, the visitor to a tropical island invariably takes an expensive taxi ride to an establishment of evening entertainment, where the prices are high indeed—another wad of dollars a day. Such entertainment is included in the price of a cruise, and comprises movies and daytime lectures and classes as well. Also included on cruises is the cost of virtually all sports equipment and facilities—items that are often charged for in the better resorts.

One segment of the cruise-ship market would never dream of participating in loony games or potato-sack races, or in the noisy amateur shows and audience-participation nights that some ships offer to lower the expense of hiring professional entertainers.

• The cost of mixed drinks on most cruise ships is rarely more than $2 per drink. The same drinks routinely are priced at $4 and $5 in most first-class or deluxe resorts.

Thus, for tropical winter vacations of at least a first-class standard, the cost of cruising compares very favorably indeed with the expense of first flying to, and then staying at, an island resort. On cruise ships of the least expensive category, one can vacation in winter for $150 per person per day, including round-trip air fare from one's home city. In the medium standard, the same can run as low as $200 per person per day; in the top-quality ships, $250. And discounts off these levels can often be obtained through travel agencies specializing in cruises.

A final budget tip: Except on the *QE2*, all public facilities and amenities of the ship you choose are standard in quality and one-class in nature for all passengers; the only item that differs in size and standard is the cabin for which you opt. Otherwise, you enjoy the same food and menus, the same public areas, the same access to entertainment, the same deck privileges, regardless of whether you're travelling cheaply in a small inside cabin with upper and lower bunks or splurging on a resplendent outside suite. Therefore, some smart travellers seek out the cheaper cabins on the better ships, in preference to the better cabins on the cheaper ships. Often they spend less money by doing so, and yet enjoy the complete run of a fine vessel and the very same meals as everyone else. Even on the winter cruises of the *QE2*, passengers in the cheapest cabins enjoy every facility other than the more exclusive dining rooms reserved for those in the larger quarters.

The Trend to the Tiny Ship

On the quays leading to a store-lined main street, a scraggly group of hawkers fidgets nervously as they await the imminent onslaught of 1,400 visitors. At curbside stands bearing English-language signs, they will have short minutes to dispose of their cheap straw hats, their gaudy T-shirts.

As the tenders deposit a regiment of humanity from the giant vessel anchored offshore, noise and confusion erupt. A military band blares away. The first arrivals go dashing to a celebrated perfume

The small-ship advantage: just steps from ship to shore.

shop, while others rush to ranks of foul-smelling tour buses or to stand in line for casino admission.

A market is growing for yacht-like vessels with shallow drafts enabling them to go directly onto palm-lined shores or to small marinas in cozy bays.

And that is the scene encountered as many as seven times in a single week by Americans sailing through the Caribbean on certain massive cruise ships. Others, repelled by the urban qualities they travelled so many miles to avoid, are opting for a wholly different sea-going experience, on a "tiny" ship—one that accommodates from 60 to 150 passengers and goes to quiet ports or secluded beaches.

In a backlash from current cruise-ship trends (one line is contemplating construction of a 5,000-passenger behemoth), a market is growing for yacht-like vessels with shallow drafts enabling them to go directly onto palm-lined shores or to small marinas in cozy bays.

Their customers often are an affluent but unpretentious lot who relax on board in shorts and sandals, follow no schedules at all and attend no ship "events"—there aren't any.

Ashore, they dine quietly in the fresh-fish restaurant of a backwater town, or lie reading a paperback novel in a rope hammock, hearing nothing but sea gulls and waves.

Among the "tiny" ships that bring you that form of paradise are:

Windjammer Cruises: Like that cabin boy in *Two Years Before the Mast*, you'll stumble in dazed excitement onto the teakwood decks of an actual ocean schooner with sails—as sleek as a greyhound, but with the tiny, cot-equipped cabins you'd expect on so narrow a vessel.

You have the run of the entire ship: bowsprit, rigging, even crow's nest and at the wheel—and are actually encouraged to help the professional crew with steering the ship. Each day you anchor off a quiet beach or tiny port, to which your

INCREASING NUMBERS OF VACATIONERS ARE OPTING FOR INTIMATE VESSELS ABLE TO TAKE THEM TO SECLUDED PLACES

lunch is brought by kitchen crew wading through the surf. You live throughout in shorts and sandals, in sheer relaxation or happy camaraderie with like-minded, unpretentious, adventure-seeking people from all over the world who have heard of these renowned ships. They range in size from the "giant" S/V *Fantome* (126 passengers) and S/V *Polynesia* (126 passengers) down to the S/V *Flying Cloud* (80 passengers) and M/S *Yankee Trader* (84 passengers, a former scientific survey ship equipped with two large sails). You sail through the Grenadines, the exotic Leeward Islands of the Caribbean, the British Virgin Islands, the Out Islands of the Bahamas, and the Bahama Banks. And you pay only $675 to $750 for a six-day cruise in most cabins, plus air fare from the U.S. ($249 from the East Coast, $349 from the West Coast). For literature, contact **Windjammer Barefoot Cruises, P.O. Box 120, Miami Beach, FL 33119 (phone toll free 800/327-2600, 800/432-3364 in Florida).**

American-Canadian Line: Budget-priced cruises of the Caribbean in winter, the inland waterways of New York and Québec in summer, on yacht-like ships carrying as few as 60 and 70 passengers apiece. Rates range from a low $80 to $160 per person per day, not including air fare to embarkation cities. On each ship, "bow ramps" allow passengers to walk, not climb, from the ship to the most isolated and inviting beaches. For literature, contact **American-Canadian Line, Inc., P.O. Box 368, Warren, RI 02885 (phone 401/247-0955, or toll free 800/556-7450).**

Yugoslavian Sailing Yacht: On the 48-passenger *Marco Polo*—a "motor/sail yacht" operated by a crew of 11—you sail

> You have the run of the entire ship: bowsprit, rigging, even crow's nest and at the wheel.

in summer along the enchanting Dalmatian coast of Yugoslavia, on seven-day cruises costing $85 per person per day, plus air fare to Dubrovnik. For literature or reservations, write the ship's U.S. representative, **Love Holidays, 15315 Magnolia Boulevard, Sherman Oaks, CA 91403.**

Ocean Cruise Lines: On the borderline of bigness, this company's 250-passenger

Ocean Islander has all the facilities of a much-larger ship, but the intimacy of a private yacht. In the summer of 1988 (early May to late September), it will cruise between Venice and Nice, yet at the surprisingly low rates of as little as $156, an average high of $300, per person per day (plus air fare from the U.S. to Italy). For literature, contact **Ocean Cruise Lines, 1510 S.E. 17th Street, Fort Lauderdale, FL 33316 (phone 305/764-5566, or toll free 800/556-8850, 800/528-8500 in Florida).**

Exploration Cruises: Largest of the

FOR ALL THEIR EXQUISITE ATTENTIONS AND AMENITIES, PRICES ARE MODERATE

mini-ship fleets, and owned by the wealthy Anheuser-Busch brewery company, these consist of half a dozen vessels with drafts so shallow that they can take you where the big ships can't. You cruise to such odd and lightly touristed places as Glacier Bay and the magnificent Prince William Sound of Alaska; to Jost Van Dyke, Norman Island, and Virgin Gorda in the Virgin Islands; the Columbia, Snake, and Willamette Rivers of the Pacific Northwest; to Tahaa and Raiatea in the Tahitian Islands.

The line's largest ship, the *Explorer Starship*, carries 158 passengers; but its average-sized vessel—the *Colonial Explorer, Majestic Explorer, Pacific Northwest Explorer, Glacier Bay Explorer*—is limited to 96, 80, or even 64 passengers. Though some of the ships resemble large ferry boats or multideck catamarans, they are wonderfully endowed with modern comforts and generally cost a hefty $200 to $300 per passenger per day, but usual-

ly including air fare from the U.S. to their embarkation points. For literature, contact **Exploration Cruise Lines, 1500 Metropolitan Park Building, Olive and Boren Streets, Seattle, WA 98101 (phone 206/624-8551, or toll free 800/425-0600 outside Washington).**

Clipper Cruise Line: Elegant luxury yachts carrying only 100 passengers apiece, the *Newport Clipper* and the *Nantucket Clipper* limit themselves to "American" waters, even in the Caribbean. Winter, they ply the Virgin Islands, visiting such peaceful ports as Cruz Bay in St. John, and Christiansted in St. Croix. Spring, they explore the "Colonial South" —the ports and historic coastal cities and islands of Florida and Georgia. Summer, they head farther north, to Yorktown, Annapolis, Chesapeake City, Newport, and Nantucket. For all their exquisite attentions and amenities, prices are not extreme: $200 to $250 per person per day for most cabins, but plus air fare of $150

charge about $375 per person per day in high (winter) season, $280 or so in off-season—which is not as high as you'd expect for an experience as exclusive as this. In summer, a sister ship called the *Wind Song* joins the fleet in Tahiti, from which it will sail each week through the Society Islands of the South Pacific, for approximately the same rates. For literature, contact **Windstar Sail Cruises, Ltd., 7415 N.W. 19th Street, Suite B, Miami, FL 33126 (phone 305/592-8008, or toll free 800/258-SAIL).**

I have not mentioned the *Sea Goddess* ships of the Cunard Lines because their rates are truly high, and out of reach for the great majority of our readers; nor have I included several vessels whose 500-passenger size disqualifies them from inclusion in this discussion. Here we're interested in proving that "Small Is Beautiful." Viva the smaller ship!

to $300 for Caribbean departures, $80 to $100 for domestic embarkation points. For literature, contact **Clipper Cruise Line, The Windsor Building, 7711 Bonhomme Avenue, St. Louis, MO 63105 (phone 314/727-2929, or toll free 800/325-0010 outside Missouri).**

Windstar Sail Cruises: Newest (January 1987), longest (440 feet), tallest (masts 20 stories tall), and maybe the largest of the world's sailing ships is the *Windstar* berthed at the island of Martinique, from which it makes weekly one-week cruises to such magical spots as Mustique, Bequia, Tobago Cay, Palm Island, St. Lucia, and other unlikely ports of call (for the standard ships). It places its passengers in cabins 185 square feet in size, and plies them with every luxury (like impulsively buying 300 pounds of lobster at a native market for consumption at a beach barbecue that day). The total passenger complement is 150, on ships whose sails are directed by computer; the mood is casual elegance, the

VII

The Cheapest of Everything: New Ways to Save Money While Travelling on Land

The Travel "Cheapstakes"

*A*fter 30 years of searching for travel values, it still feels good to stumble upon an extraordinary bargain. "Feels good," did I say? It feels phenomenal, *makes me ecstatic, fills me with rapture! Provided they're cheap enough, and important enough, travel bargains can provide the reason for an entire trip. What follows are 14 recent discoveries, of which 8 fall into the "significant" category, while six are simply happy oddities.*

(1) The Cheapest Round-the-World Air Fare on Earth: Is $1,163—yes, one thousand one hundred sixty-three dollars—as packaged by **Avia Travel, 441 California Avenue, Palo Alto, CA 94306 (phone 415/321-3824).** A trendy little agency near the grounds of Stanford University, Avia uses barely known air fares, discounted air fares, various bucket-shop devices, and fairly weird airlines (Royal Nepal Airways, Aeroflot, Czechoslovak Air, Thai Air, but TWA too) to undercut the $2,100-plus round-the-world air fares of United Airlines and others. You fly a combination of carriers, enjoy fewer stops than on the costlier plans, but still manage to hit all the highlights, on one of a dozen itineraries (of which some require

The Cheapest Round-the-World Air Fare on Earth.

$1,163

The Cheapest One-Way Air Fare on Earth.

$149

The Cheapest Major Sightseeing Attractions on Earth

FREE

30 days of advance booking, while others are capacity-controlled or available only on short notice). It's all explained in an ingenious, do-it-yourself chart supplied free by Avia to persons mailing in a request. Examples of what you can do: for $1,163—Los Angeles/San Francisco–Vancouver–Hong Kong–Manila–Bangkok–London–San Francisco/Los Angeles; for $1,279—Los Angeles/San Francisco (or Albuquerque, Las Vegas, Phoenix, or Salt Lake City)–London–Prague–Singapore–Bangkok–Hong Kong–Taipei–Tokyo–Honolulu–Los Angeles/San Francisco (or other U.S. cities); for $1,550—Los Angeles–Tahiti–Auckland–Nouméa–Sydney–Jakarta–Singapore–New Delhi–Moscow–Amsterdam–New York–Los Angeles. Most routings can be flown in the other direction, starting or ending in still other U.S. cities; some segments require "modified standby" arrangements.

(2) The Cheapest One-Way Air Fare on Earth: Is the **Icelandair** new off-season "Get Up and Go" rate of $149 from New York to Luxembourg, $159 from Baltimore, $189 from Chicago or Orlando—all for a normal ticket, but one on which reservations can be made only within 48 hours of departure. You can buy a round-trip ticket at the same time for exactly double the above prices, but your return ticket is again an "open" one, on which reservations can be made only within the two days before use. While the one-way "Max Saver" rate of $149 between New York and San Francisco is also a contender for cheap honors, that fare isn't necessarily available in high season, as Icelandair's is for $50 more than the off-peak rate.

(3) The Cheapest Major Sightseeing Attractions on Earth: Are in Washington,

LOW-COST RECORD HOLDERS AMONG TRAVEL FIRMS AND TRAVEL PRODUCTS

D.C. They are the eight associated museums of the **Smithsonian Institution,** all clustered on the Mall between the Capitol and the Washington Monument, each one of them utterly, totally, remarkably, free of charge to enter (except for certain major films shown in them). Where else on earth are so many world-class museums packed into so small a geographical space? Where else on earth are admission charges waived to attractions of such importance? From the historic space capsules of the National Air and Space Museum, to the uniform worn by George Washington at the National Museum of American History, to the masterworks and exhibits of the Freer Gallery of Art, the Hirshhorn Museum and Sculpture Garden, the Smithsonian Castle, the National Museum of Natural History, the Arts and Industries Building, and especially the National Gallery of Art, these are cultural resources so rich as to shame the parents who haven't yet taken their children to view them. That activity requires a minimum of two full days, but the cost, once more, is utterly nil.

(4) The Cheapest Transatlantic Ocean Crossing on Earth: Is from the island of Antigua to Southampton or Portsmouth, England, or to Cherbourg, France—utterly free, if you'll work as "crew" (setting sails, cooking, cleaning) on any of the yachts or sailing ships returning to their home ports after Race Week in Antigua. Usually scheduled for late April—but check with the **Antigua Tourist Office, 610 Fifth Avenue, New York, NY 10020 (phone 212/541-4117),** for the exact dates—that event attracts large and lavish vessels from Europe, whose crews break up when the race is finished and scatter to all directions. So new hands are needed

The Cheapest Transatlantic Ocean Crossing on Earth.

FREE

The Cheapest High-Fashion Clothing on Earth.

PARIS

The Cheapest Gourmet Feast on Earth

$10.50

The Cheapest Good-Quality Major City Hotels on Earth

$29

The Cheapest Cruise on Earth

$32.50

for the return trip. In English Harbour, Antigua, you need only check the bulletin boards or ask around for those ships seeking a "delivery crew." Most boats carry a small crew of four to eight for the "delivery" home, and some of those are amateurs; a pleasant personality and willingness to work (so they tell me) are more important than sailing experience.

(5) The Cheapest High-Fashion Clothing on Earth: Is found on the **Rue Alésia** on the outskirts of Paris (Métro stop is Alésia), to which many of the most famous French couturiers send the styles that haven't sold in the six-or-so-months they've been on sale. From no. 76 to no. 117 on that distinctly nondescript street, in a working-class district of Paris, discount outlets bearing the finest tradenames are lined side by side. Their windows display dresses for $80 that sold, just short months earlier, for $500; blouses, skirts, coats, both men's and women's suits, other outerwear, that shriek with chic at markdowns of as much as 60%. Among the standouts: Cacharel, Dorothée Bis, Daniel Hechter, Courrèges. Early in June, in a sea of plain pipe racks, my daughter and I purchased her a cocktail dress priced at $700 when it was first manufactured; we got it for $110 (in it, the Frommer fille outshines the British royal family!). Remember the name: Rue Alésia. But go only to the segment bearing the above street numbers.

(6) The Cheapest Gourmet Feast on Earth: Is the four-course, weekday luncheon-with-coffee sold for $10.50 (but not including wine or tip) at **Commander's Palace, 1403 Washington Avenue (phone 504/899-8321),** in **New Orleans,** which some consider to be that city's finest restaurant. In the evening at the

TRAVEL BARGAINS SO EXTRAORDINARY THEY CAN PROVIDE THE REASON FOR YOUR TRIP

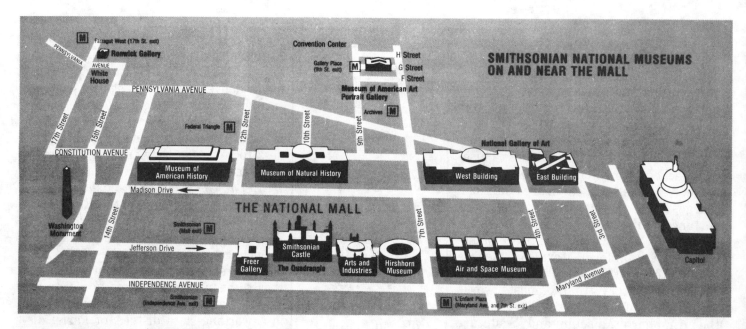

same establishment you'll pay well over $80 for two, for a glorious dinner featuring Créole specialties. Go at lunch instead, Monday through Friday, and you can be a thrifty epicure, paying even as little as $8.50 for the "light luncheon" of only two succulent courses with coffee (without wine or tip), as I did just a month ago. (Try the grilled redfish.)

(7) The Cheapest Good-Quality, Major-City Hotels on Earth: Are three quite comfortable specimens in the very center of New York, Chicago, and Detroit, where you can pay only $29 per room (yes, per *room*, not per person) by simply reserving at least 29 days in advance at the **Days Inn** in each city. When the Days Inn organization issued literature and advertising for a $29, 29-days-in-advance policy (the "Simple Super Saver") for their chain of inexpensive roadside motels—starting many months ago—they apparently failed to provide an exception for the much-higher-priced, central-city hotels that they were later to acquire in New York, Chicago, and Detroit (these, too, are

Days Inns). Result: When you phone the central Days Inn toll-free reservations number at 800/325-2525—as I recently did—the telephone clerk will confirm the $29 rate at the Days Inn in midtown Manhattan or downtown Chicago or Detroit, provided only that the reservation is made at least 29 days in advance and secured by a deposit paid that far in advance (nonrefundable if you cancel or change within 15 days of arrival). Though the mention in this essay may put an end to the entire practice—drat!—it's currently possible to obtain that rate for a room housing as many as four persons!

(8) The Cheapest Cruise on Earth: Is from Hong Kong to Shanghai on the Chinese maritime lines, leaving twice a week and requiring three nights (60 hours) for the trip. For the full "cruise," you'll pay as little as $32.50 in a several-bed dorm in the bowels of the ship, an absolute top of $100 per person in a "deluxe" double-occupancy cabin. While neither price includes meals, the latter cost only $1 for breakfast, between $2 and $3 apiece for

lunch and dinner, and are "gourmet" in quality, according to my informant, Fredric Kaplan, author of the definitive guidebook to China. On board, you enjoy swimming pools, Mah-Jongg, and Chinese bands; to return, you fly for $88 to Canton, then proceed by train back to Hong Kong. To book, visit the **China Travel Service, 77 Queens Road Central, Hong Kong** (making sure not to go to the China *International* Travel Service); they'll procure your visa overnight for a $20 charge, or for only $5 if you'll give them three working days.

(9) through (14) The Cheapest of Everything Else: Is rather minor, but fun. Cheapest opera on earth? The **Royal Opera of Stockholm,** charging as little as $4.50 for good balcony locations to spectacular productions. Cheapest shoe store on earth? **Los Guerrilleros, 5 Puerta del Sol, Madrid,** selling both men's and women's varieties, substantial and stylish, for as little as $11 per pair. Cheapest subway on earth? The 3¢ **Mexico City metro.** Cheapest public transportation on earth to an international airport? The 60¢ **Boston subway ride** to Logan Airport. Cheapest all-you-can-eat cafeteria on earth? **Duff's Famous Smorgasbords, 4118 West Vine Street, Kissimmee (near Orlando), Florida (phone 305/847-5093), or 2404 S. Volusia Avenue, Orange City (phone 904/775-9590),** and elsewhere throughout the South, charging $4.15 at lunch, $5.41 at dinner, for a staggering assortment of courses and plates, including make-them-yourself ice-cream sundaes and banana splits that *alone* would cost $5.41 in most other towns. Cheapest sit-down restaurant on earth? **Restaurant Casa Miguel, 48 Rue St.-Georges, Paris,** charging 9 francs (about $1.50) for a three-course meal with wine, but not including service charge. Because this is a

Here are the cheapest high-fashion articles of apparel, the cheapest transatlantic crossings, the cheapest shoe stores, the cheapest opera, the cheapest subway.

private operation, not meant for charity, no one has ever been able to explain why it is that cheap.

Guinness Book of World Records, move over! The travel industry could fill your every page!

The New World of Travel 1988

The lifeblood of the Arthur Frommer travel guides is the correspondence received from readers, commenting on the establishments recommended in the texts, and recommending new establishments. Each such letter is carefully studied, and when a particular lead seems promising, it is followed up and personally checked.

It is hoped that *The New World of Travel* will receive similar assistance from its readers. A yearly publication, issued near the start of each year, the *New World* will constantly grow. And since much of its content relates to organizations that lack the means to properly market themselves, or come to the attention of a travel journalist, your help is invaluable in alerting me to the organizations—hospitality exchanges, alternative resorts, new travel clubs, and the like—that you have discovered.

If you become aware of a new travel organization, program, or development that deserves to be described in our next edition, *The New World of Travel 1989*, won't you please let me know about it? Send your letters to Arthur Frommer, *The New World of Travel*, c/o Prentice Hall Press, One Gulf + Western Plaza, New York, NY 10023. All letters will be acknowledged, and all are warmly appreciated, in advance, by the author.

My Own "Little Black Book" of Cheap Destinations

A rather cynical Boston tour company once operated charter flights to Copenhagen in the frigid month of February, when snowdrifts pile up five feet deep. Because the trip cost only $299, including everything, passengers returned with stars in their eyes. "Whatta city!" they cried.

Now, cheapness alone is scarcely a reason for travel; North Yemen is cheap, but not exactly thronged with visitors.

But cheapness combined with other attractive features is a valid basis for choosing a travel destination. When everything is cheaper than you are normally accustomed to paying, you tend to love the city or country in which those prices prevail.

Based on that powerful truth—that travel enjoyment generally runs in inverse proportion to cost, that places are unusually pleasant if unusually cheap—I've searched for the world's cheapest (but at least minimally attractive) destinations. Discarding the many "cheapies" that lack any appeal at all (Albania, Bangladesh), eliminating others that

> Cheapness alone is scarcely a reason for travel; North Yemen is cheap, but not exactly thronged with visitors.

Three "addresses" from the Little Black Book: Rio. . .

aren't cheap enough, I remain with six that combine dramatic cheapness with dramatic travel excitement:

(1) Orlando, Florida: Cheapest of all the world's resort cities, cheaper even (on a relative basis) than Barcelona and the Costa Brava in the 1950s, Orlando got that way (in my view) because of unjustified expectations as to its future growth following the opening of Walt Disney's EPCOT in late 1982. Not content to predict a simple doubling or even tripling of tourism, it now appears that the citizens of Orlando were convinced it would rise tenfold. Because each of its most solid citizens—every taxi driver and dentist, every housewife with a nest egg stashed away—proceeded to build a motel (I am only exaggerating slightly).

With 65,000 rooms now available, Or-

SIX HOLIDAY AREAS WITH PRICES IN PENNIES AND VALUES GALORE

lando suffers from an unprecedented hotel glut, and units at good-quality, medium-level establishments (not simply budget motels) are often available for $25 per night and less during at least seven scattered months of the year (mid-August to mid-December, January, May, and June). Add the prevalence of all-you-can-eat buffet breakfasts (with grits!) for $2.99, add the endless offers of western-style chuckwagon lunches or dinners for $3.99, add the Duff's Cafeterias serving multi-course, Rabelaisian repasts for $5.41 (which include make-it-yourself ice-cream sundaes and banana splits that alone would cost $5.41 in most other cities)—and you have price levels lower than Las Vegas once offered to its frantic clientele.

The result is that Orlando has now become a resort area of broad appeal, and not simply a place to bring children. I suggest that smart adults without a single child in tow—utter misanthropes without the remotest intention of visiting the Magic Kingdom—can now enjoy a proper, adult-style vacation of tennis, sunning, nightlife, and swimming in the Orlando area for less than they'd spend anywhere else on earth.

Portugal. . .

(2) Cities of Central Mexico: As unlikely as this may seem, the Mexican peso presently sells at a rate of 1,435 to the dollar (it was 23 to the dollar short years ago). But don't expect dramatic savings in the popular, typical coastal resorts of Mexico (the Acapulcos, Puerto Vallartas, and Ixtapas on the Pacific; the Cancúns and Cozuméls on the Caribbean). There, with tourists numbered in the millions each year, people charge what the traffic will bear.

Rather, it is within the deep interior of Mexico—and especially in that diadem of colonial locations surrounding Mexico City—that the normal, remarkably low price structure of Mexico asserts itself. In the fabled urban centers of the 17th-century conquistadors—in such cities as San Miguel de Allende, Patzcuaro,

PLACES ARE UNUSUALLY PLEASANT IF UNUSUALLY CHEAP

Guanajuato—quite decent hotel rooms rent for $30 and under, quite adequate meals are available for $4, long intercity bus rides cost less than $2 an hour, and every other expenditure is a happy surprise.

Most important, one encounters a culture in these storied cities of Mexico's past that is fully as colorful, fully as profound and important, as any other on earth—but available here at a fraction of normal costs. One may fly to Mexico City (using reduced, midweek fares of several airlines) and rent a car from there to descend in three hours into a deeply enjoyable and reliably safe area of colonial sights so cheap as to warrant inclusion on any list of the "cheapest six."

(3) The Nation of Portugal: Cheapest country in all of Western Europe, cheaper even than Greece, Portugal is also the least developed of the Old World nations, a time machine transporting you to the past, poor but proud. Even in Lisbon, modern structures are few; but in the countryside outside the capital, life is simpler still, intensely human. And thus on the beaches of Portuguese fishing villages, anxious wives still peer out to the sea at dusk, awaiting the return of their fishermen husbands; in time-worn roadside cafés, grizzled farmers sit nursing a glass of raw red wine as they discuss the harvest or the prospect for jobs abroad, never too preoccupied to offer a seat or a kindly glance at the tourist who wanders into their midst.

The Portuguese escudo, which sold at 38 to the dollar a few years ago, is now exchanged at a rate of 140 to the dollar, and the always-inexpensive Portugal has clearly become the bargain paradise of Europe. Only the most elegant of Lisbon

But when everything is cheaper than you are normally accustomed to paying, you tend to love the city or country in which those prices prevail.

hotels charge more than $70 for a double room with two breakfasts; other quality establishments lower the price to $50, while budget lodgings in pensions and small hotels sell for under $30—often for $25—for two persons. Pay particular heed to the *pousadas* (government-owned inns, in period buildings, the equivalent of Spain's better-known *paradors*) in the north of Portugal; although priced as high as $40 or $45 for a double room, with dinner at $12, their castle-like settings and amenities will remain in your memory for years to come.

(4) Rio de Janeiro and Buenos Aires: Here, local currencies haven't simply fallen against the U.S. dollar, but virtually "collapsed" against it. At current rates of exchange, a pair of men's shoes can be bought for as little as $12 in both cities, a high-fashion women's suit for $40 and other exquisite articles of apparel for a fraction of what you'd spend at home. Because the world's most celebrated designer fashions are manufactured under license in both Brazil and Argentina, you obtain the most stylish of dresses, blouses, coats, and boots at ridiculously cheap rates.

At restaurants, steak dinners are served in Buenos Aires for $3.50 and less, high-quality meals in Rio for $6 or so. Long taxi rides cost $2. Hotel rates are appropriately low, movies cost half the rate in North America, and there is scarcely anything (except scotch whiskey) that doesn't sell for well below the levels you are normally accustomed to paying. As chic and glittering as they may initially seem, these are among the world's most remarkable bargain spots for possessors of the U.S. dollar.

(5) The Soviet Union: Though it may be

and Nova Scotia

depressing at times, it is never uninteresting. And the USSR is also among the cheapest of European nations for high-quality hotels and meals at the lowest of costs. In Moscow and Leningrad, skilled French and Scandinavian construction firms, brought in for the job, have now erected deluxe hotels (swimming pools and all else) for use on package-tour programs priced at wonderfully low levels; the tourists requesting these properties receive one of the greatest of all tour values. At mealtime, in the hotel restaurants of most Russian cities caviar is often available at no extra charge to your tour package, as are such appetizers as smoked salmon, delightful hors d'oeuvres (*zakuski*), succulent borscht (beet soup), and other gourmet-level dishes. So eagerly sought is the hard currency spent by European and American tourists that the Russians respond with extraordinary tour features: tickets to the Bolshoi Ballet, continual sightseeing, long flights within the country to destinations thousands of miles away, yet all for a price that would barely purchase a scaled-down trip by escorted motorcoach in the Europe to the west. For satisfying the most demanding of tastes at the lowest of costs, Russia vies with Portugal and Greece.

(6) Nova Scotia: Finally there is Canada, and that most quaint and underdeveloped of its provinces, Nova Scotia. In a country where the U.S. dollar sells at a full 30% advantage against its own currency, almost all Canadian areas have become refreshingly priced, but Nova Scotia is cheaper than most. You'll find lobster dinners for $8.95 (U.S.), motel rooms for $40 and less, local crafts at bargain rates, and inexpensive recreational and sporting activities conducted in the clearest, briskest air in all of North America.

And Nova Scotia is accessible, almost ridiculously so. The U.S. tourist in the eastern United States need only drive north along the Atlantic coast to Portland or Bar Harbor, Maine, from which car-ferries make the six-hour crossing (from Bar Harbor) to Nova Scotia. Once there, one roams the villages and towns, or urban Halifax, seeking that perfect lobster, that ocean trout, that exquisite seafood dinner that the "Scotians" prepare and price so well.

The site as well of a fascinating history (which includes the exile here, for a time, of Victor Hugo, banished from France), Nova Scotia is excitingly foreign, pleasantly friendly, a bit backward (in modern structures and amenities), always close to nature—in short, the type of vacation destination of which most of us dream.

America's Best-Kept Travel Secrets

Why, *in a nation of 240,000,000 people (latest census statistics), do only 2,000,000 possess "Entertainment Books" enabling them to cut restaurant and theatre-admission costs by nearly 50%? Why do fewer than 2,000,000 Americans belong to the Encore Club, receiving their second hotel night "free"? Why do so few make use of the family-operated spa resorts charging a fraction of the levels at La Costa and the Golden Door for much the same facilities?*

Some travel bargains are puzzling travel secrets, so cheap that you can't afford not to use them, yet confined to a tiny segment of the population. Let's review them quickly, and set things right:

King of the Discount Books: Though more than 2,000,000 are sold each year, scarcely a copy appears in bookstores, and use of the so-called Entertainment Books is thus confined to those relatively few savvy Americans who purchase them from nonprofit clubs, service groups, and other civic organizations. Yet each book entitles the bearer to near-50% discounts at restaurants, sporting events, movies, live theatres, and other recreational facili-

Encore has become the largest discount club in travel history. But will success spoil Encore?

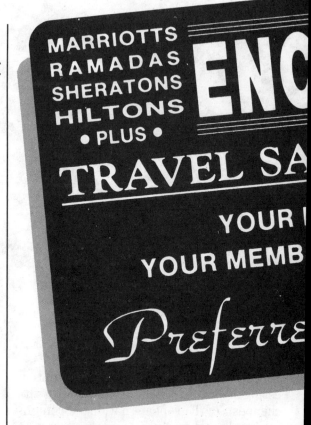

ties, even at scattered hotels in that person's home city—or in the 73 other major U.S. cities for which Entertainment Books are published.

Bulky as dictionaries, the books consist of perforated cardboard discount coupons offering "two-for-one" dining or admissions, or straight 50% reductions, at scores of establishments. Some 74 books are published each year, one for each of the 74 largest American cities.

Of course, the discount doesn't always work out to 50%. When two of you order a $15 and $11 entree, respectively, at a listed restaurant, it is the cheaper entrée (the $11 one) that comes free; and drinks and dessert aren't included in the "two-for-one" offer. As for the hotel discounts,

MOST OF US ARE STILL UNAWARE OF "ENTERTAINMENT BOOKS," THE "SECOND NIGHT FREE," AND "POOR MAN'S SPAS"

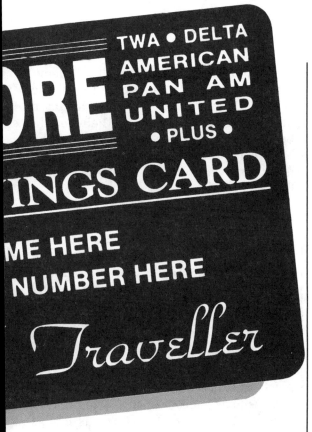

Though the dining discount works out to only 30% on average, the savings are substantial indeed.

a major portion of them are valid for lightly booked weekend stays only. Yet though the dining discount works out to 30% on average, and some of the weekend hotel discounts are of dubious value, the savings overall are substantial indeed. Two million families wouldn't budge from their homes without their Entertainment Books.

Individual-city books cost $25 to $45 apiece, depending on the city, and often pay for themselves in one or two days of travel or use. Almost all are sold in bulk to nonprofit organizations that then quietly resell them to members in fundraising programs. But since Entertainment Publications, Inc. (a 27-year-old publicly owned company), has offices in most of the

74 largest cities, they can usually be contacted directly by the public (and books purchased) by simply looking up the words "Entertainment Publications" or "Entertainment Passbooks" in your local phone directory. Or you can go directly to the headquarters of **Entertainment Publications, Inc., 1400 North Woodward Avenue, Birmingham, MI 48011 (phone 313/642-8300).** If you do contact them directly, consider buying the condensed, one-volume, nationwide Entertainment Book called *Travel America at Half Price* ($24.95).

The "Second Night Free": With nearly two million members currently enrolled, the Encore Travel Club of Lanham, Maryland, has become the largest discount organization in travel history. Reason: It has signed 2,000 hotels to provide "the second night free" to Encore members (usually without weekend limitations). Thus, stay for two nights and you pay for only one; stay for seven nights and you get two free nights; and so on. If you are constantly travelling and staying in hotels, you can scarcely afford not to join (membership is $48 a year).

But will success spoil (or even ruin) Encore? As an ever-greater percentage of the American public joins, won't these 2,000 hotels find that they are giving discounts to almost everyone, thus eliminating the potential for purely incremental business that led them to give "the second night free"? That's a problem that puzzles me. Still, until the day when hotels dig in their heels and say no to Encore's entreaties, it remains an attractive organization for frequent travellers. And it supplies its members with a growing list of other services: the lowest air

THOUGH MORE THAN 2,000,000 ARE SOLD EACH YEAR, SCARCELY A COPY APPEARS IN BOOKSTORES

fare available on domestic flights, a quarterly magazine listing discounts on tour programs and packages, still more.

For further information, or to join, contact **Encore Travel Club, 4501 Forbes Boulevard, Lanham, MD 20706 (phone toll free 800/638-0930).**

Finding the "Poor Man's Spa": A glossy, four-color publication called "Spa Finders" ($4 through the mails) is cur-

> The average U.S. spa is a small, family-owned resort hotel, chronically strapped for cash,

The industry has for years been dominated by the glitzy names—La Costa, the Golden Door, Maine Chance—charging a king's ransom for a week of their health-bestowing attentions. Most Americans have consequently assumed these slimming spa vacations to be outside their financial reach.

Unless they had a copy of "Spa Finders," that is. A remarkable product of nationwide research, presented with glamorous flair but punctilious attention to detail (prices to the penny, seasons, facilities), it claims to contain listings and descriptions of all major U.S. spas, bar none, alerting us to underutilized facilities that have long catered to a purely local clientele. Included are places with all the features and facilities of the big-name resorts—Jacuzzis and rubdown tables, saunas, aerobics, and scientifically measured meals—but at rates as low as

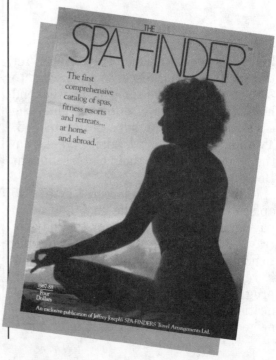

rently enabling a narrow segment of the public (those who know about it) to enjoy wholesome spa vacations here in the United States at a fraction of the cost that others incur. It achieves that feat simply by revealing the existence of a broad range of spas heretofore known only to spa-lovers residing in the immediate vicinity.

A cottage industry by normal commercial standards, the average U.S. spa is a small, family-owned resort hotel, chronically strapped for cash and barely able to advertise outside its own small region.

There is no trade association of spas, no publication devoted to the activity.

$200 a week for room, all meals, and all traditional spa treatments and programs. Some of the establishments in it are making their first appearance before a nationwide audience.

("Spa Finders" also lists and describes the higher-priced varieties, of course, but proudly claims to be the first such publica-tion to gather particulars on every one in every price range, in a widely dispersed activity).

For a copy of the 100-page, magazine-size catalogue, send $4 to **Spa-Finders, 784 Broadway, New York, NY 10003 (phone 212/475-1000, or toll free 800/ ALL-SPAS).**

Learn to Bargain in the Marketplace of Hotels

*I*f the class—ahem!—will come to order, we shall discuss the single most important skill in all the world of travel: how to "bargain down" the price of hotel rooms. That talent can save you thousands in the years ahead.

Start from the premise that nothing in this life is more "perishable" than a hotel room. If such a room should go unrented on a particular night, its value for that night can never again be recouped by the owner of that hotel.

Accordingly, it behooves that owner to rent the room for almost any price rather than leave it unoccupied. Why? Because the cost of placing a guest in the room, as opposed to keeping it empty, is measured in terms of a dollar or two: a change of towels and sheets, a bit of electricity, a cake of soap. A reduced (but still a reasonable) amount of room income is therefore better than no income at all.

Such reasoning has led smart hoteliers the world over to authorize their front-

> To bargain over hotel rates does not require that you act like a hysterical fishwife or a tobacco auctioneer.

desk clerks to respond favorably to requests for discounts, if that should be what's needed to fill rooms on a slow night. And every nationality of traveller the world over is aware of their willingness to do so, and therefore bargains—except the American.

Why not Americans? Because to most of us the very act of bargaining is vulgar and degrading.

No one else regards it as such. If you will stand in the lobby of a large Venetian hotel on a November afternoon, when 60% of the rooms in Venice are empty, chances are that you'll soon spot a well-dressed English tourist or an affluent German tourist or a French one approaching the desk and politely stating: "I am looking for a room that costs no more than 50,000 lire" (nearly $40).

This tourist knows full well that there is no such thing here as a room for 50,000 lire. He is bargaining. He is saying, in effect: "If you will rent me a room for 50,000 lire, I will stay in your hotel. Otherwise, I will stroll down the street and seek another hotel."

In other words, to bargain over hotel rates does not require that you comport yourself like a hysterical fishwife or a tobacco auctioneer. It can be done—as in the above example—with dignity, by indirection.

Often it requires only that you use a "code word" to convey to the desk clerk that you are "shopping." How many times have you heard a traveller inquire as to whether the hotel grants a "corporate rate" or a "commercial rate"—thus bargaining, and usually successfully, for a reduced rate?

What's to prevent you from doing the same? Why can't you name the corpora-

BY RIDDING YOURSELF OF POMPOUS DIGNITY, YOU CAN SAVE THOUSANDS IN THE YEARS AHEAD

tion or firm for which you work and then speculate: "I'm sure we must have a special rate at this hotel." If the hotel is empty and you appear disposed to leave the hotel unless a discount is granted, will anyone challenge the statement? Does anyone really care whether your company has made such arrangements? Or are they anxious to fill their hotel?

Or else you name your occupation and ask for a reduction based on that. You ask for a "teacher's rate," or for a "student's rate." You request a "civil servant's rate" or a "minister's rate" (that always works). You might as well ask for a "stenogra-

pher's rate" or a "dentist's rate." What matters is that you are subtly (and politely) communicating the message that you will stay at the hotel only if they grant you a discount.

When I was a travel agent, I used to phone from the airport, announce that I was seeking a room, but only if I could have a "travel agent's rate." And in that fashion I was usually able to cut my hotel costs in half.

It just so happened that I was telling the truth; I *was* a travel agent. Yet in 20 years of using the tactic, not once was I ever asked to prove it. For, in reality, the hotels didn't care. If the night was a slow

TO MOST AMERICANS, THE VERY ACT OF BARGAINING IS VULGAR AND DEGRADING. NO ONE ELSE REGARDS IT AS SUCH

one and they needed the business, they were quite happy to accept any assertion of status as an excuse for cutting the rate and keeping the guest.

Recently I phoned two professors at the prestigious Cornell University School of Hotel Administration to confirm these hotel policies, and although both pleaded to remain nameless, they instantly did.

Why, then, I asked, do some hotel

"Ask and it shall be given," says the Bible.

guests encounter rejections of their requests for reductions?

It is primarily because, they replied, most people phone nationwide toll-free "800" numbers to seek reservations and rates. The minions who man the phones at central reservations headquarters of the large hotel chains have no authority to cut rates. Rather, one should place the call directly to the hotel and speak to someone more entrepreneurially inclined. If those

local, and directly interested, people are made to know that you will stay at the hotel only if a lower rate is found, they'll often find that rate.

All hotels quote from "the top down," added one professor. "When you tell them the rate is unsatisfactory, they'll quite frequently find a lower one."

The second frequent mistake, say my informants, is to make the request—tired and burdened with luggage—in the lobby of the hotel. Once at the front desk, you are presumed by most hotel personnel to be in no position to walk out if discounts aren't given. A better course, they say, is to phone from the airport or train terminal, and announce from there that you are seeking a room that costs "no more than $—." Such a call is obviously from a "shopper," and the desk clerk will take pains to do what's necessary to make the sale—provided, of course, that the night is a slow one.

Best of all is to write ahead. In scheduling a vacation trip to Barbados or Jamaica in the dead month of June, for instance, you advise the hotel: "I am planning a stay, but only if I can secure a room for no more than $40 a night." "It so happens we have such a room" will come the instant reply.

"Ask and it shall be given," says the Bible.

The final error, say my academic friends, is to bargain at the wrong time of year. Obviously, bargaining will not work during peak hotel seasons, when hotels are confident they will fill up. But all hotels have slow weeks or months, or slow "down cycles" during a week. Hotels in business centers like New York, Chicago, or Philadelphia are packed to capacity from Monday through Thursday, then

empty and hurting from Friday through Sunday. The traveller who pays full rate —who fails to bargain—on weekend nights is a chump. That traveller is simply subsidizing the weekend stays of package tourists enjoying rooms at half the rate.

Conversely, in resort locations like Atlantic City or Las Vegas, hotels are full on Friday and Saturday nights but often quiet at other times. If you're a Monday arrival at Harrah's or the Golden Nugget, bargain!

In a country that currently deifies the "free market" and worships the likes of Adam Smith and Milton Friedman, isn't it surprising that we as individuals should be reluctant to bargain over the price of a hotel room? Who decrees that hotel rates are fixed in stone? Who denies us the right as free consumers to flex our economic muscle?

Travellers of all nations, unite! You have nothing to lose but your pomposity! You have savings to win!

VIII

Just-Plain Motoring Through the U.S.A.: The Way to Do It, and Some Recommended Itineraries

In America, Motoring Vacations Are Better Than Ever!

*I*t's early May of 1988 and we stand at the brink of a summer motoring season predicted to be the best in many years. With gasoline prices in a moderate range, millions of Americans will take to the road— yet thousands among them, oddly enough, will malign the very activity in which they're engaged.

scarcely dreamed. As we enter the season for cruising by car, it's important to wise vacation planning that we review the blessings of a remarkable travel era:

• Emergence of the Interstate Highway System. Begun in the 1960s, completed in the 1970s, these 42,000 miles of four-lane and six-lane roads now provide American motorists with quick, comfortable access to major sightseeing and vacation destinations in every part and clime. Though only a bare fraction the size of our three million miles of rural roads, the

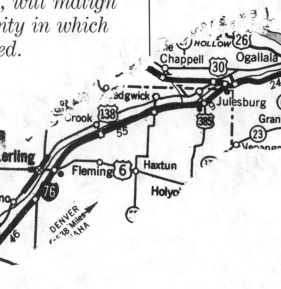

Interstates already account for nearly 25% of all motoring, and bring us quicker and easier to ever-more-remote and exotic (and thus ever-more-enjoyable) locations.

• The advent of high-quality, modern budget motels. While the standard modern motel was launched in the late 1940s, the wholly different "budget motel"— with rates astonishingly low ($6 per room initially, as little as $18.88 today)—is a phenomenon barely 25 years old. It began with the $6-a-night Motel 6 of Santa Barbara, California, was soon emulated by Cecil Day with his $8-a-night Days Inns, then proliferated into Red Roof Inns, La Quintas, EconoLodges, and endless others. Today, thousands of budget motels provide Americans with the cheapest

"It's plastic," they'll say. "Contrived. Artificial. It just isn't the same, a trip by car, not the wholesome adventure we once enjoyed, say, 25 years ago."

Not nearly the same? Not a wholesome adventure? It's better than that! In the 25 years that have just elapsed, some 20 splendid achievements have raised the level of U.S. self-drive vacations to heights of which previous generations

THIS SUMMER, WE CELEBRATE 25 YEARS OF REMARKABLE IMPROVEMENTS TO OUR LIVES ON THE ROAD

costs for modern, high-quality lodgings in all the world—a remarkable travel achievement too often overlooked.

• The rise of the fly/drive holiday. Time was when we would exhaust ourselves on long coast-to-coast drives, or from Chicago to Florida, or from St. Louis to the great national parks of the West. No more. Using Super-Saver fares or cheap airlines, we now fly by speedy, low-cost jet to L.A. or Albuquerque, and there pick up a self-drive rental car for localized touring at low weekly rates. Here is a literal revolution in the way we conduct our vacation travels.

• The ferocious competition of three dozen regional car-rental companies. Once there were only Hertz and Avis,

> Some 20 recent achievements have raised the level of U.S. self-drive vacations to heights of which previous generations scarcely dreamed.

in accident rates, and we are all the better off for them.

• An end to segregated vacation and motoring facilities. The towering achievements of Martin Luther King, Jr., and the civil rights movement of the 1960s have erased, among other things, the constant indignities to which our black fellow-

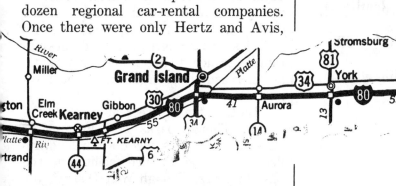

challenged perhaps by a rather insignificant Budget Rent-a-Car. Today, dozens of major car-rental companies compete for your loyalty on a national or regional basis, nearly all of them born in the last two decades. The resulting competition—a classic free-market brawl—has reduced rates and improved service, and made cars available for vacation purposes in a breathtaking range of circumstances.

• Safer motoring, reduced injuries. We may not like them, but: the 55-mile-per-hour speed limit, the increasing use of seatbelts, the drive to raise the minimum age for drinking—all products of the past 25 years—have brought about a sharp cut

citizens were once subjected as they travelled by car within the United States. This, too, is a joyous travel advance of the last 25 years.

• Better roadside aesthetics. Thanks this time to the environmental movement of the past 20-or-so years, we've eliminated some of the eyesores that once marred our roads, and encouraged highway planners to thwart the commercial pollution of our verdant countryside. And because the largely billboard-free Interstate highways have siphoned traffic from the lesser roads and made them less commercially interesting, fewer garish signs are being placed on the latter—an unexpected dividend of the Interstate Highway System.

• Better roadside air. Stringent emission controls on cars, greater regulation of our smoke-producing industries, have

WE NOW POSSESS A CHOICE BETWEEN SPEED AND DAWDLING, BETWEEN GUARANTEED LEVELS OF COMFORT AND RISKY ELEMENTS OF QUAINTNESS AND CHARM

brought a measure of relief from the worsening condition of our roadside air noticed some years back. We must all work to improve matters still more.

• A major, discernible decline in the use of abusive speed traps. Because of crusading journalists in many states, especially in the 1970s, abuses of the motorist by avaricious local magistrates and police have declined perceptibly, and less and less do we hear of notorious highway towns or tin-pot dictators of the road.

• The increasing availability of useful motoring guidebooks. Led by the redoubtable Mobil guides to accommodations and travel facilities in towns large and small, the American travel-book industry for domestic vacations came of age in the 1960s and 1970s, and is continuing to improve. Never before have the bookstores been better stocked with such exceedingly helpful guidebooks and maps for the motoring American.

• The availability of toll-free numbers for making hotel reservations. Scarcely known before 1963, the toll-free "800" system and the increasing number of "800" directories permit motoring Americans to secure a room for every night of their trip, and even in the most distant domestic locations, without incurring the crushing expense of making multiple long-distance telephone calls to hotel after hotel.

• The near-universal acceptance of bank credit cards. And who could overlook the convenience brought into our travelling lives by widely available bank credit cards and long-distance credit-card phone privileges? Remember the days when you would laboriously round up $2.45 in nickels, dimes, and quarters to

> We are no longer condemned to suffer the uneven programming of local radio stations as we drive; we now slip in a cassette and out comes Beethoven or a reading from Thoreau.

make a three-minute call?

• The ability to choose one's in-car entertainment. We are no longer condemned to suffer the uneven programming of local radio stations as we drive. We now simply slip in a cassette, and out comes Beethoven or a reading from Thoreau. Hallelujah! It took a long while to bring about this emancipation from ear-shattering, mind-benumbing sound, but improvements to the dashboard, of less than ten years' standing, have now assisted the cultural side of our motoring life.

• Better travel for the handicapped. Legislatively mandated facilities for the physically impaired, all of the most recent vintage, have measurably improved the quality of their travels. Special rest room facilities, access signs, reserved parking, ramp entrances to hotels and restaurants, are increasingly seen (although much remains to be done).

• Better travel recreation for the young. Theme parks and imaginative water amusements now dot our land, reflecting a surge in such facilities in the past 15 years. Though Walt Disney's epochal Disneyland opened as far back as 1955, raising children's amusement standards to a new realm, it was really the creation of his Florida-situated and vastly improved Walt Disney World in 1970 that sparked a giant wave of new theme-park construction, adding education to recreation. Rather than relegate our children to mindless carnivals and midway amusements, we now drive them on our holidays to attractions enjoyed as much by us as by them!

• The near-explosion in the growth of bed-and-breakfast facilities. It began as recently as a dozen years ago, in San

Francisco, initiated by public-spirited citizens anxious to re-create the tradition of the Italian *pensione* in the United States. Today the burgeoning B&B movement found in every major city—the willingness of private families to rent a spare room to transient visitors—has resulted not simply in lowered costs for accommodations, but in people-to-people contacts that are immensely satisfying and broadening, a major expansion of the benefits derived from motoring and tourism.

• Higher quality cuisine in small towns across the land. The same 600-mile-an-hour jets that began shuttling passengers across America in the 1960s are now also delivering fresh Maine lobsters to Minnesota and South Dakota, tangy Gulf Coast shrimp to Arizona and New Mexico. A quite definite improvement has occurred in the food available to motoring tourists as they stop for meals in unfamiliar towns. There, too, they currently find graduates of new culinary institutes, and a flood of French, Italian, and Japanese chefs in every state. Why, even Salt Lake City has its favored spot for sushi and sashimi!

• Highway access to inexpensive, fast-food chains of consistent quality. For cheaper meals, the motoring routes have erupted these last two decades with fast-food chains that are often the object of gentle ridicule. They shouldn't be. To motorists of mature years, who remember the greasy spoons and ptomaine taverns of the past, they are a distinct improvement, supplying us with reliably tasty and nutritious snacks and meals at exceedingly low cost.

• Simplified luggage, informal clothing. Finally, our suitcases are no longer made of heavy metal or leather, but of durable,

> The backroads of America haven't ceased to exist. As we travel the great Interstates, we always have the option to turn off into the lesser paths.

lightweight parachute cloth and other high-tech materials; and this, too, is a travel advance of the past 20-or-so years. Simultaneously, once-stuffy restaurants all over America have dropped their objections to women's pantsuits and other informal attire; those attitudes were once a considerable burden to the motoring tourist.

By contrast with these advances in the ease and availability of recreational motoring, have we suffered any corresponding declines? From all sides we hear of a dulling homogeneity in highway travel, that our roads and small cities no longer harbor local dishes, accents, outlooks, distinctive architecture. What prattle! The backroads of America haven't ceased to exist. As we travel the great Interstates with their admittedly standard facilities, we always have the option to turn off into the lesser paths. And if we do, we immediately rediscover the local grills, cafés, and shops with their strong regional flavor, their sturdy individualists and eccentrics. One has only to read the motoring bestsellers of recent years—*Blue Highways* by William Least Heat Moon, *Zen and the Art of Motorcycle Maintenance* by Robert M. Pirsig—to realize that backroad America continues to flourish amid the Interstates.

What we now possess, and did not have before, is a motoring choice—between speed and dawdling, between guaranteed levels of comfort and risky elements of quaintness and charm. Some opt for the one, some for the other. But all enjoy that most precious of rights: a choice. And therein lies the greatest triumph of American motoring over the past 25 years.

Surviving the Summer Motoring Crush

*I**t's your cherished summer vacation, but it could become a nightmare. With gasoline prices in a moderate range, record numbers of Americans will "take to the road" this July and August, cramming highways, parks, and motels to an extent unwitnessed since the OPEC oil shocks of the mid-1970s.*

At Yellowstone and Yosemite, in Walt Disney World and Disneyland, at Tanglewood and Taliesin, the prospects are for crowds, lines, jams, and, worse yet, for ripoffs in hotel rates and sightseeing charges.

How do you beat the crush? And avoid the overcharges? You obviously opt for the lesser-known locations (provided they're properly attractive), and save the Yosemites for periods other than the peak of summer. Having crisscrossed this nation on countless occasions over a long travel career, I've savored (and saved) four motoring itineraries that take you

where the tourists aren't. (That's a relative claim, of course, for even local resorts are heavily visited in summer by residents from nearby; but the aim is to avoid the mega-attractions inundated by crowds from all over.)

(1) New Mexico: The Enchanted Circle and the Santa Fe Trail

Here's your first sanctuary, far from the madding throng. In all of New Mexico (our fifth-largest state in geographical size), fewer people reside than in metropolitan Phoenix, Arizona. The tourist becomes all but invisible in this vast expanse of cactus and conifers, confining their stays almost entirely to Albuquerque, Santa Fe, and Taos. I'll briefly follow that path, reserving Santa Fe and Taos for quiet weekends, but I'll devote fully as much attention to the Enchanted Circle and Santa Fe Trail of ghost towns and Indian pueblos, abandoned gold mines and stunning rock formations. On much of the latter route, the only car you'll see will be your own.

Saturday: Arrive **Albuquerque** ("Old Town," Sandia Peak Tram), stay overnight at Conrad Hilton's first hotel, La Posada de Albuquerque (1939), attend Sunday mid-morning mass at the San Felipe Mission (1706), stroll and shop the galleries and Indian jewelry stalls of Old Town Plaza, then drive early that afternoon on State Highway 14 (the Turquoise Trail) past the gold-mining towns of Golden, Madrid, and Cerrillos to **Santa Fe**

FOUR MOTORING ITINERARIES THAT TAKE YOU WHERE THE TOURISTS AREN'T

(visiting Old Plaza, restored homes, Palace of the Governors, San Miguel Mission, six state museums, and far more). Monday at midday: Tour the Indian pueblos on U.S. 84/285, then head for **Chimayo** (Spanish weavers and woodcarvers) and **Taos** for overnight (at either the Taos Inn or La Fonda).

Tuesday: Tour Taos (birthplace of southwestern art, home to 80 art galleries in a town of only 3,400 persons), then begin your tour of the Enchanted Circle in late afternoon by driving to little **Red River** (a gold-mining village of the 1860s), where you can stay at one of six guest ranches and hike trails through secluded side canyons to old mining sites.

Wednesday: Panning for gold worth $462 an ounce may be a rewarding activity; then spend the afternoon horseback-riding and a second overnight "on the ranch."

Thursday: Drive past the ghost town of Elizabethtown, and the modern village and "lake" of Eagle Nest (windsurfing), to **Angel Fire** (an all-year resort) for lunch, then double back to Eagle Nest, and enjoy the 23-mile drive on "Scenic U.S. 64" through Cimarron Canyon State Park, with its granite cliffs, to the Santa Fe Trail town of **Cimarron.** Here, you stay overnight at the St. James Hotel, whose barroom ceiling still carries bullet holes from the gunfighters of 1872.

Santos Sotello
Robbed Stages in Kern and
Los Angeles counties
in 1877

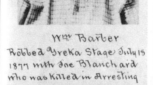

Wm Barber
Robbed Yreka Stage July 15
1877 with Joe Blanchard
who was Killed in Arresting

Geo Adams
Robbed Stage from Newhall
to Soledad alone
Dec 3 1879

Friday: Tour "Old Cimarron," then head south on State Highway 21, then due east on Highway 199 to **Springer,** from which you next head south on Interstate 25 to the village of **Wagon Mound** (so-named from the image of a prairie schooner pulled by oxen formed by nearby hilltops). Continue to **Watrous,** detour to **Fort Union,** then return to the Interstate for 18 further miles to **Las Vegas** (New Mexico), with its shaded, grassy plaza (the way all plazas were in bygone years) and stay overnight at the Plaza Hotel. Next morning (Saturday), tour the many Victorian homes of Las Vegas, then take Interstate 25 past the Pecos National Monument to Albuquerque for your homeward flight—or still another overnight stay in enchanting New Mexico.

(2) Missouri: The Lake of the Ozarks

One of the few states to have experienced almost no major population growth since World War II, uncrowded Missouri remains pleasantly rural and old-fashioned, a mirror of small-town America in the best sense of the term. And in the remarkable, 138-mile-long Lake of the Ozarks, it possesses one of the nation's finest recreational resources.

Start your trip by car with a weekend stay in **Kansas City** (visiting the Harry S. Truman Home and Library in nearby Independence, eating heavenly spiced pork and steak at Arthur Bryant's Barbecue, detouring for 50 to 55 miles to the Pony Express town of St. Joseph, where Jesse James was shot).

YOU OPT FOR THE LESSER-KNOWN LOCATIONS AND SAVE THE YOSEMITES FOR PERIODS OTHER THAN THE PEAK OF SUMMER

Monday: Drive due south on Highways 7, 13, and 60 to Clinton, Springfield, and **Branson,** the latter on meandering Table Rock Lake near the Arkansas border. Spend two nights in rustic but lively Branson, in the rolling Ozarks hills dotted with 7,000 widely scattered motel rooms, housekeeping cabins, camping sites—and some 30 country music shows. Lacking the more developed, upscale resort hotels of the Ozarks to the north, Branson offers instead a human-scale form of lake-connected activity (fishing for trout, bass, and catfish; paddleboats and sailing ships), as well as a major theme park, Silver Dollar City, featuring 19th-century arts and crafts.

Wednesday: Head east and north on Highways 76 and 5 to **Osage Beach,** directly on the heavily indented Lake of the Ozarks (so crenellated that it has 1,300 miles of shoreline) for two days and nights of water sports, boating, public beaches, and again country music shows, staying at one of a multitude of lodgings, from cheap (housekeeping cabins) to expensive (Marriott, Four Seasons). Though your hosts aren't "hillbillies," they're authentic, laid-back folk of the Ozarks, refreshing in their candor and simple warmth.

Friday: Follow Highways 42, 17, and 44 to **Rolla** (re-created Stonehenge, "Memoryville" roadside museum, among its highlights) and **St. James** (center of the state's thriving wine industry, where eight wineries offer free tours and

In northern Minnesota, temperatures drop in August, reducing crowds and mosquitoes.

On the road with American history, from anonymous con men to genius Thomas Edison

tastes). Then take Highways 44 and 19 to the mid-1800s German community of **Herman** (on the historic National Register), using the Herman Chamber of Commerce, 115 East 3rd Street, Herman, MO 65041 (phone 314/486-2313, or toll free 800/HERMANN) to obtain overnight lodgings in one of three striking B&Bs of Herman.

Saturday: Take Highway 100 and Interstate 44 to **St. Louis,** seeing the Botanical Gardens and Zoo, visiting the suburb of St. Charles (main street of authentic late-18th-century structures), the city of **Hannibal** two motoring hours away (Mark Twain Museum, Becky Thatcher's House, Tom Sawyer's Fence), or a Mississippi paddle-wheeler for short river excursions.

And thence to the airport for home, pleasantly full of Americana.

(3) Minnesota: The "Boundary Waters" and the "Iron Range"

In northern Minnesota temperatures drop in August, reducing crowds and mosquitoes, making conditions perfect for isolation-loving tourists like us.

Start, as always, on a Saturday morning, this time in the dynamic urban setting of **Minneapolis/St. Paul,** alive at that time with summer festivals, exhibitions and outdoor performances of every type.

Monday morning, embark by car onto Interstate 35 for a three-hour drive north to mighty **Duluth,** inland port for the shipment of grain all over the world. Visit its Marine Museum, then follow a skyline drive around the city for awesome views, and continue northward on Highway 61 along the upper shore of Lake Superior. On this "seaside drive" (for the lake is a giant freshwater sea, second only to the Caspian in size), people and settlements

YOU CAN AVOID CROWDS, LINES, JAMS, AND, WORST OF ALL, RIPOFFS IN HOTEL RATES AND SIGHTSEEING ADMISSIONS

dwindle in number as you pass small, old-fashioned lakeside towns, experiencing life as it was many decades ago.

Stay overnight at a motel near the oft-photographed Split Rock Lighthouse, then leave early Tuesday for **Ely** (via Highway 61, then Route 1), gateway to the Boundary Waters Canoe Area. In and around Ely, at one of many canoe outfitters that you have presumably contacted at least two weeks in advance (the Minnesota Tourist Office in St. Paul will provide the addresses; phone toll free 800/328-1461), you'll be equipped with the vessel itself, all camping gear (even a down jacket), trail meals, and a guide, for a one- or two-night, once-in-a-lifetime canoe cruise on the lakes and streams of a unique, federally protected wilderness area—untouched by man, uninhabited, pristine.

Wednesday or Thursday evening (depending on the length of your Boundary Waters stay), take Highway 169 south to **Hibbing,** center of the hilly "Iron Range" of Minnesota, explained and dramatized

> Though your hosts aren't hillbillies, they're authentic, laid-back folk of the Ozarks, refreshing in their candor and simple warmth.

by exhibits at the nearby Iron World complex, and you can tour an underground mine at Tower-Soudan. Late afternoon, continue on Route 169 to the resort city of **Grand Rapids** on the Mississippi River. A former lumbering town, with an interesting Forest History Center, Grand Rapids offers a broad range of lodgings, fishing boats, and other recreational gear.

On Thursday or Friday, take Highway 2 back to Duluth, passing first through the Fond du Lac Indian Reservation, and then return on Interstate 35 to Minneapolis/St. Paul.

(4) The Two Coasts of Florida—In One Week

All of southern Florida, all of central Florida other than Orlando, shifts into a decided "off-season mode" in July and August as a result of reports that it is unbearably hot at that time. It isn't. Sultry at most, but always tolerable, the bad reputation of Florida's weather has caused the most luxurious resort hotels to remain yawning wide open, the roads to stay clear and uncrowded, in the most popular vacation months. The result is that Florida can be toured in near elegance (but affordable elegance) at the very peak of the summer motoring season.

Start on a Saturday in **Miami** (to which numerous airlines offer bargain-priced fares in summer), rent a car at least seven days in advance at reduced summer rates, and check in near the airport at the celebrated Doral Hotel Resort and Country Club, whose rates plummet by 50% in summer. Luxuriate there for two days (amid multiple golf courses and pools, tennis courts, and flowering gardens), and then drive on Monday, in an easy 2½

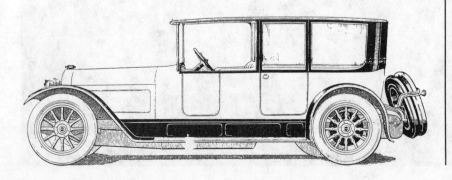

hours, up Interstate 95 (for speed) or U.S. Highway 1 (for seaside views) to other-worldly **Palm Beach,** our nation's richest small town.

In this capital of what are literally palm (fringed) beaches, treat yourself first to

an overnight, off-season-priced room in historic The Breakers on the sea, then dine at the world-renowned Café à l'Europe on glittering Worth Avenue (you couldn't get close in winter) and scan the shops of that pricey thoroughfare; drive past the estate of Rose Kennedy and other fairytale mansions on the sea; and then, on Tuesday morning, head three hours farther north on I-95 or U.S. 1 to **Cocoa Beach, Cape Canaveral,** and the **NASA/Kennedy Space Center.** Now a

Florida's weather is sultry at most, but always tolerable. Yet its bad reputation has caused the most luxurious hotels to remain yawning wide open, the roads to stay clear and uncrowded, in the most popular summer vacation months.

national shrine as much as a scientific facility, this home of both our triumphs and tragedies in space exploration simply must be visited.

From here it's but an hour along the "Bee-Line Highway" (Route 528) to **Walt Disney World,** where you'll be pleasantly surprised over the ease in finding well-priced rooms and meals. Though **Orlando** and its attractions enjoy a firming-up of business in July and August, they still receive fewer visitors then than in winter, and have ample facilities for everyone. More important, they stretch their operating hours. Both EPCOT and the Magic Kingdom stay open till midnight, provide late-night fireworks and "electric parades," offer a long, cool, seven-hour stretch of viewing (starting at 5 p.m. or so) to tourists who have otherwise spent the day around their motel pool.

Spend two nights (Tuesday and Wednesday) in the Orlando area (where scores of motels charge less than $40 a room in summer), then drive farther west on Interstate 4 for an hour and a half to **Tampa, Clearwater Beach, St. Petersburg,** and **St. Petersburg Beach** (seeing Busch Gardens on the way, staying in the grand, rococo Don Cesar Resort on Thursday and Friday nights).

Finally, on Saturday morning proceed along the Gulf of Mexico (Highway 41) to **Fort Meyers** (the Thomas Edison Home and Museum) and **Naples** (deep-sea fishing), where you turn sharply east on the Tamiami Trail through the swampy Everglades, past Seminole Indian trading posts, to Miami and your homeward-bound flight. In one week you have seen the uncrowded highlights of a home-grown tropical paradise that perhaps *should* be best visited in summer!

Weekends of History, by Self-Drive Car

*H*ow do Americans travel in the 1980s? Over a "long weekend," it seems. A rather startling recent study by Marriott Hotels Corporation reveals that more than 70% of all American vacations are for no more than three days at a time.

And how do we spend that time? Badly, in my view. On these mini-tours and quick trips, we head for casino cities or overcrowded beaches, or we spend long, languid, and often mindless afternoons with relatives or friends in the next town.

We can do better. In every major region we can, quite easily, base ourselves in a historic city from which—within a 60-mile

radius—are dozens of equally historic sights. In a self-drive rental car, driving in easy stages from that urban base, we can then quickly and conveniently relive our country's past. No other holiday experience can be more memorable, more necessary to your children's growth, a better use of your time.

Let's sample five weekends of American history:

In and around Boston is perhaps the most concentrated array of important historic attractions in all the nation.

(1) Minutemen and Muskets: Boston comes first; in and around it is perhaps the most concentrated array of important historic attractions in all the nation: colonial and Revolutionary War sites, early-19th-century sites, and those of the later Industrial Revolution.

Except on graduation weekends, the city's hotels are lightly booked on Friday and Saturday nights, when promotional reductions cut rates by a third and more. You can afford at that time to stay in the deluxe Four Seasons Hotel or equally resplendent Ritz-Carlton; you can dine on renowned seafood specialties in the historic setting of the Union Oyster House, oldest in town, dating from 1826.

From information booths at the Tremont Street side of the Boston Common, or at 60 State Street, you then gather maps for an eminently "walkable" itinerary called the Freedom Trail: it starts at the Common, ends at the U.S.S. *Constitution*, passes the Old North Church, Paul Revere's Home, Bunker Hill Monument, Old Granary Burying Grounds, and at least ten other heart-stirring sights of revolutionary times.

Your second day, a rental car brings you to Lexington, Concord, and the Minuteman National Historical Park ("Here once the embattled farmers stood and fired the shot heard round the world"), both only 15 or 20 miles from downtown Boston. A couple of miles from Concord is Thoreau's Walden Pond—enchanting. Later you drive to Salem, where witches were hung (House of the Seven Gables, Whaling Museum), 16 miles away; or to Old Sturbridge Village, 50 miles away (re-created 18th-century village); or to the partially preserved, old 19th-century mill town of Lowell, again 50-or-so miles

FIVE AMERICAN REGIONS CRAMMED WITH HISTORIC SIGHTS, ALL WITHIN AN HOUR OF A KEY HUB CITY

Old State House, Boston

away, whose industrial relics are now part of both state and U.S. national parks.

You end your short stay with a "pilgrimage" to the re-created, open-air Plimoth Plantation, only an hour from the heart of Boston. There, April through November, you board the *Mayflower II*, tread the marvelous evocation of the 1627 Pilgrim Village, see Plymouth Rock, speak about crops and the weather with "interpreters" who never step out of their historic roles.

(2) Sherman's March to the Sea: Just as

weary millions must now "change at Atlanta" to fly from place to place, so Atlanta, Georgia, was a key rail hub (and a less important town) in the 1860s. In the winter of 1864, Generals U. S. Grant and William Tecumseh ("War is hell") Sherman chose Atlanta for a key role in their end-the-war strategy.

While Grant attacked the armies of Robert E. Lee from the north, Sherman would destroy Atlanta, then march to Savannah on the sea, then north to crush the Confederacy between his own anvil and Grant's hammer. On the way he

IN A RENTAL CAR, DRIVING IN EASY STAGES FROM THAT CENTRAL POINT, WE CAN QUICKLY AND CONVENIENTLY RELIVE OUR NATION'S PAST

would destroy southern morale by devastating the civilian economy.

This he did. His troops burned and pillaged as they went "marching through Georgia," but left enough untouched to enthrall today's visitor with scenes of the antebellum South.

Your base is Atlanta; the giant convention hotels here are quiet on weekends and willing to entice you with reduced rates. Start at the Atlanta Historical Society (open seven days a week) in the Buckhead district, whose permanent exhibit, "The Campaign for Atlanta," displays the actual uniforms, gear, and photos of the Confederate soldiers depicted in the giant Cyclorama (a must-see) in a downtown park. Drive then to the re-created plantation complex (slave quarters, overseer's house,

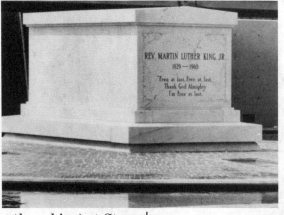

kitchen for open-hearth cooking) at Stone Mountain, a state-owned theme park 19 miles from town.

If you have the time, make a side excursion 15 miles north of Atlanta to Roswell, Georgia, whose antebellum homes and mansions include the famous Bulloch Hall (like "Tara"), where Theodore Roosevelt's mother was born and married, much in the style of Scarlett O'Hara.

Next morning, follow Sherman's route by car, driving east on I-20 for 36 miles to Covington (antebellum homes), then on to Madison, the largely preserved town that Sherman felt was "too pretty to burn" (numerous other Georgia towns claim this

Springfield was his home for 23 years; Springfield was his springboard to the presidency.

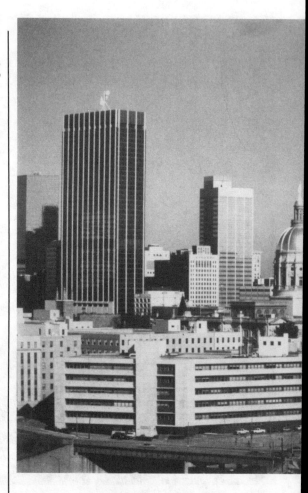

was said about them). Apart from the renowned antebellum homes, visit the Madison-Morgan Cultural Center, restored by a donation from the late, superwealthy president of Atlanta's Coca-Cola, Robert Woodruff. Proceed south then on Highway 29 to Eatonton (more antebellum homes)—Alice Walker, author of *The Color Purple*, was born here.

Then on to Milledgeville, capital of Georgia at the time of the Civil War, and today an enchanting period city once you pass through its outer, commercial "strip." Though it was a key target of Sherman's march, his army left it largely

Downtown Atlanta

Just as weary millions must now "change at Atlanta" to fly from place to place, so Atlanta was a key rail hub (and less important town) in the 1860s.

the late 1800s and its inevitable clash with the American Indian. Your dramatic protagonists: the rash and romantic George A. Custer, general of the U.S. Army, and the defiant, imperious Sitting Bull, chief of the Sioux. They met in the Valley of the Little Bighorn River on June 25, 1876, in a battle that saw Custer and his troops slaughtered to the last man. Everything about the event is hotly disputed, complex in origins, and the subject of fascinating new speculations drawn from recent archaeological work on the site.

From Billings (where you might stay at the well-preserved, turn-of-the-century Northern Hotel, with its much-acclaimed Golden Bell Restaurant), you drive east on Interstate 90 to Hardin (39 miles away) and the nearby (15 further miles south) Custer Battlefield National Monument and its visitors center. The latter is surrounded by the Crow Agency Indian Reservation (phone 406/638-2601), whose annual fair in mid-August is heavily attended by outsiders.

Follow Custer's route through the surrounding hills, then head west on state highways to Bighorn Canyon National Recreation Area (boating, and the nation's finest trout fishing, on the Bighorn River), staying overnight, however, at the motels and B&Bs of Hardin. Continue west to Red Lodge, then northward to the Yellowstone River and Columbus, on the route of the Lewis and Clark Expedition of 1804–1806.

The classic journals of Captain Meri-

intact. See the original capitol, the governor's mansion, the many period homes.

Savannah itself is too far to reach on an easy trip. From Milledgeville, return to Atlanta via a different route, on Highway 212 to Monticello (many period homes), making a side excursion to the state-owned Jarrell Plantation, probably the most authentically preserved of all such structures in the state (original cotton gin, original furniture); and back to Atlanta.

(3) Custer's Last Stand: Your base now is Billings, Montana. Your theme: the westward surge of the American nation in

NO OTHER HOLIDAY EXPERIENCE CAN BE MORE MEMORABLE, A BETTER USE OF YOUR TIME

wether Lewis and Lieutenant William Clark, rich diaries and maps, are widely sold hereabouts, and are still applicable to the evident and unchanged natural sights you pass as you drive. Let your spouse or children read them aloud and identify the landmarks as you drive east and then slightly north on I-90 back to Billings. En route, but on I-94, you'll pass famous Pompey's Pillar—a sandstone monolith jutting up from the rocky ground—on which Meriwether Lewis carved his initials (you can still see them). Atop the pillar, Custer peered out at the horizon, seeking the Indian community and thus the battlefield where he met his death.

Back in Billings, the hallways of the old and unusually inexpensive Hotel Lincoln are filled with historic photos that you'll want to view. Near the Custer site, you may encounter native Americans. It's enlightening to hear their views on "Custer's Land Stand."

(4) Lincoln as a Lawyer: Though he was born in Kentucky and brought up in Indiana, Abraham Lincoln moved as an emancipated young man of 21 to the tiny village of New Salem, Illinois, about 20 miles from the current capital city of Springfield. There he worked as a surveyor, in a tavern, and then in a post office, while "reading law" for admission to the bar. In 1837, at the age of 28, he took up life as a lawyer in Springfield, formed several law partnerships, followed the state court as it went travelling "on circuit" throughout the state—and entered politics. Springfield was his home for 23 years, Springfield was his springboard to the presidency, Springfield is where he is buried, and Springfield makes for a memorable weekend of history, via self-drive car.

The city is amply stocked with hotels,

Your theme is the westward surge of the American nation in the late 1800s and its inevitable clash with the American Indian.

all anxious for weekend guests. Though none of the hotels or restaurants of Springfield dates from the era of Lincoln, a restaurant called Maldaner's has served the residents for several generations, and is always pleasant.

Within the city, six major attractions require at least a full day to be seen: (1) Lincoln's home is the only one he ever owned, purchased after his marriage to Mary Todd; its interior has been restored as it was in the 1850s, and contains original pieces: horsehair furniture, daguerreotypes of the family, and a shaving mirror positioned for Lincoln's 6-foot 4-inch frame. (2) Lincoln's law offices are also completely restored, and found on the third floor of a building whose second floor was the site of the only federal court of that time in Illinois. (3) Lincoln's tomb is the burial site of all the family except for Robert Lincoln, buried at Arlington. The tomb's nearby bronze bust of Lincoln is rubbed for luck by tourists and visiting politicians ranging from George Bush to Michael Dukakis. (4) The Old State Capitol Building is also completely restored to its appearance in the 1840s and 1850s. It was here that Lincoln, who had once served in the state legislature, proclaimed in a campaign speech: "A house divided against itself cannot stand." (5) The Great Western Railway Depot is where Lincoln gave his farewell address to Springfield, upon boarding a train to Washington, D.C., as the president-elect in 1861. And (6) the Governor's Mansion, which dates from the 1850s, is one of the oldest, continually occupied such residences in the U.S.A.

Your second day, the obligatory (and fascinating) visit is to the New Salem Historic Site, 20 miles from Springfield.

This is the fully re-created log cabin village where Lincoln spent his early years, open all year, and maintained as if he were still living there. You smell fresh bread baking, watch candlemakers and blacksmiths at their work, observe the use of spinning wheels and crude cobblers' tools. In summer, the "Great American People Show" presents nightly evening performances of historical pageants. And a riverboat called the *Talisman* takes you up and down the Sangamon River.

In the same general area as the New Salem Village is the Clayville Rural Life Center, re-creating life of the 1850s in an old stagecoach inn. Back in Springfield, a visit to the home of Vachel Lindsay, the 20th-century poet and chronicler of Lincoln, caps a visit to a city of unforgettable memories.

(5) The California Gold Rush: The old railroad town of Truckee, California, is your touring base for this final weekend of history, but Reno, Nevada, across the border, 35 miles away, is your best source of hotel rooms in all price ranges; its 3,000-room Bally Grand Hotel is a phenomenon that must be seen, if not used.

Returning to Truckee, you tour its wonderfully preserved "Commercial Row" of 19th-century western stores two stories tall, now a useful shopping area for gifts and clothes, every sort of snack, and two small—but historic—hotels (Cottage Hotel and Star Hotel).

In 1846, in a foretaste of the later movement that brought gold-hungry prospectors to the area in 1849 and later, a party of Illinois farmers led by the Donner family came here to cross the Sierra Nevada mountains on their way to the "promised land" of sunny winters and flowering earth: the valleys of California.

> You see the towns the miners built, the mines they dug into the earth, the springs, creeks, and rivers where they panned for gold—and where you can "pan" today (sometimes a grain turns up).

Tragically, an attempted shortcut had delayed their arrival for three weeks, and an early severe winter soon mired them in deep snows. Throughout the winter of 1846–1847 they fought to survive, huddling in crude shelters, eating the flesh of those who perished first.

All around Truckee are chilling memorials and relics of the doomed group: the Graves Cabin Site on the Donner Pass Road; the Emigrant Trail Museum, Donner Party Monument, and Murphy Cabin Site in the Donner Memorial State Park; the Alder Creek Campsite in the Tahoe National Forest.

It is well worth a day of your long weekend to read briefly about the Donner party (in numerous guidebooks sold in Truckee), and then to follow the markings of their movements and those of rescue teams coming from the west.

Emigrant farmers like the Donners, travelling in wagon trains, scouted the routes that thousands of "49ers" took in their quest for gold. From Truckee, drive north to Sierraville, then northwest into the Sierra Valley and Sierra City, with its many surviving historic structures of a once-important Truckee, and head north to Calpine, White Sulphur Springs, Plumas-Eureka State Park (with its authentic mining site), Portola, the cabin of pioneer explorer James Beckwourth, and Chilcoot. Then return to Truckee or Reno, having passed the several large ranches that provisioned weary miners in the 1850s, the towns the miners built, the mines they dug into the earth, the springs, creeks, and rivers (like the North Yuba River hereabouts) where they panned for gold—and where you can pan for gold today. Sometimes a grain or two of the gritty, yellow sand shows up!

IX

Travel Opportunities for the Older American—What's Helpful, What Isn't

Our Greatest Retirement Bargains—Extended-Stays Overseas

If I could bestow an Academy Award for travel, it would be to the operators of extended-stay vacations to Spain, Yugoslavia, and Australia in the winter months. Next to the values offered by these one-month (and longer) sojourns, all other tour programs seem tawdry ripoffs, high-priced scams.

I am standing, in my fantasy, on the great curving stage of the Dorothy Chandler Pavilion in Los Angeles. I rip open the envelope and shout to the world: "The winners are:" (pause) "Sun Holidays of Stamford, Yugotours of New York, and Aero Tours International—for their 'Extended Stays'!"

And as they drag me to a psycho ward (overlooking the blue Pacific), I struggle to explain the concept:

Almost by definition, an extended-stay vacation takes place overseas in the off-season setting of a popular summer resort.

The hotels are desperate. Built to accommodate the great warm-weather crowds, they now stand empty and losing in the chillier months. Along comes a U.S. tour operator with the following pitch: "If you will rent us your rooms for $6 a night, we'll fill them off-season with retirees staying for at least 30 days. You'll still lose money, but you'll lose less. And your staff will be happy to stay active and receiving tips."

There you stay for four weeks in a studio apartment with fully equipped kitchen, enjoying the mild winter climate of Spain's southernmost shores.

To the airlines, a similar appeal: "Our one-month clients don't need to leave on the popular dates. Give us round-trip seats for $300, and we'll fill your flights on Tuesday nights."

To the public: "Why go in the winter to a mildewed motel and the plastic meals of fast-food chains? We'll fly you for less to glamorous foreign resorts. Sure, it's no longer hot in those places. But it's sunny and mild, and filled with exotica."

Thousands of mature U.S. travellers (and their numbers are growing) now say "Yes" to these attractive offers. They receive one of the great travel bargains, which seem particularly well packaged by the following companies:

Sun Holidays, to Spain's Mediterranean Coast ($765): The undoubted price champion of the extended-stay companies, Sun charges a flat $765 for a full month in winter on the Costa del Sol of Spain, including air fare. It flies you there and back from New York, Boston, or Miami ($50 more from Miami) on Iberia Airlines, meets you at the airport of Malaga, and transfers you by bus to the modern, high-rise Timor Sol Apartments on the beach of bustling Torremolinos (Europe's most heavily visited resort city in summer) with its dozens of hotels and varied tourist facilities. And there you stay for four weeks in a studio apartment with fully equipped kitchen, either making your own meals or taking them at restaurants nearby, enjoying maid service, an entertainment program, and the mild winter climate of Spain's southernmost shores (where it's too chilly at that time for ocean swimming, but otherwise entirely pleasant—and emptied of its often-oppressive summer crowds). For $140 more per person, you get a one-

bedroom apartment for the month; for $69 per person per week, you get additional weeks. And thus, for $1,041 per person, including air fare, you can stay for a full eight weeks on the Mediterranean coast of Spain!

Sun Holidays has been operating these tours in close concert with Iberia Airlines for seven years. Though a dozen other companies attempt the same thing—including such well-known senior-citizen specialists as Grand Circle Travel ($855 for a month in Torremolinos) and AARP Travel Service ($898 for the same), no one else comes remotely close in price or value. An Oscar is clearly deserved. For a

colorful, free catalogue describing several such lengthy stays in various resort areas of Spain, contact **Sun Holidays, 26 6th Street, Stamford, CT 06905 (phone 203/ 323-1166 or toll free 800/243-2057 outside Connecticut).**

Yugotours, to the Dalmatian Coast ($1,260): Some six years ago, the leading tour company of Yugoslavia—a remarkably elegant organization despite its somewhat brutish name—discovered ahead of everyone else that a large number of Americans could greatly enjoy a long-stay winter vacation in the then largely empty modern hotels of the medieval resort cities of the Dalmatian (Adriatic) Coast of Yugoslavia.

Thirty thousand U.S. travellers, mostly 55 and older, have since leaped at the

A MONTH IN SPAIN FOR $765, INCLUDING AIR FARE— AND SIMILAR STAYS IN YUGOSLAVIA AND AUSTRALIA

chance. Somehow they sensed that the colorful atmosphere, setting, cuisine, and deliciously old-fashioned pace of these ancient ports would provide a unique vacation. They had heard, of course, that the Dalmatian Coast was among the most scenically awesome spots on earth. And they were soon to learn that it is also remarkably cheap.

Today, from a busy office in New York's Empire State Building, Yugotours publishes an eagerly awaited and quite handsome, 16-page catalogue of "extended stays" in the fall, winter, and early spring to Dubrovnik, Opatija, Hvar, and Split, among others. Their rates are like from a Slavic fairytale. They include not only air fare and accommodations, but two meals a day—and other remarkable features (like

> Thousands learned that the colorful atmosphere, setting, cuisine, and deliciously old-fashioned pace of these ancient ports resulted in a unique vacation.

a trip by passenger steamer between one resort town and another, on tours that feature more than one resort).

The best of the tours (but not the cheapest) are those assigning you to three different cities in your three-week stay—with the option to stay an extra week. For a grand total of $1,156 to $1,246 per person (depending on dates), you fly on Yugoslav Airlines from New York or Chicago ($80 more from Chicago) to Zagreb, go by bus to Opatija, proceed from there by steamer to a week apiece in Hvar and the walled city of Dubrovnik, stay in modern seaside hotels with heated swimming pools, eat two meals a day, and receive all sorts of charming extra features: cocktail parties and candlelight dinners, a Dalmatian band at several meals, orientation tours, films about Dubrovnik and Hvar, much else. This short summary can't begin to do justice to the program as a whole.

From all resorts you have cheap, and almost daily, optional excursions to a variety of enchanting, unspoiled villages and seaside locations—especially to those in historic Montenegro: Sveti Stefan and Budva, the Bay of Kotor. So hand me that golden statuette for Yugotours! And for a free catalogue, contact **Yugotours, 350 Fifth Avenue, New York, NY 10118 (phone 212/563-2400, or toll free 800/223-5298 outside New York).**

AeroTours, to Australia's "Gold Coast" ($1,521): Here is the sole exception to the "off-season" timing of most extended stays: our American winter is Australia's summer, and the ocean is filled at that time with swimmers, who later bask in the 80° sun. The low value of the Australian dollar, which sells for only 65¢ U.S. (you almost double the value of your

money there), explains why the six-year-old AeroTours International can sell such a reasonably priced, month-long holiday to a high-quality, peak-season resort so far away.

For a total of $1,605 from April to November, $1,805 from December to March, AeroTours will fly you round trip from the U.S. West Coast direct to Brisbane and then bus you 40 minutes south to the 26-mile-long beach known as the Gold Coast; it is lined with luxury hotels, condominiums, and even a casino or two. Near a town called Surfers Paradise (its actual name), you'll stay for a full month in a 15-story beachfront apartment-hotel (the Equinox Sun Resort) in a balconied studio with wall-to-wall carpeting, fully

equipped kitchen, and dining nook. Downstairs are restaurants, shops, squash and tennis courts. Fifteen minutes away are rain forest–covered mountains with horseback and walking trails, and most of the wildlife sanctuaries of Australia.

When you consider that the peak-season air fare from the West Coast to Australia is alone $1,360, you glimpse the value this package represents. And if you can yourself improve on the air fare to Australia—using a local bucket shop, for instance—AeroTours will sell you just the accommodations, at a considerable saving. Once in Australia, you enjoy marvelously low prices for everything else, including the memorable trip to the Barrier Reef.

Persons of any age can book these tours (and so can retirees of any age on the programs of Sun Holidays and Yugotours).

For brochures and further details, contact **AeroTours International, P.O. Box 602, Lenox Hill Station, New York, NY 10021, (phone 212/594-7575, or toll free 800/223-4555 outside New York)**. And for giving me this chance to tell you about AeroTours, I want to thank the Academy, my travel agent, the Rand McNally Atlas, my typewriter repair shop. . . .

The Battle for the Older American Traveller, I

*I*n the world of travel, what do older Americans really want?

That inquiry is the topic of the year among airlines and tour operators. As if, without warning, a new planet had swung into their sight, they've discovered that a startling portion of all travel expenditures are made by persons 55 and older. Not yuppies, not preppies, not even baby boomers, but rather senior citizens are today the "name of the game" in travel.

Young folks, it appears, go to the movies; older ones go on vacation.

"Our senior citizens," says one tour operator, "are feeling better about themselves, and that's why they're travelling more. They're healthier, living longer, more affluent. They have a new conviction that life is to be enjoyed for quite a while more, and this fairly recent attitude makes them the fastest-growing segment of the travel market."

Given that fact, it is surprising, as an initial note, to find so few companies serving the needs of the older American traveller. Apart from local motorcoach operators and purely ad hoc programs by regional firms, only four really major U.S. companies deal exclusively with the marketing and operation of far-ranging tours

> Tour companies earn their allegiance by providing arrangements that are significantly different from those designed for a general clientele.

for seniors, and three of these are headquartered in one city: Boston. They are: **Saga International Holidays, 120 Boylston Street, Boston, MA 02116 (phone toll free 800/343-0273); Grand Circle Travel, Inc., 347 Congress Street, Boston, MA 02210 (phone 617/350-7500, or toll free 800/221-2610); Elderhostel, 80 Boylston Street, Boston, MA 02116 (phone 617/426-7788); and AARP (American Association of Retired Persons) Travel Service, P.O. Box 92964, Los Angeles, CA 90009 (phone toll free 800/227-7737).** A fifth firm, **Passages Unlimited, 48 Union Street, Stamford, CT 06906 (phone 203/323-1441, or toll free 800/472-7724),** is less than five years in existence and still comparatively small, but breathing hard down the necks of its longer-established contenders.

Having journeyed to Boston to view the first three, and phoned the others in Connecticut and California, I've been alternately impressed, startled, dismayed, and educated by several uniform ways in which they do business. Travelling seniors may want to consider the following observations on the major "tour operators for older Americans":

They mainly sell "direct." Not one of the "big four" deals with travel agents or sets aside a single percentage point of income for the latter. Each one heatedly insists that the processing of seniors' tours is a specialty requiring direct contact between them (the tour operators) and their clients (the actual senior travellers), usually via toll-free "800" numbers. Just as heatedly, the people at Passages Unlimited—which does deal through travel agents—insist that the senior traveller requires the personal assistance of an impartial human being seated across a

FIVE MAJOR TRAVEL FIRMS ARE FOLLOWING A UNIQUE APPROACH IN THEIR SALE OF VACATIONS TO SENIORS

desk and not the disembodied voice of a far-off, salaried telephone reservationist. Because the first four firms adhere fiercely to their position, their brochures and quest their brochures by writing to the addresses listed above. Once you do, you'll soon receive a heavy packet of attractive, four-color literature.

catalogues are unavailable in travel agents' racks and can be obtained only by mail. Nor do they advertise in the general media. If you are not already on their mailing lists, you must specifically re-

They cater to "older" Americans. Although people can theoretically use the services of the senior citizen tour operators when they reach the tender ages of 50, 55, or 60 (50 for AARP, 55 for Grand

THE BAD NEWS IS THAT THE TOURS PLANNED FOR SENIOR CITIZENS ONLY ARE GENERALLY HIGHER PRICED THAN SIMILAR TRIPS SOLD TO ALL AGES

Circle and Passages, 60 for Saga and Elderhostel), in practice they don't. The average age of Grand Circle's clients is 68, that of the others only slightly less. The apparent reason is that Americans no longer feel removed from younger age categories until they reach their early or mid-60s. Advances in health care and longevity, better diets, and attention to exercise keep most of us youthful and vigorous into our late 50s, and reluctant to cease socializing—or vacationing—with younger people. (I recall growing apoplectic with rage when, on my 50th birthday, the mail brought an invitation to join

Not yuppies, not preppies, not even baby boomers, but rather senior citizens are today the "name of the game" in travel.

AARP.) Who any longer even retires at the age of 65?

Their clients insist on the exclusion of younger passengers. But when those mid-

60s are, in fact, reached, the newly elder turn with a vengeance to services of the specialists. After an initial reluctance to confine their travel companions to a single age group, today's 65-year-olds discover that they are of a different "mind set" than their younger co-citizens. Brought up during the Depression, sent to fight or work in World War II, denied the easy travel opportunities enjoyed by our blasé younger set, they better appreciate the joys of international travel, react with gratitude and awe to wonders of the world, enjoy the companionship of people who feel the same way.

They possess a historical perspective denied to the younger generation; share a wealth of experience and a common outlook; come from an education in the broad liberal arts as contrasted with the crudely materialistic, vocational outlook of so many of today's youth. And when they travel with younger people, they are often upset by the young folks' failure to share the same values or to be familiar with the events that so shaped their own lives. What mature American can enjoy a trip through Europe or the South Pacific with people who are only dimly aware of Franklin Roosevelt or Winston Churchill, of Douglas MacArthur or Field Marshal Rommel, of the Invasion or the Holocaust? Accordingly, they respond with eagerness to tour programs limited to persons of their own age.

Their clients receive distinctly different, custom-tailored travel arrangements. In addition to confining their groups to an older age range, the major tour companies earn their allegiance by providing arrangements that are significantly different from those designed for a general clientele. "We avoid the modern hotels, with their small public spaces, their in-room videos and bars," explains one specialist. "We look for traditional buildings with large lobbies for congregating and sitting—our clients prefer ca-

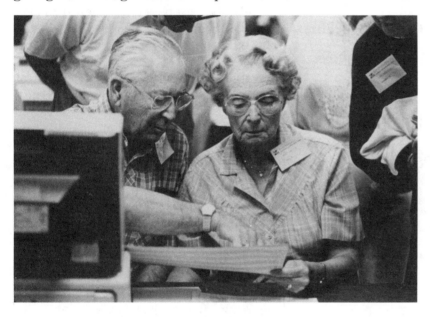

maraderie to in-room movies! We also insist on a location within easy walking distance of everything important."

"We pace our tours to avoid overly long hours on a bus," explains another. "But we keep our passengers active, always on the move. Older travellers have had enough of sitting around at home; they want constant experiences and encounters."

Though the tours are of a longer duration than the normal variety, they are rarely for more than three weeks at a time. "People in retirement like to take two and three trips in a year," says the president of Passages. "They tour a particular destination for two or three weeks, then want to try something else."

In planning tours for the older Ameri-

can, the great majority of departures are scheduled for off-season periods—not in July or August to Europe, for instance, but in the "shoulder" and "off-peak" months when retired people are the best possible prospects for travel. "We get better rates for them that way," says a tour official. "And they're better appreciated at that time by the suppliers. They get more and better attention."

But their prices are higher than the norm. So much for the good news. The bad news is that the tours planned for senior citizens only are generally higher priced than similar trips sold to all ages. This is not to say that the former do not use better hotels, provide closer and more personal attention, supply more tour ingredients. They may or may not. But except for Elderhostel—whose prices are truly remarkable—not one of the senior-citizen specialists has opted to service the needs of intensely cost-conscious Americans; their tour products are generally $100 to $300 higher than the motorcoach programs or "stay-put" holidays available from several of the low-cost tour operators serving a general public, sometimes for suspiciously similar features. This, to me, is a serious mistake on their part, limiting their programs to an upper-middle-class clientele and bypassing the budget-limited majority of the older generation. When a tour company—perhaps a wholly new one—begins offering modestly priced tours for exclusive use by older citizens, they will, in my view, be flooded with bookings (as Elderhostel is).

What programs do the current companies offer? And what are their prices? How do the companies compare in their personnel and policies? Those are the subjects of our next essay.

The Battle for the Older American Traveller, II

*T*hink hard. "What major tour operators refuse to deal with travel agents, sell directly to the public, schedule most of their departures for off-season months, and require their customers' hair to be silvery white—or at least heavily speckled with gray?"

To this variant of a children's riddle, the answer is: "Saga, Grand Circle, AARP, and Elderhostel." A fifth firm—Passages Unlimited—also confines itself

On board the buses, frolicsome passengers quip that Saga means "Send-A-Granny-Away" or "Sex-And-Games-for-the-Aged."

to older people, but deals with those pesky travel agents.

In the immediately preceding essay I explored the reasons why Americans in their mid-60s are increasingly opting to travel only with persons of their own age, on trips planned by the specialists listed above. As one such tour operator puts it, "They've become, with age, more outer-directed, less impressed with status or position, intensely curious about the ultimate questions. They're more interesting than younger people, and anxious to travel only with other interesting people."

In serving their travel needs, what do the specialists offer, and how do they differ one from the other? Here's a quick rundown:

Saga International Holidays, 120 Boylston Street, Boston, MA 02116 (phone toll free 800/343-0273), is perhaps the largest of the lot, resulting from the activity of its British/Australian parent company, which each year sends over 300,000 senior citizens on vacation. To tap into that major movement (and the bargaining power it represents), the U.S. organization routes all its transatlantic tours through London, there to combine its older American travellers into one group with older British and Australian passengers. Such blending of English-speaking nationalities adds "zip" to any tour, they claim, and I agree. On board the buses, frolicsome passengers quip that Saga means "Send-A-Granny-Away" or "Sex-And-Games-for-the-Aged" (the latter very much tongue-in-cheek).

Headed by an ebullient, walrus-mustached, former educator named Jerry Foster, a one-time official of Elderhostel, the Saga staff also provide technical travel arrangements for Elderhostel's programs

APPRAISING THE FIVE SPECIALIST FIRMS AND THEIR FIVE DIFFERENT APPROACHES

(see below) to Britain, Ireland, Spain, Portugal, and Turkey—a potent endorsement. Saga's passengers (who must be 60 or older) are later invited to join the Saga Holidays Club and receive a quarterly magazine supplemented by newsletters. The latter's most appealing feature is a page of travel "personals"—older people seeking other older people to join them on a trip.

Saga's major stock in trade is escorted motorcoach tours: heavily (and throughout the year) within the United States, heavily to Europe, but also to Mexico, in Australia, and in South America. Although it also offers cruises and extended stays, it is the escorted motorcoach, competitively priced, that most of its clients demand.

Grand Circle Travel, Inc., 347 Con- **gress Street, Boston, MA 02210 (phone 617/350-7500, or toll free 800/221-2610),** is the oldest of the U.S. firms dealing only with senior citizens, but recently rejuvenated through its acquisition by a dynamic, young travel magnate, Alan E. Lewis, who has injected considerable new resources and vigor (quarterly magazine, *Pen Pal* and travel-partner service) into it. In business for 30 years, it enjoys a large and loyal following who respond, especially, to offers of extended-stay vacations in off-season months, to low-cost foreign areas with mild climates. The greater number of Grand Circle's passengers are those spending, say, 2 to 20 weeks on the Mediterranean coast of Spain, in a seaside, kitchenette-apartment supplied with utensils, china, and cutlery. Others go for several weeks to Dubrovnik on the awesome Dalmatian coast of Yugoslavia, or to Madeira, the Canary Islands, the Balearics. Wherever, the tour company argues (and quite successfully) that older Americans can enjoy a "full season" at these exotic locations for not much more than they'd spend to Florida or other domestic havens. While neither Spain nor Yugoslavia offers swimming weather in winter, their low prices enable seniors (even those living mainly on Social Security) to vacation in dignity, enjoying good-quality meals and modern apartments in place of the fast-food outlets and shabby motels to which they're often relegated here at home. Grand Circle's extended stays are supplemented by nearly a dozen other programs—Alaskan cruises, Canadian holidays, tours to Europe and the Orient—booked by thousands, but not yet as popular as those "stay-put" vacations for several weeks in a balmy, foreign clime.

PASSAGES IS THE MAVERICK, WORKING EAGERLY WITH TRAVEL AGENTS

AARP Travel Service, P.O. Box 92964, Los Angeles, CA 90009 (phone toll free 800/227-7737), is the "new boy on the block," less than five years old, but obviously destined for big things. As the official travel arm of the 25-million-member American Association of Retired Persons, it draws upon a massive potential following and contacts them quickly and efficiently via the organization's impressive bimonthly magazine, *Modern Maturity,* sent to all members. They, in turn, can request upward of 30 separate travel catalogues dealing with cruises, motorcoach holidays, "long stays," and jaunts of every description.

But though the audience is of such a mass scale, the programs themselves are operated for AARP by a "carriage trade" tour operator, Olson Travelworld, known for its quality accommodations, careful attention to travel details, and substantial price structure. Olson, in its early stewardship of the AARP program, has surprised the travel trade by placing a heavy emphasis on cut-rate cruises; it offers (with considerable success) a lengthy series of sailings on celebrated ships already heavily patronized by seniors, but discounted for the AARP membership by as much as $150 to $2,000 per person. While the strong response to these ocean-going values has tended to overshadow the remainder of the program, AARP's buses, planes, and traditional tours are operating to every major destination.

Elderhostel, 80 Boylston Street, Boston, MA 02116 (phone 617/426-7788), is, in a nutshell, the much-discussed, increasingly popular, nonprofit group that works with 1,000 U.S. and foreign educational institutions to provide seniors 60 and over with residential study courses at

The greater number of Grand Circle's passengers are those spending, say, 2 to 20 weeks on the Mediterranean Coast of Spain, in a seaside, kitchenette-apartment supplied with utensils, china, and cutlery.

unbeatable costs: $195 to $250 per week for room, board, and tuition (but not including air fare) in the U.S. and Canada; an average of $1,500 for three weeks abroad, this time including air fare. Accommodations and meals are in student residence halls or underused youth hostels.

Those are the "nutshell" facts, which can't do justice to the gripping appeal of Elderhostel's course descriptions. Who can withstand "The Mystery and Miracle of Medieval Cathedrals" (taught at a school overlooking the Pacific)? Or "Everything You Always Wanted to Know About Music But Were Too Afraid to Ask" (at a university in Alabama). Or "Gods, Kings, and Temples" (at a classroom in Cairo)? They make you yearn to be 60!

With more than 160,000 travelling students anticipated for 1988, Elderhostel is the once-and-future travel giant, fervently acclaimed by its elderly devotees. "Thank you, Elderhostel!" wrote one senior in a recent publication. "We've built beaver dams in Colorado, explored temples in Nepal, ridden outrigger canoes in Fiji, sat on the lawn sipping coffee at Cambridge University, eaten with our fingers at private homes in Bombay, where they venerate older people!"

Passages Unlimited, 48 Union Street, Stamford, CT 06906 (phone 203/323-1441, or toll free 800/472-7724), smallest of the group, is also the maverick: unlike the others, it pays commissions to travel agents (up to 17.5% of package prices), lauds their services, and works eagerly—and only—through them. Its airline is primarily Pan Am; its European motorcoach operator, the long-established Global of London; its minimum age for

tour members, 55; its chief innovation, travel specially designed for "mature singles." Having discovered, in its words, a "formidable constituency" of older Americans "who do not wish to be one of three or five singles in an enormous group of couples," Passages now sets aside particular departures on its major programs (to London, Spain's Costa del Sol, Russia) for mature singles. Response to the singles policy has been strong, despite the substantial prices Passages tends to charge for most of its trips, cruises, and tours.

So why aren't they cheaper? With such huge resources and immense followings, the senior-citizen specialists are capable of achieving major price breakthroughs for their elderly clientele. The disquieting thing is that they don't.

In the area of extended stays, a well-known nonspecialist, **Sun Holidays, 26 6th Street, Stamford, CT 06905 (phone 203/323-1166, or toll free 800/243-2057),** takes persons of all ages to modern, apartment-hotels on Spain's Costa del Sol, in winter, for a charge per month (the first month) of $765 per person, including round-trip air fare from New York on Iberia Airlines. Two of the major senior-citizen specialists (I am of course excluding Elderhostel) charge $855 and $1,124 for virtually the same one-month stay (although the $1,124 tour includes a night, with meals, in London at both the start and end of the trip, and a slightly larger apartment). The senior-citizen companies also include insurance worth about $30.

In the field of escorted motorcoach tours, the well-known **Trafalgar Tours,** selling to young and old alike, charges $1,399 for a 16-day tour of Britain, air fare included, and $1,449 for a classic 18-day tour of Europe, air fare included. Two of the major senior-citizen specialists (I am again excluding Elderhostel) charge $1,498 and $1,895 for a shorter, 15-day tour of Britain, air fare included, and one charges $2,350 for a quite similar 18-day tour of Europe, air fare included. While hotels on the highest priced of these tours are marginally better than Trafalgar's, they do not support (in my opinion) a differential of that magnitude; and most other features of the tours are similar.

Should companies be surcharging the senior citizen by $100 to $400 per person for the right to travel only with other senior citizens? Shouldn't older Americans, of all people, enjoy the lowest of travel costs? Especially when they are dealing directly with the tour operator, saving that company a travel agent's commission?

In private conversations, travel industry people will speculate as to whether the senior-citizen companies are relieved of normal competitive pricing pressures by the semi-captive nature of their clientele—who have no independent travel counselor to steer them to a cheaper course. Whether or not this is so—whether, as the companies claim, their tours are worthier because of their attention to needs of the elderly—those prices quite obviously need analysis, and perhaps revision.

A Guide to Mature Travel, I

When I was barely 22, at the time of the Korean War, the long arm of Uncle Sam plucked me from law school, dressed me in khaki, and flung me to Europe. That was 34 years ago, and I've been travelling ever since. First in the army, and then as the author or publisher of more than 70 travel guides, I've journeyed to foreign continents like other people commute to the suburbs—daily, weekly, unremittingly, traversing millions of miles to nearly 100 nations.

Have I learned anything from all this? As a mature adult, do I travel differently from when I was younger? You bet I do! With age comes travel wisdom, and wisdom consists of life-improving rules and reflections, healthy lessons for future conduct. In my case, I now vacation better than I ever did before, by following 12 basic courses of mature travel:

1. *I combat jet lag by going to sleep immediately upon arrival.* Time was when I would "hit the streets" after an overnight ocean crossing and go dashing into museums and shops, enjoying that false sense of vigor that the excitement of a foreign land often brings. No longer. As the years have passed, jet lag becomes

As a mature adult, do I travel differently from when I was younger? You bet I do! With age comes travel wisdom. . . .

Arthur then

harder, not easier, to overcome, and the mature traveller who fails to nap on arrival becomes so overly tired as to be unable to sleep—and thus condemned to a "white night" and disoriented fatigue thereafter —when evening falls. Having tried every "jet lag" diet and routine ever suggested, I now simply pass up that immediate round of sightseeing and instead go immediately to sleep for a few hours upon arriving at my overseas hotel (and this, regardless of whether I've been able to sleep on the plane). In midafternoon, upon arising, I devote the few remaining hours of daylight to casual, relaxed activity, and then fall asleep again for a fresh, full night of rest. While, to some, I may be "wasting" my first full day in London or Bangkok or Seoul, I have instead, to my mind, achieved the transition to a new time zone; I have regained a clear head and make more effective use of the days ahead; I do not wander like a zombie in my first week abroad, as do so many younger travel zealots who go charging off their overnight flight to the counters at Harrod's or the halls of the Louvre. Frommer's time-tested, mature remedy for jet fatigue? Go to sleep!

2. *I prepare for my trips with histories and art appreciations, more than with guidebooks.* In my early years of travel I thought nothing of flinging myself to the most remote, exotic foreign

AT THE AGE OF 56, I FOLLOW 12 NEW APPROACHES TO VACATIONS AND TOURS THAT IMPROVE UPON MY TRAVELS OF EARLIER YEARS

destinations without spending so much as a single evening in a library studying the history and culture of the places I was about to visit. Result: I arrived in Zurich, or Cairo, or New Delhi, literally as an untutored ignoramus, confused and bewildered, unable to discern the age or history of the structures about me, puzzled by the comments of people or the lectures of tour guides, failing to derive 90% of the enjoyment—and intellectual growth—that could have been mine had I come mentally equipped. No more. I now prepare for my trips. I approach them with mature deliberation, without youthful impetuousness. If I am going to the Far East, I read about the concepts and institutions of Buddhism. If I am off to the cities of Germany or France, I refresh my

> **I shed that juvenile modesty and bargain at the drop of a hat, openly, unabashedly, proudly.**

Arthur now

memory about the history and evolution of the Gothic Cathedral. If I am visiting Scandinavia, I read appropriate articles about the provocative new social experiments of the Danes, the Swedes, the Finns. Although I consult the practical guidebooks for hotels and shops, I spend far more time reading about the political developments, contemporary achievements, cultural treasures, historical trends, in the cities or countries I am about to see. I arrive with an advance framework for understanding. And through this mature preparation, my trips at the age of 56 have become infinitely more meaningful than those headlong travel flings into the unknown that proved so painfully confusing, and ultimately lacking in satisfaction, when I was 22.

3. *I pack less and enjoy more.* Youthful vanity once dictated that I bring an outfit for every conceivable and far-fetched social occasion. Yuppie morals required that I avoid repeating an item of apparel on successive days. I traveled like a beast of burden, with multiple suitcases, collapsing in sweat at every hotel, laboriously packing and unpacking suitcases of unwashed laundry, carting about trendy sports jackets, or dress shoes, or silk neckties never once worn in the course of a trip. No more. Just as I now accept that I will never be president of the United States, so does my increasing age cause me to reject unjustified travel expectations: I've come to peace with the probability that I will not be invited to a garden party on my two-week holiday to Spain; that I will not attend the sold-out opera in Sydney or Vienna; that I will not be asked to meet the Queen. I no longer pack with those possibilities in mind. And as for the repeated use of the same pieces of cloth-

NO MATURE STOMACH CAN POSSIBLY TOLERATE AN ENDLESS ROUTINE OF THOSE OVERLY RICH, OVERLY SAUCED RESTAURANT MEALS ABROAD

ing, I rejoice in the mature wisdom of doing exactly that! I bring a quarter of what I used to, pack only one replacement set of underwear, socks, and sport shirts, wash them out in my hotel room at night, travel with a single, medium-size suitcase half full, and thus go about the world with more "youthful" freedom and lighthearted independence than certain popinjays of the new generation, who groan under the weight of their self-imposed fashion needs!

4. *I equip myself with the names and addresses of competent, English-speaking physicians.* No longer the eternal optimist about health and illness, I travel ready for that unsettling event—becoming ill in a foreign land—that sooner or later always occurs as you travel through the mature years. And sometimes it occurs on safari in far-off Kenya,

> I take advantage of the single most significant phenomenon in travel: the utterly perishable nature of rooms and airplane or cruise tickets.

or in an isolated village in the south of France, or in the remote suburbs of Rio. A doctor arrives, his command of English shaky, his competence questionable; he prescribes for you, and yet you become sicker and sicker as the trip proceeds, until a new doctor is summoned; he visibly recoils as he reads the prescription of the earlier savant, cancels it forthwith, and brings you back to health. This, believe it or not, has happened to me on two occasions in my recent travels, once because the first physician's command of English was insufficient to catch the nuances of the symptoms I described; once because the doctor in question was simply a dolt.

I now phone up my own doctor on the eve of a trip and obtain his recommendations of a colleague or two in the places I am about to visit. If he has none to suggest, I contact the life-saving **International Association for Medical Assistance to Travellers (IAMAT), 417 Center Street, Lewiston, NY 14092 (phone 716/754-4883),** and obtain their list of capable, well-trained, English-fluent doctors in every major tourist destination. And ever since I've achieved the mental calm that comes from such a list, I have never once become sick again in the course of my travels!

5. *I bargain over the prices of travel purchases.* In my 20s, 30s, and 40s I regarded the act of bargaining as beneath youthful dignity, something for hysterical fishwives or tobacco auctioneers, but certainly not for proud young achievers like me. What errant nonsense! As I've grown wiser to the ways of the world—seen the rampant rebating and discounting in the travel industry, the notorious last-minute "sales" and cut-rate disposal of rooms, seats, and cabins, the ability of tour oper-

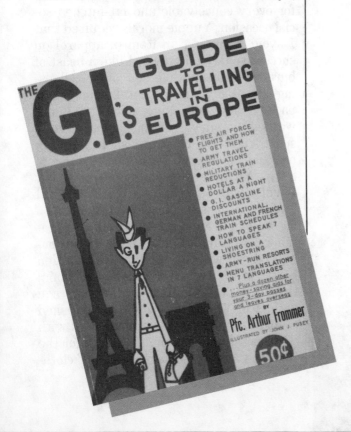

ators to negotiate the rates in half for purchasers of travel "packages"—I now shed that juvenile modesty and bargain at the drop of a hat, openly, unabashedly, proudly. I walk to a hotel counter and announce that I am looking for a room, "but only if it costs less than $45." And somehow, mysteriously, such a room is found for me.

With the years, I've learned that attitudes toward bargaining are all in the mind; that bargaining is neither degrading, demeaning, nor humiliating; that it can be done courteously and without loss of face. By acting like a smart senior determined not to waste money, I now take advantage of the single most significant phenomenon in travel: the utterly perishable nature of all hotel rooms, charter-airplane seats, and cruise-ship cabins. Since these items are a complete loss to their owners if unsold for a particular date or departure, such people react favorably to requests for discounts if that is the course required to sell off their last remaining rooms, seats, or berths. "Ask and it shall be given," says ancient wisdom. As a mature traveller, rid of my youthful modesty, I now ask—and it is given more often than you'd ever expect!

6. *I take one meal a day "picnic style."* Entering into my mid-40s, travelling all the while, it slowly dawned on me that no mature stomach could possibly tolerate an endless routine of those overly rich, overly sauced restaurant meals abroad. As metabolism slowed and waistline increased, I resolved—and have ever since succeeded—to make one meal a day out of simple, cold ingredients purchased in a foreign grocery or delicatessen and consumed from a park bench, a river's bank, or in the privacy of my hotel room. In this

The mature traveller who fails to nap on arrival becomes so overly tired as to be unable to sleep—and thus condemned to a "white night" and disoriented fatigue thereafter—when evening falls.

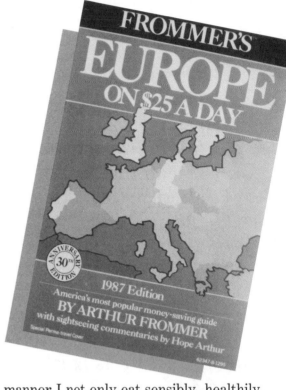

manner I not only eat sensibly, healthily, and cheaply—but better! Why? Because the ingredients of a picnic meal overseas are a gourmet's delight, almost always superior to the same food items enjoyed at home. It is a fact, as unfortunate as it may be, that the quality of the bread, for instance, found in nearly every foreign country, is superior to the bread we bake in the United States. The same for pâtés, cheeses, fresh olives, tomatoes, local red wine—all the other ingredients that make up those memorable picnic-style meals consumed while travelling in foreign climes. I now invariably have a simple, cold lunch from items I've purchased at a grocery counter abroad, and then wait patiently until evening to dig into those garlicky escargots or escalopes, those subtly flavored fish fillets swimming in sauce au vin blanc, or juicy tournedos doused with sauce béarnaise. Mature travel has taught me that meals like that can be had with safety perhaps once a day, but never twice!

Rules 7 through 12 of "mature travel"? Turn the page.

A Guide to Mature Travel, II

Though it may seem like a dream come true, a life devoted to constant, unending, almost-weekly foreign travel isn't nearly as romantic as you might think, dear readers: it is fiercely fatiguing (listen to me complain!), full of both tedium and mishaps, disorienting. And it gets harder, not easier, as you move into the mature years—as I am now doing, at the age of 56. In the first part of this discussion, I wrote that a lifetime of near-continuous travel had at last caused me

to adopt 12 totally new approaches to my trips, wholly different from the rash fashion in which I used to fling myself abroad. Specifically, I now (1) combat jet lag by going to sleep immediately on arrival, (2) prepare myself culturally for the cities I'm about to visit, (3) pack less and enjoy more, (4) equip myself in advance with the names of competent, English-speaking physicians at the destination, (5) bargain over the prices of travel purchases, and (6) take one meal a day "picnic style."

What else do I do? Read on!

7. *I bring along a small but select assortment of travel products.* And I emphasize the reference to "small"; the aver-

My mature travel tastes are for the places as yet uninundated by commercial tourism.

age trip requires only a handful of tiny gadgets or medicines, but smart older tourists are clear about what they should be: eyeshades to ensure your continued morning sleep when sunlight invades the room and easily pierces middle-aged eyelids; earplugs to blot out the occasional snores of your travel companion; a small immersion heater for that late-night coffee indulgence; Tums or Maalox for indigestion; Lomatil for greater upsets. And, of course, adapters and converters for enabling your electric appliances (travel

Arthur in Berlin, 1955

irons, hair dryers, and the like) to work on foreign currents and in foreign sockets. Don't take another thing! The traveller who arrives in London or Paris—birthplaces of the pharmacy—with suitcases of Band-Aids, Kleenex, and iodine, is simply woefully uninformed about the highly developed state of most foreign capitals; even Katmandhu has a late-night drugstore!

RULES 7 THROUGH 12 OF PAINFULLY ACQUIRED VACATION WISDOM

But there is one final product that mature travellers will almost always procure in advance of arrival abroad: comfortable walking shoes, even ultra-comfortable walking shoes, however unsightly the latter may be. Cushioned, crepe-soled shoes, even some of the new cushioned running shoes, are travel footwear rarely found on youthful feet—but they're the losers for all of that! When one has marched for miles on the uneven cobblestones of a medieval city, or sloshed along the muddy paths of a Bangkok, or shuffled through the yellow clay of Aswan or Abu Simbel, one begins to envy those senior citizens who have rejected style and conformity in favor of bouncy, springy, comfy, molded walking shoes.

8. *I acquire, in advance of departure, the names and addresses of people to look up at the destination.* Ultimately, the experienced traveller concludes that people are the highlight of any vacation trip —people in the form of foreign residents with whom one converses by chance on a train or in a café, and who sometimes invite you to their homes. We all know that these are the single most memorable events of travel, yet in our early trips abroad we approach such contacts helter-skelter, without a plan. After many years of random approaches to people, I now devote time to ensuring that such encounters will in fact take place. I pester friends, associates, or relatives for the names of their own acquaintances in the cities I am about to visit. If I have more time, I apply for the names of people who have indicated to several nonprofit organizations that they are willing to provide hospitality in their own home cities to visitors from overseas. Among such groups are **Servas, 11 John Street, New**

A lifetime of near-continuous travel has at last caused me to adopt a new approach to my trips, wholly different from the rash fashion in which I used to fling myself abroad.

Arthur in Mallorca, 1955

York, NY 10038 (phone 212/267-0252), or INNter Lodging Co-Op, P.O. Box 7044, Tacoma, WA 98407, or Visiting Friends, Inc., P.O. Box 231, Lake Jackson, TX 77566. With maturity, with the personal humility that comes with years, I now want to know what other inhabitants of this planet are thinking, and I value the chance to meet them as a supreme travel goal, fully as important as the many minor museums and lifeless monuments to which the younger tourists are madly dashing.

9. *I make use of government tourist offices and "institutes."* In the early years of travel we tend to be "do-it-yourselfers," arriving in cities without advance information of any sort, stumbling from festival to festival without knowing their dates, bereft of addresses, learning only from hard knocks and chance discoveries. It only gradually occurs to us, as the

years unfold, that every major city, every island, every country seeking to attract tourists, maintains offices in the United States for the purpose of aiding would-be visitors to their land. And only then do we write to these entities for lists of hotels and private homes, events and services, the advance information that proves such a balm to mature travel. The most experienced of travellers actually pay visits to these government tourist offices, in New York and Miami, in Chicago and Los Angeles.

Such was the "wisdom" I finally acquired after, say, 20-or-so years of aimless travel. I'm even more ashamed to disclose that it was only in the past two years that I became aware of a parallel organization—the government "institutes"—that most nations maintain, some with offices in the United States, others only in their home capitals (for which addresses will be provided by the tourist offices). Unlike the tourist offices, these have the broad goal of promoting their nation's culture and image by assisting the formation of study tours, or by scheduling appointments and interviews with experts for travellers pursuing special interests in their countries. By simply writing to the Swedish Institute, or the Danish Institute, the British Council, the Institut Français, or any number of others, Americans can obtain the most extraordinary free assistance toward meeting and conversing with the single most accomplished individuals in those nations, enjoying a "program" of timed interviews with professors, government officials, technicians, and artists. By taking the time to do just that in my latter-day trips, I've experienced the most profound forms of mature travel. You can do the same.

10. *I stay calm and roll with the travel "punches."* If maturity teaches anything, it is that the world is a turbulent place filled with people who often err— especially in travel. Uncertainties and omissions, delays and goofs, are an inherent element in travel, and part of what makes the activity so dynamic and appealing. How dull the world would be if all the countries in it hummed and purred and worked like Switzerland! Recognizing this, I no longer rant and rail when the airport clerk announces a two-hour delay; I whip out a paperback book and savor an interlude of leisure. I no longer gnash teeth and feel the ground swaying underfoot when the hotelier admits an overbooking; having experienced the futility of protesting against such a situation on so many occasions, I ascribe it all to "karma" and, Zen-like, begin calmly exploring the alternatives. In short, I now accept the inevitable vagaries of vacations, and travel to undeveloped and inefficient lands precisely because they are so unlike the mechanical society we know at home. If the point of life is simply to enjoy an uneventful, slumbering routine, then why travel? Maturity, instead, is the acceptance of the improbable and unexpected, the spice of life; and mature travellers stay relaxed and unperturbed in the face of unscheduled problems.

11. *I buy various forms of cheap travel insurance before departing on a foreign trip.* I never did so when I first travelled, but oh, how I learned, I learned! Travel, let me tell you, is a complex activity in which many things can and sometimes do

WE'VE SEEN THE WORLD AS NONE OF OUR FOREBEARS COULD, AND WE CAN CONTINUE TO DO SO—EVEN BETTER—INTO OUR MATURE YEARS

go wrong. Luggage is lost or misplaced. Strikes or weather delay your return flight. Cables arrive advising of the illness of a relative at home, requiring that you prematurely cut short your trip, forfeiting hotel deposits or the benefit of your return air ticket. The door of a Paris subway closes on your arm, severely bruising it.

The financial consequences of each of these potential mishaps can be offset by various forms of inexpensive travel insurance, yet only a tiny fraction of all American travellers ever buy such policies before departing on a trip. Youthful optimism is one explanation. Youthful inexperience or confusion about the whereabouts of such policies is another. The mature traveller, by contrast, takes time to survey the field, and soon discovers that both Citicorp and BankAmerica travelers checks are currently making available quite respectable policies (covering baggage, trip interruption, and trip accident losses) for as little as $8.50 total per person; you simply apply for the policies in the same transaction at the bank in which you purchase your traveller's checks. With rates so low, and policies so accessible, no mature traveller should ever forgo the peace of mind, and real protection, afforded by reputable travel insurance; and that, too, is a lesson derived from three decades of travel all over the world.

12. *I avoid the heavily touristed and opt for the undiscovered.* Finally, having had my fill of all the massively popular destinations—the Londons and the Acapulcos, the Romes and the Honolulus— my mature travel tastes are for the places as yet uninundated by commercial tourism: the Bonaires and Nova Scotias, the

Ultimately, the experienced traveller concludes that people are the highlight of any vacation trip and takes time to ensure that encounters with people will take place.

Maltas and the peninsulas of Jutland. Give me a beach where I alone lie sheltered by a waving palm, reading a paperback classic undisturbed by chattering charterloads of people. Take me to the village cafés whose patrons look up startled but genuinely pleased to see an outsider in their midst. Show me the shopkeeper for whom a tourist is still an event! There remain such places on earth, and the mature traveller searches them out. We've learned, with age and experience, how tawdry and dull are the contrived nightspots, souvenir shops and mindless tours of the mass-volume cities and resorts. We crave good music, not discos; good talk, not loudspeaker commentaries; good companionship, not crowds. And we find these in the quieter spots not yet on the tourist map.

Think back on it: your fondest travel memories are of the islands and towns where you arrived before the others did, where prices and amenities were gently human in scale, where residents smiled as you approached. In the last analysis, mature travel consists of continuing to act as a travel pioneer, always seeking out the new, keeping juices and spirits flowing, pursuing the dream of discovery and challenge, retaining the very best form of "youth," that of an ever-questing open mind.

Travel: it is today an essential requisite for a civilized life. We who are now in our mature years have been the first generation in history to enjoy travel in its fullest. With jet airplanes at our disposal, crossing from continent to continent in a few short hours, we've seen the world as none of our forebears could, and we can continue to do so—even better—into our mature years.

Travelling Alone in the Mature Years— Plight or Opportunity?

*O*ut-of-breath and weary, I end my eager speech—that overlong lecture on travel that I deliver, somewhere, each month—and throw open discussion to the floor. Within four minutes, never more, it comes, that inevitable, inescapable, and utterly harrowing question: "Can a single woman travel safely, and enjoyably, alone?"

Amazing how persistent the inquiry, how it reveals a major, near-universal concern among a large portion of all potential travellers.

The questioner is usually a widow in her late middle age, her forehead furrowed with worry. She explains that she and her husband had enjoyed memorable trips abroad, that travel for her is a cherished activity, but that now she is anxious, even frightened, about undertaking further journeys on her own.

As she talks, a nervous movement occurs in the auditorium among men of a similar age. Though they—the men—never initiate the question, they now lean forward in rapt attention, concentrating on every word. And suddenly it is obvious: the problem is not confined to women; the question should be rephrased to ask: "Can a single woman, or a single man, travel enjoyably alone? And can this be done at a mature age?"

Before discussing the ways to travel alone, it's important to note that you don't have to.

The glib response

Though my answer, generally, is "Yes," I wish I could state it with greater conviction than I do. But the issue is complex, surrounded by ifs, perhapes, and maybes.

In this respect I differ from a great many more impulsive travel lecturers who teach one-evening courses at urban night schools, under the title "Traveling Solo: The Joys of Going It Alone." These people claim that we should always travel unaccompanied, even if we don't have to. Why? Because such is the road to romance and adventure, to chance encounters with foreign citizens, invitations to foreign homes. And the practice, as they tell it, is deliciously selfish: you do only what you

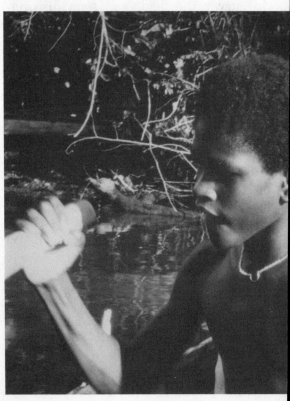

THE PROBLEM IS NOT CONFINED TO WOMEN; THE QUESTION SHOULD BE REPHRASED TO ASK: "CAN A SINGLE WOMAN, OR A SINGLE MAN, TRAVEL ENJOYABLY ALONE? AND CAN THIS BE DONE AT A MATURE AGE?"

desire, without compromise. You do not alter your itinerary or schedule to suit the tastes of another human being. For the first time in your life, you are Free.

The message of these trendy singles (almost all in their mid-20s) is of course based on the assumption that a compatible travel companion doesn't exist; that, almost as if by some law of nature, two people travelling together must necessarily have widely divergent views, inclinations, and tastes. Having themselves never experienced true friendship, love, or compatibility, they proclaim the resounding advantage of travelling alone.

I can't go quite that far. For surely, only the most naïve pollyanna can believe that the pleasure of travelling with a cherished companion—the joy of sharing

reactions to renowned sights and experiences—can now be duplicated or replaced in the absence of that person. At best they can be experienced differently, with adequate enjoyment, but not usually with the profound satisfactions of discovering them in the company of a like-minded friend.

The alternatives to solitude

Therefore, before I discuss the ways to enjoy a solitary holiday trip, to "make a go" of travelling alone, it's important to note that you don't have to. By simply mailing $5 for a three-year membership in the Saga Holidays Club operated by **Saga International Holidays Ltd., 120 Boylston Street, Boston, MA 02116, (phone toll free 800/343-0273)**, or $5 for a similar membership in the Grand Circle Travel Club, operated by **Grand Circle Travel, Inc., 347 Congress Street, Boston, MA 12210 (phone 617/350-7500, or toll free 800/221-2610)**—both of them companies dealing exclusively in travel for mature persons—you can obtain the names of potential companions for your next trip. Both clubs distribute quarterly magazines with "Pen Pal" or "Penfriend" features listing dozens of applications by mature singles for travel partners. These, in effect, are "travel personals," but proper to a fault, and fascinating to read as they detail the varied characteristics and goals of the mature, experienced travellers submitting them.

For more extensive listings (nearly 200 "travel personals" per bimonthly publication), send $40 for a one-year subscription (but only $25 for six months) to **Partners-in-Travel, P.O. Box 491145, Los Angeles, CA 90049 (phone 213/476-4869)**. Its newsletter, issued every 60 days, is by the

AS ONE CANNY VOYAGER PUTS IT: "TRAVEL ISN'T SOMETHING YOU DO IN OLD AGE; IT IS SOMETHING YOU DO *INSTEAD OF* OLD AGE"

irrepressible Miriam Tobolowsky, who attracts a zestful following and ads peppered with jaunty exhortations: "Let's go—life is for living!" One recent listing assures that the applicant is "caring and considerate, but won't hover. Want ardent traveller who travels light, dependable driver, honest and open communication, brisk walker." Though Partners-in-Travel does not limit its services to mature persons, a full 70% of its subscribers appear to be over 50, most in their 60s.

And for a near-guarantee that you will find a suitable travel "match-up," but at rates varying from $3 to $11 per month (with a six-month minimum), contact **Travel Companion Exchange, P.O. Box 833, Amityville, NY 11701 (phone 516/454-0880)**, founded by the well-known travel figure, Jens Jurgen. His is the most elaborate of all travel match-up services, supplying you with literally thousands of available listings, all carefully grouped by computer into helpful categories ("special interests," "special travel plans," and the like) to enable a wise choice.

Travelling only with singles

As a substitute for seeking a travel companion, one can travel with groups consisting only of singles. The nationwide tour company known as **Passages Unlimited, Inc., 48 Union Street, Stamford, CT 06906 (phone 203/323-1441, or toll free 800/472-7724)**, which operates tours confined to those over the age of 55, now schedules certain departures on its programs—cruises, motorcoach tours, "stay-put" holidays—only for "mature singles," guaranteeing that everyone on the tour will be of that status. Such departures in 1987 were entirely sold out,

> As a substitute for seeking a travel companion, one can travel with groups consisting only of singles.

and more are scheduled for 1988. Although another long-established company, the prestigious **Singleworld Cruises & Tours, Inc., 444 Madison Avenue, New York, NY 10022 (phone 212/758-2433, or toll free 800/223-6490, 800/522-5682 in New York State)**, does not limit participation to mature persons only, its Seniorworld passengers are over 45 and its tours are only for single people. Join them and your problems of "singlehood" vanish.

Loners on Wheels, Inc., 808 Lester Street, Poplar Bluff, MO 63901, is still another travel organization confined to singles. An RV club, it forms caravans of singles only, and takes them to rallies and campouts all over the country.

Activities where it doesn't matter

Your other option is to travel abroad with groups pursuing an intense social, political, scientific, or educational purpose. In that context, the fact that some are singles, some couples, becomes of minor significance: people are engaged in a communal activity, living helter-skelter in improvised or group lodgings, so intent on their work that they mix and mingle to an extraordinary extent.

The study tours operated by the famous **Elderhostel, 80 Boylston Street, Boston, MA 02116 (phone 617/426-7788)**, are that kind of program. Elderhostel sends people over the age of 60 to attend one- to three-week classroom courses of instruction in the U.S. and around the world, using university residence halls—sometimes even dormitories, segregated by sex—for lodgings. It makes no guarantee of single or double rooms, charges one standard fee without single supplement, and thereby attracts a heavy number of singles to its continually fascinating curriculum (singles make up a full 30% of Elderhostel's volume, and two-thirds of those singles are women). But because Elderhostel passengers are focused so intently on ideas outside of themselves, the fact that they are alone or accompanied dwindles in importance, fades from consciousness; and people glory in the camaraderie and joint activities of the entire group.

The trips sponsored by **Earthwatch, P.O. Box 403, Watertown, MA 02172 (phone 617/926-8200),** are also that sort of program. It sends its volunteers on scientific research projects (tagging fish, measuring acid rain, interviewing rural residents), making use of a catch-as-catch-can array of housing accommodations (local schools and community centers, tents, and private homes) in which people are lodged as conditions permit. Its charges ("contributions") are one uniform flat fee, with no single supplement, and the composition of its "teams" is heavily slanted to singles. "We were an unlikely group," wrote one recent Earthwatch participant, ". . . a history teacher from Ohio, a Long Island college student, a retired real estate investor from Arizona. . . ."

Similar in character, largely erasing the distinction between couples and singles, and attracting a heavy percentage of singles, are the "adventure tours" (camping safaris, treks in Nepal and the Andes, outdoor nature expeditions) sponsored by an increasing number of tour operators. Though they require a certain minimum vigor (but less than you might think), they cater to people of all ages, attract a heavy turnout of mature singles, and house them in tents or improvised accommodations. Scan the catalogues of **Over-**

> Your other option is to travel abroad with groups pursuing an intense social, political, scientific, or educational purpose. In that context, the fact that some are singles, some couples, becomes of minor significance.

seas Adventure Travel, 6 Bigelow Street, Cambridge, MA 02139 (phone 617/876-0533, or toll free 800/221-0814)—which carried an 82-year-old woman on a recent camping safari to Tanzania—or **Sobek Expeditions, Inc., P.O. Box 1089, Angels Camp, CA 95222 (phone 209/736-4524),** for additional examples of purposive trips in which all participants became undifferentiated members of a cohesive group, without regard to marital status. The same applies to volunteer "workcamp" tours engaging in socially conscious projects around the world: contact **VFP International Workcamps, Tiffany Road, Belmont, VT 05370 (phone 802/259-2759),** and specify the trips open to all ages), or to politically oriented trips, some heavily feminist in nature, organized by such as **Schilling Travel Service, Inc., 722 Second Avenue South, Minneapolis, MN 55402 (phone 612/332-1100).**

While all such trips appeal to only a segment of the mature audience, they provide the perfect antidote to the "single travel blues."

It is primarily—let me suggest—on the standard, traditional trips, with their single supplements and couples-only atmosphere, that the problems of travelling alone are most sharply felt.

Enjoying the standard trips

So how, then, do you travel alone for normal sightseeing or recreational purposes? How, as a mature single person, do you best vacation in new lands, or travel to visit important cultural exhibits or simply to refresh the mind and body?

The problem centers on that edifice known as a hotel—that ultimately boring and impersonal institution, with its inescapable "single surcharges." (One wise

observer recently speculated that Hell consists of being condemned to stay, unto eternity, in a different modern hotel each night.)

The obvious solution is to avoid the use of standard hotels, and replace them with a people-friendly form of lodgings. Staying with families while abroad serves the triple purpose of avoiding loneliness, gaining new friendships and insights, and lowering costs: you not only escape from that burdensome single supplement, but start from a radically lower base of costs. Indeed, some mature singles even lower their lodgings expense to zero by joining the public-spirited, worldwide membership of **Servas, 11 John Street, Suite 706, New York, NY 10038, (phone 212/267-0252)**, which believes that free and frequent people-to-people contacts, through home visits, serve the cause of world peace. On the eve of a trip, they obtain from Servas the names and addresses of families in every major city who have expressed their willingness to receive other Servas members into their homes (for short stays) free of charge, because they believe in the profound moral aspect of such hospitality.

Other mature singles opt for a more commercial form of homestay, but inexpensive and without the single supplement, by utilizing the services of homestay organizations in every major country. For a comprehensive list of several dozen national homestay organizations (and of other interesting travel activities), send $4.95 (plus $1 for postage and handling) to **Pilot Books, 103 Cooper Street, Babylon, NY 11702,** for a copy of the 72-page *Vacations with a Difference.* This little book lists homestays in Canada, France, Australia, Tahiti, and Scandinavia; homestays with Unitarians, humanists, Mennonites, and Quakers; homestays with farmers and wine growers; homestays for as little as $85 a week, including all meals. What you yourself may have done as a teenager—a month and more abroad with a foreign family—is now available in your mature years, and for reasons obvious and profound, no other travel experience quite compares to it.

The most relaxed and adventurous of mature singles stay in youth hostels both here and abroad, now that the international youth-hostel organization has removed all maximum-age restrictions on the right to use their facilities. Particularly in the fall and winter months, when young people are in school, the predominant clientele of many youth hostels is today middle-aged and elderly! But even when one shares these multibedded rooms or dorms with young people, one pays a standard, uniform, and very inexpensive charge, without a single supplement. And one stays in a lively setting of international conversations and encounters. For information contact **American**

Youth Hostels, Inc., P.O. Box 37613, Washington, DC 20013 (phone 202/783-6161).

One rather affluent and mature U.S. lawyer of my acquaintance, who has travelled extensively by herself in the South Pacific, actually favors hostels, though she could afford much better. "They offer a wonderful way to meet people, including local people travelling in their own country," she points out. "The kitchen is a great social center, with perhaps 12 people each attempting to cook dinner for one—a hilarious scene. By the time the various dinners are ready, you're all old friends."

Revising your attitudes

If, despite this advice, you're determined to keep going on the standard trips and to use standard hotels, you may need a new mental outlook for coping with the problems of solitary travel—a confident and positive outlook. Though I was careful to stress, at the outset, my own view that travelling in twos is usually superior to travelling alone, there are nonetheless some attractive aspects to the latter experience.

You might regard that first experience as a zesty challenge, a chance to shape yourself for the better. Whatever your usual personality, you must of necessity attempt to be more outgoing and convivial.

Introduce yourself to the people around you. Ask other tourists for advice on restaurants and sights. Suggest the sharing of a meal at some celebrated establishment. Just as the same human necessities breed invention, so travelling by oneself often leads to increased openness, receptivity to new people and ideas, greater

> Because Elderhostel passengers are focused so intently on ideas outside of themselves, the fact that they are alone or accompanied dwindles in importance; and people glory in the camaraderie and joint activities of the entire group.

self-assurance and pride.

Among some single travellers—certainly not all, but some—the experience soon takes on a mood of surprised exhilaration. They find they're more sensitive to the people and culture of the destination. The absence of a familiar companion removes them from the familiar cocoon of their own language and culture, and teaches them a new language, a new culture. (And, incidentally, travelling alone is the fastest—some say the best—way to learn another language).

These new solitary travellers become less self-conscious. After that first nerve-wracking dinner alone in a large hotel restaurant—when every eye seems focused, accusingly, on them—they suddenly realize that in reality no one is terribly concerned with or interested in the fact that they are dining alone. It is a liberating bit of knowledge. On all subsequent evenings they bring a book or magazine to the dinner table, and revel in the luxury of thus relaxing at a high-quality meal.

Though it may not be all that it once was, travelling while alone is soon recognized to be immeasurably more satisfying than the alternative: moping at home alone. And with every succeeding trip, the experience gains in pleasure, ease, and depth; it keeps us alive. As that canny voyager (Miriam Tobolowsky) who operates Partners in Travel puts it: "Travel isn't something you do in old age; it is something you do *instead* of old age."

Travel is thus far too important to be dispensed with when a companion is unavailable; it is part of a civilized life, our birthright. The most vital of our fellow humans travel, whether alone or not—and so should you!

Some Travel Options—Good, Bad, and Indifferent—for the Mature American

Maybe it's my widening girth, my whitening hair, my increasing nostalgia for "slow music." But the travels of senior citizens interest me more and more, and provoke these comments on recent developments:

That 10% lure: Call me a grouch, but I'm not impressed with the discounts for mature travellers offered by most hotel chains and airlines. In the majority of cases these consist of 10% reductions off room rate or air fare. Since that's the exact amount that hotels and airlines pay out to travel agents, and since most senior citizen travel programs require (in effect) that passengers avoid the use of travel agents in making reservations, the hotels and airlines are frequently saving 10% on their senior citizen programs—and then simply passing on that 10% saving to the senior citizen.

In other words, they're not spending a red cent to obtain their senior business. Which seems a bit chintzy.

Does anyone do better by America's elderly? A few do. And they deserve acclaim as a means of nudging the others to do more. Here's a sampling:

Sheraton Hotels: Though they caution that the discount can be withheld during periods of peak business, and is not applicable to minimum-rate rooms, most Sheratons give a 25% discount to persons 60 years of age and older.

Ramada Inns: Many (about half) give

Entertainment, accommodations, and three grand repasts daily are provided for one fixed and remarkably low price.

the same 25% off to persons 60 and up.

Marriott Hotels: At more than 100 Marriotts in the U.S., Europe, and the Caribbean, a 50% discount off regular weekday rates is given to persons 62 years of age and older, and 25% off on lunches and dinners (the latter whether you're a guest or not). Reductions are subject to availability and occasional seasonal close-outs, and require advance reservations at the reduced rate.

La Quinta Inns: Offer 15% off to people age 55 and older.

Holiday Inns: Give 15% off weekday, 25% off weekend rates to guests 55 and older who belong to their Travel Venture Club (P.O. Box 7642, Mt. Prospect, IL 60056).

Days Inns: From 10% to 50% (usually 15%) off at 536 participating inns, to members (50 years and older) of their September Days Club; send $12 to **September Days Club, P.O. Box 4001, Harlan, IA 51593 (phone toll free 800/241-5050).**

Howard Johnson's: Take 15% off for seniors 60 years and older at more than 85% of the nation's H.J. hotels.

As for the airlines, some of them also confine their senior-citizen discounts to 10% and simply pass on the 10% they've saved by subtly influencing senior citizens to book direct. To add insult to injury, they then charge a $25 "membership" fee to enjoy that 10% off, and a $100 charge for the "companion" who accompanies the senior (American Airlines' "Senior SAAvers Club" and Continental's "Golden Travellers Club" are typical examples; United Airlines' "Silver Wings Plus" charges $50 for life membership, but does give two $25 travel certificates good for the first year, in addition to the standard 10% discount). In fairness, they also pro-

AS THE TRAVEL INDUSTRY SCRAMBLES TO WIN OVER THE SENIOR CITIZEN, A MIXED BAG OF PROGRAMS EMERGES

vide self-promoting newsletters and diverse other discounts and features. Braniff, in handsome, contrasting style, gives 15% off to travellers 65 and older, and asks no fee. TWA sells coupon booklets or yearly $1,399 passes entitling the senior citizen to unlimited domestic travel for one year; international flights are an add-on option.

Such programs have been overtaken by events. The introduction of radically reduced "MaxSaver" fares, and the continuation of "Super-Saver" fares—as little as $49 to fairly distant points—lessens the worth of these programs considerably. Unless one travels with absurd frequency, it is often cheaper simply to pay individual advance-purchase rates than to commit to the use of a yearly pass.

Clearly, unless the airlines devise new programs keyed to the levels of, and kept below, their own "Saver" fares, they must —in my view— brace for outcries of protest from seniors who purchased their fixed-price coupons or year-long passes.

Rehearsals for Retirement: Happier news—of a bright, new use of holiday travel to scout potential sites for retirement. Though the idea is obvious, it's easier said than done.

When middle-aged people go off to test the retirement attractions of Florida or Arizona, of Costa Rica or Cuernavaca, they often return as uncertain as when they left. Simply to look at a retirement area is not to ensure that you obtain reliable, relevant information about its suitability for retirement. For the latter, you need to meet with real estate people and lawyers, with municipal officials and other retirees.

So reasoned Jane Parker, a retired schoolteacher of Saratoga, California.

> Call me a grouch, but I'm not impressed with the discounts for mature travellers offered by most hotel chains and airlines.

And thereupon she formed a tour company called Retirement Explorations that performs all the advance preparations for a meaningful research trip. Arriving at the destination, her groups engage in scheduled interviews, appointments, seminars, and briefings on the pros and cons of that area's retirement possibilities. The information is supplied by on-the-spot specialists, who undergo a withering cross-examination by tour participants; the latter stay at the area's best hotels and enjoy gala dinners while doing so.

Retirement Explorations' most popular trip is to Costa Rica. Three tours are scheduled each year, in February, July, and November, and at least two of these consist of two groups at one time. The cost for ten days from Miami is $1,010, with a single supplement of $165. Groups are limited to 30 people.

Twice a year, Retirement Explorations sends groups to the Algarve coast of Portugal and Spain's Costa del Sol (on the Mediterranean). The 15-day trip is $2,020 per person, with a $260 single supplement, and can be booked by up to 40 persons per departure.

For additional information, or to book, contact **Retirement Explorations, 19414 Vineyard Lane, Saratoga, CA 95070 (phone 408/257-5378).**

A "Club Med" for Seniors: At $22 to $27 per person per day (based on double occupancy), including three meals, private facilities, and morning-till-night activities— all limited to people over the age of 60, from November until April 30—that, in a nutshell, is the pricing policy of "Florida's Club Meds" for senior citizens: three large hotels in highly desirable cities on the west coast of the Sunshine State.

DOES ANYONE DO BETTER BY AMERICA'S ELDERLY? A FEW DO, AND THEY DESERVE ACCLAIM AS A MEANS OF NUDGING THE OTHERS TO DO MORE

Unless the airlines devise new programs geared to the levels of their "MaxSaver" and "Super-Saver" fares, they must brace for outcries of protest.

These are not, of course, real "Club Meds"—that's only my term for them. The owning company is Senior Vacation Hotels of Florida, in business for 25 years —longer than any Club Med in the Western Hemisphere.

But the offerings—and atmosphere (adapted for an older generation)—are exactly that of a Club Med: you receive not only your room but also three grand repasts daily, parties, live entertainment and free movies, bus excursions, theme nights, beach trips, and more—for one fixed, and remarkably low, price.

What's the catch? Well, first, there's the required minimum age, and I should point out that most guests appear to be over the age of 65 (but they're an unusually lively lot of over-65ers). More important, you must normally stay for a minimum of one month, usually starting at the beginning of the month. Provided you do, you pay only $650 per person per month (based on double occupancy) in November, December, and April; $750 per month in January; $800 per month in February and March. A single-room supplement runs about $175 per month.

The hotels in question are the large Sunset Bay and Courtyard in St. Petersburg, the Regency Tower in Lakeland, and the Riverpark in Bradenton. For a lively four-color brochure on these veritable "Club Meds for Senior Citizens," and for application forms, contact **Senior Vacation Hotels of Florida, 7401 Central Avenue, St. Petersburg, FL 33710 (phone 813/345-8123, or toll free 800/247-2203, 800/872-3616 in Florida).**

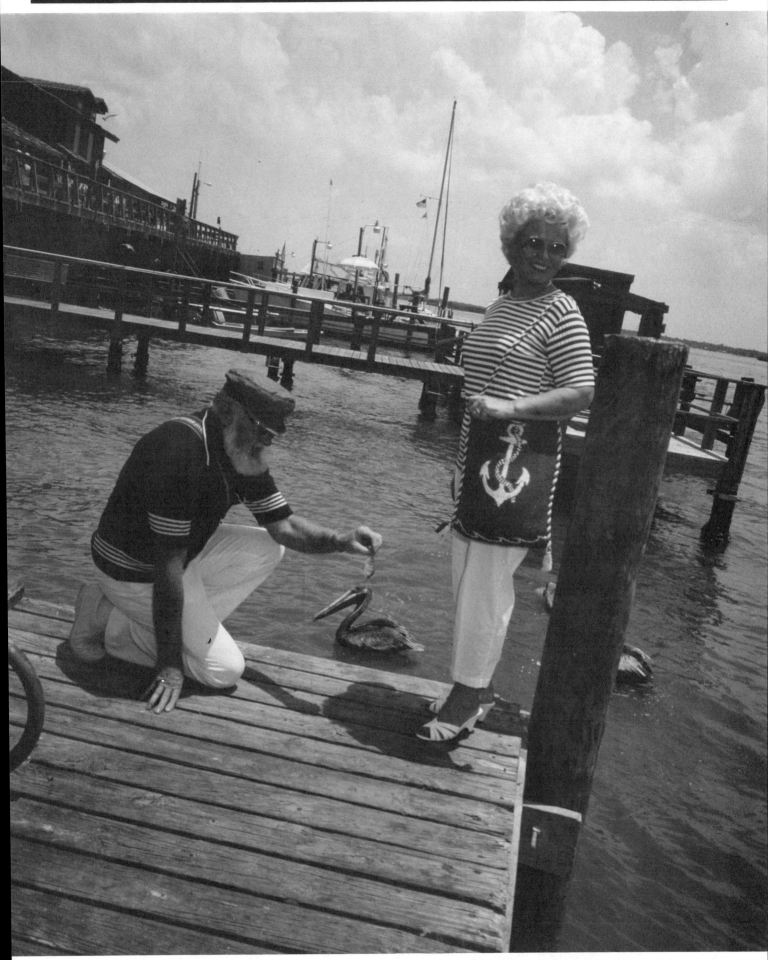

Removing the "Youth" From "Youth Hostels"

It was a mixed-up scene, to say the least. But strangely affecting. In a corner of the lounge, a middle-aged pianist sat rifling off a Schubert cadenza while a teenaged music lover turned the pages of her sheet music. At a chessboard nearby, two college students stared at their rooks and knights, while a white-haired senior offered occasional advice. And at an overstuffed couch under a notice-filled bulletin board, several eager young people sought travel advice from a couple in their 40s.

If you were now to learn that this jumbling of the generations—young with old, newly retired with newly wed—was occurring not in a school, but in a youth hostel, you'd probably be startled. Unknown as yet to the vast majority of American travellers, every youth hostel organization in the world (other than in the German state of Bavaria) has eliminated the maximum-age limitation on youth-hostel membership or the right to use youth-hostel facilities. A small but growing population of every age and condition—married and single, elderly, middle-aged, baby boomer, yuppie, and preppie—are today flocking to make use

of the cheapest lodgings and most dynamic travel facilities on earth.

And what are these structures that now accept "young people of all ages"—to use a newly coined slogan of the hostels? They range from ancient castles to modern farmhouses, from Buddhist temples to converted water mills, from rambling Victorian mansions to four-masted sailing ships to glass-walled high-rises in the center of great cities—some 5,000 hostels in all (in 60 different countries), of which 280 are here in the United States. While the beds they offer are often double-decker cots in privacy-lacking dormitories (but segregated by sex, with men in one wing, women in another), their facilities are otherwise comfortable and clean, closely supervised by "hostel parents," social, cheery, priced in pennies—and now multigenerational in clientele, as I was recently able quite personally to confirm.

The scene that began this essay was one I witnessed recently in the public areas of the Washington, D.C., youth hostel short blocks from the White House. I had arrived in Washington on a Friday afternoon, without reservations, never dreaming that every hotel in town would be sold out. They were. Shaken and dismayed, but vaguely aware of the revolution in youth-hostel policies, I rushed from the Capitol Hilton (where I had just been turned down) to the Capitol Hostel, if it could be called that. And moments later I was ensconced in a quite decent (if somewhat dreary) single room at the grand rate of $29 a night, tax included. I could have stayed in the dorms for only $10 a night.

If the locale had been Europe, Mexico, or the Far East instead of Washington,

A REVOLUTION HAS ALTERED THE CHARACTER OF THESE INEXPENSIVE LODGINGS, MAKING THEM AVAILABLE TO MATURE ADVENTURERS OF EVERY AGE

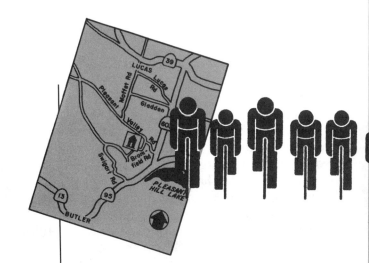

D.C., I could have enjoyed similar facilities for as little as $5, $6, or $7 a night, sometimes with breakfast included. Only in the United States, and only in the nation's capital at that, do youth-hostel prices rise to the princely levels encountered that night. Almost everywhere else they amount to a near-negligible expense, permitting seniors to enjoy a major extension of their time spent on travels.

Prior to retirement most of those seniors had money but no time. Now they have time but less money. The ability to use $6-per-person hostels instead of $50-per-person hotels suddenly enables mature citizens—even those on Social Security—to enjoy the same three-month stays abroad that many younger Americans experience on their summer vacations. How many retired Americans could undertake trips of that length if they were compelled to pay normal hotel rates on each and every night?

What brought about this revolution? Some hostelers point to the laws against age discrimination enacted in numerous enlightened countries. Some mention the growing realization by youth-hostel organizations of their need for income and patronage in those nonsummer months of the year when young people are in school and unable to use hostels. Still others suggest that the lowering of age bars, occurring gradually in different countries, came about when hostel-loving "baby boomers" approached their middle years and insisted on the right to continue using hostel accommodations. "Hosteling gets into your blood and you can't get rid of it," say Hal and Glenda Wennberg of central Maryland, who met at a hostel in 1946 and soon were husband and wife. Though the American youth-hostel orga-

nization has always, in theory, been open to people of all ages (unlike its European counterparts), it is only recently that youth hostels have openly advertised the right of seniors to join and participate. In Europe, formal decisions were required, and taken, to accomplish the same goal.

"The reason we use hostels," says an elderly hosteler and former college lecturer from Nebraska, Jane Holden, "is because hosteling is an attitude, not simply

WHETHER MARRIED OR SINGLE, ELDERLY, MIDDLE-AGED, BABY BOOMER, YUPPIE, OR PREPPIE, YOU MAY NOW MAKE USE OF THE CHEAPEST ACCOMMODATIONS ON EARTH

a source of cheap accommodations for penniless young people. That attitude never changes. To me, the finest moments of life are in meeting people from different countries and backgrounds, and extending friendship to them. Even if it means trading off a bit of comfort and privacy."

Do mature hostelers find it difficult to mix with members 40 years younger than they? "Not at all," say Edwin and Jeanne Erlanger, hostelers since the mid-1950s. "Once people work together in the kitchen or begin discussing that day's news, the barriers just fade away. Wherever it is—Japan, Austria, Mexico—the generations have far more in common than you'd think." One prominent San Francisco member of Golden Gate Youth Hostels, the sassy, 72-year-old Miriam Blaustein, is also a leading activist in the highly political Grey Panthers. "I am still as youthful mentally as I ever was!" she states. "But I know my limits. I will not exceed them, nor will I impede what the younger people are doing. My work in youth hostels is part of a broader effort against 'ageism.'"

When seniors first began using youth hostels in heavy numbers, some youth-hostel "parents" (managers) persisted in giving preference in reservations to young members; that's now ended, says Robert B. Johnson, director of American Youth Hostels, Inc.; in nine years in that position, he hasn't received a single complaint of age discrimination. Other mature guests were a bit nonplussed by the dormitories assigned to them, although many soon found that hostel managements were at pains to provide them with such private rooms as existed. Director Johnson points out that the trend in youth-hostel construction around the

They range from ancient castles to modern farmhouses, from Buddhist temples to converted water mills, from rambling Victorian mansions to four-masted sailing ships.

world is to rooms housing no more than four or five persons, and occasionally to the standard twin-bedded or single room variety.

An often-heard proposal is to formally eliminate the word "youth" from the organization's title. Though that idea was recently rejected by the organization's board of directors, individual hostels have taken steps to do just that. In the Washington, D.C., structure, the word "Youth" in a large neon sign has been replaced with the word "International"—Washington International Hostel—and staff members inside patiently explain that the "youth" in the title of their sponsoring organization means "young in spirit" or "young in outlook," and not in chronological terms of age. As if the dream of Ponce de León were finally at hand, today's mature citizens find "eternal youth" in a youth hostel.

Enter Elderhostel

But now a caution. This newly acquired ability by mature and senior citizens to make use of youth hostels should not be confused with a wholly separate program of study tours called Elderhostel. Limited to people over the age of 60 (but open as well to their spouses of any age), "Elderhostel weeks" are conducted by the Elderhostel organization of Boston, Massachusetts, at more than 1,000 universities and other educational institutions in the U.S. and abroad. Domestically, Elderhostel programs last for one week and cost $195 to $250 per person, plus air fare. Internationally, Elderhostel programs are of three weeks' duration—a week apiece in each of three foreign centers—and average $1,500 per person, including air fare. In each case partici-

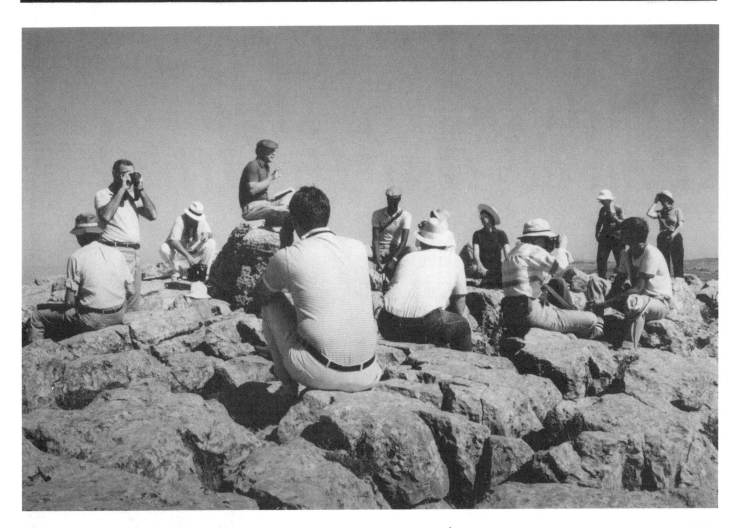

pants stay in unused or temporarily vacated university residence halls or youth hostels, receive all three meals each day, and attend at least 4½ hours a day of classroom instruction.

What sort of instruction? The courses range from "Modern Italian History" to theories of Albert Einstein to "The Architecture of Jerusalem"—to any topic at all, in fact, so long as that subject does not deal with problems of aging or other issues uniquely affecting senior citizens. The goal of Elderhostel is to permit senior citizens to remain vital and alive to current concerns, and the formula has proved immensely popular. Reacting to course announcements in Elderhostel's thrice-yearly free catalogue (supplemented by intermittent newsletters), nearly 180,000 people over age 60 will pursue such instruction in 1988. That catalogue is today stocked in most public libraries, but can also be obtained by contacting: **Elderhostel, 80 Boylston Street, Suite 400, Boston, MA 02116 (phone 617/426-7788).**

Meanwhile, to simply stay at youth hostels regardless of your age, get a youth-hostel membership card from: **American Youth Hostels, National Administrative Offices, P.O. Box 37613, Washington, D.C. 20013 (phone 202/783-6161),** or a local youth hostel council in your own city, if one exists. Enclose $10 (plus $1 for postage and handling) if you are 17 and under, or age 55 and older; $20 (plus another dollar) if you are age 18 to 49; $30 for family membership. You'll receive the card, and a manual listing youth-hostel facilities of the United States. For an additional $7.95, (plus $2 for postage and handling), you'll receive a similar but more extensive handbook of youth hostels in Europe and the Mediterranean area, and still another $7.95 (plus another $2 for postage and handling) will bring you the same for Africa, Asia, Australia, and New Zealand. And suddenly a brave new world of remarkably inexpensive lodgings becomes available to you, permitting almost constant travel—month after month—for an outlay that would barely secure two or three nights at the average hotel!

Vacations at Pritikin Centers Are High Priced But Healthy

The good news is that the approach seems to work, restoring your health, lengthening your longevity.

The bad news is that it's rather expensive: an average of $3,500 for two weeks, $6,000 for a month.

Yet Americans continue to throng the three Pritikin diet centers, devoting their two- to four-week vacations to a disciplined regimen of bland meals and mild exercise. And a major expansion of the Pritikin facilities—as planned by the 35-year-old son of the company's founder, the late Nathan Pritikin—will soon bring Pritikin-style vacations or treatments into the geographical reach of more and more people.

Residential Pritikin centers are currently in operation in Santa Monica, California; Miami Beach, Florida; and Downingtown, Pennsylvania.

Each of the centers advances the message first proclaimed by Pritikin in 1974: that most of the major degenerative diseases of our time—heart disease, diabetes, atherosclerosis—are largely caused by excessively high blood-fat levels, and that their prevention and cure could be brought about by reducing those levels through diet and exercise.

Sounds commonplace now, doesn't it? But it was revolutionary then. Heart-disease patients were being routinely treated by drugs and surgery, told to avoid exercise, and then sent back to eating the standard American diet of

Each of the centers advances the claim that most degenerative diseases are caused by excessively high blood-fat levels.

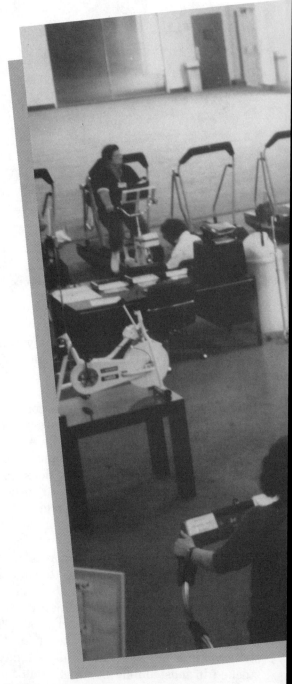

meat, eggs, and dairy products.

Instead, Pritikin advocated a diet that consisted only 10% of fat, only 15% of protein, but a full 75% of complex carbo-

BLAND MEALS AND MILD EXERCISE AT MIAMI BEACH, SANTA MONICA, AND DOWNINGTOWN, PA.

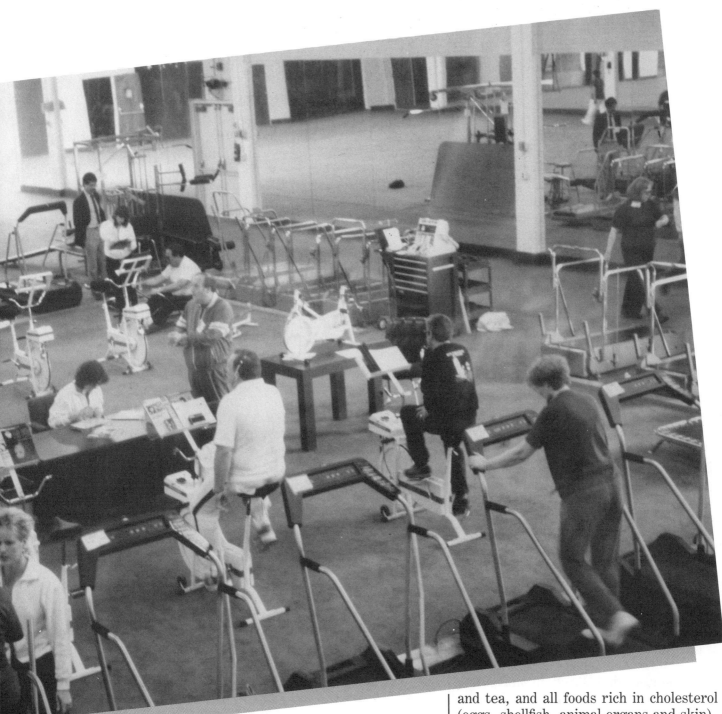

hydrates, the latter mainly from fruits, vegetables, and whole grains. He counseled an avoidance of all extra fats and oils (other than those naturally in grains and lean meats), all simple sugars (honey and molasses as well as sugar), all salt, coffee, and tea, and all foods rich in cholesterol (eggs, shellfish, animal organs and skin).

And each Pritikin patient or vacationer, regardless of age, was to engage in daily exercise, mainly walking.

On such a program, he maintained, the middle age of life could be stretched to cover the years between 40 and 80, rather than those from 40 to 60. Old age would

IS IT NECESSARY FOR THE PRITIKIN EXPERIENCE TO BE SO EXPENSIVE?

begin at 80, not at 55 or 60.

Pritikin staff will cite all sorts of statistics—I won't repeat them here—to bolster their claims that the treatment has had remarkable results for the 10,000-odd people who have thus far passed through the three residential centers. What is unarguable is that strong word-of-mouth comment has kept all three facil-

ities busy and well occupied, despite the founder's death from leukemia in 1985.

Each center offers programs for 13 and 26 days. The shorter course is for those overweight or interested in preventing future illness or reducing stress, or who have hypertension or mild diabetes (currently treated by oral medication). The second program, while available to anyone, is primarily designed for those suffering from the more serious health problems of heart disease, insulin-demanding diabetes, obesity, gout, or claudication.

No matter which program you select,

you're busy from early morning till early evening, taking pre-breakfast walks along the beach or on country lanes, exercising three times a day, attending cooking classes, lectures, or supermarket expeditions.

Personalized medical supervision is a major feature of the program. Depending on their health needs, guests are assigned to a specialist in either cardiology or internal medicine (Pritikin physicians are all Pritikin enthusiasts and live the programs themselves).

As for the meals, they are—reportedly —much better than in the early years of Pritikin. Although no extra fat is added to foods, and no salt, sugar, or caffeine is permitted, chefs still manage to turn out tasty fare. Meals are largely vegetarian, but with some fish served several times a week. You eat six times a day, so you never get hungry. Snacks might consist of vegetables and soup, Pritikin "chips" and salsa, fresh fruits. Dishes include "enchilada pie," potato pancakes, Moroccan orange-and-carrot salad, sweet-and-sour cabbage, ratatouille, paella, vegetable pot pie, and yogurt-marinated chicken. Desserts might be carrot cake or strawberries Romanoff.

For all this, you pay a substantial price if you are travelling alone, but considerably less on a per-person basis if you are accompanied by spouse or companion. For a 13-day session, including medical costs, the fees total $4,805 for one person, but only $6,970 for two. For a 26-day session, fees are as much as $8,308 for one person, but only $12,281 for two. Major-medical plans may cover that portion of the cost that is attributed to medical attention. And some guests have been known to treat the entire expense as tax deductible, provided they have been directed to take the program by their doctor (consult your tax adviser).

Is it necessary for the Pritikin experience to be so very expensive? Physicians with whom I've spoken think it well worth the price and not out of line with costs in the more exclusive spas (not to mention alternative costs of surgery, hospitalization, time lost from work).

The other, lower-cost alternative is a planned new chain of health-and-fitness clubs for people over 40, embodying the Pritikin principles. Three are currently in operation in Los Angeles and Houston, with several more due to open soon. These, in essence, are "outpatient" facilities, with Pritikin-style restaurants on the premises and a 30-hour program of instruction presented three nights a week for four weeks, all at the moderate charge of $300 to $400.

Meanwhile the better course—if you can afford it—is to spend a two-week or four-week vacation at an actual Pritikin residential facility. The **Pritikin Longevity Center, 1910 Ocean Front Walk, Santa Monica, CA 90405 (phone toll free 800/421-9911, 800/421-0981 in California)**, is the largest (150 guests) and the mother center (some would call it the "mother church"). It enjoys a superb beachfront location facing ten miles of boardwalk on which, conceivably, you might walk from Malibu to Palos Verdes.

The **Pritikin Longevity Center, 975 East Lincoln Highway, Downingtown, PA 19335 (phone 215/873-0123, or toll free 800/344-8243 outside Pennsylvania)**, in rolling hills an hour and a half from downtown Philadelphia, at the gateway to the quaint Amish country, provides both indoor and outdoor swimming, tennis, a

> Each attacks that condition through radical dietary discipline—avoiding all fats and oils—and through constant mild exercise.

golf course across the street, two driving ranges within walking distance, and bowling available less than 100 yards from the main building. There's also a climate-controlled indoor gym for the 45 to 60 guests enrolled per session.

And finally, the **Pritikin Longevity Center, 5875 Collins Avenue, Miami Beach, FL 33140 (phone 305/756-5353, or toll free 800/327-4914 outside Florida)**, is housed in a small resort hotel on an ocean beach that is swimmable year round. It takes about 50 guests per session at this writing, but will be able to accommodate 100 when a current expansion is completed. There's a large beachfront pool, and an oceanfront gym.

Pritikin Center, Santa Monica

At all the centers, visitors are welcome to take a free tour. At Miami Beach, says the general director, you may even be invited to take a meal with guests.

Vacationing with the Seventh Day Adventists

You are 55 and you feel yourself—faintly but perceptibly—slowing down. You are overweight and high in cholesterol. You are anxious and stressed. You have heard of the Pritikin Centers, where health can supposedly be restored, but you can't afford the tab (as much as $6,000 for a month).

So what do you do?

You call the Seventh Day Adventists (and I am perfectly serious). For prices averaging $2,400 a month they offer residential health retreats all across the U.S.A., where diet, exercise, and atmosphere are akin to those maintained in the costly health resorts, but at less than half the price.

The Adventists have long been known for their interest in health and nutrition, and for the consequent longevity of their lives. Studies in California have revealed a

much smaller incidence of heart attacks and strokes among them, as compared with other population groups in the state. Early in the century an Adventist named Kellogg began producing strange but effective breakfast foods called "wheat

A LESS COSTLY FORM OF PRITIKIN-LIKE TREATMENTS FOR MATURE AMERICANS

Hawaii—from which smaller, no-frills, nonprofit, inexpensive health retreats have been spun off.

At each such center the policy is determinedly vegetarian. Adventists are normally advised (but not required) to consume a purely "Vegan" diet of fruits, vegetables, legumes, and for those able to handle them, modest amounts of such high-fat foods as nuts, avocados, and ol-

ives. No "free fats"—i.e., those not found in whole foods—are used.

Which means no butter or marmalade on rolls, no oils in salad dressings, and foods sautéed in water rather than oil (the Adventists and the Pritikin people are in agreement on the total elimination of "free fats"). Complex carbohydrates are the basis of their diet (again in agreement with Pritikin; Pritikin, however, does allow small amounts of poultry, fish, and dairy products).

For all its spartan features, Adventist food can be surprisingly tasty. At my own recent lunch in the Adventist-run Living Springs of Putnam Valley, New York, I took repeated helpings from a buffet of salad, steamed vegetables, and cashew chow mein.

flakes" and "corn flakes," while his brother in the same town founded the famous Battle Creek (Michigan) Sanitorium. Today Adventists operate large and prestigious hospitals—notably, Loma Linda in California and Castle Medical Center in

WHAT DOES NOT TAKE PLACE IS RELIGIOUS PROSELYTIZING

Careful attention to diet is combined, at the centers, with exercise in the open air, sunbathing, a mammoth intake of water (six to eight glasses a day), hydrotherapy treatments (saunas, alternate hot and cold showers), and temperance: the total avoidance of coffee, alcohol, tobacco, and irritating spices.

Those strictures are translated into programs that begin early in the morning with brisk outdoor walking, followed by a hearty breakfast, daily lectures by physicians, hydrotherapy, classes on remedies utilizing water, vegetarian cooking classes, more walking, a large meal at lunch, educational seminars, more walking or exercising, a light evening meal, then perhaps a slide show on some aspect of health.

What does not take place is religious proselytizing. "People of all persuasions and no persuasion come here," says Leatha Mellow of the center known as the Weimar Institute, in California. "We've had Catholic priests, Jews, Christians, and atheists. We do maintain a spiritual emphasis, but it is nondenominational and nonsectarian."

In health matters, by contrast, the centers are fierce advocates. Like Pritikin, they believe a proper diet can avoid the major degenerative diseases of our time— heart disease, diabetes, atherosclerosis— and pursue their cures intensively in two- to four-week programs at the following locations:

Living Springs Retreat, Route 3, Bryant Pond Road, Putnam Valley, NY 10579 (phone 914/526-2800): In the foothills of the Berkshire Mountains, about an hour's drive from New York City, it is a large but homey building overlooking an 18-acre pond with swans. Guests occu-

> Says one Adventist nurse: "We believe our services should be made available to all, and not simply to those with money."

py attractive private and semi-private rooms, all with private bath, for which they pay weekly high-season rates (Memorial Day through Labor Day) of $595 in a semiprivate room, $695 in a private room, $875 for two persons staying together. Off-season weekly rates are $495, $635, and $805 respectively, including all three meals daily and all treatments.

Hartland Institute of Health Education, P.O. Box 1, Rapidan, VA 22733 (phone 703/672-3100): On over 500 acres of gently rolling hills, an hour from the Blue Ridge Mountains and two hours from Washington, D.C. When its current expansion program is completed by the spring of 1988 it will house up to 30 guests in two lodges. Programs are 25 days long, and cost $3,250 for one "patient," $2,425 for a companion. Says head nurse Linda Ball: "We believe services like these should be made available to everyone, and not just those with a lot of money. Some people call and say, 'I'll pay any price.' Others still say, 'I can't afford it.' "

Wildwood Lifestyle Center and Hospital, Wildwood, GA 30757 (phone toll free 800/634-9355): A modern facility on 500 acres of trails and hills, at an elevation of 700 feet, between Mount Raccoon and Mount Lookout. Rooms are attractive, and each has its own sunny patio. On a 24-day program, rates are $2,495 in a semiprivate room, $3,095 for a private room with bath, $2,927 for a private room with shared bath. On the 17-day program, rates in a semiprivate room are only $1,950, a private room with bath is $2,375, $2,256 without bath.

Uchee Pines, Route 1, Box 440, Seale, AL 36875 (phone 205/855-4764): In a climate that is generally warm the year round (though rainy in winter), this is a

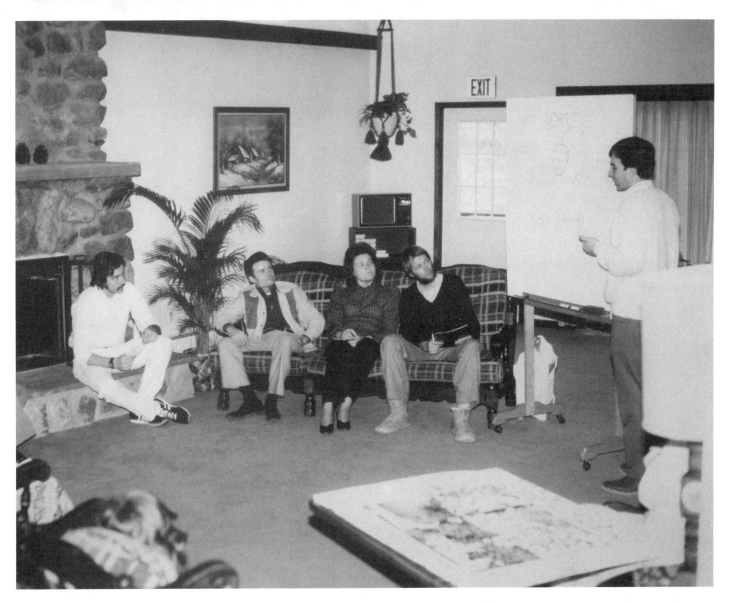

country house set in 250 wooded acres, with lovely gardens and trails. A 21-day program is offered, at charges of $2,520 for the first "patient," $2,320 for a patient/companion. Occasionally guests will be accepted for shorter programs, and fees will then be prorated.

Poland Spring Health Institute, RFD 1, Box 4300, Summit Spring Road, Poland Spring, ME 04274, (phone 207/998-2894): Smallest of the retreats (seven guests only), but with a broad variety of activities, including cross-country skiing in winter. It is an old New England farmhouse with attached barn housing the guests and various hydrotherapy facilities. Down the road is a clinic with medical offices. Rates are $525 a week for semiprivate rooms, $745 a week for private rooms; but most rooms share a bath. The average stay is two weeks. And, oh

yes, this is the same Poland Spring of the world-famous mineral waters; the institute has its own well, and guests therefore drink the same water as in the bottled product.

Weimar Institute, P.O. Box 486, Weimar, CA 95736 (phone 916/637-4111, or toll free 800/525-9191): It enjoys the most idyllic of Adventist retreat locations—on some 450 acres in the foothills of the Sierras, about 50 miles northeast of Sacramento, off Interstate 80—but is atypically expensive: $4,200 for the first "patient" on a 25-day program, $3,350 for that patient's companion. Guests do a great deal of walking through hundreds of acres of hiking trails, and occupy rooms that are all supplied with private bath.

Write for literature, then call. Staff members at all six centers are, in my experience, gentle, caring people.

X
A Fresh Way to Visit Old Destinations

Sweden: A Return to the World of Tomorrow

To a teenager in the late 1940s (myself), magazine articles on Sweden supplied the same improbable combination of erotic urges and high-tech fantasies that Playboy provides today. Imagine! Swedish men and women, it was seriously claimed, were living together before they got married. Wow! Day-care centers, like apparitions from Mars, were sprouting up for the children of working mothers. Neat! As wintry as its weather was said to be, Sweden seemed a dream of the rational future, and I longed to view it.

So did thousands of other foreign admirers, who flocked to Stockholm for special tours of contemporary life that the Swedes, with uncharacteristic immodesty, called "the World of Tomorrow." Then, as the rest of the world began cohabiting before marriage, and women flocked to offices and assembly lines, as progressive schools and cradle-to-grave security became a commonplace in dozens of nations, that special interest in Sweden began to wane, and all but disappeared by the mid-1970s.

Well, it's time to return, but fast. Be-

> Then, as now, Sweden seemed a dream of the rational future, and I longed to view it.

Royal Palace, Stockholm

cause those sly ol' Swedes are at it again, testing the limits of the possible, once more enacting the visions of social planners, revamping the rules of commerce, industry, and even family life. And since the rest of the world tends to emulate the Swedish model on a time lag of about 30 years, no thinking person can pass up this foretaste of what, arguably, the world of the future may be.

As early as the ride on the airport bus into Stockholm, you begin to glimpse the Swedish penchant for innovation, if only in a trivial sense. It is a sunshiny, summer day. Yet all the cars have their headlights on. "Why is this?" you ask the stately Swedish woman in the seat ahead. "Sta-

THERE'S NEW FERMENT IN THE GREATEST SOCIAL LABORATORY ON EARTH—AND SPECIAL "INSTITUTES" CAN REVEAL IT ALL TO YOU

tistics show," she answers rather archly, "that even daytime accidents are sharply cut if pedestrians and motorists are made more aware of traffic by oncoming headlights. Our parliament now requires them on, throughout the day."

Once in town, engaged in conversation with the largely English-speaking Swedes, you quickly meet up with matters more monumental: all talk is of the awesomely ingenious, new "wage-earners' funds" designed to overturn the very basis of industrial ownership in Sweden. Created in 1984 by Sweden's then-governing Social Democrats, the funds are entitled to 20% of the pretax profits of all corporations above a certain size. These monies are then reinvested in exchange for new stock whose voting rights are held by labor unions and other public representatives of the employees in those firms. The aim is nothing less than to transfer control of all such corporations from shareholders to the employees in them, by 20 to 30 years down the road (although the initial legislation expires in 1990), in addition to ensuring the reinvestment of profits instead of their distribution to shareholders. While Sweden's opposition parties have pledged to dismantle the funds if they should win the next election, the razor-thin margins by which most Swedish governments gain and remain in power, and thus the probable Social Democratic reaccession in any event, makes the funds a lively topic for investigation and debate, both within Sweden and abroad.

A lighter topic for study (unless you're 12 or younger): spanking is now illegal in Sweden. Corporal punishment of the young in any form, even "humiliation" visited upon a child (like being made to

> They are at it again, testing the limits of the possible, once more enacting the visions of social planners, revamping the rules of commerce, industry, and even family life.

stand in a corner), can now subject Swedish parents to a fine or term in jail. Though no one has yet been imprisoned, Sweden's child experts expect the altered home environment resulting from this legislation to produce no less than a better human race, at least in Sweden.

How do you, as a curious student of world trends, gain access to these experiments? How do you progress beyond the purely touristic realms into the actual test-tube settings of Swedish innovation?

You write to an "institute"—in this case, the Swedish Institute. Unknown to 99% of all American visitors, most European governments supplement the work of their tourist offices with "institutes" offering assistance far more profound to visitors pursuing special interests. Unlike the tourist offices, whose function is simply to attract more and more tourists, the institutes are broadly charged with promoting the culture and image of the nation. And although many of the institutes are primarily concerned with language courses or library services—the Institut Français/Alliance Française, the Goethe Institute, the British Council, the Austrian Institute do that—another batch (including, most prominently, the Swedish Institute and Danish Institute) are heavily involved in arranging interviews and meetings with distinguished local figures or authorities for visitors from abroad.

You are, we'll presume, the vice-president for labor relations of your company, or a teacher of political science, or vice-chairman of your local political club, heavily involved in matters of social welfare. Or you're a medical administrator anxious to visit the Scandinavian hospitals, especially in a country whose life-expectancy rates are two years higher

NO THINKING PERSON CAN PASS UP THIS FORETASTE OF WHAT, ARGUABLY, THE WORLD OF THE FUTURE MAY BE

than ours. You advise the Swedish Institute that you'll be in Stockholm, say, from February 3 through February 12 (having first made all hotel and transportation arrangements yourself), and then: you describe your background, enumerate the topics you're desirous of pursuing, and ask whether a "program" might be prepared for your stay. Within a few weeks (faster in winter), and free of charge, you receive a carefully formulated schedule of appointments. At 11 a.m. on February 3 you're to meet for an hour or two with Professor Rasmussen of Uppsala University, an authority in the field you've cited. At 9 a.m. on the 4th, the appropriate English-speaking committee of the Center Party will wait to brief you at their party headquarters in downtown Stockholm. That afternoon, their opposite numbers at the Social Democratic Party will do the same. And so on and on. While none of this will be arranged for persons who simply describe themselves as members of the public (no matter how studious, sympathetic, or concerned they may be), it should not be hard to dredge up the titles or qualifications that will entitle you to receive these introductions to your "professional" counterparts in Sweden.

Next time you visit Europe, try an institute! No more fascinating travel activity exists. Contact the **Swedish Institute (Svenska Institutet), Sweden House (Sverigehuset), Kunstradgarden, Box 7434, S-103 91 Stockholm, Sweden.** Or the **Danish Institute (Det Danske Selskab), #2 Kultorvet, DK-1175 Copenhagen K, Denmark (phone 135-448).** And thus replace those rather mindless vacation weeks of sand and sea with intelligent travel, to destinations that may indeed presage the World of Tomorrow.

How do you, as a curious student of world trends, gain access to these experiments? You write to an "institute"—in this case, the Swedish Institute.

Stockholm

Home Stays in the British Isles

*I*n tweed jacket and suede tie, his bushy white moustache twitching with glee, the ruddy old squire stood beaming at the gates to an imposing English estate, as an American tourist couple came driving up the gravel path. "I'm Underhill!" he boomed. "The bed-and-breakfast man! And if you can stow your gear post-haste, we still have time to view the horse auction in the village!"

In actual fact, this gentleman-farmer was not a bed-and-breakfast host. Britain's B&B proprietors are often fully as warm and spirited, but they tend to be a far more ordinary lot, not given to living in stately country homes. And their offer of bed-and-breakfast means just that: bed, a breakfast the next morning, then a cordial but conclusive good-bye.

Rather, the people of whom Squire Underhill is typical are a wholly different lot whose conversation and companionship are themselves a prime reason for your visit to Britain. They are the source of unique home stays designed to produce a very special travel benefit: the experience of gracious country living, yet in a lively atmosphere of intellect and discourse, among individuals of distinctive social views and lifestyles. The sojourns they offer take place in country homes of

The sojourns they offer take place in country homes of Great Britain.

the British Isles. The proprietors in question are a form of landed gentry, an aristocracy of sorts, but nontitled, democratic, close to their middle-class origins, and not at all like their often otherworldly counterparts on the continent, the latter frequently removed from life, acting as cultural ornaments or loosely overseeing hereditary estates. English gentry are more often active types, merchant bankers (investment counselors) and retired magistrates, functioning business executives and art dealers, muchtraveled former army officers from "good regiments," professors, writers, and dons of awesome reputation.

Why should such persons accept paying guests into their homes? It is because their wealth is often in land and structures, in paintings and heirlooms, and not in cash—which is always welcome. About a decade ago, when various British organizations began discreetly soliciting their willingness to receive overseas visitors, many of them cautiously agreed, some with initial hesitation, some insisting that visitors first be screened for compatability. Thus it was that various firms emerged to match up hosts with guests. It is these screening organizations—some identified by the words "at home" in their titles—that provide the most curious of tourists with the profound delights and insights of a proper British "home visit."

Among the oldest of the "at home" firms is Esther Eder's At Home in England and Scotland, Inc. The Argentineborn wife of the former theatre critic of the *New York Times*, she agonized in the mid-1970s that friends going to England weren't seeing "her England" because of their limited access to Britons of distinction. She began approaching prospects,

A NUMBER OF IMPRESSIVE ORGANIZATIONS NOW PERMIT AMERICANS TO VISIT WITH BRITONS OF DISTINCTIVE SOCIAL VIEWPOINTS AND ACHIEVEMENTS

explaining, cajoling, and assuring, ultimately tapping into an extraordinary wealth of human resources that proceeded to host hundreds of fortunate Americans in the ensuing years:

• The one-time private secretary to Winston Churchill, now a merchant banker living in Dorset, from which he commutes to important meetings in London, accompanying his guests on the ride into town;

• A retired general, later a professor of political science at the University of Exeter, now a consultant from his home in Wales on responses to international terrorism;

• An active, though middle-aged, administrator of the Bodleian Library of Oxford, his wife a writer in her late 20s, both living near a picture-postcard village near Oxford;

• A woman "don" at the University of Cambridge, an imposing raconteur whose field is the history of architecture, her own Tudor home an impressive example;

• A former governor of the Bank of Scotland, his wife a magistrate, their household completed by the elderly nanny of their now-grown children (for which reason they especially enjoy receiving families);

• And scores more, of every calling: an international stockbroker, once with the Tenth Hussars Regiment, living in the horsey country outside Bristol; an intensely contemporary theatrical agent, also the business manager for a renowned duchess; a retired judge now serving as the arbitrator for industrial disputes. Plus an executive with British Petroleum, and another with Cadbury Chocolates. And leavening the political leanings of these gentlemen farmers, art dealers and

Why do such persons accept paying guests? It is because their wealth is often in land and structures, and not in cash—which is always welcome.

auctioneers, chartered surveyors and retired officers: a prominent member of the British Labor Party, now retired to a charming cottage both thatched and covered with vines; a leading left-wing journalist still passionately contributing columns to a literary weekly. Their homes range from 16th-century manors to 18th-century rectories, from rambling Queen Anne country estates to narrow, four-story Georgian townhouses (of "Upstairs, Downstairs" memory), from 17th-century farmhouses outside tiny Cotswold villages to modern, but classically elegant, mansions surrounded by miles of open ground. They are in England, Scotland, and Wales, in Lancashire and Gloucestershire, in London and near Brighton. And their charge for hospitality, guest rooms, full English breakfast daily, and use of the entire estate, in Mrs. Eder's program, averages $50 to $60 per person per night, including Mrs. Eder's rather extensive services in matching you up with a suitable host. Minimum required stay is three nights.

The larger country homes, each with two or three guest rooms to rent, are the specialty of a competing organization known as At Home Country Holidays. But though the latter's appeal is primarily to small groups—say, a family, or two or three couples travelling together—the goal remains the same distinctive and intensely private, noncommercial, and leisurely home stay offered by the others: no paying guests other than your own party of travellers are ever accepted in the same house at the same time. Hosts of At Home Country Holidays tend also, in the view of some observers, to fewer political or business interests than Mrs. Eder's. Practi-

THEIR CONVERSATION AND COMPANIONSHIP ARE THEMSELVES A PRIME REASON FOR YOUR VISIT TO BRITAIN

tioners of the good life, they stress the art of country living, and warm to the visitor who shares their admiration for 19th-century prints, hunting and sailing, antiques and gardens. When one possesses a country estate, not simply a country home; when one lives in a near-stately structure of turrets and towers, with croquet lawns and walled kitchen gardens,

in dozens of surrounding acres—as so many At Home Country Holidays hosts do—one apparently cares less about Dow-Jones statistics or North Sea oil. "Your host," says one typical At Home Country Holidays entry in their illustrated catalogue, "is a former Master of Foxhounds and a member of the Coaching Club. Guests may have the opportunity of hunting in wintertime and driving round the forest in a four-in-hand in the summer. They may also join the family on their 36-foot mahogany yawl, built in Denmark in 1966 and meticulously cared-for." Another points out that he "is a writer and art historian, and his wife lectures and writes on the history of food and garden design." Others stress that "being collectors ourselves, we are happy to act as guides to nearby antiques markets." Most take pains to assure that "there is a swimming pool in the garden and tennis courts in the village." "Our guests dine with candles and flowers in the dining room either with us, or on their own, as they prefer." For such elegance and grace, which always includes a private

"suite" (bedroom, bath, sitting room, and garden) and full English breakfast, the charge is £85 ($127.50) per couple per night, £60 ($90) for a single. They now offer the same service in smaller homes for £60 ($90) for a double, £45 ($67.50) for a single. Dinner, at an extra £12.50 ($18.75) per person, can also be arranged.

The most expensive of the home-stay firms is Country Homes and Castles, headed by Susan Uda, who uses a carefully defined ratings system to set apart her renowned member establishments. "Grade A" consists of "Stately Homes and Castles in Extensive Parklands," charging £232 ($348) per couple per night, including cocktails, a three-course dinner with wine, coffee, and liqueurs, overnight accommodations, full English breakfast, and the many facilities individual to each home—a very considerable value. "Grade B" comprises "Country Mansions and Castles," and costs £169 ($253) per couple per night, again including dinner for two and full English breakfast the next morning. On arrival at each home, usually in late afternoon, one joins the family for cocktails in the drawing room, then enjoys that full-scale dinner with wine, and retires to an elegant bed, steeped in the history and heritage of each house and family.

Typical of the firms offering budget-priced home stays are Wolsey Lodges, a loose marketing association of independently owned country houses clustered in the southern half of England, heavily in the Cotswolds and East Anglia. Though some resemble the more commercial variety of bed-and-breakfast, they are all a cut above, and by studying the Wolsey literature carefully, one can find homes owned by Oxford graduates, retired lieutenant-colonels of the Royal Air Force, people actively engaged in demanding professions and business activities. Their charges range from as little as £15 ($22.50) per person to rarely more than £20 ($30) per person, a cooked breakfast included, and although they engage in none of the elaborate screening and matching of guests with hosts, of the sort promised by the costlier firms, they offer the opportunity (through careful selection of homes, this time by yourself) to socialize with English people of above-average intelligence and tastes.

Having made the choice of firms, how then do you comport yourself as a house guest in Britain? You act exactly as if you were staying with friends or relatives. You make your own beds. Except at Wolsey Lodges, where it obviously isn't expected, you bring a small house gift. Again except at Wolsey Lodges, you make no on-the-spot payments of any sort to your hosts—you have already prepaid through your "at home" booking organization. Primarily, you talk—about wide-ranging topics, enjoying the lively, articulate views of the obviously gregarious people who engage in hosting. In the morning, you wander through home and grounds. You take long walks. Sometimes you are escorted by your host to worthwhile sights of the vicinity. One host in London invariably takes her guests to an unforgettable luncheon in Parliament!

In the predominantly countryside settings of home stays, you also gain a rare opportunity to observe British attitudes toward leisure, which they take as seriously as work, pursuing the life of sport, which they practically invented, and to which they devote ever-constant atten-

> Your hosts are a form of landed gentry, an aristocracy of sorts, but nontitled, democratic, and close to their middle-class origins.

tion. In this, and in still other areas, you witness the life of England from an utterly unique vantage point.

In short, you act as a traveller, not as a mere tourist, enjoying intellectual growth as well as profound pleasure.

For the descriptive literature and booking forms of the firms I've cited, contact **Esther Eder, c/o Carol Sherr, At Home in England and Scotland, Inc., 66 Edgewood Avenue, Larchmont, NY 10538 (phone 914/834-3944)**—Mrs. Eder requests completion of an elaborate questionaire, including an optional short essay on your background and interests; **Angela Rhodes-James, At Home Country Holidays, The Stone House, Great Gransden Sandy, Bedfordshire SG19 3AF, England (phone 076-77-300); Susan Uda, Country Homes and Castles, 118 Cromwell Road, Kensington, London SW7 4ET, England (phone 01-370-4445 or 370-0322, or 404/231-5837 in the U.S.);** or **Wolsey Lodges, 17 Chapel Street, Bildeston, Suffolk IP7 7ED, England (phone 0449-741-297).**

For still another organization somewhat similar to Mrs. Eder's, contact the Countess of Denbigh's **Welcome Stranger Ltd.,**

Stable Cottage, Newnham Paddox, Monks Kirby, Rugby, Warwickshire CV23 ORX, England (phone 0788-832-173), represented in the United States by **Laurie Holmes, 137 East 36th Street, #2B, New York, NY 10016 (phone 212/689-1088).**

Seeing Britain Differently: Industrial Visits

*I*n the business of commercial tourism, most people follow the path of least resistance, packaging the sights admired by the greater number of visitors and conducting you to them in effortless form. From the moment of your arrival in Britain, you will be assaulted by mass-volume offerings of scheduled motorcoach tours to silent Stonehenge and Salisbury Cathedral, or to rollicking, Tudor-style entertainments and medieval banquets, to the Beefeaters of the Tower and the Changing of the Guard. It all requires so little effort.

It does require effort, but only a modicum of it, to enter into another world, of contemporary achievement, fascinating to witness, and providing valuable lessons for application to one's own concerns at home. The essential act is a letter, written well in advance of arrival, requesting a guided industrial visit to one of the 100-or-so major British companies that have expressed themselves to

A dozen recent Nobel Prizes attest to the undoubted, continuing vigor of British scientists, inventors, and theoreticians, whose work finds quick application in the British industries available for visits.

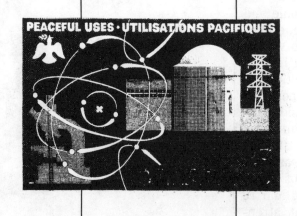

travel officials and others as willing to conduct such tours and consultations, but only by appointment. By contrast, if the firm is one that conducts regularly scheduled tours of its premises for tourists who simply show up unannounced—as famous breweries or the makers of celebrated chinaware do—you can bet that the visit is of little interest to serious students of the subject, and is conducted for public-relations reasons only. The best requires an effort: a letter.

And why do such firms respond favorably to such letters? Partly because of pride in their activities, but also out of a conscious respect for international connections formed through contacts with their counterparts or possible customers from other lands. And why should you send off such letters? Because the current-day activities of certain British firms are advancing the very frontiers of science and technology, promising breakthroughs in many fields, and offering an added dimension of profound interest to your British holiday. Viewed quite selfishly those activities may provoke valuable new approaches to your own business opportunities, but even on the most disinterested level, they lend fascination and lively intellectual content to a British trip.

To the uninformed, British science and industry are a weary grouping, diminished in vigor since the decline of the British Empire. Don't believe a word of it! In basic research, in discovering entirely new technologies, Britain remains a world leader, and the past 20 years is a period

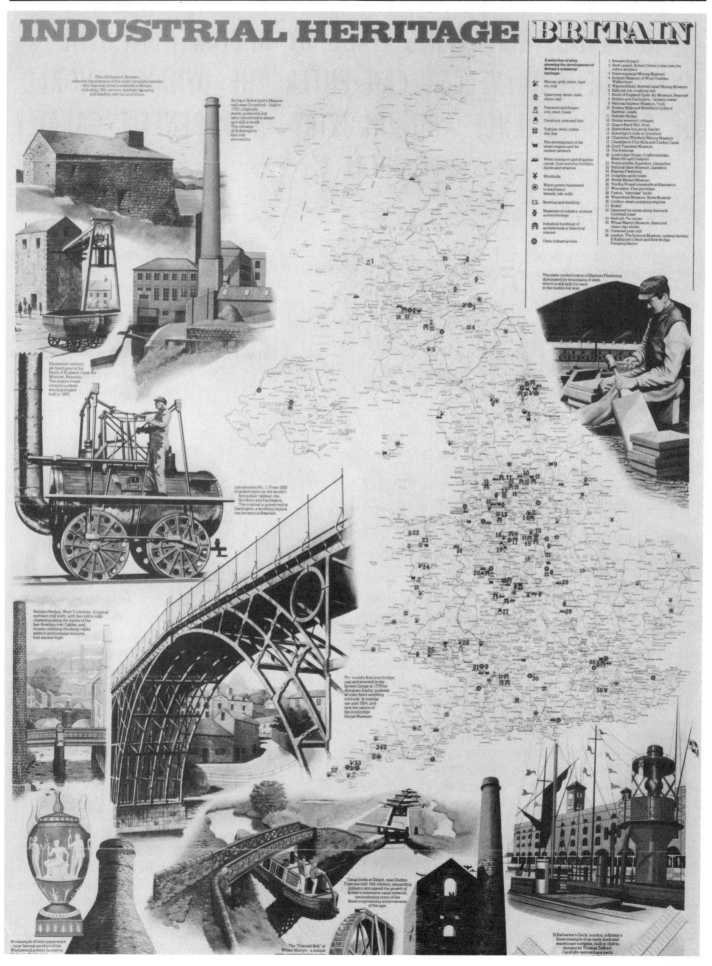

ON INDUSTRIAL VISITS MADE BY APPOINTMENT, THE INTELLIGENT TRAVELLER CAN ENTER THE DYNAMIC WORLD OF BRITISH SCIENCE AND INDUSTRY—AND BENEFIT GREATLY FROM IT

of staggering achievement for the island kingdom in robotics and aerospace research, in biotechnology and a score of other disciplines. Britain's "viewdata" services and telephone transmissions by optical fiber are years ahead of all other nations; its "beta blockers" revolutionized the treatment of cardiovascular diseases; its recent inventions and developments include creation of the vectored-thrust aircraft engine (by Rolls-Royce), vertical/short-takeoff and landing aircraft (the Harrier), monoclonal antibodies for the treatment of human virus diseases (first produced at Cambridge), glass-reinforced cement, livestock breeding by embryo transfer, synthetic insecticides, remote-control mining of coal and lead, deciphering the structure of DNA, hovercraft, the technique of "melding" fabrics, charcoal in cloth form (as filters), interferon, the "distributed array" microprocessor, solid-state radar, the optical fiber, the medical CAT scanner, the nuclear magnetic resonator (again for body scans), the fuel-cell-powered electric car, and hundreds more. A dozen recent Nobel Prizes attest to the undoubted, continuing vigor of British scientists, inventors, and theoreticians, whose work finds quick application in the British industries available for visits.

Of the scores of plants and offices willing to receive you, a sample seven provide some indication of their quality:

(1) Cambridge Science Park, on the northern outskirts of the famed university town, leads the list (as well it should). It is a breakthrough collaboration, as yet new to the English, between the pure scientists and academics of the great British universities (in this case, Cambridge) and British industry, who in the past have rarely spoken with one another, let alone

collaborated. More than 50 ultra-high-tech companies (of which some are from the United States) have already established plants and research centers on the grassy site—a large, rolling expanse of campus-like appearance and serenity—and dozens more are rushing to put down their bids.

All are drawn by the relaxed approach of Cambridge dons (professors) toward sharing their knowledge with others, proffering scientific advice and engaging in brainstorming sessions without worrying overmuch about "intellectual property" or advance compensation. As one tenant of the park put it, "there is an extraordinary network of information here, available simply to those who master the network." Twelve of the companies occupying quarters are in stratospheric realms of studying human intelligence for computer software applications, and in computer hardware design; another handful pursue the microscopic mysteries of biotechnology, while still others approach the commercial use of lasers, fiber optics, electronic signal-processing systems, energy conservation, ultraviolet-light systems, medical monitoring equipment, veterinary vaccines and hormones, human pharmaceuticals. One tenant universally acknowledged as being of seminal importance, the Cambridge Microelectronics Research Laboratory, organized by the university itself, researches the ever-smaller "microfabrication" of electronic devices.

By writing to the project managers of the park—**Bidwells, Trumpington Road, Cambridge CB2 2LD, England, attention Mr. Henry Bennett (phone 0223-841-841)**—you can obtain a glossy 40-page listing of all the participating companies, with fulsome descriptions of their activities and staffs. By then writing directly to the companies that interest you, you can arrange a visit to take place in the course of your British trip.

(2) Britain's Robotics Centre: Unique to the U.K., the Robot Development Centre at Melton Mowbray, in the English midlands, is a combined exhibition center, research laboratory, school, and conference facility solely concerned with industrial robots, and under management of Britain's Production Engineering Research Association (PERA), a private group of over 2,000 member companies from 30 nations. It exists to be visited. Plant managers dazed or befuddled by robots, thinking of introducing them or encountering difficulties in their use, come here as to the Mayo Clinic for succor and assistance. An expansive exhibition floor displays dozens of robots, some on permanent loan from prominent companies, while a permanent staff of robotics experts provides custom-tailored advice as well as periodic classroom instruction; others engage in continuing research, de-

> Because the current-day activities of certain British firms are advancing the very frontiers of science and technology, promising breakthroughs in many fields, they offer an added dimension of profound interest to your British holiday.

sign, and development. Call ahead to **PERA, Melton Mowbray, Leicestershire (phone Melton Mowbray 0664-501293),** and ask to speak with Mrs. Jill Swann, who directs the full-day tours of the center given to visiting business people and groups; a week ahead is usually sufficient time. And then, from London's St. Pancras Station, take the train to Leicester, there to be picked up by the center's car, if they've been given notice.

(3) The Longbridge Plant of British Leyland: Here you see an actual application of the center's research—the world's most highly automated auto factory, surpassing anything in Japan. Its tireless robots (and humans) produce impressive daily numbers of that standout of the Austin-Rover Group, the Mini-Metro, perhaps the most economical small car built in Europe (58.3 miles per gallon at a steady 55 miles per hour). The 2½-hour tours of the robot-served assembly lines, the engine building, and the vehicle testing departments are had by writing or phoning **British Leyland Cars Ltd., Longbridge, West Midlands B31 2TB (phone 021-475-2101,** and ask to speak with Mrs. M.A. Moisy). Distance: About 2½ hours by car or train from London.

(4) Nuclear Power Stations: To an extent unimaginable in the United States, nuclear power plants in Britain encourage visits by the public, enabling you to see for yourself, to pose hard questions about disposal and safety to their managements and staff. Both the **Sizewell "A" Nuclear Power Station, Leiston, Suffolk (phone Leiston 0728-830444, ext. 436),** and the **Dungeness "A" Nuclear Power Station, Romney Marsh, Kent TN29 9PP, U.K. (phone Lydd 0679-20461,** asking to speak with Public Relations), are easily accessi-

THE ESSENTIAL ACT IS A LETTER WRITTEN IN ADVANCE OF ARRIVAL, REQUESTING A GUIDED INDUSTRIAL VISIT. THE BEST ESTABLISHMENTS REQUIRE A LETTER

ble to London, an hour or so away, and both will accept visitors (but by advance appointment only) every day of the year. In northern Wales, more remote (about four hours by train from London), both the **Trawsfynydd Power Station, Trawsfynydd, Gwynedd, Wales LL4 4DT, U.K. (phone Trawsfynydd 076-687-331),** and the **Wylfa Nuclear Power Station,** on the rugged coast at **Cemaes Bay,**

Anglesey, Gwynedd, Wales LL67 ODH, U.K. (phone Cemaes Bay 0407-710-471), pursue a similar policy.

(5) Dinorwic "Stored Energy" Station: An eighth wonder of the world, only recently completed, it brilliantly illustrates the propensity of British engineers, using basic thinking, to turn simple artifacts of nature into highly effective technical applications. Essentially, Dinorwic is a giant mountain of solid slate in North Wales, near the top of which is a lake, with another lake near its base. By boring out the interior of the mountain, creating giant "tubes" of slate leading from one lake to the other, the tubes regulated by equally giant valves, it is now possible to "drop" the water of the upper lake to the lower one in a mammoth "flush" operation, driving turbines along the way and

In basic research, Britain remains a world leader, and the past 20 years is a period of staggering achievement for the island kingdom in robotics and aerospace research, in biotechnology and a score of other disciplines.

creating a giant surge of electrical power. The operation can be put into effect in a few seconds. Instead of maintaining slow-starting, excess power capacity throughout the day, Britain's electric grid uses Dinorwic to supply peak-time "surges" as needed—for example, when the entire nation turns on an electric tea kettle following the conclusion of a popular TV program. The water so used is later pumped back up to the top of the mountain during periods of low, cheap power use—like the middle of the night. Saving to the nation over conventional methods of storing or providing power for peak-time use: £52 million a year. Ten years in construction, and the largest pumped-storage hydroelectric scheme in Europe, it was so perfectly designed to meet ecological specifications that it is all but invisible to the visitor wandering the mountain scenery of Wales's Snowdonia—who sees only a small door cut into the side of the mountain. But visitors are given an entire tour and explanation of the cavernous underground complex, touring the control room and seeing the main inlet valves and drop valves. Write to **Visits Officer, Dinorwic Power Station, Llanberis, Gwynedd, North Wales, LL55 4TY, U.K. (phone Mrs. Jennifer Parry at Llanberis 0286-870-935).** Then take the train from London to Bangor in North Wales, from which Llanberis and Dinorwic are an 11-mile bus or taxi ride.

(6) Welsh Plant Breeding Station: For visits here, of interest to dedicated professionals in the agricultural field, contact **Patricia Twig, Plas Gogerddan, Aberystwyth, Dyfed, Wales SY23 3EB, U.K. (phone Aberystwyth 0970-828-255).**

(7) And finally: **James Pringle Ltd., Holm Woollen Mills, Inverness, Scot-**

land IV2 4RB, U.K. (phone Inverness 0463-223-311), weaver of notable sweaters and such; **Robert Noble Ltd., March Street Mills, Peebles EH45 8ER, U.K.** (phone Peebles 0721-20146), maker of English tweeds; and **Trafford Carpets, Mosley Road, Trafford Park, Manchester M17 1PK, England (phone 061-872-1665)**, manufacturer of Axminster and Wilton carpets—all are representative of British achievements in high-quality textiles, and all can be visited, even without notice in the case of Pringle, but by appointment only for the other two.

The **British Tourist Authority, 40 West 57th Street, New York, NY 10019**, publishes a list of still other "Visits to Workplaces in Britain," grouped under such headings as Agriculture, Airports, Astronomy, Beer, British Rail Engineering, Broadcasting, Cars, China and Pottery, Cider, Dairy Products, Drugs, Film Studios, Foodstuffs, Glassware, Institu-

tions, Lighthouses, Newspapers, Papermaking, Power Stations, Schools, Sport, Textiles, Theatres, Whiskey, and Wine. Unfortunately, too much of the list relates

Some firms are drawn to British university centers by the relaxed approach of their dons (professors) toward sharing knowledge with others, proffering scientific advice without worrying overmuch about "intellectual property" or advance compensation.

to plants of mere consumerist appeal—the breweries and the scotch makers, the chinaware companies and the cider bottlers, the purveyors of food and apparel seeking a wider public audience—and to hardly any of the more important firms making heavy contributions: the Courtaulds and the British Celaneses, the National Coal Board and Taylor Woodrow Construction, British Aerospace and Thorn EMI, the IMI Titaniums and the Tate and Lyles.

To visit the premises of the latter, you write them a letter; we share a common language, too little used in direct, written communications between us. Failing that, you write to the major trade associations requesting an introduction to leading firms. The latter include the **Society of Motor Manufacturers, Forbes House, Halkin Street, London SW1X 7DS, England**; the **British Clothing Industry Association, 6 Upper St. Martins Lane, London WC2; England**, the **Society of British Aerospace Companies Ltd., 29 King Street, St. James's, London SW1Y 6RD, England**; the **Royal Agricultural Society of England, 35 Belgrave Square, London SW1X 8QN, England**; or the **British Textile Confederation, 24 Buckingham Gate, London SW1E 6LB, England.**

Are visits such as these a valid activity on a vacation trip? Or are vacationers presumed to check their brains at home? To the intelligent traveller, holiday pleasure flows not from simple inactivity or mindless recreation, but from the pursuit of one's deepest interests. If, even partially, those interests lie in business pursuits, then scores of your counterparts, and counterpart activities, are available in Britain to enhance your vacation stay.

Viewing Their Cities vs. Our Cities

When Americans travel on vacation to Europe, they tend to devote their time almost exclusively to museums and theatres, art galleries and cathedrals, spas and trendy boutiques.

I think they might profitably pay some attention to the organization of cities. The growing difference between the pattern of European cities, and that of the newly emergent, major cities of the United States (especially in the South), is so very pronounced as to touch off the most provocative ideas and comparative lessons. Nothing in travel can be more instructive.

Here's a short "travel guide" to the difference between European and American cities: what to look for, what to consider.

The average European city is a high-density metropolis, not a sprawling, spreading ink blot like Los Angeles, but a tightly compressed area like Boston or San Francisco.

Some major European cities have resisted the trend to decentralizing suburbs by surrounding their town limits with compulsory "greenbelts" in which further commercial development other than farming is prohibited. Others maintain programs encouraging the construction of high-density, multi-unit housing in the center of town.

By influencing the bulk of people to remain in or near the center, those policies have preserved that area as the focal point of all community activities. The downtown is a vibrant, colorful place in

They have resisted the trend to suburbs; the typical example remains a concentrated metropolis, not a spreading ink blot.

which people of all income classes mix and mingle, enjoying a sense of community.

The large numbers of people going downtown for their evening entertainment support a prolific theater and cultural activity—not the civic "art centers" or solitary, 2,000-seat auditoriums of our U.S. cities (with their bland and bloodless productions designed not to offend), but dozens of private theaters, cafés, cabarets, and art galleries, experimental and daring.

European cities are fanatical about preserving their historic and/or period buildings. In many cities, when one pulls down a turn-of-the-century (or older) structure to modernize it, one is required to rebuild its façade to the earlier design, down to the last millimeter, sometimes using the very same bricks as were there before.

In those several major cities whose historic inner centers were destroyed or badly damaged in World War II—London, Prague, Warsaw—people did not take ad-

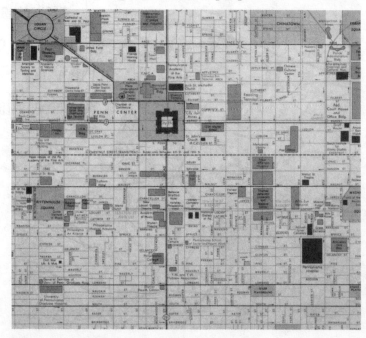

A NEW POINT OF REFERENCE FOR YOUR EUROPEAN TOUR

vantage of that devastation to build a modern, new city, but rather they restored the historic inner centers to precisely their prewar appearance.

In such cities as Paris and Madrid, after some much-regretted deviations from the same path, people have now reached a near-universal consensus to locate modern, high-rise buildings away from the center, in districts of their own, preserving the city's inner core in its earlier, classic form.

In London, constraints have been placed on the construction of downtown office buildings; people believe that to erect more of these towers in place of older, smaller structures is to create oases of death in a living city, to reduce vitality and excitement rather than to improve matters.

Those are the policies. You may want to discuss them with the Europeans you meet in your hotel or pension, in the

Their downtowns are vibrant and colorful, the meeting place for people of all income classes.

theatre bars or sidewalk cafés. Now, in the further course of your stay, relate those views to the wholly different paths taken by the major new cities of the American Sun Belt—Houston, Dallas, Atlanta, and Phoenix, among others. Here, the downtown in its traditional form has all but disappeared, to be replaced by office buildings, office buildings, office buildings. At night the streets surrounding these towers are scenes of desolation and death.

For the grand, rococo theatres that once were downtown, substitute the tiny cinemas in the suburban shopping malls. For a life of window-shopping and camaraderie, substitute long hours in an automobile, endlessly spent on highways cutting like an ugly scar through a once-pleasant scene of tree-lined streets and small or medium-sized buildings.

For high density, substitute the very opposite: sprawling tracts of one-family homes in areas a dozen miles and more from the city center. There live the middle class and rich who no longer see, meet, hear, or suffer the poor.

As for historic preservation, our most "dynamic" cities again follow a totally different course from that of Europe. In place of neo-Gothic churches, distinguished Victorian homes and clubs, modest but attractive department stores, they have erected still more of the office towers. On the former sites of magnificent train terminals, demolished without thought or contrition, they have thrown up box-like skyscrapers.

Now come the lessons and benefits of travel. Having made the comparison, ask yourself which form of city supports a higher quality of life? Which type—high-density European or low-density Amer-

ican—creates a greater sense of community, reduces the alienation of modern life? Which maintains a higher level of culture, discourse, and learning: London or Los Angeles, Munich or Phoenix?

Talk to the Europeans you meet. Ask

Compare and contrast: Albuquerque

them about their city as a city. How do they feel about having no automobile and making use instead of public transportation? Do they yearn for the suburbs? Would they prefer to replace their visits to the heavily attended theatres and mov-

ies of downtown with a smaller cinema in a shopping mall? You will receive a variety of answers—all of them instructive and a possible guide to your own life.

This year, as you rush from the Uffizzi Galleries to the Pitti Palace, from the

and Bruges

Louvre to the new Musée d'Orsay, pause to consider the contemporary life of Europe, and especially the organization of its cities. Nothing, as I have said, could be more instructive—a major dividend of your European trip.

XI
New Destinations

"Frommer's Favorites"

*T*hink back on it. Your fondest travel memories are always of the islands and cities you visited before *they were discovered by hordes of others. Beaches on which you alone dozed beneath a sheltering palm. Cafés in which you chatted for hours on end with residents eager and open to a newcomer's questions. Places unique in their distinctive characteristics, excitingly foreign or fresh, as unfamiliar in appearance and attitudes as a South Seas island.*

Do they still exist? They're obviously harder and harder to find! Yet in a world crammed with sightseeing buses, amid the wailing jet engines and the cacophony of tourist voices, five refreshingly unspoiled destinations come immediately to mind. Some are small and only slightly known, others are giant urban centers, but all are places not yet thronged with visitors from remote cities—the key to a magical sojourn of the sort you once knew.

(1) The Island of Bonaire. Here is the Caribbean as it used to be, without highrise hotels or daily charter-loads of "packaged" tourists. A member of the politically stable Netherlands Antilles, located

less than 30 miles from the coast of Venezuela, Bonaire is a good-sized island but one with only 8,000 permanent inhabitants; a destination serviced on direct

THE LARGELY UNVISITED DESTINATIONS THAT HAVEN'T YET BEEN SPOILED BY MASS TOURISM

flights by major airlines, but with only two major hotels (neither more than three stories tall) and a handful of smaller ones; the proud possessor of two tiny casinos, a disco, and nightly entertainment by native dance troupes, but a haven of calm and repose for all of that. In the village square off the stone counters of a tiny fish market, residents still smile at the tourist —as if they were the first to visit the site —and lead you by the hand to view that morning's catch of rainbow-colored fish.

The chief attraction is scuba-diving, practiced here with an intensity found elsewhere only in the Red Sea; scuba-diving experts rank Bonaire with Elath as enjoying the two top underwater sites of the world. Off the white sand beaches fronting the island's two large hotels are coral reefs and sea life famed throughout the world. Numerous certified divers provide you with "resort courses" enabling you to don a tank and mask after only two days' instruction and attempt a dive of, say, 40-foot depth. Nothing you ever viewed from the surface of the sea while snorkeling can possibly prepare you for the awesome beauty far below; though you may never have considered this rather difficult sport before, you'll quickly yearn to be a diver of ever-greater depths—in Bonaire.

For less venturesome sorts, the island offers almost constant sun throughout the year, magnificent beaches, a high level of continental cuisine in several restaurants (more than enough for your needs), birdwatching of

great variety and appeal (the island's second major attraction), pink flamingoes roaming in flocks over expansive salt flats —and relatively moderate prices by Caribbean standards. For detailed information, contact the **Bonaire Government Information Office, 275 Seventh Avenue, New York, NY 10001 (phone 212/ 242-7707)**, and for tours to Bonaire, contact either a travel agent or the airlines flying directly to Bonaire (ALM Antillean Airlines) or to nearby Curaçao (Eastern and American Airlines), from which small planes then shuttle you to Bonaire, 20 minutes away.

(2) The Resorts of Silicon Valley. With more BMWs per capita than anywhere else on earth (Germany included), Santa Clara County south of San Francisco is home to the golden youth of high tech, the scientific yuppies whose microchip factories and computer think tanks have caused the entire area to be known as Silicon Valley. Their very presence here has, in turn, spawned a secondary resort industry well known to most residents of San Francisco, but to scarcely anyone else at all. It is centered about four remarkable towns: Los Gatos, Santa Cruz, Aptos Beach, and Capitola.

The inland gem of Silicon Valley is little Los Gatos, sandwiched between a double range of low-lying mountains about 30 miles from the sea. A relatively compact city by California standards, its trendy downtown area can be covered on foot, passing boutiques by the dozen, chic eth-

THE UNDISCOVERED DESTINATION—DOES IT STILL EXIST? IT'S OBVIOUSLY HARDER AND HARDER TO FIND

nic restaurants, crafts stores and art galleries, a movie house showing foreign films, and—most delightful—a block-long garden/courtyard fronting a theatre in a restored old mercantile building, all of this alongside still other restaurants patronized by many of the most accomplished young and middle-aged people of America.

The chief seaside location is sprawling Santa Cruz, almost wholly suburban in appearance, but with that most appealing of urban attractions: a pleasant boardwalk lined with ferris wheel, roller coaster, and other smaller entertainments for families with kids. Behind the boardwalk are suburban-like areas of charming modern residences, as well as wooden Victorian homes made into low-cost apartments. These, and the city's mild, year-round climate (better than San Francisco's), have attracted flocks of writers, artists, and musicians to a community that grows ever more vital with their arrival. Immediately adjoining Santa Cruz: the more sophisticated Capitola (again, art galleries, colorful restaurants and boutiques, hotels in Spanish style directly facing the sea) and Aptos Beach, where waters are warm enough for swimming in almost every month. If hotels in these stylish sections are too pricey for your budget, you'll find numerous lower-cost bed-and-breakfast establishments nearby.

If you were now to proceed southward along coastal Highway 1 for another 30 miles, you would reach that stretch of Pacific Ocean beachfront of which everyone in America knows: the famed Monterrey Peninsula, with its awesome "17-Mile-Drive." But don't neglect the resorts of Silicon Valley in your search for the better-known sight. While these havens

> Cafés in which you chat for hours with residents eager and open to a newcomer's questions.

of high tech can be contrived—a bit pretentious—in their architecture and decor, sometimes "tea shoppe" in character, screamingly quaint, they house a special breed of American, alive to every human possibility, ambitious and educated in the best sense, open and eager to new ideas and people—like you.

(3) Malta, in the Mediterranean. The British tourist goes there. And so does the German. But to date, very few Americans have experienced the unique charms of this odd Mediterranean island, a former member of the British Commonwealth, located 60 miles south of Sicily. It is accessible via cheap flights (as little as $224 round trip from London) on its own flag carrier, Air Malta, operating from major European capitals to a coral-covered surface of about 100 square miles. And once there, the tourist discovers top

hotel resorts (the Malta Hilton, the Phoenicia) charging but $82 to $110 a night for a double room, lesser hotels for much less, restaurants with an Italianate flavor charging $6 and under for meals, an outgoing, sociable population of about 300,000 people, well-disposed to visitors —and sun, sun, and more sun.

After a checkered history of successive domination by many different foreign lands, Malta burst into world prominence in the 1500s when it came under the control of the historically important Knights of the Order of St. John, a quasi-military organization of the Roman

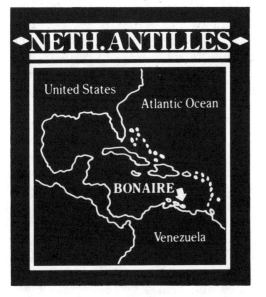

Catholic Church. In later centuries—particularly the 17th and 19th—the "Knights of Malta" brought artistic riches to the island's many churches, and covered its cities, particularly the capital of Valletta, with white stone structures of great architectural merit; most of these ancient buildings still stand and impart a distinctive cast to the island's appearance. In World War II, as a key outpost of the British Empire, Malta withstood the most constant but unavailing attacks by the German air force.

For today's tourist to Malta, there are more intact historical remnants per square mile than perhaps anywhere else in the world: both Megalithic and later Roman temples, catacombs and palaces, formerly inhabited grottoes and caves. There are medieval fortifications and structures built by the Knights, more recent façades from the era of the ba-

In a world crammed with sightseeing buses, amid the wailing jet engines and the cacophony of tourist voices, five refreshingly unspoiled destinations come to mind.

roque, the homes of ancient nobles, art treasures of extraordinary value and variety—it requires a full week to take in the most minimal list of sights.

For less exalted recreation: low-priced resort hotels with pools, casinos, and tennis courts; intermittent beaches scattered about (particularly on the small neighboring islands of Gozo and Comino); sightseeing boat cruises through the Grand Harbor and along the coast; those Italianate restaurants to which I referred; and those friendly Maltese people, themselves an attraction. Among the undiscovered gems to which you haven't yet been, Malta ranks high; don't omit it when planning your next European itinerary. For more information, contact **Air Malta, 345 California Street, Suite 2560, San Francisco, CA 94104 (phone 415/362-2929).**

(4) The Colorful Nation of Belgium. Neglected by the tourist throngs, lightly visited and often casually dismissed—"If it's Tuesday, it must be Belgium"—Belgium is a nation with museums to rival the Louvre, a cuisine rated tops in the world, a friendly, sympathetic population, and low to moderate prices. Why, then, is it so widely bypassed by the major travel movements?

The fault, I suggest, lies in the tourist and not in Belgium. We tourists were incorrectly taught that the Middle Ages —the period of Belgium's greatest glory —was a time of "darkness," when nothing much happened, and mankind passed into sloth and illiteracy. Because the greatest Belgian sights are medieval cities preserved from that period—Bruges, Ghent, Antwerp, Tournai—we assume them to be unimportant, and either eliminate a stay from our itinerary or schedule only a scant two days for Belgium.

In actual fact, the latter half of the so-called Middle Ages—the High Gothic era—was a time of extraordinary human achievement, in which Belgium was a world leader. It was then that people embarked upon construction of the great Gothic cathedrals, began painting the never-again-equalled masterworks of the Flemish primitives, erected the gilded city squares and soaring belfry towers that so enchant us today, and formulated

GRAND MASTER MANOEL DE VILHENA (1722-1736)

most of the legal, commercial, and theological concepts that continue to govern our lives. As you pass beyond Brussels to the magnificently preserved medieval cities of Belgium, you literally stagger under the impact of great art and architecture, revising all your previously mistaken notions about those "terrible Dark Ages."

In addition to drinking in these remark-

able visual sights, you eat—oh, how you eat! You dine from the wares of chefs as celebrated as movie stars. You choose from 300 varieties of Belgian beer. Suitably aglow, you watch ballet companies and colorful religious processions, outdoor markets and masked revelers, festivals peopled by papier-mâché giants, massed ranks of dedicated diamond cutters, equally intent croupiers at elegant seaside casinos on the 60-mile Belgian coast.

Don't pass up Belgium—it is the example par excellence of another undiscovered geographical delight! An enthralling nation well represented by the capable **Belgian National Tourist Office, 745 Fifth Avenue, New York, NY 10151 (phone 212/758-8130)**, from which further information is readily available, it more than repays the tourist who approaches its resplendent city sights with the proper, advance historical preparation—and attitudes.

(5) Wales and Its People. For most of us, our awareness of Wales—that separate "country" in the western part of the British Isles—is based on poems by Dylan Thomas, as read by Richard Burton, or from *How Green Was My Valley* and its picture of the harsh life of coal miners occupying the section's southern industrial belt. Mainly it is a grim image we remember, and grimmer still now that the coal mines are mainly abandoned and Britain's "sunset" industries (steel, in particular) winding down. In actual fact, the greater part of Wales is a green and verdant landscape, given over to large national parks and impressive mountain ranges, to white sheep with black feet grazing on heather-covered slopes, to picturesque villages and terraced farms,

with scarcely a single soot-darkened miner trudging wearily home at dusk. Though the Welsh economy is sharply depressed, its tourist appeal is undiminished and increasingly looked to as a source of Welsh employment. Yet only a bare handful of Americans travel on to this unusual "nation" found only three-or-so hours by train from London.

You reach the underpopulated center of Wales, or the alpine-like north, in less than four comfortable hours from London's Euston Station, usually changing at Shrewsbury (pronounced "shroze-berry") and proceeding from there through the "harp-shaped" hills of Wales (Dylan Thomas's phrase) either through the center or to the northwest. If you choose the central route heading toward the quaint and dreamy town of Machynlleth (pronounced "mah-hun-lith"), with its several hotels and guesthouses, you can pause for a day or two to view an oddity (described in a separate essay in Part III)—the Centre for Alternative Technology—located atop an abandoned slate quarry just outside the town. A utopian community of 30-or-so extreme ecologists, fully self-sufficient from the use of renewable energy sources only (solar power, wind,

water), the Centre actively encourages visits and conducts all guests on extensive tours of the grounds, seven days a week. One continues from Machynlleth to the delightful Welsh university town of Aberystwyth on the sea, or northward to Snowdonia Park containing the highest mountain peaks in Britain.

With its distinctive national culture and history, its use of the Welsh language by nearly 25% of the population, Wales is an exotic travel experience too complex to summarize here, but one that shouldn't be passed up. It is the classic example of an untouristed (by Americans) "find," possessing all the attributes and attrac-

tions of more heavily visited destinations, but reserved, for the time being, just for you!

U.S. Winter Vacations—Mostly Odd and Unexpected

A sk an experienced friend or travel agent to recommend a wintertime vacation in the United States and it's likely the response will be so standard and limited as to be utterly infuriating.

The two coasts of Florida. Aspen and Vail. Los Angeles and Orlando. Though the same savants can name dozens of holiday havens in Mexico and the Caribbean, they get tongue-tied and tentative in contemplating the vast expanses of the U.S.A.

Well, obviously we have more places to go than the tired old favorites. While some of them are hot, most are faintly chilly or worse—and are therefore inexpensive and so seldom regarded as winter destinations as to be pleasantly uncrowded and unpressured. Here are 11 "picks," both hot and cold:

1. A Long Theatre Weekend in Minneapolis/St. Paul

Meet the "sleepers" of the travel scene, the oddest capitals of culture to emerge in many years—and a remarkable destination for avid, incessant theatre-going. Though their more extravagant claims may be open to doubt, boosters of Minnesota's "Twin Cities" will argue with passion that on at least four nights of the week, more high-quality presentations in the performing arts are given here than in any U.S. city other than New York.

As to the quality (if perhaps not the quantity) of those spectacles, they have a

Meet the "sleepers" of the travel scene, Minnesota's Twin Cities.

point. Critics have ranked St. Paul's new opera house, the Ordway, and its presentations as among the world's best. They rank the Guthrie in Minneapolis as the nation's finest regional and repertory theatre, bar none. The Children's Theatre here is widely acclaimed, as are half a dozen symphonic, concert, recital, and dance stages hosting major soloists and troupes, and a horde of smaller off-Broadway and off-off-Broadway–type playhouses devoted to heavy-duty, avant-garde, experimental, or classic plays. Obtaining tickets at a fraction the price of New York's (and far more easily available), a great many of the nation's most intense theatre-goers are opting to substitute a winter weekend in Minneapolis/St. Paul for all the bright lights of Broadway, as improbable as that might seem.

Weather, of course—the most dreadful, appalling conditions—is a drawback. But second-story "skyways" vaulting over the streets and connecting a great many downtown buildings often enable you to walk from place to place without venturing outside. It was ten degrees below zero on my last visit, yet I had to be dragged away once I saw the ads for *Cyrano de Bergerac* at one theatre, a Eugene O'Neill revival at another. For additional information, write the **Minnesota Office of Tourism, 375 Jackson Street, 250 Skyway, St. Paul, MN 55101 (phone 612/296-5029, or toll free 800/**

DOMESTIC DESTINATIONS FOR YOUR DECEMBER-THROUGH-MARCH HOLIDAY

328-1461, 800/652-9747 in Minnesota). And welcome to the new "Athens of America."

2. *Nashville by Night*

Though it's obviously milder than most northern cities, Nashville can be cold in winter—let's agree on that. But the attractions of the country-music capital are weather-resistant indoor and evening ones, in taverns showcasing aspiring country-music greats, in "Opry Land," and at the Grand Old Opry.

Because the major country stars spend much of the spring-through-fall season at out-of-state shows and country fairs, winter is the best time for catching them on home grounds. That's when you're almost certain to see the likes of Loretta Lynn and "Cousin" Minnie Pearl at the famed "Opry," where the price is only $11 ($9 and $7 at matinees) plus tax for seats widely available (at that time) without

> The attractions of our country-music capital are weather-resistant, indoor and evening ones, in taverns showcasing aspiring talent.

long-in-advance reservations.

Time was when just outside the Opry's backdoor you could stroll to a number of musical taverns with lesser country entertainers. The disappearance of that cluster has led some visitors to conclude, mistakenly, that the "showcases" no longer exist. They do, as vital and thriving as ever, but in scattered locations. At one, the Nashville Palace, a certain Randy Travis—the ordinary "house act" for two years—broke out into country stardom with a major album. At the Bullpen Lounge in downtown Nashville, and at the Station Inn and Bluegrass Inn nearby, you, too, might see a similar "star of tomorrow" in their apprentice mode.

Daytimes, about 12 miles to the east of the city, the major attraction is Andrew Jackson's plantation-style Hermitage, as fascinating as his own personality and career. Weekends in winter you can board a 300-foot packet-type paddlewheeler for an outing on the Cumberland River, including live musical entertainment. In December you supplement other evening events with dinner and an hour-long

Tennessee State Capitol

265

WHILE SOME OF THEM ARE HOT, MOST ARE FAINTLY CHILLY OR WORSE—AND THEREFORE INEXPENSIVE AND UNCROWDED

stageshow, *Country Christmas*, at the 1,000-room Opryland Hotel.

But mainly there's that Grand Old Opry, and the several smaller stages of the country-music taverns. They provoke such hoedown enthusiasm that some visitors end their stays with a visit to Nashville's Recording Studios of America. Why? Because this small professional establishment has a library of prerecorded 24-track backgrounds for country and pop songs, enabling them to record you against a full orchestral background, as you bellow your favorite country hit for the folks back home ($10.95, including a minute or two of rehearsal time, and one cassette). For further Nashville details, contact the **Nashville Convention & Visitors Bureau, 161 Fourth Avenue North, Nashville, TN 37219 (phone 615/259-3900).**

3. *Wandering by Car Through Southern Arizona*

Thronged with tourists in the spring and summer, the national parks and monuments of Arizona—more numerous, more heavily visited, than in any other state—are pleasantly uncrowded in the winter months, and many are just as

Winter is the time to visit one of the greatest sightseeing attractions in the world—Washington, D.C.

pleasingly warm in climate. Though, if you're like most people, you won't want to make a winter tour of such northerly attractions as the Petrified Forest or the Grand Canyon (whose north rim is actually closed to tourists in winter), the south of the cactus state is another matter.

In the so-called Desert Country—the southeastern quadrant of Arizona—viewing conditions are at their yearly best in winter. Average temperatures range from 65° to 75° in January, February, and March, drawing hordes of "snowbirds" from other states to the costly resorts and city attractions of Phoenix and Tucson.

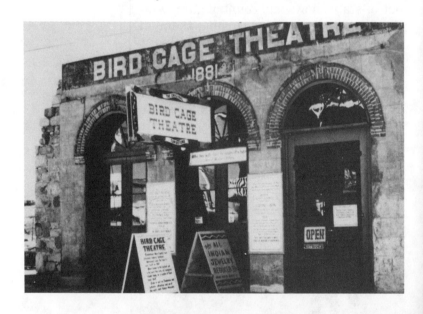

San Xavier del Bac

Old Tucson

But to the south of Phoenix, and to the south and east of Tucson, a remarkable array of other pleasures await, all interspersed with moderately priced highway motels. On any number of classic motoring itineraries—well described in an "Arizona by Auto" booklet issued by the state tourist office—you'll make an inexpensive, warm-weather swing to such enthralling locations as Saguaro National Monument (40-foot-high cacti, some 150 years old, largest found in the U.S.), the adobe ruins of historic Fort Bowie, Organ Pipe Cactus National Monument, the several sections of the Coronado National Forest, the Chiricahua National Monument (volcanic rock formations), and the abandoned ghost towns and mines surrounding Bisbee and the well-preserved Tombstone ("Shoot-Out at the O.K. Corral," with its Crystal Palace Saloon and other simple wooden buildings looking exactly as they did more than 100 years ago). For literature so attractive that you'll instantly yearn to make the trip, contact the **Arizona Office of Tourism, 1480 East Bethany Home Road, Phoenix, AZ 85014 (phone 602/255-3618).**

4. *Washington, D.C., When the Crowds Have Gone*

In spring and summer, it teems with tourists in sweaty T-shirts and jeans. They in turn convoy irascible young children sticky with the remains of Dove Bars and Popsicles. All in all, that's not the most auspicious company for viewing the Rembrandts at the National Gallery.

Winter is the time for visiting Washington, D.C. With tourism then sharply reduced, the hearing rooms of congressional committees offer easily visited drama; the marble chambers of the Supreme Court serve up oratory to savor—and with no great wait.

And the exhibits, the collections! Surely the eight clustered museums of the Smithsonian Institution (Air and Space, Natural History, Arts and Industries, American History, Freer Gallery, Hirschhorn, the "Castle," and the Nation-

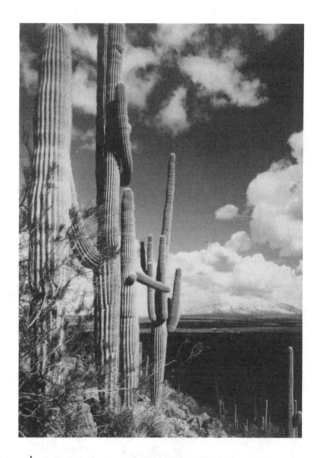

Symbol of the Southwest

al Gallery)—all on the Mall, within an easy stroll of each other—are, in their totality, among the greatest sightseeing attractions on earth (and underrated by our cultural elite). They can all best be visited, in profound comfort and quiet, in the slow winter months.

In winter here, hotel rates plummet on weekends and during congressional recesses. They are always low when booked as a "package"—in those glossy brochures filling your travel agent's racks. If you can't find a package, then bargain over the phone when requesting a room reservation, and more often than you'd dream possible a special rate will be found for you.

THE GOLDEN ISLES OF GEORGIA ARE RICH WITH RESORTS AT REFRESHING WINTER PRICES

5. *New Orleans in Its Finest Hour*

New Orleans is overbuilt with hotels (temporarily, at least). That's the big news affecting travel to this classic American attraction, whose climate is best—mild and refreshing, for shirts and light jackets—in the deep winter months. The city's disastrous 1983 World's Fair (still causing political repercussions) left a legacy for us tourists of several thousand new hotel rooms. Result: What was once the nation's most expensive hotel city, vying with San Francisco and New York for that dubious honor, is now appreciably cheaper. Reasonably priced hotel rooms join reasonably priced meals as a potent tourist magnet.

And the meals are reasonable indeed. At one of the city's finest restaurants—Commander's Palace—the average dinner check (according to management) averages $50 for two persons; at lunch, special

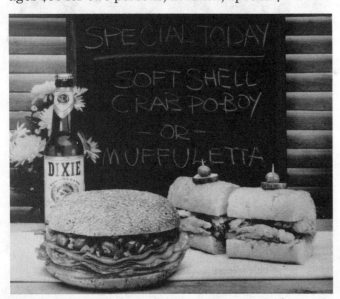

four-course meals of gourmet level can be had for $10.50.

So why hesitate? With its irresistible

Because the temperatures are perhaps ten degrees cooler than in southern Florida, the winter of the pleasantly uncrowded Panhandle is a technical "off-season."

Créole cuisine, its French-colonial architecture, its "foreign" ways and no-holds-barred morality, its open-to-the-air jazz hangouts, its Mississippi setting and black-coffee-with-crullers in the late night chill, New Orleans is an indispensable winter visit: at some point in your life, it must be seen.

6. *The "Golden Isles" of Georgia*

At the turn of the century America's wealthiest families—the Rockefellers, Vanderbilts, Goodyears, Pulitzers—spent the winter on these barrier islands off the Atlantic coast of Georgia, in elaborate "cottages" on grounds of what was then the nation's most exclusive resort: the Jekyll Island Club.

At that location, roughly halfway between Savannah and Jacksonville, winter conditions are about as mild, measured, and moderate as you can get in these United States (average mean temperatures of 55° from January through March), but not of the sort that attract the heat-seeking crowds. Yet the islands are rich with beaches, lush year round with foliage, laced with marshes and marsh rivers teeming with wildlife, and dotted with widely scattered hotels in all price ranges on the three islands that take overnight visitors: St. Simons, Sea Island, and Jekyll. All are easily reached by causeways from the port city of Brunswick, Georgia ("Shrimp Capital of the World"). A fourth—Cumberland Island—is a "national seashore" of hiking trails and historic ruins, but without hotels or restaurants and reached only by boat.

Though the ultra-wealthy have long since pushed further south to Palm Beach, people of normal means will continue to find the most remarkable lodgings here—the historic and newly refurbished Jekyll Island Club (reopened in December 1987 after a 45-year sting as a state monument), the glamorous, thoroughly deluxe The Cloister on Sea Island, numerous hotels of lesser rank—at refreshing winter prices. At the legendary The Cloister, where some guests still dress formally for dinner, rates on the American Plan (three lavish meals daily) are as little as $85 a day per person in most winter periods. For rarified vacation activities—riding stables and deep-sea fishing, wine lectures and "big bands," golf and skeet shooting, but all without bankruptcy—the coastal islands of Georgia are hard to beat in winter.

7. *The Panhandle Coast of Florida*

They call it "air-conditioned sand" because it's cool to the touch on the hottest of days. Small particles of pulverized mountain quartz brought south by melting waters of the last Ice Age, those remarkably uniform granules have created here one of the whitest, softest, most pleasant beaches on earth. It stretches, with some gaps, for 130 miles along that thin, lengthwise rectangle of Florida (the Panhandle) lying directly below Alabama on the Gulf of Mexico—from Pensacola in the west to Panama City in the east. In between are Destin and Fort Walton Beach.

Because the temperatures are perhaps ten degrees cooler than in southern Florida, the winter of the pleasantly uncrowded Panhandle is a technical "off-season," though averaging a comfortable winter mean of 60°. While few visitors go sea-bathing at that time, they swim in heated pools, play golf at 34 nationally famous courses (a major activity), go sportfishing

(for marlin and sailfish) from Destin, visit the Spanish quarter of historic Pensacola—and all at winter lodging rates as low as $35 a room in good-quality motels, far less than they'd pay at the wall-to-wall hotels of central or southern Florida. And they dine magnificently, on scamp and amberjack, grouper and blue-shell crabs, Gulf shrimp, oysters and red snapper, and other famed seafood wonders of the Gulf Coast.

Though in past years the Panhandle has primarily been a destination for low-income tourism from Alabama and Mississippi, it has sprouted in the most recent times with important high-quality resorts: Marriott's Bay Point Resort in Panama City Beach, the Sandestin Beach Resort, the new Sandestin Hilton, among others; all are the equal of the more celebrated names to the south, but relatively unknown among a national audience. Get there quick before the crowds arrive. And for additional information, try the helpful **Greater Fort Walton Beach Chamber of Commerce, P.O. Drawer 640, Fort Walton Beach, FL 32549 (phone 904/244-8191).**

8. *San Diego and Its Winter Sun*

If you can't decide between city attractions and country-like pleasures, between sports and nightlife, shopping and sunbathing, then San Diego is the perfect winter destination for you: it has both. A sprawling city of nearly a million souls, with 90 museums and countless stores, it offers miles of Pacific Ocean beaches and endless acres of parks, deserts, and mountain ranges, and so many recreational activities that it has been called "the fitness capital of the United States."

Everything is accompanied by constant

DOES THE "REAL, UNTOUCHED" HAWAII STILL EXIST? YES—JUST BARELY

sun: 265 days a year of it, less than ten yearly inches of rain, average high temperatures in winter of 65°, rarely a chilly day. In any other section of the country its winter weather would be acclaimed as a tourist magnet, yet because the winter is a tiny bit cooler than in other seasons, hotel rates tend to drop somewhat in the January-through-March period. Because the city possesses a massive hotel plant in every price range, those winter hotel rates then become moderate indeed.

In addition to important cultural attractions, the city operates major maritime attractions, a zoo considered to be one of the world's finest, an important harborside area. Its main downtown streets have been greatly upgraded in recent years, and made cosmopolitan with futuristic shopping and entertainment complexes. It is among the nation's fastest-growing cities.

Yet it is mainly that near-perfect climate which attracts the wintertime visitor—and isn't that reason enough?

9. *Mendocino, the Mild Massachusetts of the California Coast*

When producers of the TV mystery series "Murder, She Wrote" want to film Angela Lansbury in the Maine-like setting of the story line, they take their cameras to the Pacific Coast town of Mendocino, California, 170 miles north of San Francisco. Settled in the 1850s by fishermen from New England, developed by them in the ensuing decades of the late 19th century, and unaltered since, Mendocino is a perfectly preserved National Historic District—an authentic New England fishing village in appearance, protected from change by Draconian regulations. Today, when Californians want a

> Though not nearly as famous as Carmel, Mendocino is the same species of "getaway" in the north, but without the excessive crowds and at much lower cost.

respite from modern life, they head to the small hotels (25, 50 rooms, at most) in Mendocino's historic buildings, or to some of the $40-a-night B&Bs in authentic historic homes. There they sit by the fire, or soak in hot tubs, or go walking along the sea or fishing in it for salmon (from party boats), or ride horseback through the surf, or dine late and leisurely in trendy ethnic restaurants ranging from Cajun to Mexican to pure, classic French. Blessedly, there are no chain hotels in the area, no fast-food shops, no modern structures at all. "Romantic" is the word for Mendocino, and also describes the instant mood of many tourists.

The climate is exactly that of San Francisco: rarely above 75°, rarely below freezing. The winter is mild, and tourism continues through it. The seaside terrain and coastline are like those of Maine, all jagged with headlands, bluffs, coves, tiny beaches—but backed, in this instance, by the giant redwoods of California.

The chief business activity, apart from tourism, is arts and crafts, and the resultant shopping occupies a great many visitors. For other forms of commerce, you go ten miles farther up the coast to the almost equally interesting old port city of Fort Bragg.

Though not nearly as famous as Clint Eastwood's Carmel, found 150 miles south of San Francisco, Mendocino is the same species of "getaway" in the north, but without the excessive crowds and at much lower cost. Next time you're tempted to head the car south, drive north instead. For further details, and for making B&B bookings, contact the **Fort Bragg–Mendocino Coast Chamber of Commerce, P.O. Box 1141, Fort Bragg, CA 95437 (phone 707/964-3153).**

10. *A Skiing Vacation Outside Reno, Nevada*

In the winter when its weather turns cold, Reno, Nevada, no longer enjoys the casual tempo and appeal of its sunny sister resort, Las Vegas. Hotel rates plunge and avid gamblers enjoy a stay that, if not for their gambling losses, would barely dent their purses.

Nowadays their ranks are joined by an unlikely lot of youthful, apple-cheeked, outdoor sorts whose tastes run to fruit juices at the casino bars. Fed up with the price-gouging and overcrowding of the more celebrated ski areas (particularly those in Colorado), a sizable number of winter skiers now take moderately priced winter-season accommodations at the most glamorous Reno hotels—like the 2,000-room MGM Grand—and drive from there each morning to ski lifts and slopes less than an hour away. After a day of hard skiing, they return not to expensive-but-spartan bunks in muddy lodges, but to the warmth and lush comfort of a casino hotel room, with mirrors on the ceiling yet.

Within a 60-mile radius of Reno are a dozen major ski areas amply supplied with lifts. As close as 24 miles away are two quite decent slopes with lifts and other facilities. Less than 20 miles due south of Reno is the awesomely lovely Lake Tahoe and the start of the Sierra Nevada mountains, with still other exciting ski possibilities, all priced well below the levels in other states. By opting for the unlikely base of Reno, you save a considerable amount on ski facilities, save even more on your lodgings expense, enjoy top room comforts and scintillating nightlife, and become that rarity in a Nevadan gambling center—a big winner.

> Fed up with the price-gouging and crowds of the more celebrated resorts, a sizable number of winter skiers seek accommodations and slopes in and around Reno.

11. *The Other Hawaii*

You walk the streets of crowded Waikiki, passing couples in matching aloha shirts and muumuus, and if you've a modicum of taste or sensitivity, you yearn to escape to the "real Hawaii," the traditional or untouched Hawaii. Does it still exist?

Just barely. And it requires precise instructions, a dogged persistence, to find.

You encounter it best (and most cheaply) by choosing to stay in bed-and-breakfast establishments on each of the major islands. **B & B Hawaii, P.O. Box 449, Kapaa, HI 96746 (phone 808/822-7771)**, is typical of several major organizations that have persuaded hundreds of ordinary Hawaiians to open their homes to transient guests.

Or you write well ahead to the few surviving indigenous Hawaiian resorts, like Coco Palms north of Lihue on the lush garden island of Kauai. Alternatively, you "rough it," staying at the national-park-operated dormitory cabins in Haleakala on Maui, or at the rustic Kokee Lodge near Waimea Canyon in Kauai. Best yet, you travel from Oahu to the island of Molokai, which is where the Hawaiians go when they want to "get away from it all." The last of the major islands to be developed, its main town is like a set from a Wild West movie, its facilities a bit weatherbeaten, its shopping poor; but it is laid-back and rural, like Hawaii itself 50 years ago. (Increasingly it is becoming the residence of serious artists and craftspeople.) And it is cheap: try the Pau Hana Inn outside the main town of Kaunakakai, at $35 per oceanside room. Contact the **Hawaii Visitors Bureau, 2270 Kalakaua Avenue, Honolulu, HI 96815 (phone 808/923-1811)**.

A Pilgrimage to Arcosanti

Like an immortal among the living, he is perhaps the leading architect of our time.

Colleges would kill to have him on their staffs. Others would pay fortunes to have him design their skyscrapers, homes, and hotels.

Yet he sits in shorts and undershirt in the Arizona desert, 65 miles north of Phoenix, enduring ridicule, stretching funds, but building, always building, his dream city, Arcosanti. To tour through Arizona and not to visit the urban vision of 68-year-old Paolo Soleri is to miss a view of the future as seen by a possible Leonardo da Vinci, at least a sublime Don Quixote, of our century.

The quest for Arcosanti starts in the setting that Soleri detests. From the sprawling tract homes of Phoenix's hushed and endless suburbs (a two-dimensional city in a three-dimensional world, Soleri would say), you at last pass

The trip begins in the setting that Soleri detests: Phoenix, Arizona

in your rental car into awesome desert mountains, their lower slopes lined with tall saguaro cactus, like toy soldiers guarding the approach to Soleri's domain.

An hour and a quarter's drive brings you to the tiny, uplands community of Cordes Junction (occasional cowboy-types in dusty pickup vans), where you turn onto a bumpy dirt road and follow signs for several miles into the horizon-wide emptiness of the construction site, on a mesa overlooking a dry riverbed valley and facing cliff.

At a visitors' center splashed with sunlight from great round windows, you pay $4 for an hourly tour, and join a daily average total of perhaps 50 Americans, rarely more, who make their arduous way to this site of titanic conflict with prevailing urban concepts. That paltry income helps fund the construction, as does a few hundred dollars of weekly profit from the appearance of periodic Elderhostel groups who live in the few completed apartments, attend daily lectures, and then mold and fire their own tiles to adorn the concrete walls of high-tech arches scattered about. Near the end of their week, they meet Soleri. He descends a rough-hewn ladder from a balcony-studio,

SOLERI'S CITY OF TOMORROW, ON A BARREN DESERT FLOOR

and for one or two hours stolen from work, gently and patiently, with good humor and respect for the elders' views, he fields questions and doubts about the monumental project.

To complete Arcosanti would require upward of half a billion dollars and perhaps 20 more years; it is now 3% done, largely from the labor of volunteer college students who flocked here in the 1960s and '70s to pour concrete and shape stone. It is obvious from the current lessened pace of construction that today's young people, intent upon their entrance into the corporate culture, are not providing Arcosanti with the support that a more idealistic earlier generation did.

So how, apart from visitors' fees, does Soleri continue to construct Arcosanti? Largely from the sale of windbells. Fiercely refusing to deal with mortgage brokers and venture capitalists, innately unable to beg and solicit at cocktail-party fundraisers, thoroughly unsuited for foundation grants and rich widow's handouts, he devotes off-hours to designing these ravishing works in bronze and ceramics, and raises, through their sale, most of the income needed to keep Arcosanti alive. "If 30 years ago, someone had

A central hall at Arcosanti

The unfinished Arcosanti

told me that windbells would build Arcosanti, I'd have thought him mad," he smiles.

The object of these expenditures is a complex series of interconnected structures—almost like a single building, one part of which will be 25 stories high—designed to house 6,000 persons and to supply them, in the same building, with their workplace, entertainment, culture, and support systems.

HE LABORS IN A SPARE WORKROOM, ENDURING RIDICULE, STRETCHING FUNDS, BUT BUILDING, ALWAYS BUILDING, HIS DREAM CITY, ARCOSANTI

Arcosanti from afar

It is a city so densely populated and compact as to use only the barest fraction of the land on which it sits—in Arcosanti's case, 14 acres out of 860 surrounding and unused acres. It thus preserves nature instead of paving it over. Its inhabitants are city people and rural folk at one and the same time. From their city, they have only to step outside into vast, adjoining countryside.

Though it houses people to the highest population density on earth, it provides family units with as much as 2,000 square feet of apartment space apiece—far more than most Americans enjoy. That feat is achieved by "miniaturizing" other traditional structures of today's cities, and particularly by eliminating the automobile, with its space devouring streets, freeways, intersections, garages and parking spaces, curbs and lots. In Arcosanti, one simply walks from one end of the city to the other in ten minutes.

The city of Soleri's dream is intensely energy-efficient. It is flanked with vast sloping greenhouses that create a "chimney" effect, wafting sunwarmed air to the adjoining megabuilding, to create both heating and air conditioning, as the seasons require.

It is complex to an extent unimaginable until seen, even in the model you will peruse on the top floor of the visitors' center. In this respect, according to Soleri, it is an upward step in man's evolution, leading to higher and more developed forms of social interaction—and perhaps to higher consciousness.

It is an "arcology," in Soleri's phrase, a blending of the best in architecture and ecology. And it is one of several score of single-structure "arcologies" he has designed, whose sketches and detailed drawings appear in his remarkable *The City in the Image of Man* (Cambridge, Mass.: MIT Press, 1969), unfortunately now out of print. There you find the plans for "Novanoah" (a floating, ocean-based city for 400,000 people), "Arcodi-ga" (a city atop a dam, whose 280,000 residents enjoy unlimited cheap energy and unparalleled water sports and recreation), "Stonebow" (constructed like a giant bridge over a canyon or ravine, for 200,000 persons), "Astcromo" (a city in space, designed like a giant lightbulb to house 70,000), and "Infrababel" (for 100,000, partially underground).

Does all this set your teeth on edge? If so, says Soleri, consider the alternative: the sprawling, low-density, energy-inefficient cities of one-family homes in the sunbelt of America.

They spread like permanently enlarging inkblots over once-verdant fields and gardens, devouring ever-greater portions of our remaining countryside. Their geographical expanse is so immense—so dispersed, of such low density—as to separate humanity from its institutions. Every simple function of life—attending a film, shopping, visiting friends—becomes a major undertaking. In them, residents spend interminable, inane hours in highway lines, anxiously tuned to traffic reporters, enduring gridlock and jams, boredom and fatigue. Isolated by distance from their fellow human beings, people are prisoners in their homes, condemned to sit in darkened living rooms staring at TV.

They are retrograde cities, backward and simple, cultural wastelands. Their

sheer sterility, in its impact upon the young, cannot help but create a generation to dread.

And so Soleri builds. To demonstrate, to prove. Though his writings are profuse and in every library, he feels compelled to physically create the new metropolis. Without funds or proper assistance, without junior architects to draft the detailed work, without help in a hundred areas, he labors on, doggedly, without complaint.

And Arcosanti grows, but at an infuri-

Soleri

atingly slow pace, in a race against the mortal condition of Soleri's own life.

How can you and I help Paolo Soleri? First, we can visit Arcosanti, in the manner just described. The address is: I-17 at **Cordes Junction, Mayer, AZ 86333 (phone 602/632-7135).**

Second, we can devote our vacations to his five-week "workshops" on the site. There, after a week of instruction primarily in concrete-pouring (the basic material of the city), participants work for four weeks in the actual construction of a tiny unit in the jigsaw-puzzle-like structure of Arcosanti. Cost for the entire five weeks is a remarkable $560—precisely $16 a day—including accommodations, instruction and supervision, and all three meals daily. Workshop schedules are prepared in late fall, and you can write for application forms to: **Registrar, The Cosanti Foundation, 6433 Doubletree Road, Scottsdale, AZ 85253 (or phone 602/948-6145).**

Finally, we can all help search for a benefactor. Among your acquaintances is there a millionaire seeking immortality as the patron or patroness to a great man? Just a few of those millions could bring in a professional construction company that could speed the development of Arcosanti and draw in further capital.

In an America sprouting with trivial theme parks, deathly parking garages, and redundant shopping centers, aren't there funds for a city that might advance mankind?

A Memoir of Bruges

When we first wander through it, astonished and silent, we try to rein in our excitement. After all, on our trips throughout Europe before visiting Bruges, we have seen other perfectly preserved medieval communities: Carcassonne, Siena, Ávila, Rothenburg.

But those were mere villages, small secondary towns. Bruges is a medieval *city* perfectly preserved, a giant, sprawl-

A natural phenomenon caused it to miss the Industrial Revolution. If only more ancient cities had suffered such misfortune!

ing, ancient metropolis once of world significance, and yet today almost unaltered

Bruges by day

in its former splendor, its awesome beauty and size.

Suddenly those people of the Middle Ages cease, in our minds, to appear a quaint and backward species. All at once we realize, if we hadn't before, that people have nearly always had aspirations and achievements equivalent to ours. And if we were born, as I was, an American, optimistic and arrogant, rarely looking back, believing in the constant upward progress of human civilization, we feel shaken by Bruges; we learn decisively that mankind has both advanced and declined, that aspects of the past were perhaps superior to the present, that an age nearly 700 years ago, and later reviled as "dark," enjoyed artistic, commercial, and physical prowess of a sort that many later eras and nations have still to attain.

Bruges is a city arrested in time. A Pompeii or a Brigadoon. An urban portrait caught as if by stop-frame photography, of a community that died while it was still young. The most heavily visited touristic site in all of Belgium, it is the victim of one of the strangest natural events of history—the "silting of the Zwin"—which snuffed out its commercial life in the late Middle Ages, caused it to miss the Industrial Revolution, and thus paradoxically saved its unique medieval legacy from the wreckers' ball. If only more ancient cities had suffered such misfortune!

Bruges, in medieval times, was the greatest trading center in northern Europe, a multinational marketplace for importing and exporting, storing, and displaying cloths and spices, herrings and wine, every variety of goods. Along its canals and in central squares dozens of wealthy foreign merchants maintained exotic commercial palaces, virtual embas-

ARRESTED IN TIME, A POMPEII OR A BRIGADOON

sies of their countries in which they lavishly entertained and dealt with the thousands of traders who flocked to a city renowned for its glitter and importance.

The focus of all this movement, the vital access road, was the Zwin, a waterway that connected Bruges to the North Sea. In the mid-1300s, at the height of Bruges' renown, and for reasons still not fully understood, the Zwin began to fill with sand, denying passage to deep-draft ships. By the 1400s it was clogged and impassable.

And Bruges died. Literally died. With the ending of ship traffic, commercial activity virtually ceased, and large portions of the population—some estimate as many as half—left to seek employment in Antwerp and other cities, abandoning their stunning homes, their commercial palaces, their magnificent squares. For 500 years, through the late 19th century, Bruges dozed and declined until a Belgian writer, Georges Rodenbach, inadvertently broadcast its charms to the world in a novel called *Bruges La Morte* (Dead Bruges) and set off a wave of tourism. Soon thereafter, wise minds forbade any further tampering with the façades of Bruges, and the city embarked on its second career, this time as a monumental European tourist destination. I have often felt that if the international airport of Belgium were located outside Bruges, rather than Brussels, overseas tourism to Belgium would triple.

Bruges today is a city of dreams, where every walk brings reveries, every stroll results in unexpected discoveries of beauty. You walk behind a gate, and there is a ravishing courtyard, the kind you'd imagine from the last scene of *Cyrano de Bergerac*, or one you'd find in a monastery

Bruges by night

cloister, peaceful and green. You walk down a lane and there is a canal and regal swans upon it. You gaze up at buildings and there are exquisite carved-stone emblems of the guilds or functions they once served. Everywhere are canals (in this "Venice of the North") and small arched bridges, cobblestoned streets, ranks of aged medieval structures covered by

277

A CITY OF DREAMS, WHERE EVERY WALK BRINGS REVERIES, EVERY STROLL RESULTS IN UNEXPECTED DISCOVERIES OF BEAUTY

vines, interspersed with trees—for there are large, flowering trees everywhere—guardians of peaceful repose and quiet, except of course in the majestic main squares where towering belfries, cathedrals, market halls—themselves supreme works of art—draw sightseers to gaze upon them.

And the homes! They all have pointed roofs and are of brick, but brick used for an aesthetic purpose, set in patterns that draw the eye to a focal point, or create designs of beauty and purpose in even modest dwellings, bricks set in curved archway fashion, or bricks set aslant, or

bricks that criss-cross upon themselves to make the architect's statement. Just as Italy in the Middle Ages excelled in marble, and France in stone, so medieval Bruges was the creator of brickwork never again equalled in its variety and charm. Compare even the modest commercial structures of Bruges with the mindless and squat, vapid rectangles that constitute the retail architecture of most cities in North America.

How to describe, in my limited remaining space, the facilities and attractions of

A canal in Bruges

The Lake of Love

Town Hall

Bruges? You stay in hotels of architectural distinction, not a single one of modern construction (even the Holiday Inn occupies a period building). You eat in Belgium's finest restaurants. As you pass from meal to meal, in even the modest establishments, you thrill to plates of tissue-thin and palely pink smoked salmon sprinkled with strawberry-flavored vinegar and spiced with red and yellow peppercorns. You precede the meat course with a bowl of tender tiny scallops boiled in a fish-stock soup; you suck the delectable stuffing from a tray of steamed "langoustines" (small crabs) in melted butter-garlic. You exult, at the entrance to even a three-star restaurant, to find yourself treated as a human being whose patronage is welcomed (in sharp contrast to the treatment in great restaurants of other European lands).

You visit and view masterworks of art so numerous and sublime as to rival collections in cities three times the size: Jan van Eyck's *Madonna with Canon Van der Paele* in the Hall of the 15th Century Flemish Primitives at the Groeninge Museum; Hans Memling's *Mystic Marriage*

of St. Catherine in the 12th-century Hospital of St. John, Memling's *Shrine to St. Ursula* in the same enthralling structure. In the 13th-century Church of Our Lady you find the only statue by Michelangelo —*Madonna and Child*—to have permanently departed from Italian soil.

You wander a Beguinage where elderly women lived in the 13th century; you shop at tiny lace stores; you are awed by the Palace of Gruuthuse, by the Town Hall (oldest in Belgium—1376) resembling a Gothic wedding cake of pointed spires and elaborate statuary. At the Basilica of the Holy Blood you gaze at the stained cloth said to be from the cloak of Jesus and brought to Bruges in 1150 by a leader of the Second Crusade. In between, you sail the canals dotted with swans, as themes from Mozart filter through your mind and send you into dreams.

Have I exaggerated the charms of Bruges? Ask anyone who has been there. It is a stellar sight of Europe, yet bypassed by the bulk of American tourists in their head-long rush to better-known attractions.

XII

Thirty Largely Unknown Travel Organizations That Can Alter, Even Revolutionize, Your Vacation Trips—For the Better

Companies That Make Travel as Broad as Life Itself

When I was courting my wife and attempting to persuade her that the legal profession was not the dull and stultifying activity she thought it to be (I was practicing law at the time), I told her that law was as broad as life, that whatever happens in life is ultimately reflected in law.

Well, travel is as broad as life (I am now in the travel field). And everything that happens in life is sooner or later the subject of a tour program, a vacation offering, or a resort hotel. As witness:

The Iran-Contra Connection: Though no one ever dreamed of going there in the days of Somoza—a tropical paradise it wasn't—today you can't beat them away. So many Americans are currently travelling to Nicaragua, to "see for themselves," that a sizable segment of the travel industry (at least a dozen specialized tour operators) has emerged to service the trend.

One of the largest is NICA (Nuevo Instituto de Centroamerica), which sends you to study Spanish in the town of Esteli (pop. 70,000; Nicaragua's second largest) in the north of the country, quite near to Contra activity, but thus far unscathed by it. There you live with a Nicaraguan family for either four weeks ($875, including meals but not air fare) or five weeks ($950), sharing their lives in toto, studying Spanish in classrooms for four hours

Permanent members of the Fourth World Movement share the actual lives of the most abject poor in shantytown communities all over the world. Nonpermanent "volunteers" spend three weeks each summer in workcamps at the movement's headquarters in France.

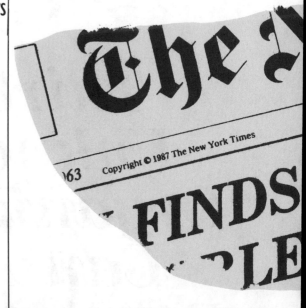

each morning, performing volunteer work on two afternoons weekly, attending seminars and lectures (by Sandinistas and oppositionists alike; you even meet one weekend with U.S. Embassy officials) several times a week. Median age of participants is 31 years, but people of all ages make the trip. For literature, contact **NICA, 1151 Massachusetts Ave. (P.O. Box 1409), Cambridge, MA 02238 (phone 617/497-7142).**

Shorter, one-week ($695 from Miami) or two-week ($900 from Miami) study tours on topics ranging from "Health and Education in Nicaragua" to "The Role of Women in Nicaragua" are operated throughout the year by **Marazul Tours, Inc., 250 West 57th Street, Suite 1312, New York, NY 10107 (phone 212/582-9570)**, from which brochures are available. Rates include economy-style hotel accommodations, two meals a day, all transportation to and within Nicaragua,

THEIR FOCUS: ON NICARAGUA, PSYCHOLOGY, WORLD POVERTY, HELEN NEARING

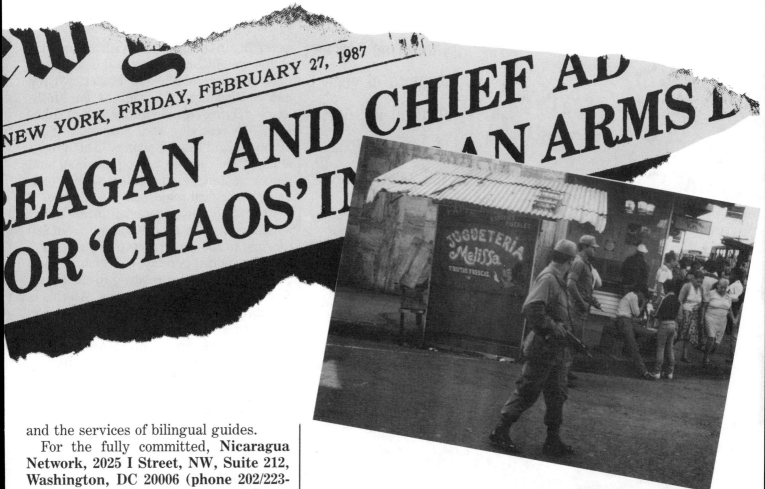

and the services of bilingual guides.

For the fully committed, **Nicaragua Network, 2025 I Street, NW, Suite 212, Washington, DC 20006 (phone 202/223-2328)**, works with regional organizers all over the country to coordinate volunteer work brigades to Nicaragua. (There are three types of brigades: coffee harvesting, construction, and reforestation). Stays are for four weeks, and cost a total of about $700 from Mexico City. Monthly, the **Casa Nicaragüense de Español, 853 Broadway, Room 1105, New York, NY 10003 (phone 212/777-1197)**, provides four-week stints of Spanish-language study in the capital city of Managua, plus meetings with political leaders, family living, and community work. At other times the organization known as **TECNICA, 2727 College Avenue, Berke-**

ley, **CA 94705 (phone 415/848-0292)**, sends skilled Americans to consult with or assist their counterparts in several business or technical areas for periods of two weeks to one year. If you're worried about such things, ask to be assigned to southern locations, as Contra attacks are mainly directed at civilian activities and civilian communities in the north.

Popular Psychology: In the Santa Cruz Mountains of California overlooking Monterrey Bay—you can't imagine a more enthralling location—the Mount Madonna Center is America's leading conference and "retreat" facility for the discussion of

EVERYTHING THAT HAPPENS IN LIFE IS SOONER OR LATER THE SUBJECT OF A TOUR PROGRAM, A VACATION OFFERING, OR A RESORT HOTEL

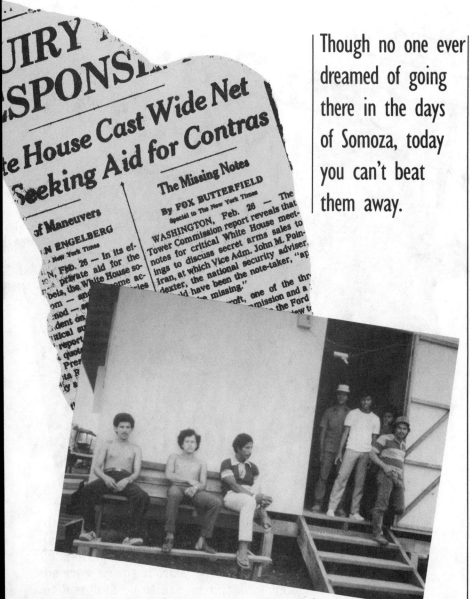

Though no one ever dreamed of going there in the days of Somoza, today you can't beat them away.

cavorting in the open air, with attendance at the weightiest of talks and discussions (like an ultra-intellectual Esalen): "Eros and Spirituality," "A Retreat for Mothers," "Dying—Opportunity of a Lifetime," "Creativity and Success," "Self-Hypnosis and Inner Balance." Though the staff of the center is yoga-trained and yoga-oriented, seminars deal with broader psychological issues, as you can see.

Room and two vegetarian meals daily, supplemented by snacks, ranges from $30 (dorms) to $35 (semiprivate rooms) to $50 (private rooms) per day, to which you add $70-or-so for tuition relating to the courses and seminars you've chosen. All this is but an hour from San Jose Airport, an hour and a half from San Francisco Airport. For descriptive literature, contact **Mount Madonna Center, 445 Summit Road, Watsonville, CA 95076 (phone 408/722-7175 or 408/847-0406).**

World Poverty: Like the fictitious priest who lived among the lepers, beggars, and cart-pullers of *The City of Joy*—that massive bestseller found on all the newsstands—so permanent members of the Fourth World Movement share the actual lives of the most abject poor in shantytown communities all over the world. Without making quite the same commitment, nonpermanent "volunteers" spend three weeks each summer in workcamps at the movement's international headquarters in Pierrelaye, France, held late June to mid-July, mid-July to early August, and early to late September. No knowledge of French is needed; total cost for the three-week stay is 300 francs (around $50); work includes carpentry, painting, masonry, cooking, followed by evening discussions and readings, sometimes with the movement's much-revered

every psychological issue, every spiritual conundrum, including the very latest and hottest topics. Unlike other centers which rent their premises to self-confined groups, Mount Madonna invites members of the public to every session, and thousands head there each year for long-weekend or weeklong vacations that combine hiking in the redwood forests and

founder, Fr. Josef Wresinski.

Other volunteers devote three months, at any time of the year, to an internship at the movement's New York headquarters, again working with families living in extreme poverty on projects designed to draw them back into society: street libraries, literacy and computer programs, family vacations. Interns share housing (free) and housing duties with permanent Fourth World members, but are asked to make a small contribution to food costs during the first month only.

Because the movement is painfully strapped for funds, be sure to enclose an already-stamped, self-addressed envelope (and perhaps a contribution, too) when requesting further information and literature: **Fourth World Movement, 172 First Avenue, New York, NY 10009 (phone 212/228-1339).**

Homesteading: The late Scott Nearing, who remained handsome, vigorous, and creative until his recent death at the age of 100, was a 1920s radical ousted from teaching positions because of his far-advanced views. He and his wife, Helen, determined to end their dependency on society by moving first to Vermont and then to an abandoned farm in Maine, where they developed the practice of homesteading to a fine art: producing goods and services for their own consumption, self-sufficiently, without the intervention of a market or the use of cash.

A stream of books from their fertile pens—*Living the Good Life, Continuing the Good Life,* and *Simple Food for the Good Life,* among others—brought thousands of visitors each year to their Forest Farm and stone house built with their own hands, where Helen and Scott demonstrated the virtues of a fresh-food diet,

gardening, composting, pond and dam building, and lectured on other, broader social themes. Despite Scott's death, 83-year-old Helen is still willing to receive visitors, provided they make advance contact with the nearby **Social Science Institute, Harborside, ME 04642 (phone 207/326-8211),** to which royalties from the Nearings' books are assigned, and which also sells their books through the mails (request a catalogue). According to Helen Nearing, it is possible to visit Forest Farm during the summer and fall. She devotes the other seasons to travel and writing. Accommodations and meals are available in the town of Blue Hill, approximately 20 miles away.

Care to change your life? The farm and books of Scott and Helen Nearing have done that for multitudes before you.

Student Exchanges, Hospitality Stays, Volunteer Workcamps

Bed and full American breakfast in 400 U.S. cities for $7.50 per person per day. A month in Israel, including air fare, lodgings, and all meals, for $424 to $616. A summer camp for adults for $175 a week, all inclusive. Ten months in Europe, on a student exchange, for $3,590. Three months of the same, in summer, for $1,675.

Bargains like these—mind-bogglers, eye-rubbers—are not to be found in glossy brochures or big ads, or from standard travel sources at all. Rather, they emerge from a little-known, nonprofit or partially nonprofit segment of the travel industry. Lest any go unused, let's bring them to the fore, quick.

• **A nonprofit student exchange:** The very finest form of travel, bar none, is a several-month stay in a foreign home, enjoyed in the teenage years of one's life. I weep for those students who miss out on these life-enhancing, maturing experiences simply because their schools haven't publicized the offerings (which happens more than you'd expect).

The solution: Acquire the information yourself and then deal directly with the sponsoring organization.

A 104-page publication from the Council on Standards for International Educational Travel describes the student pro-

At an armored camp near Ashkelon, you grease or paint tanks. At a bivouac in the Negev, you cook for the troops. At a supply depot near Jerusalem, you sort uniforms.

grams offered by 36 reputable U.S. organizations and provides the facts for selecting the group from which to request further information. Listed are not simply the "giants"—Experiment in International Living, Youth for Understanding, American Field Service—but also the smaller, specialized ones as well—like the Educational Foundation for Foreign Study ($3,590 all inclusive, for ten months in Europe with volunteer host families, while attending European public schools; note its full scholarship for students creatively talented in the arts); or the Iberoamerican Cultural Exchange Program ($550 for a six-week stay with a Mexican family, $1,300 for a full school year, excluding air fare). Scholarship aid is heavily stressed.

Request the *Advisory List of International Educational Travel and Exchange Programs 1988–1989* from **CSIET, 1906 Association Drive, Reston, VA 22091,** and enclose $5 for the cost of the booklet, postage, and handling.

Volunteers for Israel

DIG FOR A WHILE ON THE NONPROFIT SIDE OF THE U.S. TRAVEL INDUSTRY, AND YOU'LL QUICKLY DISCOVER NUGGETS OF GOLD

THE BEST OF THE TRAVEL BARGAINS EMERGE FROM A NONPROFIT OR PARTIALLY NONPROFIT SEGMENT OF THE TRAVEL INDUSTRY

• **A next-to-no-profit lodging service:** Just when you thought the bed-and-breakfast movement had lost its passion for low cost, along comes the Evergreen Club to restore your faith. Just $10 a night for a single, $15 a night for a twin, is its charge for rooms in more than 700 homes found in 45 of the 50 states.

Amazingly, the price includes full American breakfast—juice, eggs, toast, coffee—for each guest. At $7.50 per person per day, double occupancy, these are among the lowest bed-and-breakfast rates in all the world.

But there are conditions. First, membership is limited to persons over the age of 50. They pay $35 a year single, $40 a couple, to receive a directory of Evergreen hosts (who also must be over 50). Because Evergreen's prices are essentially profit-less, psychology rather than finance explains the willingness of hundreds of mature Americans to participate.

At their age, the kids have left the house, which now stands empty and eerily quiet. Spare rooms abound. Evergreeners quite obviously enjoy having new company, especially when it consists of people their own age.

Why, then, the fee? Club officials think the $10 and $15 charge adds a sense of discipline to normal attitudes of hospitality (in addition to offsetting out-of-pocket costs). Paid for their empty room or rooms, hosts will patiently await their guests' often-tardy arrivals, then rush to serve their every need.

Finally, on applying for membership prospects are asked to list their own accommodations for use by other members. But no one requires that members necessarily accept all or even most of the book-

> The very finest form of travel is a several-month stay in a foreign home, enjoyed in the teenage years of one's life.

ings phoned in to them. They have complete discretion in that regard.

Evergreen's officers are even studying creation of an "associate member" category for people whose small apartments or infirmities might prevent them from listing the possibility of accommodating another member.

You'll be pleased to know that the club enjoys strong sponsorship. It is the offshoot and brainchild of the powerful American Bed & Breakfast Association (16 Village Green, Crofton, MD 21114), whose 12,000 member establishments charge normal B&B rates nowhere near $10 or $15. You can send $17.95 to the parent organization for its yearly directory of standard bed-and-breakfast houses (still excellent values).

But for information on the remarkable Evergreen, send a self-addressed, stamped envelope to **Evergreen Bed & Breakfast Club, P.O. Box 44094, Washington, DC 20026.**

• **Israel on zero bucks a day:** Well, almost. You'll need to supply the air fare, of course. That costs as little as $465 for a student travelling to Israel in off-season, $650 for adults in other months.

But once there, "they" take care of everything else: room and board for two or three weeks (preferably three), even a set of boots and khaki fatigues.

"They" are the Israeli Army. As a "Volunteer for Israel"—aged 18 to 65, male or female, Jew or gentile—you're housed at an Israeli military base, working at light, unskilled chores for 5½ days a week to free up Israeli reservists for actual military training.

At an armored camp near Ashkelon, you grease or paint tanks, tighten the screws on howitzers, make careful inventories of spare parts. At an infantry bivouac in the Negev, you cook for the troops or serve in the mess hall. At a supply depot near Jerusalem, you sort uniforms, pack kit bags, clean rifles, or cut grass.

The working day is from 8 a.m. to 4 p.m. In the evenings, there's a "rec room" and subtitled movies or an Israeli professor (doing reserve duty) happy to deliver a lecture (in English) on the Dead Sea Scrolls or the current Mideast conflict.

You sleep in barracks segregated by sex, but take your meals with both male and female soldiers, enjoying mammoth Israeli breakfasts of yogurt and fresh vegetable salads, hard-boiled eggs, bread, and black coffee.

If, following your stint, you wish to stay on for extra weeks in Israel (this time, at your expense), your air ticket is easily extended for up to 180 days.

Some Americans devote every one of their yearly vacations to the work I've just described—and then can't wait to return. Some older Americans go several times a year.

"It can be tedious," wrote one volunteer-grandmother in her 60s, in a newsletter for alumni of the program. "I packaged coffee beans for distribution to the troops. But I was happy to do it.

"Some grandmothers take their grandchildren to the park—and some grandmothers volunteer for the Israeli Army."

(Incidentally, though you assist that army, you do not join it or otherwise endanger your U.S. citizenship.)

Groups depart on three-week programs as often as eight times a month in the busy summer season, four times a month in the winter. Participants apply either to the New York office of Volunteers for

Just when you thought the bed-and-breakfast movement had lost its passion for low cost, along comes Evergreen.

Israel or to volunteer representatives.

Contact **Volunteers for Israel, 40 Worth Street, Room 710, New York, NY 10013 (phone 212/608-4848).**

• **Summer camp for progressive adults:** Proud and unrepentant, happy and defiant, liberals from all over the nation (of all ages, families and singles) converge each summer on the World Fellowship Center in the White Mountains of New Hampshire for a special vacation.

With its 300 acres of forest, mile-long Whitton Pond for swimming and boating, cookouts, campsites and rustic lodge buildings, WFC would seem at first glance to be a standard resort for standard, warm-weather relaxation.

But from mid-June to early September every week of the summer there is devoted to such atypical, even unsettling, "resort" themes as "Care for the Poor," "Central America—Witness to War," "Cracks in the System," "Bretton Woods Revisited," "Peace Priorities." Noted lecturers (including literary great Dr. Annette Rubinstein in 1988) take to the stump on each week's topics. Twice-daily discussions, at 10:30 a.m. and after dinner at 8 p.m., alternate with lighthearted blueberry-picking, exercise sessions, swimming.

All three meals are included in the room rates, and yet those charges amounted last season to only $175 or $200 per person per week (depending on room) or to only $120 per week if you bring a tent. At those price levels, space fills up fast.

For information and application forms contact **World Fellowship Center, RR2, Birch Street, Box 53, North Conway, NH 03860 (phone 603/447-2280).**

Cracking the Codes of the Travel Trade

When travel-industry professionals speak to one another, they use a weird jargon of curt abbreviations, cryptic references, and horrific contractions of the English language. *"Didja see the latest Jax Fax?" "Didja go to Henry Davis?" "Whyncha get it on a barter?" "Whyncha use a bucket?" "Does anybody rep 'em?" And "Aw, nuts, they don't wanna hotel; try Elsie from England!"*

Each one of these puzzling references can make all the difference to the cost or enjoyment of your next vacation. Each refers to a behind-the-scenes organization, publication, or method for obtaining remarkable savings or services. And each is far too important to be left to the travel professionals—rather, they can all be used, with varying degrees of difficulty, by the public at large.

Here's a translation of "traveltalk":

(1) "Didja see the latest Jax Fax?" *Jax Fax* is a monthly magazine, the size of a tiny telephone directory, that lists just about every charter flight scheduled to depart from every American city to every destination in the world over the next several months. It also lists the departures for a great many packaged holidays using scheduled air transportation, more

It isn't necessary to make expensive overseas phone calls, or to write endless and successive letters, to the hotels you need. Use a "rep"!

numerous than the charters.

Published for many years by a group of former airline executives in Darien, Connecticut (280 Tokeneke Road; phone 203/655-8746), *Jax Fax* is sheer travel excitement, alerting you to exotic itineraries, little-known programs, flights from secondary cities or going to lesser-used cities abroad, supplying information of the sort rarely seen in ads or commercials.

But you needn't send off for your own copy to use it. Since nearly every travel agency, almost by definition, subscribes to *Jax Fax* (their prime source for charter information), you need only appear at such an agency and courteously ask to look at the most recent edition. Most agents will be happy to let you leaf through a copy, taking copious notes of travel bargains, in the hope that you'll then book the charter through that agency, earning them a commission. Everybody benefits, and a publication intended for the travel trade alone is then better able to perform its near-divine mission.

(2) "Try Elsie from England!" "Elsie from England" is a Cockney from south London named Elsie Dillard, who emigrated to the state of Washington in 1957, tried her hand at real estate and insurance, but preferred offering advice to friends about travel to the British Isles. "You don't want a dull hotel," was her most frequent litany. "I've got this darling bed-and-breakfast house for only 32 shillings 6 pence."

Soon she was a retail travel agent, and then a wholesaler, the single leading source to other travel agents of low-cost bed-and-breakfast accommodations in scores of locations throughout England, Scotland, Ireland, and Wales. Her product currently ranges in price from $20 per

SOME HIGHLY TECHNICAL TRAVEL ORGANIZATIONS TOO IMPORTANT TO BE LEFT TO THE "PROS"

person per night (breakfast included) for the standard English guesthouse, to $30 for an upgraded version that can sometimes be a comfortable country estate. (She charges $7.50 additional for every reservation made.) And although her clientele originally was mainly travel agents from the western states, she is perfectly willing (indeed, eager) to deal directly with the public from every state.

If you've a craving for the "real England," call Elsie for even a single reservation in a single location. Or else put yourself entirely in her hands for a full three-week tour. She'll start you in a B&B in London, then place you in a self-drive car, and provide you with other prepaid B&Bs for all remaining nights, as you follow a classic, planned-by-Elsie itinerary into Wiltshire (Somerset) and the West Country (Devon and Cornwall), up to Bath and through "the Potteries" into North Wales, thence to Chester, on up to the Lake District, and all the way up to the Hebrides and northern Scotland, then south to Edinburgh, and into York, the Cotswolds, and Heathrow or Gatwick Airport for the homeward-bound flight. With pre-reserved, classically British, marvelously cheap guesthouse rooms all the way! Write or phone **"Elsie from England," P.O. Box 5107, Redondo, WA 98054 (phone 206/941-6413).**

(3) "Whyncha get it on barter?" "Barter" is the exchange of product for product, and nowhere is the activity more intensely pursued than in the travel industry. Airlines trade seats for radio commercials, cruise ships trade cabins for stationery and supplies, hotels trade rooms for ads on the sides of buses. Since each of the "traders" has unused capacity or excess merchandise, they are exchang-

jax fax (jaks faks) *n.* [see prec.] **1.** source of charter flight data **2.** compendium of tour packages **3.** travel research tool

barter (bahr´ tuhr) *n.* [OFr. L] **1.** exchange of travel product for advertising space **2.** act of obtaining trade credits from travel supplier

rep (rehpp) *n.*, also *v.* **1.** agent of hotel or hotel chain **2.** person authorized to confirm reservations **3.** (*v.*) to represent

elsie (elí see) *n.* [proper name] **1.** legendary source of British guesthouses **2.** company arranging low-cost visits to England, Scotland, Wales

ing items that might have gone unsold in any event—thus the trade costs them nothing (so goes the theory).

But who ends up sitting in the airplane seats, or sleeping in the hotel rooms and cruise-ship berths, that have been "bartered"? Since there's an obvious limit to the number of trips that radio station personnel and staffs of advertising agencies can themselves use (or else they'd be on perpetual vacation!), the excess "travel credits" are sold by dozens of so-called barter companies to large corporations or special groups, at prices heavily discounted from normal levels. Among those firms, a small but growing number (a handful, really) are currently selling their credits—sharply reduced air tickets, cruises, car rentals, tour packages, hotel stays—directly to individual members of the public, among others.

In the Southeast, the behemoth of the barterers is **All Advertising, Inc., 5665 Central Avenue, St. Petersburg, FL 33710 (phone 813/384-6700),** and it is willing to deal with the public (I asked). Call, write, or visit, and you'll pick up a broad variety of trips and tickets at substantial discounts. In the East and West, the leading firms are **Travel World Leisure Club, Inc., 225 West 34th Street, Suite 2203, New York, NY 10122 (phone 212/239-4855),** and **Communications Development Corp., 1454 Euclid Street, Santa Monica, CA 90404, (phone 213/458-0596),** respectively. Both sell deeply discounted tour packages, cruises, and air tickets, and have no objection to selling them in "ones and twos," to even a single person or couple contemplating a trip. For precisely what were these tours, cruises, and tickets originally exchanged? For a TV spot late at night, or a billboard in the

TRAVEL IS TOO IMPORTANT TO BE LEFT TO THE TRAVEL "PROS"

country, or even a paint job in the airline's office!

(4) "Whyncha try a bucket?" As I've mentioned in two separate essays in Part V, the "buckets," or "bucket shops," are those utterly respectable, but ill-named, retail travel agencies that sell off air tickets at considerable discounts from the published rate. Some of the "buckets," in turn, obtain their discounted tickets from a "national bucket shop," the well-reputed, long-in-business **Unitravel, 222 South Meramec, St. Louis, MO 63105 (phone toll free 800/325-2222)**. It supplies tickets not only to local "buckets," but to hundreds of normal travel agencies anxious to enjoy "a deal." And it is quite willing (again, I asked) to handle an occasional direct request from members of the public seeking a cut-rate air fare to somewhere.

If you live in a town that has no "bucket," or are anxious to deal only with a major, nationwide firm, then try a call (or have your agent place the call) to Unitravel, usually at least 21 days in advance of departure (a requisite for many, but not all, of the tickets they sell). Their discounts run as high as 40% off normal excursion fares on departures scheduled well into the future, from every major city, and extend to car rentals and tour packages as well. Here's a "bucket" totally unlike the notorious stock market "buckets" of the 1920s.

(5) "Who reps 'em?" Literally thousands of hotels around the world, on every continent—large ones and small, high-priced and budget, independent and chains—are assisted in the United States by companies familiarly known as "hotel reps." Such major hotel representatives as Loews Reservations, Inc., Utell, Inc.,

Each cryptic name refers to a behind-the-scenes organization, publication, or method for obtaining travel savings or services.

Robert F. Reid and Associates, plus dozens more, can instantly confirm space for you at a multitude of hotels in a short phone conversation over toll-free lines.

It isn't necessary, therefore, to make expensive overseas phone calls, or to write endless and successive letters, to the hotels you need. You simply ascertain the name of their U.S. "rep" and phone them up, free.

And how do you secure those names? Every major library carries a thick directory known as the *Hotel & Travel Index*. It lists the pertinent facts on nearly every one of the world's hotels, and indicates which of them are "repped" and by whom. If your resulting call reveals that your preferred hotel is booked for the dates you wish, you normally obtain an alternative hotel in the very same phone conversation. How's that for rational behavior?

(6) "Didja go to Henry Davis?" "Henry Davis" is the leading trade show of the travel industry. Twice each year, in the 30 largest cities of the United States, it rents a convention center or mammoth hotel ballroom to display the brochures and leaflets of hundreds of travel suppliers: airlines, cruise ships, tour operators, hotel chains, you name it. Travel agents by the thousands then roam through those display areas, talking to exhibitors, but more important, stocking up on the literature, which they cart away in giant plastic shopping bags or even shopping carts. In effect, they have equipped themselves with all the hot new travel products for the coming season.

Now the Henry Davis staff restricts admission to members of the travel trade. In fact, it tries very hard to restrict admission to the "pros." But they can't really tell. Since admission is simply upon presentation of a business card, a number of travel agencies have favored their large or more important customers by lending them a card with which to visit the show. If you'd like an early, advance preview of all the cruises and tours for the coming months, including a massive set of brochures describing the trips in full, simply ask your travel agent to alert you to the dates when "Henry Davis" is coming to

town, and to lend you one of his business cards. It isn't quite cricket, and you'll be ousted if you're caught, but isn't the ultimate purpose to get that information into the hands of the travelling public?

Someone said that war is too important to be left to the generals. Travel is too important to be left to the "travel pros"!

Five Outstanding Travel Organizations Known to Very Few

"Time is the thing *we have least of,"* said Ernest Hemingway, and he could have added that space in this book is second in short supply. With so many important new (or newly discovered) travel organizations surfacing each week, the only way to keep reasonably current is to compress five of them into a single essay. Here goes:*

(1) The Ultimate Travel Club: Its only membership requirement is that you have "an aenemic wallet," and a zest—despite that condition—to rove the farthest reaches of the world. Its members of all ages make the readers of my $25-a-day books seem like plutocrats. They walk across all of Nepal; take local buses, regional jitneys, occasional mule trains, to cross the wastes of sub-Saharan Africa; sleep in the huts of Indonesian villages, cadge meals at the communal fires of New Guinean fishermen, trade bars of soap for trinkets crafted in the yak tents of Ladakh.

And then they return home to tell about it, at monthly public meetings in St. Martin's Lane, London; in southern California or New York; or in the pages of their six-times-a-year newsletter, *The Globe.*

Surely the most distinguished travel group on earth—despite their "aenemic wallets"—is the 40-year-old **Globetrot-**

In theory, it's simplicity incarnate: you offer to accommodate people free of charge as they pass through your home city; they offer to accommodate you as you pass through their home city.

ters Club, c/o BCM Roving, London WC1N 3XX, England (an oddly truncated, but perfectly adequate, mail-drop address). Since officers are all volunteers lacking a full-time office and frequently changing, they use that simple pickup point to receive membership applications and communications. The fee is $14 per year, $24 for two years, for receiving *The Globe* every other month, as well as *The Globetrotters Directory,* listing names, addresses, ages, and travel experience of members (be sure to provide that information while applying), as well as purely optional offers by them of free accommodations or advice to other members. Because a great many members do, in fact, make such offers of lodging (in spare beds or cots of their living rooms or dens), the *Directory* is a rich source of free travel opportunities, though not primarily designed as such.

THEY CAN MAKE A MAJOR DIFFERENCE TO THE COST AND ENJOYMENT OF YOUR TRIP

London Globetrotters (and visitors from abroad) meet at 3:30 p.m. the second Saturday of each month in the Friends Meeting House, 52 St. Martin's Lane, (entrance at 8 Hop Gardens), London WC1; monthly sites and dates for the same in New York, Toronto, and southern California are listed in *The Globe*—as are those accounts of members' adventures in touring the Third World.

(2) Networking the "A.T.'s": "Appropriate Technology" or "Alternative Technology" ("A.T.") is a massive worldwide movement of people who believe in a simpler, gentler, human-scale life, non-industrial, cooperative, participatory—the dramatic opposite of the factory-polluted, harshly competitive and hierarchical world of autos and metallic wastes in which most of us live. Its advocates are found in every nation, on organic farms and in vegetarian restaurants, at "New Era" bookshops and solar-energy centers, in consumer co-ops and small utopian communities. And because they believe in pressing their views on others, they are the easiest people on earth to get to know. Regardless of your own beliefs, you add a new dimension and intellectual growth to your travels when you meet and interact with these mild-mannered but highly motivated, free-thinking people.

But how do you meet them? Though it wasn't intended for that purpose, the quarterly newspaper/newsletter called *TRANET*, for *Transnational Network for Appropriate Technologies*, is a highly useful "guidebook" to alternative technology people in every nation. Its primary goal is to apprise alternative technology advocates of developments in their specialties in other lands. But recent editions

Alternative technology

have contained extensive directories of addresses for the specific purpose of encouraging well-focused, carefully planned, international travel by persons exploring "A.T." Thus, issue 42 for the summer of 1986 listed organizations engaged in "cross-cultural, people-to-people linkages" across national boundaries; by contacting them, one arranges to meet "people who are changing the world by changing their own lives . . . adopting alternative technologies." Issue 43 for Winter 1986 was called "Alternatives Down Under" and provided the addresses of scores of contacts in Australia and New Zealand for experiencing those approaches. The spring 1987 issue has a similar directory to alternative movements and peoples in the otherwise highly conformist nation of Japan.

Such contacts are the supreme essence of meaningful travel, says *TRANET*. Journeys should produce not simply a "tolerance" of foreign people, but "a love of our differences. . . . We need to invite them to our homes, to visit them in theirs. We need to participate in their alternative celebrations, to eat their foods, to honor their ceremonies, to explore their wild

295

ITS MEMBERS OF ALL AGES MAKE THE READERS OF MY $25-A-DAY BOOKS SEEM LIKE PLUTOCRATS

places, to understand their human-rights issues, to see how they confront their governments."

Though a one-year subscription to *TRANET* is a hefty $30, back issues will be sent to you for $5 apiece. You'll want to start with the remarkable directory to Australia and New Zealand (no. 43), then perhaps go back to the previous directory on "People-to-People Networking" worldwide (no. 42). Contact **TRANET, P.O. Box 567, Rangeley, ME 04970 (phone 207/864-2252).**

(3) The Other "Elderhostel": You've just been placed on your third waiting list for a popular Elderhostel course; your first two choices are hopelessly sold out. Soaring in popularity, the 12-year-old system of foreign and domestic study tours for seniors over 60 is expected to draw 180,000 participants in 1988, causing a moderate, but still irritating, number of "close-outs."

So try Interhostel. It's administered by the same University of New Hampshire officials who created Elderhostel, but then "spun it off" when the baby grew too big for the campus. The university continues to operate Interhostel, which at this time sends people over the age of 50 to pursue intensive two-week tours and bouts of classroom instruction at foreign universities around the world. While topics are a bit more general and geographical than Elderhostel's, they're taught by leading academic figures. Price: $1,095 for two weeks, including everything (housing in university residences, all meals, all tuition) except air fare, usually from Boston or New York.

For information, contact **Interhostel, University of New Hampshire, Division of Continuing Education, 6 Garrison Avenue, Durham, NH 03824 (phone 603/862-1147 Monday to Friday from 1:30 to 4 p.m. EST).**

"TRANET" caters to that massive, worldwide movement of people who believe in a simpler, gentler, human-scale life, non-industrial, cooperative, participatory.

(4) The "Readers' Digest" of Travel: Once a week throughout the year Miriam Tobolowsky of West Los Angeles—a part-time English teacher—travels to a public library to scan the Sunday travel sections of two dozen major newspapers. Pausing for breath, she then proceeds to read every major U.S. magazine, searching for their occasional words on travel. That done, she composes highly abridged "précis" of the latest travel news and publishes them in her bimonthly newsletter, *Partners-in-Travel*, sent to several thousand subscribers.

No matter how extensive your own reading of the travel press, you will always encounter surprising new tidbits of travel lore in her chatty but incisive condensations. Though her focus is on the mature traveller, and her newsletter was initially intended as a match-up service for retirees seeking travel companions (and still performs that function), *Partners-in-Travel* is fast emerging as a valuable compendium of travel discoveries that would otherwise appear in only isolated form, lost to the great majority of us.

Where else would you learn about a club for single persons owning recreational vehicles ("Loners on Wheels")? Or about swim-up blackjack tables in Las Vegas, a golf school for senior citizens, a pet hotel in Arizona? One issue even preserves the advice of a certain Arthur Frommer (on how to override the airline computers when they show an absence of discount fares) for those deprived communities, dark holes of ignorance, where this book isn't sold.

People-to-People, Japan

A subscription to *Partners-in-Travel* (still devoted in part to "Travel Personals") is $25 for six months, $40 for a year, from **Partners-in-Travel, P.O. Box 491145, Los Angeles, CA 90049.**

(5) Hospitality Exchanges: In theory, it's simplicity incarnate: you offer to accommodate people free of charge as they pass through your home city (using a spare room or cot in your home); they offer to accommodate you as you pass through their home cities. Both of you live for free on all your travels, whenever they occur.

In practice, this intermittent exchange of hospitality requires a great deal of administration, and a number of well-meaning "hospitality exchanges" have collapsed under the weight of address chang-es, heavy correspondence, and other pesky paperwork.

One with considerable staying-power—possibly because it is not entirely free—is **INNter Lodging Co-Op, P.O. Box 7044, Tacoma, WA 98407 (phone 206/756-0343).** With several hundred members well scattered across the country, it provides you with instant friends (and accommodations) in all the states other than Utah and Nevada for an initial fee of $45, plus $4 or $5 per person per night paid to your actual hosts (for the cost of fresh linen, towels, and other usables). Children with their own sleeping bags pay only 25¢. On an INNter Lodging Co-Op trip, says founder Bob Ehrenheim, you learn that "strangers are friends you haven't met yet."

Slightly smaller, but growing fast, is **Visiting Friends, Inc., P.O. Box 231, Lake Jackson, TX 77566,** the "guestroom exchange network." It charges $15 for a "lifetime membership," then a total of $20 for your stay of up to six nights at a member's home. It also centralizes the reservations process, keeps all addresses to itself (and not in a published directory), and thus preserves both your privacy and occasional desire to receive no inquiries at all for a number of months.

Note that a "hospitality exchange" is different from a "home exchange" or "vacation exchange"; it does not require a simultaneous swapping of accommodations. You use the service, or provide accommodations, only when you choose, and without having to coordinate your travel plans with the simultaneous travels of another.

Surely there are other, struggling "hospitality exchanges"; if you'll send me their names, to the address listed in the Introduction, I'll spread the good word.

Travel "Davids" Against Travel "Goliaths"

Success stories in the travel industry are always pleasant to relate. They prove that new ideas and innovation can still prevail against stodgy policies and closed-minded people:

The Ghost of People Express: It walks again. Just when you thought that all the "cheap" airlines were finally defunct (Capitol, World, Air Florida, People), along comes the new **Challenge Air** to fling down a fresh gauntlet to the larger lines (and it's doing quite well, thank you).

Headed by a highly respected former executive of Air Florida, the new Challenge flies daily at cut-rate prices between Newark and Miami ($79 one way), and on from there to the Caribbean and Central America. Recently Washington, D.C., joined their domestic stops, and Aruba and Jamaica will soon be added to their island destinations. Phone 305/594-0017 or toll free 800/343-1222 to book.

Could it be that on the second go-around, a "cheap" airline will finally survive?

The Ship That Turns Around in the Panama Canal: Into a cruise-ship industry glutted with capacity, a new, one-ship line called **Regency Cruises** made its entrance two years ago.

Skeptics sneered. Today they're gasping. By sailing an itinerary that goes halfway through the Panama Canal (from the Caribbean), then turns around in Gatun Lake and goes back out again (re-

Just when you thought that all the "cheap" airlines were finally defunct, along comes the new Challenge Air to fling down a fresh gauntlet.

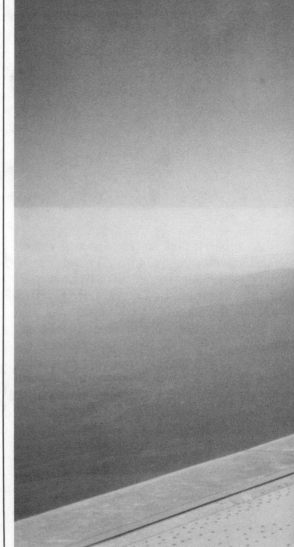

Approaching Mexico City, you can see the famous twin volcanoes, Popocatepetl and Ixtacchihuatl

SIX SMALL BUT EMERGING COMPANIES THAT ENJOY A GROWING CLIENTELE

BY STUFFING FOUR UNRELATED PERSONS INTO A QUAD ROOM, SINGLEWORLD REDUCED THE RATE RADICALLY

turning to the Caribbean), Regency transformed an overly long 14-day cruise (because ships making the full passage must then sail to far-off Pacific ports) into a popular 7-day cruise.

The public responded with record book-

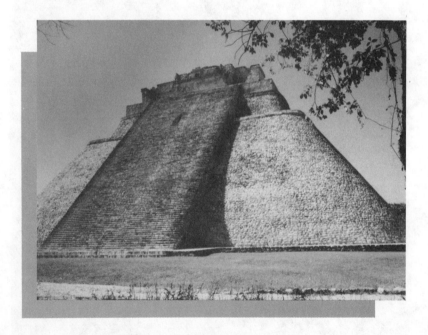

Largest pyramid at Uxmal, the Yucatán

ings. Profitable from the first sailing, Regency has now added a second ship—the *Regent Star*—to its former one-ship "fleet" of the *Regent Sea*. One of the two ships will always ply the halfway-through-the-canal route (going up one lock, then down one lock on the return).

Apparently, once you've seen one lock, you've seen them all. For brochures and bookings, contact any travel agent.

The Cheapest Cruise Going: It's not a sailing offered by the lower-quality ships, or even a cruise heavily discounted in price by the cruise "bucket shops." Rather, it's a cruise on which four people squeeze into a single cabin. Though travel agents told them they were crazy to try, a small-but-distinguished tour company called Singleworld (formerly known as Bachelor Party Tours) recently offered to guarantee quad accommodations for individuals travelling alone. By stuffing four unrelated persons (of the same sex, of course) into a quad "room," Singleworld reduces the price of some Caribbean cruises to less than $800 a person, including round-trip air transportation to the embarkation point from nearly every major U.S. city.

Do people then chafe at their cramped condition? Are they at each others' throats after only a few hours? Not so, says Singleworld—they're rarely *in* the cabin assigned to them!

For a free catalogue of Singleworld's offerings, write: **Singleworld, 444 Madison Avenue, New York, NY 10022.**

Herding Cattle for $70 a Day: Consider, now, the latest initiative of the tireless Patricia Dickerman of New York City.

In 1948, alone in a battered coupe, she bumped along the rural dirt roads of America, persuading skeptical farmers to accept her guests and thus create a new holiday industry and a new source of income for themselves: farm vacations. She later did the same at working ranches. Her classic book of 1949, *Farm & Country Vacations* ($11 postpaid from Pat Dickerman, 36 East 57th Street, New York, NY 10022), updated approximately every three years, is the oldest continually published travel guide in America.

Now, fulfilling everyone's secret desire to lead the life of a cowboy, she arranges for actual participation by us city types in real-life cattle drives in Wyoming, Nevada, Colorado, New Mexico, and Montana, moving herds to pastures with better grass. Costs range from $60 to $100 per person per day, including everything: chuckwagon meals, tents or sleeping bags under the stars, your own horse to ride. If nothing else, says Pat, "you'll have a new respect for a hamburger and the hard work that goes into producing it."

For a free newsletter on cattle drives, send a self-addressed, stamped no. 10 envelope to **Adventure Guides, Inc., 36 East 57th Street, New York, NY 10022 (phone 212/355-6334).**

Mexico Study Groups: Jim and Gayle Savelsberg, of Phoenix, Arizona, are teachers who felt that school-based Spanish-language courses were lacking in one key element: immersion in the home life and conversation of a Spanish-speaking family.

So they darted from Cuernavaca to the Yucatán, from San Miguel de Allende to Guadalajara, laboriously persuading Mexican families to put up students (aged 15 to 85) in their homes, on a three-meals-a-day basis. That exposure to everyday Spanish, coupled with four hours a day of instruction in distinguished Mexican schools, catapulted their courses over those of the competition—while keeping prices at rock-bottom levels. The fame of Mexico Study Groups soared, and it is now a well-established travel company.

The study tours last for 30 days, are each accompanied by Gayle and Jim (who stay near you, but at a discreet distance, and without intruding into your Spanish-speaking life); and they are operated at renowned "institutos" or "academias" in San Miguel and Cuernavaca in summer, in Merida and Cuernavaca in winter. Rates are a remarkable $1,045 for 30 days

They persuaded Mexican families to put up language students in their homes, on a three-meals-a-day basis.

(thus, $35 a day), including everything (housing, meals, instruction) except round-trip air fare to Mexico.

Contact **Mexico Study Groups, P.O. Box 56982, Phoenix, AZ 85079 (phone 602/242-9231).**

"Canaling" in America: To Peter Wiles in 1968, the idea seemed irresistible: run passenger boats on the narrow, lock-dotted Erie Canal. Nowhere else in America could one duplicate the popular canal touring of Europe.

Was it difficult to bring about? "Try going to a bank," he wryly responds, "to borrow money to build a packet boat." Then, too, the canal itself—this once-great, 365-mile-long man-made waterway crossing the width of New York State, completed in 1825—stood largely unused and forgotten, an anachronism.

Wiles began with a single vessel, advertised sparingly, developed a name. Today, his Mid-Lakes Navigation Co. is a thriving fleet of eight small boats making one- to three-day cruises from May to mid-October on the historic Erie Canal (where replacement of horse-drawn barges with self-propelled ships makes it no longer necessary, as the song would have it, to spend "15 days on the Erie Canal"). You rapidly float from Buffalo to Syracuse, or from Syracuse to Albany, or from Buffalo to Albany, for rates of $120 a day per person (double occupancy) on the three-day cruises, including all three meals aboard each day and hotels ashore each night.

For literature and details about this touch of triumphant Americana, our only true "canaling," contact **Mid-Lakes Navigation Co., 11 Jordan Street (P.O. Box 61), Skaneateles, NY 13152 (phone 315/685-5722 or toll free 800/255-3709).**

Travel Oddities (But Maybe They're Just What You Need)

Soviet cruise ships, camping tours in deepest Alaska, VCRs to plan your trips, gourmet hominy grits for your vacation meals. Though some may seem a trifle strange, each of these Ripley-like phenomena has appealed to a growing number of travelers, and deserves inspection.

The World's Finest Cruise Value: Forget the source and focus on the price. You pay as little as $125 a day (plus air fare), perhaps an average of $140 a day (more familiar cruise ships average $200 to $225). You cruise with largely English-speaking passengers on unusual routes through the Baltic Sea, or to the North Cape (of Norway) or the South Pacific, or you sail around the world in 100 days for as little as $10,000.

Only thing is: you do it on a Soviet ship. Proud possessors of the world's largest passenger-carrying fleet, the Russians have launched a determined effort to enter the international cruising market. And thousands of British vacationers, Germans, and more recently, Americans, have responded favorably, booking themselves onto the world's cheapest ocean-going cruises.

From Tilbury, England, on the River Thames, the 17,000-ton *Leonid Brezhnev* and *Azerbaidzhan* sail in summer on 14-day itineraries along the fjords of Norway's North Cape, and on alternate departures through the Baltic to Helsinki,

> Proud possessors of the world's largest passenger-carrying fleet, the Russians have launched a determined effort to enter the international cruising market.

Stockholm, Copenhagen, Gdynia (Poland), and Leningrad—the latter visited on group excursions requiring no visas. In spring and fall the same large ships depart from Genoa or Venice to wander the eastern Mediterranean, and then go to the Greek Islands and Turkey, occasionally darting through the Black Sea to Yalta or Odessa (again no visa needed). In January, and again from Tilbury, the *Leonid Brezhnev* sets off to sail around the world (at even lower daily rates than its normal $125 minimum).

From Bremen, Genoa, or Venice, the M/V *Odessa* makes similar 14-day cruises, but is best known for its yearly round-the-world sailings, on which 50% of all passengers are now Americans. From Australia, the M/V *Belorussiya* cruises through the South Pacific.

Meals on board are "continental," with Russian touches: borscht among the soups, chicken à la Kiev and beef Stroganoff among the entrees. Entertainment is so-called international cabaret adapted to Russian talents: balalaika groups perform, and sailors dance the *kasatski*. But movies, thankfully, are U.S. or British, all cabin and deck staff are reasonably multilingual, and politics are never discussed. "You are in America when you use the ships catering to the U.S. market," says a Soviet shipping official, "but on our ships, you are in Europe more than America."

For brochures and sailing schedules, contact the U.S. general agent for the Soviet shipping lines: **International Cruise Center, Inc., 185 Willis Avenue, Mineola, NY 11501 (phone 516/747-8880, or toll free 800/221-3254).**

Alaska in a Tent: How will the tourists pouring into Alaska this summer be

SOVIET CRUISE SHIPS, CAMPING TOURS IN DEEPEST ALASKA, AND MORE

housed? Already notoriously short of peak-season accommodations, the 50th state is best visited in any event on excursions into its parks and uninhabited wilderness, where few or no lodgings exist. The solution: CampAlaska Tours for tourists of all ages, and for families.

You supply the sleeping bag, they provide all else: 14-passenger vehicle with driver, state-of-the-art tents, other camping gear and cooking equipment (in the classic fashion of "cooperative camping" tours). Tours average $65 a day (plus a food kitty contribution of $6 a day), last 7 to 32 days (but average 14), depart from early June to mid-September, and transport about 12 to 13 individuals booking each departure (of which 40 such departures are available). They leave mainly from Anchorage, and include all overland and ferry transportation, entrance to national parks and campgrounds, services of CampAlaska's guide, and use of their camping equipment. You visit the continent's most spectacular natural wonders, breathe exhilarating air, go fishing, climbing, trekking, and rafting.

For irresistible literature, contact: **CampAlaska Tours, P.O. Box 872247, Wasilla, AK 99687 (phone 907/376-9438).**

Vacationing with a VCR: There's no greater bore than the average travelogue (". . . and as the sun sinks slowly in the west . . ."), yet "travel videos" continue pouring onto the market from a dozen production companies. Does anyone watch them? Is there a standout among the lot? I remain a doubter, but to prove me wrong, an outfit known as the Official Travel Video Company has just released a 90-minute, VHS color cassette called *Around the World in 80 Tapes*, previewing what they regard as the nation's 80

> Though some "tramp" cargo steamers occasionally do wander around the world (without having planned to do so), a major line will now deliberately do just that.

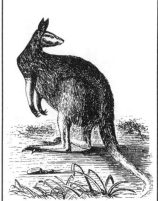

best travel videos. If, among the abbreviated clips (about a minute per video), you see something you like, you use discount coupons affixed to the package to order the full-scale video films at a specially reduced price. Send $8.95, if you're so inclined, to **MCV, Inc., 2 Mott Street, New York, NY 10013,** and they'll respond with the 90-minute "video of the travel videos."

America's Cheapest High-Quality Restaurant: To avoid offending other cities, I did not advise the Democratic Party to choose Atlanta, Georgia, for their 1988 nominating convention. But now that the choice has been made, I can at last reveal that Atlanta possesses the nation's cheapest "gourmet" restaurant—"gourmet", in this instance, referring to the classic southern cuisine and not to the "haute" variety.

At the quaintly named **Mary Mac's, Ltd., 227 Ponce de Leon, Atlanta (phone 404/875-4337),** the "Smothered Country-fried Steak" entree with one choice from the vegetable list (hoppinjohn with chow chow, squash soufflé, fresh turnip greens or sweet-and-sour red cabbage) totals all of $3.50. Extra vegetables are 75¢, as is a cup of "turnip green pot likker" with corn muffins, or a glass of buttermilk. Baked chicken with savory dressing and gravy can substitute for the steak, or perhaps you'd prefer country sausages with hominy grits—all so lightly devoured, all flavored so subtly and delectably, as to ennoble the old Confederacy. Already crowded at each meal, Mary Mac's should swell at the seams with cost-conscious Democratic delegates, and should be visited long before it comes to national attention in July of '88.

XIII

Carefully Guarded Travel Tips, New Developments, and New Travel Products

The World's 15 Finest Travel Products

Gadgets for travel: Most are the purest junk. From the factory lofts of Seoul and Taiwan (their birthplace) to the counters of K-Mart and Woolworth (their stage), they stream forth in a growing torrent of tinny new devices and elaborate inventions that somehow, consistently, never work out. Like oddly shaped pillows for sleeping on planes. Like collapsible hotplates for cooking en route. Yet on the eve of a trip, well-meaning friends rush to gift you with these bulky contraptions that swell up your luggage and snag on your clothes, adding weight-without-substance to an already heavy load of clothing, toiletries, and books.

But diamonds shine among the dross. Once every three years or so, a serious engineer or designer—inspired, you can bet, by a personal vacation experience— suddenly thinks through the logic of a travel need, perceives a childishly simple solution for it, creates a tiny machine, an

When designed by people of talent and training, they weigh less than a pack of cards, occupy the smallest of spaces, and are carried without fail on every trip.

arrangement of cloth, a container, or a tool that those of us who are constantly on the go can instantly recognize as one of the classic travel products. When designed by people of talent and training, they weigh less than a pack of cards, occupy the smallest of spaces, are a visual delight, become cherished by the world's most experienced tourists, are carried without fail on every trip.

And they make a helluva difference. They keep you well groomed and attired on the most hectic itinerary. And wake you in time for an early flight. And cook you a coffee in the middle of night or open the wine that you need to sleep. Some 15 separate products do all this and more, 15 lasting achievements that diminish the rest. And though each comes in many confusing new versions, one in each category always excels, either because it is the lightest (an important consideration), cheapest, or most reliable of the lot. After sampling a large number and seeing still others, I've chosen 15 generic products for my own packing list, and a brand or two in each category as the best of all buys:

(1) The Swiss Army Knife: This, to begin, is the "star" of them all, a masterpiece of sorts for the modern wanderer. Popular for travel since 1882, it resembles a normal, small pocketknife except in width, which is nearly an inch. Yet that tiny bulk encloses, as improbable as it may seem: a fold-out corkscrew, bottle-cap opener, can opener, blade, minuscule scissors, nail file, hole punch, screwdriver, tweezers, and metal toothpick. If you've ever lacked the means to open a bottle of wine in your hotel room late at night, or to deal with recalcitrant beer bottles or cans of pâté, you'll appreciate

SELECTING THE GADGETS, TOTEBAGS, AND TOOLS THAT MAKE TRAVEL INTO A FINE ART

the blinding insight that must have led to this marvel of miniature engineering. Though some modified versions eliminate one or two of the functions listed above, it's best to insist on the real thing, all ten components in their familiar red-porcelain casing embossed with white Swiss cross: the cost is $39, complete, plus $4.50 for postage and handling, from the prestigious **Hoffritz Cutlery, Inc., 515 West 24th Street, New York, NY 10011** (requesting product no. 11185).

(2) A Travelling Alarm Clock from Casio: It's fully as useful. Because wake-ups take on such ghastly importance while travelling—why is it that half the planes we catch leave almost at dawn?—a feather-light alarm clock is a vital supplement for those often-unreliable wake-ups at your hotel. With battery-operated, digital, quartz alarm clocks available in ever-tinier, ever-less-expensive, credit-card size, yet accurate to a fault, there's no reason not to take one. (Only the stubborn traditionalist continues to buy the bulkier, "tick-tocking" windup species). The classic brand is the popular Casio World Timer Alarm, powered by a lithium battery having an 18-month life. It measures only 2⅜ inches by 3¾ inches, is light as a spoon, thin as a bread slice, yet rings you awake with a loud, insistent sound. You can order it through the mails for $24 (including postage and handling) from **L. L. Bean, Freeport, ME 04033**; request the Casio World Timer Alarm (no. 8640).

(3) The Mighty Mini Luggage Cart: Here I go against the trend. Though the popular movement is to luggage with built-in wheels, consider the advantages of the older, collapsible luggage cart. It enables you, first, to carry all your suit-

cases and bags on one cart, including heavy carry-on items that don't come with wheels. It permits one person to cart along the several suitcases of two or three members of their party, like their children. And it doesn't break, as wheels affixed to suitcases always, inevitably, infuriatingly (in my experience), do. What brand to buy? I prefer the sturdy, fairly heavy (5½ pounds) variety made of chrome-steel tubing, to the lighter but flimsier, part-aluminum models. I also like carts that come with fairly large wheels capable of bearing up to 250 pounds in weight. Both attributes belong to the Mighty Mini (model no. 700) manufactured by **Products Finishing Corporation, 350 Clarkson Avenue, Brooklyn, NY 11226**, and available from them for $40, including freight and handling.

(4) An Over-the-Shoulder, But Under-the-Shirt, Money Belt: To safeguard their valuables from increasingly active pickpockets and purse-snatchers around the world, a great many travellers are wearing money belts. But the kind that go around your waist are often hot, bulky, and uncomfortable. I like "Le Hol$ter" instead. It's a shoulder holster, looking exactly like the form-fitting, well-concealed, revolver-toting, over-the-shoulder pouches worn by gangsters in Hollywood films, but this time made of light canvas, not leather, with tightly zippered compartments for passports and currency, not guns. You wear the body-contoured item under blouse or shirt, or simply under your jacket, and thereby conceal your cash and papers in absolutely foolproof fashion. Le Hol$ter costs $9.95 (plus $2 for postage and handling) from the Canadian manufacturer known as **Austin House**, whose U.S. outlet is contacted at

TOO OFTEN THE UNEQUIPPED TRAVELLER FEELS RUMPLED AND FIDGETY, UNPRESSED AND UNHINGED

P.O. Box 117, Station B, Buffalo, NY 14207. Austin also produces a Neck$afe for backpacking under-30s (a simple cloth pouch hanging from strings around the neck; $7.95), and a Waist$afe (which, as you'd guess, is the standard money belt, relatively light and airy in the Austin version; $8 plus postage).

(5) A Fake Aerosol Can for Hotel Room Security: Now you're again in the hotel, about to step out with your Hol$ter, but desirous of leaving a few valuables—wristwatch, earrings, good cufflinks, coins—safely in the room. Some do-it-yourselfers achieve that feat by placing a "Do Not Disturb" sign on their outer doorknob, but at the cost of never having their room made up. Others (who have come better prepared) stick the precious items into the empty interiors of a fake Gillette Shave Cream or Old Spice Deodorant can, which they then leave conspicuously on a bathroom shelf; unless chambermaids of the world are readers of this book, they rarely suspect such cans to be tiny little safes. A travel classic. Actual aerosol cans purchased from Gillette and Old Spice, but emptied and then altered to unscrew at the bottom, are available for $19 (plus $2.50 for postage and handling) from a distinguished travel accessories store, **The Passenger Stop, 732 Dulaney Valley Court, Towson, MD 21204 (phone 301/821-5888).** They're all so authentic that you can smell their former contents when sniffing the can!

(6) The Itty-Bitty-Book Light: For keeping the peace between travelling companions, this one deserves a medal. At home, when one of you reads while the other sleeps, separate bed lamps or separate rooms accomplish the feat. Not so

while travelling, in the typical, nonsuite hotel room with its single source of bedside light. The solution: Another travel breakthrough, less than five years old, yet already a massive bestseller in department stores and on variety counters around the world. The Itty-Bitty-Book Light is like a massive, white plastic paper clip that clamps to your book or magazine; from it protrudes a swiveling, antenna-like rod, at the end of which is a tiny, shaded, focused lightbulb illuminating the page you're reading without brightening the room in which your companion sleeps. On long trips particularly, when jet lag causes people to sleep at different times or stay awake throughout the night, it's an important aid for sophisticated, book-devouring travellers. Convinced? Then send $20 (plus $2 for postage and handling) to the manufacturer, **Zelco Industries, Inc., 630 South Columbus Avenue, Mount Vernon, NY 10550.** Optionally, add $5 for two replacement bulbs, $10 for a cloth travel pouch, or $10 for a battery case (if you're anxious to use the light without plugging it into a socket).

(7) A Travelling Iron: Though it's an obvious "must" for the majority of tourists, even the smallest of versions has, until now, weighed a number of pounds—an unacceptable burden on trips. That's why the "Tiny Touch Up" by Franzus—a triumph of miniaturization—is such major travel news. Only two inches wide, less than four inches long, and only six ounces heavy, it wouldn't be used to iron a bedsheet, but it's perfectly adequate for smoothing out wrinkles in sleeves, collars, pleats, neckties, blouses, all those minimal tasks of pressing for which a small, portable iron is brought. The purse-

size iron, smallest on earth, is only $17.95 (plus $4 for shipping) from various travel outlets (like **The Travel Store at 56½ Santa Cruz Avenue, Los Gatos, CA 95030**), or directly from the manufacturer, the **Franzus Company, Inc., 53 West 23rd Street, New York, NY 10011** (specify model LT12).

And incidentally, some canny travellers are beginning to prefer "steamers" to irons; these you simply pass over offending wrinkles on clothing hung in the hotel closet, after first filling the apparatus from a tap. The smallest I've seen is the Streamline Steamer by Franzus, a mail-order item costing $34 (plus UPS charges) from **The Passenger Stop, 732 Dulaney Valley Court, Towson, MD 21204 (phone 301/821-5888).**

(8) Converters and Adapters: These become mandatory, not optional, for persons planning to bring any sort of electric appliance—electric shaver, hair-blower, other heat-making products—on a foreign trip. That's because foreign voltages are different from ours (220/240 volts instead of 110), and worse, because American plugs, with their two oblong prongs, don't fit into the two or three round holes or angled rectangles of most foreign sockets. You buy a converter to overcome the difference in voltage, adapters to overcome the difference in prongs. And you buy several adapters because British sockets are different from those on the continent, which in turn differ from those in the Middle or Far East, which themselves differ from those in Australia and New Zealand. In fact, you need a kit of multiple converters and adapters, lightweight but sturdy. I like best the International Electricity Converter/Adapter Set (no. CA 1600) sold on the East Coast by

One in each category always excels, either because it is the lightest (an important consideration), cheapest, or most reliable of the lot.

The **Passenger Stop, 732 Dulaney Valley Court, Towson, MD 21204 (phone 301/821-5888)**, and on the West Coast by **The Travel Store, 56½ Santa Cruz Avenue, Los Gatos, CA 95030**, for $22.98 per set (plus $2.50 in postage and handling) in each instance. One-year warranty; spiffy plastic case.

(9) A Coffee Immersion Heater: Breathes there a soul who hasn't craved a "cuppa" at the break of dawn or late at night, in a room service–lacking hotel? Dozens of companies, in every clime, produce a metal immersion coil (attached to a heavily insulated electric wire and plug) that you dunk into a cup of water drawn from the tap, and *voilà!* a cup of boiling water. The best thing about the Insta Heat variety by Franzus is that it carries its own built-in converter (see no. 8, above) and an adapter designed for use in continental Europe; it's also a solid, heavy-duty coil that will last a lifetime if used properly. And thus a lifetime of instant cups—the philosopher's definition of happiness—stretches before you. The price is $9.95, plus $4 for postage and handling, from the **Franzus Company, 53 West 23rd Street, New York, NY 10010.**

(10) The Kanga Tote: Every well-prepared traveller needs an extra totebag that lies quietly, lightly, and compactly in a corner of the suitcase throughout most of the trip, but then unfolds into substantial size when and if the need arises—and that need arises when purchases are made along the way. The "kangaroo" reference in Kanga Tote is because it folds into its own pocket, down to a compact 5 by 8 inches, less than an inch thick, then unfolds into a big 12 by 20 inches in size, with carrying handle, all in ultra-chic design. Just $11 is the mail-order price.

Not nearly as elegant, but able to deal with a gargantuan shopping spree, is the water-repellent, acrylic-coated, nylon Utility Bag manufactured by Coglan's Ltd. of Winnipeg, Canada. It folds down to handkerchief size, then unfolds to the size of an army duffel bag. Only $3.98 through the mails.

Both items can be ordered from the reliable **Passenger Stop, 732 Dulaney Valley Court, Towson, MD 21204 (phone 301/821-5888)**, by adding an extra $2 for postage and handling.

(11) Rain Dance Rain Boots: Though all the travel ads are of sun-drenched scenes, it can rain on your vacation. The trick is to have access to a pair of galoshes without having to carry about a heavy, bulky pair of galoshes. Rain Dance Rain Boots are almost without weight, less than an ounce apiece, made of soft, clear, foldable and crushable thin plastic vinyl that wraps around your normal walking gear. They are unisex, and able to fit any size of foot; snaps at the top tighten the covering about your ankle. Best feature is that unlike some brands which completely cover your shoes, these have a hole which your normal rubber heel, of any size, sticks through; that gives you control over your steps, makes you sure-footed. Surprisingly, the handy item costs only $5.99 (plus $2 for postage and handling) from **The Passenger Stop, 732 Dulaney Valley Court, Towson, MD 21204 (phone 301/821-5888)**.

(12) A Travelling Raincoat: By which I mean a strictly utilitarian raincoat to be extracted from your luggage only when it rains (and not the fashionable sort that is draped over shoulder or arm throughout the trip). This one is for workaday holiday tourists who are hoping it will never rain! But unlike the workaday, shapeless pon-

> Once every three years or so, a serious engineer or designer thinks through the logic of a travel need, perceives a childishly simple solution for it, creates a tiny machine, an arrangement of cloth, a container, or a tool that those of us who are constantly on the go can instantly recognize as a classic travel product.

cho that's rolled into a ball and stuffed into the suitcases of so many casual tourists, the Travel Rain Coat by StarCase is smart and trim, a poor man's Burberry. Yet it rolls into the very same small ball, requiring almost no space at all, and accounting for even less weight. Made of soft, waterproof transparent nylon in "smoke colors" (a darkish gray), it is unisex and one size for all. And although it resembles a traditional raincoat, it has a permanently attached hood, like a poncho. Best of all (and true to its use), it costs only $9.95, plus $2.50 for postage, when ordered from **The Travel Store, 56½ Santa Cruz Avenue, Los Gatos, CA 95030**. Ask for style no. 157.

(13) A Travel Calculator: People adept at mathematics and the use of calculators look down on this special-interest version of the familiar electronic device. They shouldn't. In addition to converting foreign prices into dollar terms (which you can do with any calculator by simply dividing the rate into a price), a travel calculator changes meters into feet, kilometers into miles, liters into quarts and gallons, Celsius into Fahrenheit—and who can remember the ratios of all those measurements? Even in the simple area of money rates, the special travel calculator proves convenient: on entering a country, you punch in the exact exchange rate down to several decimal points, and that information stays fixed throughout your stay; from then on, you need only punch in the prices you encounter and up flashes the dollar equivalent. Faced with a bewildering array of francs, marks, or dinars in a shop window or on an elaborate menu, you enjoy instant conversions as fast as you can press the keys. Through the mails, send $20 (plus $2.50 for postage and handling) to **The Travel Store, 56½**

SWISS KNIFE, TRAVEL ALARM, LUGGAGE CART, MONEY BELT, FAKE CAN, BOOK LIGHT, TRAVEL IRON, CONVERTERS, COFFEE HEATER, KANGA TOTE, RAIN BOOTS, TRAVEL RAINCOAT, TRAVEL CALCULATOR, DETERGENTS, EXPANDING TOWEL

Santa Cruz Avenue, Los Gatos, CA 95030, and ask for the Money Exchange/ Metric Converter.

(14) Travelling Detergents: Another "must." Though you be rich as Croesus, you must never send out your laundry to be done from a hotel (an extravagance supreme), but rely instead on the bathroom sink for washing out underwear and socks. That requires detergent. Similarly, if you're a holiday traveller moving rapidly from place to place, you'll find it rarely possible to use laundries or laundromats, or even to draw very hot water from the sink, requiring cold-water detergents in this instance, and again the do-it-yourself approach. Though cold-water Woolite is by far the bestseller in this field, I prefer the lesser-known Trinse Packets, less heavily perfumed than the more popular brands, and less allergy-making, too. They cost $4 for 15 portions (each the size of a packet of garden seeds), each packet doing one wash, in any sort of water. And if you'll add a mailing charge of $1.50, you can procure same from The Passenger Stop, 732 Dulaney Valley Court, Towson, MD 21204 (phone 301/821-5888).

(15) The Miraculously Expanding Towel: No bigger than a Ping-Pong ball, and almost as light, this final tiny marvel of compression (and dehydration) is purchased in hopes that it will never be used. But the day always comes when you run out of towels, or find insufficient towels, or no towels at all, in your hotel or guest-house bathroom. Not to worry. You drop the wee ball into a basin of water and it unravels and untwists into a cotton bath towel which, once dry, is a reasonable approximation of the real thing. Smart travellers throw two or three into their suitcases, then forget all about them until

the eventual, dreaded discovery of no towels. The Magic Petit Towel costs $3.50 (in face-towel size) or $4 (in hand-towel size), plus $2 for shipping a set of two or three, from Kimura Industries, Inc., 2301 205th Street, Torrance, CA 90501 (phone 213/781-9300).

And there you have the famous 15, jewels among the junk. "Also-rans," an anguishing decision, include inflatable hangers, Wash 'n' Dri's, Berlitz language tapes, eyeshades and earplugs, and that sure-fire cure for stomach upsets, Fernet Branca Liqueur (though clearly not invented for travel). While 15 products may seem a great many, those I've recommended are tiny for the most part, light almost always, occupy a mere fraction of your suitcase, add but a handful of pounds, and cost a total of $268.23 for all 15, plus postage (I've totaled them up). Once purchased and used, they'll soon become—may I suggest—a standard inventory for all your trips.

Because they do make a difference. Without them, travel for some people is a series of vaguely uncomfortable hotel stays, never remotely involving the sense of well-being, or the comforts and convenience, of home. Too often the unequipped traveller feels mildly hungry throughout the day and night, rumpled and fidgety, unpressed and unhinged. Yet another type of traveller turns out smartly each morning, moves about carefree and lighthearted, and savors that extra vigor, that heightened sense of the world's possibilities and delights that international travel can so often bring. Though I'd never suggest that a few material gadgets account for this difference, they help, yes they help. And when they're as tiny and cheap as the 15 "classics" are, they ought to be bought!

Europe: Satisfying Champagne Tastes on a Beer Budget

*A*s the author of a guidebook that was once entitled Europe on $5 a Day, *I can scarcely be accused of having a passionate longing for luxury. But occasionally in my travels, amid the starkly simple (but pleasant) pensiones, and the plates piled high with french-fried potatoes (they taste better in Europe than here), the urge arises for a bit of sloth and indulgence. Yet the desire for economy remains. Can the two be reconciled? Can you sample the three-star meals and the four-star hotels of Europe without breaking the bank? By following some relatively simple rules, you can:*

• Seek out the oddball room in the old deluxe hotels. It was the summer of 1969. Hugging a cliff that hung above the brilliant blue of the Mediterranean, our battered Volkswagen wheezed to the top of a forested height and there it was: the single most expensive hotel on earth (in those days), the stately mansion known as the Hôtel du Cap, near Cap d'Antibes in France. "Let's stay there!" my wife impulsively cried.

"Maybe they have a room without private bath!"

And to our astonishment, they did. Of the 100-or-so rooms in the awesome structure, two or three were stuck among eaves in such odd locations that they lacked plumbing. These rented for only a quarter of the hotel's normal charges, enabling us to cavort (on a budget) for an unforgettable week among the likes of Kuwaiti sheiks and French movie stars, sharing a cliffside sunning perch with Louis Jourdan, the emir of Abu Dhabi, and their lithesome companions.

No matter how grand or luxurious, if the European hotel was built more than 60 years ago, chances are it possesses some rooms of midget size, convoluted shape, or without a tub and shower (and therefore priced considerably below a normally sky-high level). The Ritz in Lisbon and Paris, the Palace in Madrid, the Beau Rivage in Lausanne, and the Negresco in Nice—as hard as it may be to believe—all house a few budget-priced rooms with those characteristics, particularly the lack of a bath.

• Bargain for the best in the off-season months. Though it's confined to a mere five months—from November 1 through March 31—there *is* an off-season in Europe, when prices plummet in the resort hotels (namely, those alongside lakes or the sea) and in cities almost exclusively devoted to tourism (Venice, Florence, Bruges, and the like). But even off-season rates are rather high at a Royal Danieli in Venice or a Carlton in Cannes, and the smart tourist bargains for further off-season discounts at such celebrated properties. He or she walks to the front desk and politely states, "I'm looking for a

RULES FOR SPENDING A MODERATE SUM ON EVEN THE MOST LUXURIOUS OF FACILITIES

room that costs no more than . . ." (here you name a price considerably below normal levels) and more often than one would dream possible, the desk clerk responds, "Yes, we do have a room at that price." Since nothing is more perishable than a hotel room (a dead loss to its owner when unoccupied), hotel managements the world over direct their front-desk personnel to react favorably to discount requests on nights when they expect to suffer a great many vacancies. Or you incorporate the request in a letter to the hotel. And in this fashion, more often than not, you stay during off-season in the finest of the world's hotels at rates more suitable to a roadside inn!

• Devote your evenings to high-grade theatre, recitals, and concerts. You imbibe the finest champagnes, figuratively speaking, but at a cost more suited to beer, when you spend your evenings in Europe at the most exalted of the performing arts: opera and ballet, concerts, recitals, and theatre.

Around you in the gilded auditoriums of a thousand rococo structures are Europe's thoughtful elite, the most demanding audiences on earth, a large and highly trained corps of refined and cultivated spectators, whose very presence lends tangible excitement to the evening. Upon the stage: performances sublime, to the most rigorous of standards, animated by centuries of tradition and experience. Yet except in a handful of grand operas (such as Vienna's, whose ticket prices are similar to our Met's), the cost of concert and theatre tickets throughout Europe is a fraction of American levels, provided you go to the serious productions or presentations. It is the lower form of European

If the European hotel was built more than 60 years ago, chances are it possesses some rooms of midget size, convoluted shape, or without a tub and shower (and therefore priced well below the normal tariff).

spectacle—the girlie shows and loud cabarets, the "theme nightclubs" with their "serving wenches" and tired tourist appeal—that charge sky-high prices for little or no value.

With the exception perhaps of the Lido in Paris, the flamenco bars of Spain, and the fado cafés of Portugal, there's not a single European nightclub worth crossing the street for, in my view. Tourists who devote their precious evenings in Europe to the Crazy Horse Saloons, the Moulin Rouges, the Whiskey-a-GoGos, have only themselves to blame.

Rather, it is theatre, concerts, or recitals that one ought to pursue in Europe. They can be found in every city of size, and all are cheap to moderate: $16 gets you a decent seat at a play or musical on London's West End, and $18 admits you to the Concertgebouw or Stadschouwburg Opera of Amsterdam or to the Maurice Béjart Ballet of Brussels' Cirque Royale. Whatever may be your theatregoing habits (or lack of them) at home, a European vacation is an occasion for rediscovering your better self. The very fact that you have cut loose from your familiar moorings contributes to an appreciation of high art, and you should rush to concerts, even to classic plays presented in their original (and unfamiliar to you) languages—Ibsen in Oslo, Molière in Paris—all so cheap to view that you won't mind the lack of word-by-word comprehension.

• Patronize the inexpensive countries or the lower-cost parts of costly countries. Not every European country offers the same average level of prices, and indulging your champagne tastes can cost considerably less in Portugal (cheapest of

EVEN WITHIN A SINGLE COUNTRY, PRICES DECLINE WHEN ONE MOVES AWAY FROM THE CAPITAL CITY

all), Greece, Spain, or Yugoslavia, than, say, in Germany, Switzerland, Scandinavia, or France. In the first four nations named, only the most celebrated, "name" establishments (like the Athens Hilton) are priced at normal deluxe levels; most other hotels of deluxe or first-class status can be had for $70 or so per room, sometimes less. Of all the European currencies, the Portuguese escudo, Greek drachma, Spanish peseta, and Yugoslavian dinar have suffered most, devaluing to as little as a quarter their former worth. Smart tourists react accordingly in choosing their destinations.

Within a country, prices decline when one moves away from the capital city or the popular tourist areas. High-quality hotels in Manchester or Glasgow are considerably less costly than in London or Edinburgh; superb hotels along the Atlantic coast of France are a fraction of the cost of their counterparts in Paris or on the Riviera. Generally speaking, prices decline as you move southward in Europe, except, of course, in the more noted resort centers. And they become lower still when you leave the European mainland for the islands offshore—Sicily, Cyprus, or even farther south to the island of Malta in the Mediterranean.

• Visit the Eastern European countries or the Soviet Union. The nations of Eastern Europe (including the nearest areas of the Soviet Union) are also among the cheapest in all of Europe. In Moscow and Leningrad, deluxe hotels with swimming pools and all the other trimmings have been built by French and Scandinavian construction firms for use by those on wonderfully low-priced package tours.

Act like a smart traveller and share courses or dishes; the most cultivated Europeans adopt this approach in all but the most exalted restaurants.

Meals in the Soviet Union? In the hotel restaurants of most Russian cities, caviar is frequently available at no extra charge to your tour package, as are such appetizers as smoked salmon, delightful hors d'oeuvres (*zakuski*), succulent borscht (beet soup), and other gourmet-level dishes. So eagerly sought is the "hard currency" spent by European and American tourists that the Russians respond with extraordinary tour features, such as tickets to the Bolshoi Ballet, continual sightseeing, and long flights within the country to destinations thousands of miles away, yet all for a price that would barely purchase a scaled-down trip by escorted motorcoach in Western Europe.

• Use a Yugoslavian ship for your luxury cruise. As cruising soars in popularity as a high-quality method of touring the great seaside cities and associated island destinations of Europe, cruise charges have risen. They are much less, however, on the Yugoslavian liners cruising the Adriatic and Aegean.

On departures from colorful Dubrovnik (where you await embarkation in modern, first-class hotels, yet at the lowest of rates), the Yugoslavian ships provide you with facilities comparable to any Mediterranean vessel—multicourse meals of savory continental specialties, poolside buffets, white-jacketed stewards attending with great verve to your cabin needs, parties, and cabaret entertainment.

Although it costs more to fly to Dubrovnik in the first place, as compared with a Mediterranean embarkation port, the savings from taking a Yugoslav cruise far exceed this difference. The cruises venture to Venice, then up along the exotic ports of the enchanting Dalmatian

Coast (rated by connoisseurs as Europe's finest seaside area), and always in luxurious fashion that surfeits you with all the champagne, soufflés, and pâtés that you could possibly desire, at all-inclusive rates of as little as $140 a day—a great bargain.

To confirm this, simply ask your travel agent to look up the cruise charges of an impressive Dubrovnik-based vessel known as the M/S *Ambassador*, a Slavic "Love Boat," budget style.

• Share, split, and order by halves. I'm talking now about food. Craving a gourmet meal? Eager to sample those renowned European restaurants with the one, two, or three stars? Worried about cost? You should be. Though the great restaurants of Europe charge less than their New York or Los Angeles counterparts, they remain a costly extravagance. But except at the world-famous "names," their servings of food are ridiculously large. And therein lies the secret of enjoying luxurious meals at a reasonable price. Consider the following example of an oft-encountered dilemma (and opportunity):

You are seated in the beflowered splendor of Copenhagen's Belle Terrasse restaurant in the Tivoli Gardens. "Enchantment" describes the mood, until you spot the price of main courses and grimly begin ordering the dishes that will destroy that week's travel budget. You and your companion each order an appetizer. You each have a main course. You each order a dessert. The appetizer, when it comes, is enough for a small football team. The main course is presented on a silver serving tureen two feet long, and could feed a family. The dessert is in three separate portions which the waiter vainly urges you to complete. Of course it's cost-

> There *is* an off-season in Europe, when prices plummet in the resort hotels.

ly! The food you've received is enough for three!

Act like a smart traveller and share. Order an appetizer apiece and then one main course, which you divide. Split the dessert. You'll have reduced the bill by almost half, and still have far too much to eat. To follow an even more sophisticated line, ask that the dish be diminished in size. If the pâté de foie gras at $12 is irresistible but budget-breaking, ask for a half plate ("une demi portion, s'il vous plaît"); it will still prove more than you need, but for only $6. The most cultivated Europeans adopt this approach in all but the most exalted restaurants.

• Eat picnic-style at least once a day. Finally, consider the chic practice of alternating those continual visits to European restaurants with an occasional cold meal of European specialties purchased at a food shop or food section of a department store, and then consumed along a riverbank or in a park; nothing could be more elegant and satisfying (yet cheap), given the superb quality of Europe's fresh foods. What other continent matches their pâtés and cheeses, freshly baked rolls, olives and tomatoes, inexpensive local wines? The true gourmet takes a daily plunge into the European equivalent of a delicatessen, and enjoys healthy, refreshing meals of awesome quality, but of equally refreshing cost.

Champagne tastes on a beer budget? It's all in the mind. People in love with life create their own bubbles, carry effervescence within them, make no effort to match the thoughtless travel expenditures of the pampered rich. The vaunted pleasures of Europe are best available to the creative and young at heart.

The Industrial Revolution Comes to the Ski Slopes

*B*et you thought that skiing couldn't get any better, right? *Wrong. At all the major snow resorts of Colorado—at Snowmass and Vail, at Breckenridge and Buttermilk—people are turning handsprings, crowing, and cavorting over an advance in ski-lift equipment that literally transforms the nature of the sport. Though other areas are rushing to install the same devices—and some already have—Colorado's clear lead in the new technology has once again confirmed the eminence of that state in U.S. skiing.*

By intermittently removing the ski chair or gondola from its supporting wire rope, the ski lift is able to operate at more than double the normal speed.

Even within Colorado, resorts with a great deal of the new equipment are proclaiming their superiority over resorts with less of it. Popular Vail—with four installations—claims an edge over trendy Aspen/Snowmass, with only three.

I'm talking about "superchair," the "rapid lift," the "express gondola," the "detachable quad"—all interchangeable terms for essentially the same thing. By intermittently removing the ski chair or ski gondola from its supporting wire rope (I'll explain why later), the ski lift is able to operate at more than double its normal speed. And from that, wondrous benefits result: an elimination of the 35- to 45-minute waits for a chair that have bedeviled so many popular resorts; an up-to-20-minute reduction in the time needed to reach the top of a slope; a doubling of the time that skiers can now spend on the slopes in the course of a day.

It sounds almost pathetically simple—this increase in lift speed—but it requires a daunting, $2-million investment per lift. That caused a great many ski companies to put off the changeover (whose potential first came to their attention in 1981) until they could first gauge the public's reac-

MEET "SUPERCHAIR," THE "RAPID LIFT," THE "EXPRESS GONDOLA," THE "DETACHABLE QUAD"

tion (a process of four long years; 1985 witnessed the first large-scale installation of detachable chairs). Like U.S. automakers dawdling over the adoption of superior Japanese approaches, a number of laggard ski companies are now paying the price for refusing to make an early invest-

ment. Resorts with "rapid lifts" expect a record season in the winter of 1988. Resorts without them will suffer.

Prior to the new technology, ski lifts moved at a speed of only 400 feet per minute. Since chairs or enclosed gondolas were permanently gripped to fixed positions on the wire rope, a faster speed would have made it difficult or even impossible for skiers to climb aboard at the bottom of the slope.

Even at those slower speeds, beginning skiers (like me) have always found it difficult to position themselves properly to grab the passing chairs.

However hard the loading, unloading was worse, resulting in every sort of Charlie Chaplin pratfall, pile-ups, even dangerous mishaps. Attendants at emergency buttons have needed to stop the lifts, and then slowly restart them, an inordinate number of times. Start-and-stop operations, added to slow speed, caused long waiting lines to form at the bottom of the mountain. Heavily visited Vail, in particular, suffered considerably from its reputation for half-hour-and-longer waits, added to half-hour ascents, reducing the number of possible downhill runs per day to an unacceptable level. To increase those runs, skiers limited their lunches, bolted down sandwiches, allowed themselves scarcely any socializing or rest.

In 1981 came the first attempt at reform. The mighty Doppelmayr Company of Austria (whose competitor in the manufacturing of ski lifts is the equally powerful Poma of France) installed a single detachable-chair lift at Breckenridge, Colorado. A "rope" designed to run at 1,000 feet per minute (2½ times the earlier pace) brought chairs at high speed into terminals at the bottom and top of the mountain. There they detached them-

IT SOUNDS ALMOST PATHETICALLY SIMPLE, BUT REQUIRES A DAUNTING INVESTMENT PER LIFT

selves from the main line, proceeded onto a separate "track," and decelerated to permit boarding at slow speed. Once full, they then slowly returned to the fast-running line, re-gripped it, and were whizzed uphill in less than half the normal time.

Because the chairs could be boarded at slow speed, more skiers could also climb on at the same time. Chairs were widened to accommodate four skiers sitting side-by-side ("quads"). Enclosed gondolas were built to seat as many as eight. Capacity climbed so exponentially that waiting lines instantly disappeared. Able to go up and down several times a day, skiers turned to long, leisurely lunches, brightened at the prospect of constant skiing, and sang the praises of Breckenridge.

Surprisingly, nothing more was built for the next three years (perhaps because of the high cost of installing the detachable feature). Then, in 1986 activity exploded: a dozen "rapid lifts" went into

service for the winter of 1987; a dozen more are currently in construction nationwide for the coming winter of 1988. Vail and Squaw Valley, California, led in quantity of the new equipment; Aspen Mountain installed the longest new lift—13,000 feet. At 1,000 feet a minute, the latter brings you to the top of a high mountain in 13 minutes, as compared with the 33 minutes earlier required. And without a long wait in line to board the lift.

Among the resorts with "rapid lifts": Vail, Breckenridge, Aspen Mountain, Snowmass, Steamboat Springs, Mount Bachelor, Squaw Valley, Keystone—all in the West; and Gore Mountain, New York, and Stowe, Vermont, in the East.

Among the resorts that still don't have them (although some have installed wide "quad chairs," nondetachable ones): Mammoth Mountain, California, Crested Butte, Purgatory, and Aspen Highlands, in the West; and most resorts in the East.

Though eastern ski resorts probably excuse the lack on the basis of their shorter, 4,000-foot-long slopes (which compare with the 9,000- to 10,000-foot varieties often found out west), they must still contend with claims that their facilities are no longer as comfortable as those equipped with the rapid lifts. Frankly, I'd give considerable weight to the nature of lift equipment in deciding which of several competing resorts to patronize. Many skiers now make a call to the resorts they're considering and put the question point-blank: How fast are your lifts? Nothing could be better calculated to goad the recalcitrants into making the improvement.

As for the future, the "rapid lift" is now under consideration as a non-ski-related, horizontal "people-mover" in all sorts of urban and industrial situations: bringing

Resorts with a great deal of the new equipment are proclaiming their superiority over resorts with less of it. Popular Vail—with four installations—claims an edge over trendy Aspen/Snowmass, with only three.

crowds of office workers from main building to parking lot, taking shoppers from place to place in downtown areas.

But meantime, in the world of skis, the "rapid lift" is the big news—the major development—of 1988. It brings additional excitement to an already-exhilarating sport.

Aspen Mountain   Aspen Highlands   Buttermilk Mountain   Snowmass

XIV
Careers in Travel

Can You Really Become a Part-Time Travel Agent?

*I*t's a zinger, a stunner, a title bound to appeal. But to pound the point home, they place dollar signs, in boldface, at the start and the end: "$Become a Part-Time Travel Agent$."

At "urban night schools" all over the land, lecturers charge as much as $24 for three hours, even $41 for six hours, to present a topic that I think can be treated in 1,200 words. Here goes:

Anyone can become a "part-time travel agent" by 10 a.m. tomorrow morning, because part-time travel agents receive no salary, and are paid only when and if they produce clients for their agency. Though some travel-agency owners are weary of the part-timers they already employ, and will refuse to take on more, most will instantly respond "Yes" when you offer to work for them "free."

While you wait for your business card to be printed, you hang around the agency for an hour or so each day, to familiarize yourself with its personnel and with the travel packages most frequently requested of them. You browse among the brochures on the racks. You do not learn the technical end of the travel-agency business, and no one offers to teach you. As a part-timer, you are not really a "travel agent," but rather an "outside sales rep," in the parlance of the trade.

On the day when your cards arrive, you ask to borrow 200 pieces of letterhead stationery and envelopes, which you take home. You then proceed to compose a list of every human being you have ever met: relatives, friends, alumni, business asso-

> **Anyone can become a part-time travel agent by 10 a.m. tomorrow, because part-time travel agents receive no salary.**

ciates, fellow church members—anyone. To them, you compose and duplicate a letter, which might read like this:

> *Dear Friend:*
> *You will be delighted to learn that I am now associated with XYZ Travel Agency. And in that capacity, I should like to arrange your next vacation trip.*
> *Give me a chance—I won't let you down! I'll send you on journeys of unequalled joy, I'll weave rainbows into your holiday plans.*
> *And it won't cost you an extra cent. My services are free (to you), my income is from the airlines, cruise ships, and hotels I use.*
> *Hoping to hear from you.*
> *Alice or John Jones.*

To your amazement, the phone begins to ring. Why? Because most people don't already have a travel agent to whom they owe allegiance. Or else they're accustomed to making their own reservations by calling airlines and hotels direct. When you offer to take those burdens off their hands—at no cost to them—they often rush to agree.

If all you then do is refer the booking to the travel agency you represent—without performing any of the work—you generally receive one or two of the percentage points of commission they earn. After all, you have brought them a client they might not otherwise have had.

If you do more, you earn more. Thus if you consult with the client and "hone" their vague vacation desires into a finite, complete decision—get them to agree on the exact date and flight of their departure, a specific hotel property, all else—and then present that virtually complete transaction to the agency for processing, you are generally able to up your income to three or four percentage points. After all, you have saved the agency one or two

AS MANY AS 100,000 AMERICANS EARN INCOME FROM THE SALE OF TRAVEL WHILE HOLDING DOWN FULL-TIME JOBS IN OTHER FIELDS

hours of nonproductive time. Instead of engaging in repeated discussions over the phone or across a desk, the agency can limit its services to a few minutes of processing: placing the booking, then issuing tickets and documents.

Gradually you—the "outside sales rep"—learn to do even more. As your knowledge of the industry increases, you actually phone the suppliers and make the needed reservations. Though you still can't work the computer, issue tickets, or perform a dozen other tasks, you do much of the other paperwork and all of the contact with the client. And then, because you're saving the agency additional time, you ask them to "split the commission," receiving an average of five percentage points on the income your clients bring.

With growing pleasure, and while retaining your daytime position as a nurse, teacher, or paralegal, you begin receiving a steady stream of small commission checks. If you are diligent about it, you discover that you are supplementing your income with two or three thousands of dollars a year, maybe more.

And then you generally make that other all-important travel discovery: that it is often just as easy to book 20 people on a trip as to sign up one. You begin actively to "sell" travel, creating holiday motivations where none might exist. On the bulletin board of a large, nearby office, you post a notice: "Hey, gang, if I can sign 20 of you aboard a charter to Rio on September 17, I can get us a full week's trip, including air fare and a good Copacabana hotel, for only $599."

If you are good at it and enjoy a following—which most often happens if you're a "joiner" known to large numbers of people in your community—you find

> As a part-timer, you are not really a "travel agent" at all, but rather an "outside sales rep."

that your part-time "outside sales" position is so promising as to warrant your taking an evening vocational course in the retail travel business. Every city of size offers such instruction—look in the *Yellow Pages* phone directory under "schools" and then under the subheading of "travel." You do this either to improve your skills at handling entire travel transactions, remaining a part-timer all the while, or else to enter the travel world on a full-time basis. My guess is that as many as 100,000 Americans act as "part-time agents" or "outside sales reps," while holding down full-time jobs in nontravel fields.

How about free or reduced-price travel privileges? Do part-timers enjoy that fringe benefit of the travel agency? Depends on the agency. Under deregulation, no legal obstacle any longer bars airlines or others from offering free trips to anyone. But different agency owners pursue differing policies in allocating their reduced-price trips, free "junkets," or "familiarization trips." Ask before you make your choice of agencies. Certainly, if you're a heavy producer, you should be entitled to your pro-rata share.

And that, so help me, and in my humble opinion, is all there is to it. Obviously, it doesn't work for everyone, as nothing in this life does. But with so many travel bookings being placed directly with airlines, cruise lines, and hotels—and not presently through travel agents—opportunities abound for dynamic, sales-minded individuals to steer much of that business their way, earning a commission.

Thereby they not only enhance their incomes, but share in the emotional rewards of the travel industry.

And they don't have to pay $24 for a course to learn how.

The World of the One-Man (or One-Woman) Tour Operator

She had reached the well-paid pinnacle of her profession.

And she felt miserable.

After 12 years with a glamorous New York advertising agency, she had grown bored with business and began asking all the standard questions: "Is this all there is to life?"

One thing she knew: that she loved to travel. So in January of 1985 she booked a tour to view Algerian rock paintings dating to 8,000 B.C. To reach them required that her party first pass through the eerie, boulder-bestrewn, moonlike expanse of the Central Sahara. And she fell in love with it.

Forget the rock paintings! Learning that hardly anyone was travelling commercially to the Central Sahara, she extended her stay to perform the necessary reconnaissance and preparations, then returned to New York and formed a one-woman company to advertise and operate tours to that unique location. Today her desk is awash with bookings, and she has led multiple expeditions—of 4 to 12 passengers apiece—to both the Sahara and other virtually unvisited points of the globe.

Her name is Irma Turtle (it really is); her company is **Turtle Tours, 251 East 51st Street, New York, NY 10022 (phone 212/355-1404)**; and she is representative of nearly 200 entrepreneurs scattered about the country who have formed one-

The classic advertising medium for them is a thick, biannual magazine called the *Specialty Travel Index.*

SPECIALT IN

person (or at best, two-person) tour operations designed to explore the most narrow of special interests or the oddest of worldwide destinations.

In the case of Irma Turtle, savings from a lucrative career permitted her to place tiny ads for her special travel offerings in *The New Yorker* and other trendy magazines, and a heavy response to those notices gave life to Turtle Tours. For other one-person companies lacking such funds, the classic advertising medium is a thick biannual magazine called the *Specialty Travel Index.* It reaches 41,000 persons associated with travel agencies, but it should be on the desk or coffee table of every American avidly interested in travel. It can change your travel life.

Essentially, the *Specialty Travel Index* publishes inexpensive ads placed by 436 largely unknown, undersize tour operators who schedule and operate several thousands of special-interest tours. The ads appear in nearly-uniform horizontal strips in the body of the magazine, alphabetically by name, but they are preceded by indexes and cross-indexes of their subject matter and geographical emphasis.

Care to visit the Falkland Islands? Or Mauretania or Mauritius? You have only to turn to "F" or "M" in the *Index*'s geographical listings and out jump 14 tours to exactly those spots.

Longing for a tour of stamp-collecting exhibitions in northern Europe? Canoeing

OFFERING SPECIALTY TRAVEL, EXPLORING THE MOST NARROW OF INTERESTS OR THE ODDEST OF DESTINATIONS

TRAVEL $3.00

in Zimbabwe? Caving in Belize? Dying to discuss psychiatry with your counterparts in southern India? Simply turn to the several pages of small type in the subject-matter section of the *Specialty Travel Index* and there you'll find cross references to dozens of departures for exactly those purposes.

Merely to stab at random among those subjects is to find provocative new ideas for trips and tours. Would you believe that travel programs exist which explore "polo instruction," "porcelain china," "psychology," "public affairs," and "religion/spirituality"? Or that companies offer tours of "soccer," "solar energy," "space travel," "spectator sports," and "stress management"? Some 176 special interests or activities are listed—including "antiques," "bridge tours," "chocolate tours," "fashion tours," "holistic health tours," "llama packing," "military history," "whale watching," and "wine tasting"—and each subhead lists the programs of up to a dozen specialty-tour operators.

Though some of these are substantial companies—especially those involved in various aspects of "adventure travel"—upward of 200 are small, local firms, some composed of only a person or two, whose offerings would scarcely be known outside their immediate area if it were not for the *Specialty Travel Index*. So affirms its ebullient co-publisher, 47-year-old Steen Hanson.

It reaches 41,000 professionals, but it should be on the desk or coffee table of every American avidly interested in travel.

To prove it, return again to the example of Irma Turtle. Though ads in *The New Yorker* launched her offerings to the moderately familiar Central Sahara (18 days for $2,500, plus air), only constant appearance in the *Specialty Travel Index* enables her to gather sufficient passengers for departures to a set of almost totally unknown destinations. As remarkable as it may seem, she is currently operating her one-woman expeditions to:

• The "Pantanal" of Brazil: World's largest wetlands, full of river networks and 600 species of tropical birds. "Every time a passenger comments that we haven't yet seen a certain species," says Ms. Turtle, "100 of them suddenly appear. Walt Disney couldn't do it any better."

• From Ougadougou to Timbuktu, Mali: By Land Rover, over 1,500 miles of roadless terrain. "I put these groups through one very tough trip," says Ms. Turtle, "and not only do they survive it, but they thank me at the end and say they wouldn't have missed it for the world."

• And add: The Atlas Mountains of Morocco, led by Berber guides; the Ecuadorian Amazon, among the Jivaro Indians (former headshrinkers, they now do it only to monkeys); Rajasthan, India, "where camels pull our baggage in wagons as we cross the Thar desert."

American Express she obviously isn't; a tour operator in the classic and original sense, she is. For a one-year subscription to the *Specialty Travel Index*, encountering the ornery, individualistic, and slightly wonderful Turtles of this world, send $5 to **Specialty Travel Index, 305 San Anselmo Avenue, Suite 217, San Anselmo, CA 94960 (phone 415/459-4900).**

Travelling for Free as a Tour Escort, I

A *"tour escort": the words imply a dream job, the fantasy career. In blue blazer and natty scarf (one typical vision), you stroll through life with well-mannered groups of sensitive adults as they view the storied sites of antiquity.*

Just think: you are travelling for free, and getting paid, to boot!

The reality can be jarringly different. As a paid travel professional, on call around the clock, your phone rings at all hours of the night with unreasonable demands: change my room, get me more blankets or towels. You learn that awful truth: that of every 40 persons on earth, 38 are gentle, caring souls and 2 are monsters. In my own past life as a tour operator, I sent an escort to China with 20 auto dealers and their spouses, of whom two refused to eat Chinese food after the first day. The poor tour escort, in addition to her other tasks, labored in a hot hotel kitchen to prepare hamburgers or spaghetti for the obstinate duo.

Still another member of the group was a surly drunk who slipped pitchers of Mai Tais onto the bus, creating scandal and problems in a dozen Chinese towns.

Want an additional whiff of reality? Well, people get sick while on tour, and you, the tour escort, rush them to the hospital at 3 a.m. and pace the waiting room. People occasionally die while on tour—that being a tiring activity—and

It's not always a happy task: of every 40 persons travelling together, 38 are gentle, caring souls, and two are monsters.

you, the tour escort, trudge to a grisly foreign morgue to ship the body home.

Yet for all the horrors, thousands of Americans—in love with travel, in love with people—are joyfully at work as tour escorts, either part-time or full-time; and many thousands more would kill to land a like position. In this, the first of two essays, I appraise that dream vocation, and provide pointers—based on interviews with the personnel directors of nearly a dozen tour operators—on how to be hired.

The companies that hire

As travel becomes increasingly group-oriented (economies of scale bring lower prices to groups), creating an obvious need for one escort per group, more than 450 tour companies are now making use of tour escorts—some hiring fewer than 10 a year, others as many as 200.

The largest users of tour escorts are, beyond any doubt, Tauck Tours of Westport, Connecticut (for domestic trips, mainly by motorcoach), and Maupintour of Lawrence, Kansas (going worldwide). Beyond the two leaders, precise rankings are difficult to make, but the major escort-hiring firms include, quite clearly: American Express of New York City (primarily for incoming groups to the U.S.); Four Winds of New York City; West Tours of Seattle, Washington; Mayflower Tours of Downers Grove, Illinois; Olson-Travelworld of Culver City, California; Pacific Delight of New York City and San Francisco (but this one requires fluency in one or more Asian languages); Collette Tours of North Providence, Rhode Island; Paragon Tours of Bedford, Massachusetts; Globus Gateway/Cosmos of New York City and Los Angeles; Allied Tours of

PURSUING THE DREAM JOB, THE FANTASY CAREER: THE COMPANIES THAT HIRE, THE PEOPLE THEY HIRE

New York City and Los Angeles (foreign incoming tours, mainly); and Rural Route Tours of Overland Park, Kansas (the last-named, of increasing significance).

To obtain a more comprehensive list of every such potential employer, including escort-using companies in your own immediate vicinity, I'd go to a local retail travel agency and ask (politely and shyly) to look at their current copy of one of the "travel trade personnel directories." These yearly publications, some the size of a small telephone book, are issued by the three major trade periodicals: *Travel Weekly*, *Travel Agent*, and *Travel Trade*. Each lists all the major companies of the travel industry. By scanning the sections called "tour operators," and reading the descriptions of each, you can usually spot the many firms that hire tour escorts.

marc Rosenthal

PERSISTENCE, AND A PROPER RÉSUMÉ, ARE KEYS TO LANDING A TOUR ESCORT POSITION

An increasing number of companies are saying they will "give an edge" to school-trained applicants.

Two other important names in tour escorting are those of the major schools purporting to train and place "tour managers" (their loftier title for a "tour escort" or "tour courier"): **American Tour Management Institute, 271 Madison Avenue, New York, NY 10016** (classes in New York), **International Tour Management Institute, 625 Market Street, San Francisco, CA 94105** (classes in San Francisco, Los Angeles, San Diego, Chicago, Seattle, and Boston). Although I've long been skeptical about their ability to teach what seems to me a commonsense function, I was surprised to learn, in interviews, of the high regard in which both companies are held by the professionals. While the vast majority of tour escorts obtain their positions without formal instruction in the subject, an increasing number of tour companies are currently saying they will "give an edge" to

school-trained applicants; one or two even look exclusively to the graduates of such schools for openings in their ranks.

The people they hire

The activity is largely a women's profession—to such an extent that some personnel managers say they now give preference to men to redress the balance! And contrary to the popular conception of tour escorts as vigorous yuppies in their early 30s, the actual average age level is fairly high. A recent private study of tour escorts by George C. Guenther of Talmage Tours in Philadelphia (which he was kind enough to show me) asserts that the typical tour escort is, in addition to being female, between 50 and 59 years of age, married, but retired and working part-time as an escort (she is also "caring, patient, outgoing, and well-organized").

The maximum age limit for service? None, say the personnel managers, provided the applicant is physically strong and able to work the long hours (hopping on and off buses, doing considerable walking) that tour escorting entails.

The places to which you go

By a three-to-one ratio (and probably higher than that) domestic tours outnum-

ber international ones as opportunities for escorting; you are far more likely to criss-cross New England than New Zealand. And this numerical imbalance has an important part in determining the duties you'll perform.

On an international tour you'll seldom be asked to deliver the lectured commentary on what the group is seeing. That's done by local art historians or other specialists picked up along the way (who accompany the group, say, to the Uffizzi Galleries in Florence) or by full-time, highly trained British tour guides assigned to the bus for the entire tour. The tour escort from the U.S., if there is one, performs the homelier tasks: dealing with mishaps and travel emergencies, overseeing transfers of luggage, watching the air connections, acting as liaison between the group and their hotels, or between the group and the tour operator's head office. Ironically, the foreign tour is thus the easiest to escort.

In the United States, by contrast, both practice and tradition cast the tour escort, in most cases, as the commentator: you provide a running lecture on all that passes by.

Accordingly, virtually all tour companies cite "a knowledge of place," "experience in the area," as one of the prime requisites for a majority of their escort positions. That's not to say that you must memorize scores of facts about various destinations to get the job; no escort is made to "solo" on a particular tour until he or she has first accompanied a trained escort on at least two departures of the same tour. But to the extent that you are already heavily travelled, or know particular areas well, you become a prime prospect for domestic escorting.

A knowledge of place—the destinations served by the tour operator—is the key talent.

(In this respect, tour escorting is radically different from most other careers in travel. In a retail travel agency, for instance, the fact that you have travelled a great deal in life has almost no bearing upon your ability to do the job; rather, it is first and far more important that you master a body of technical details on booking and pricing flights, cruises, tours, and the like.)

Therefore: if you know New England like the palm of your hand, if you grew up on the coast of California, if Alaska was

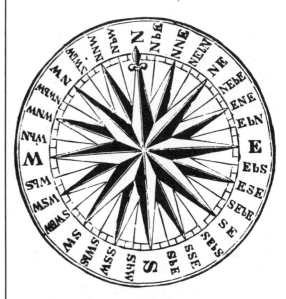

your kindergarten or Florida your lifelong home, say so. Lead off your résumé with travel experience and half the job is done.

What else do companies require in a tour escort? What causes them to pluck a single résumé or two from a stack of 20? How much do they pay? How often do they send you on tours? Will they hire you to work part-time?

Turn the page for more on the dream career.

Travelling for Free as a Tour Escort, II

*I*n they come, *résumés in search of the dream job, as many as ten a week to even the smaller tour operators. The position sought: a tour escort "paid to travel," accompanying groups of 30 or 40 Americans on international trips (where other local guides supply the lectured commentaries) or groups of 20 and 30 persons on domestic tours (where the escort provides the commentary and thus becomes less "escort" than "guide" or "director").*

With ten applications for every opening, tour escorting rivals the theatre world in the brutal competitiveness of its job-seeking process. The analogy is apt. "We're looking for stars," says Nancy Jepson of Globus Gateway/Cosmos Tours. "You have to be a bit egotistical to be a tour director, which is why unemployed actresses are often our best prospects."

To find out the criteria leading tour companies use for choosing escorts, I interviewed (by phone) the personnel managers for a dozen large tour companies. Apart from a knowledge of the destinations to which the tours go—a talent heavily stressed by most—what other attributes cause ten résumés to be plucked from a stack of a hundred?

"Let me tell you first what we're not

What causes them to pluck a single résumé or two from a stack of twenty?

seeking," says John Stachnik of Mayflower Tours, Downers Grove, Illinois. "We're not impressed by people in a mid-life crisis seeking a 'cure' through travel or escaping from reality—and we can read those aims in a great many of the applications we receive."

"We're looking for people who like being leaders, responsible for the welfare of a group," says Bruce Beckham of Beckham Travel, Boston. "I scan the résumés mainly for organizational background, prior experience as the head of a group or effort, however small: teachers, high school principals, former YMCA directors, people who have been involved in social volunteerism: Elks, Knights of Columbus."

"The underlying quality," says Betty Tilson, director of tour managers for Olson/Travelworld, "is that they be caring; they must enhance the tour on a personal level, go all out. In the very first interview with them, perhaps by phone, we are looking for that caring quality."

"Too often," says John Stachnik of Mayflower Tours, "we hear applicants stressing how much they love to travel. We would rather hear them say, 'I love to be with people.'"

"They must be a bit like psychiatrists," adds Kathy Ackers of Rural Route Tours, Overland Park, Kansas, "able to cope with varying personalities, eager to mold 40 people into a happy group, a family. If you get tired of 40 people after seven days, and have seven more to go, you're in the wrong business. And if you don't like change, you won't survive."

The subsidiary qualities for success in the field? "The strength of Superman and the patience of God" (says Joan Dunne of Pacific Delight Tours, New York City);

DIDI JONES
110 DECLAN DRIVE, #55
BROOKLYN, NY 11215
Tel. 000-000-0000

OBJECTIVE:

To lead tours to Latin America with a cultural and/or spiritual emphasis.

TRAVEL EMPLOYMENT AND EXPERIENCE:

Organized and led five tours to Peru, focusing on Macchu Picchu, Journeys Within, Travel Division of New York Institute of the Light, 1986-87.

Assistant Coordinator, "Exploring Andean Culture," Yale University Alumni College Abroad, summer 1981

Traveled independently for 18 months throughout Central and Latin America—Honduras, Nicaragua, Costa Rica, Guatamala, Mexico, Peru, Ecuador, Colombia, Chile, Bolivia. Wrote over 20 articles for five academic journals, including Globalinks and Women Around the World, 1983-85.

Anthropological research, studying women's roles in Andean society, Cajamarca, Peru, summer 1980 (Yale University Latin America Summer Fellowship).

EDUCATION:

Yale University, New Haven, CT, B.A. Latin American Studies, 1981, Magna Cum Laude; Distinction in the Major; Latin America Summer Fellowship.

University for Peace, Villa Colon, Costa Rica, M.A. in Communications for Peace, 1983.

Swedish Institute of Massage, New York City, 1986-present.

LANGUAGES:

Spanish, Quechua.

HOBBIES:

Song-writing, ceramics, motorcycle touring, hang-gliding, fishing.

REFERENCES:

Available upon request.

MORE THAN 450 COMPANIES ARE NOW MAKING USE OF TOUR ESCORTS

"good grooming; we stress appearance very, very strongly" (Bill Strickland, American Express, New York City); "good communications skills" (Bob Sanger, director of New York's American Tour Management Institute); "high energy level, liking to have fun" (Kathy Ackers, Rural Route Tours); "incredible patience, mature judgment, and the vigor to bear up under a physically demanding job: the end of the day is not the end of their day; that's when problems start" (Dick Sundby, tour escort supervisor for Tauck Tours, Westport, Connecticut).

"The ideal candidate," concludes John Stachnik of the fast-growing Mayflower Tours, "is a recent widow, completely flexible in her time requirements, still vigorous, who has feelings within herself to give, a great deal to share, and is herself well-traveled and very caring."

Possessed of such qualities, how do you bring them to the fore and snare the job? Through persistence, answer all my interviewees. The mailing of a résumé to multiple tour operators is only the first step in a protracted campaign. You follow up by phone, perhaps two or three times in a season. You regard turndowns as mere temporary setbacks—the simple lack of an opening in an industry whose needs are notoriously volatile, fluid. You shrug off rejection, press on in requesting interviews, submit updated résumés. One reason why some companies prefer graduates of the two major schools of "tour management" (see the previous essay) is because attendance at such a school evidences a profound determination to enter the field.

If some companies demand prior experience of their potential tour escorts (as American Express, for one, does), you

Tour-escorting rivals the theatre world in the brutal competition of its job-seeking process.

obtain that experience by leading a small, local tour for one of your own local tour companies or travel agencies, even for free. And then you headline your résumé with that event. Either way—with or without experience, with or without tour-school training, but through persistence —you obtain an interview and presumably obtain the job.

Once employed, do you work full-time or part-time? In most instances you work seasonally, say all my informants; at least 70% of all tour escorts do it on a part-time basis, and only 10% to 20% of the 450 companies hiring tour escorts are able to employ people year round (Collette Tours is one of the latter). Even the giant Tauck Tours employs the great bulk of its escorts during the May-through-October season only (but operates every day of the week throughout that season). Actually, according to Tauck supervisor Dick Sundby, that intense seasonality is well suited to the type of escort Tauck seeks to hire. "We like people who have other things in their lives. We look for escorts willing to work their heads off May through October and use the other months to pursue life goals."

How much do tour escorts earn? While arrangements vary broadly from firm to firm, most companies report an average of $80 to $100 a day while on tour (and tours can extend for as many as 14 to 21 days), much of it from the tips that escorts traditionally receive from their passengers. And since escorts are usually housed and fed at the tour company's expense, most of that income can be retained as savings. "You live a rather high life when you're a tour director," says Nancy Jepson of Globus Gateway/Cosmos Tours. "If you're doing it full-time, you

THOMAS HUTCHINSON VAN DELFT
27 Linden Lane
Rye, NY 10000
Tel. (000)000-0000

WORK EXPERIENCE
1986-present

Tourguide with Eurotour Inc.; organized and guided one- and two-week tours for Americans

1985-1986

Assistant to Special Attache for Economic Affairs, U.S. Embassy, Paris

1983-1985

Researcher for Department of Romance Languages, Princeton University

TRAVEL EXPERIENCE
1986-present

Accumulated 33 weeks leading tours to following countries: Austria, Belgium, Denmar, France, Great Britain, Greece, Holland, Italy, Luxembourg, Spain, Switzerland, and West Germany

1982-1985

Traveled independently during summer, especially France, Greece, Italy, and Switzerland

EDUCATION
June 1985

A.B., Romance Languages, Princeton University
Captain of Lacrosse Team
Member of Ivy Club

July 1986

Certificat d'Excellence, Ecole de l'Etude du Vin, Paris

PERSONAL

Enjoy collecting wines, unusual travel and participating in polo and lacrosse

REFERENCES

Available upon request

often don't pay rent, because the company will put you up when you're between tours. If you're away seven months, you make a lot of money."

But: "It's a 24-hour job," Ms. Jepson continues. "You have to be a little crazy to do it, and you have no social life. At the same time, it's the most rewarding job you'll ever have."

Which is why those résumés keep arriving in an endless stream, seeking the dream job, the fantasy career.

Appendix

Twenty-one of America's Foremost Discount Travel Agencies

Though some call them "bucket shops," they are simply discounters of air fares performing a function no less proper or respectable than the activities of discount pharmacies, discount record stores, discount clothing shops.

Primarily, they sell air fares to international destinations at discounts of as much as 30% and 40%. Because these tickets come from prestigious airlines, which make them available through selected retail outlets, the bucket shops have to possess some "standing"—a relationship with an international airline—to remain in business. And I, for one, have not yet heard of a single instance among them of blatant skullduggery, financial insolvency, or irresponsibility (stranding of passengers).

In the main text of this book, I've discussed the buckets at length, and provided the names of half a dozen. Here, now is a more comprehensive listing of 21, out of the 100-or-so that presently operate in U.S. cities.

ACCESS INTERNATIONAL, INC.
250 West 57th Street
New York, NY 10107
(phone 212/333-7280)

Claims to be the nation's largest bucket shop, with sales of more than 150,000 seats in 1988. Its tickets are primarily to European destinations, and Orient-bound passengers might be better advised to seek out an Asian specialist.

MAHARAJAH TRAVELS
518 Fifth Avenue
New York, NY 10036
(phone 212/391-0122, or toll free
800/223-6862 outside New York
State)

Another prominent New York discounter, with a toll-free "800" number for out-of-state clients. Primarily to Europe, but also to India, Singapore, and Tokyo. Will also handle hotel reservations.

SUDO TOURS
500 Fifth Avenue
New York, NY 10110
(phone 212/302-2860)

A long-established specialist to Tokyo. It will send you there for an amazing $820 (and less) round trip, provided you agree to go on an indirect route involving stops. "Those who know Asia, know us" is their slogan.

THE VACATION OUTLET
(in Filene's basement)
Washington Street
Boston, MA 02108
(phone 617/267-2411)

Sells tours and packages—never air fares alone—at sharply discounted prices, primarily to resort destinations. Open Monday through Friday from 9 a.m. to 6 p.m., on Saturday from 10 a.m. to 3 p.m., and claims to be the nation's only "retail travel store." Operates in a bustling, invigorating atmosphere as a result of its location in one of the busiest retail department store basements. Many packages sold are of the last-minute variety, but departures are available several weeks ahead.

JAPAN BUDGET TRAVEL
9 East 38th Street, Room 203
New York, NY 10016
(phone 212/686-8855)

Though nearly every employee is Japanese, with less-than-fluent abilities in English, it nevertheless pays to endure the language difficulties—their values are that good. Is primarily engaged in selling air fares to Japan at heavily discounted levels, but also has packages for sale, to both Japan and Europe. Sells Northwest Orient tickets to Japan at the last minute; maintains office hours Monday through Friday from 9:30 a.m. to 5:30 p.m., on Saturday from 10 a.m. to 4:30 p.m.

TRAVEL SERVICE, INC.
135-40 North Florida Avenue, Suite
206D
Tampa, FL 33613
(phone toll free 800/843-9692)

This travel service will have moved to another address in Tampa by the time this book appears, but its phone number will stay the same. Primarily deals with Europe-bound passengers (and secondarily to the Orient), and primarily sells air fares at cut-rate levels. Does some last-minute work, but is mainly interested in bookings made at least 21 days in advance. Ask for Trish or Fred.

TRANS-AM TRAVEL
3101 Ford Avenue
Alexandria, VA 22302
(phone 703/998-7676)

Orient only, air fares only, at "the best levels offered." Hours are Monday through Friday from 9 a.m. to 6 p.m., on Saturday from 10 a.m. to 3 p.m. Claims to offer the best prices to the Orient of any East Coast travel agency.

SUN INTERNATIONAL TRAVEL
6000 Dawson Boulevard
Norcross, GA 30093
(phone 404/446-3111)

Sells Japan Air Lines tickets at "wholesale rates"; in phoning, ask for "wholesale division."

TRAVELOW INTERNATIONAL
136-75 37th Avenue
Flushing, NY 11354
(phone 718/445-1302, or toll free
800/231-5561)

Another substantial source of discounted international tickets to just about anywhere overseas. Prides itself on ability to obtain such tickets down to three days before departure.

EURO-ASIA, INC.
4203 East Indian School Road
Phoenix, AZ 85018
(phone 602/955-2742)

Proud to be called a "discount travel agency." Its international tickets are both transatlantic and transpacific, at considerable reductions.

COAST CONSOLIDATORS, INC.
2019A East Orangethorpe
Placentia, CA 92670
(phone 714/528-3366)

Sells air tickets to Europe and the South Pacific at discounts of 15% to 30% off published rates. Tahiti is among its destinations, in addition to the standard European gateways.

EXPRESS DISCOUNT TRAVEL
5945 Mission Gorge Road
San Diego, CA 92101
(phone 619/283-6324)

The heavyweight of the West Coast shops, owned by people prominent in the field of air-fare discounting for several years. Many other West Coast agencies procure their cut-rate tickets from this firm. Air-fare discounts of up to 50%; discounts of 20% to 30% on tour programs. Handles South America as well as Europe and Asia. Also has discount hotel packages in some locations.

SUNLINE EXPRESS HOLIDAYS
210 Post Street
San Francisco, CA 94108
(phone 415/398-2111)

"We're the lowest on the West Coast," they claim—to Europe, Mexico, South America, Hawaii, the Orient. "Our discounts range up to 40%; our prices are sometimes cheaper than the children's fare!"

EXPRESS FUN TRAVEL, INC.
1169 Market Street, Room 809
San Francisco, CA 94102
(phone 415/431-7512)

Sells discount tickets to the Orient, often at reductions of 30%.

ALL UNIQUE TRAVEL
1030 Georgia Street
Vallejo, CA 94590
(phone 707/648-0237)

Needs three weeks' advance notice to procure you a good discount on tickets to Mexico, Hawaii, Europe, Africa, the Middle East.

COST LESS TRAVEL, INC.
674 Broadway
San Francisco, CA 94133
(phone 415/397-6868)

Discounts of 25% to 30% on most international air fares, specializing in the Orient.

COMMUNITY TRAVEL SERVICE
5237 College Avenue
Oakland, CA 94618
(phone 415/653-0990)

Particularly good discounts on air fares to the Orient.

GETAWAY TRAVEL, INC.
1105 Ponce de Leon Boulevard
Coral Gables, FL 33134
(phone 305/446-7855)

Discounts on fares primarily to Europe; "we accommodate people planning late."

TRANSOCEANIC TRAVEL
209 Post Street
San Francisco, CA 94108
(phone 415/362-0390)

Specializes in long-haul, cost-efficient air tickets. The more stops you make, the better is this agency able to help you. Can sometimes achieve 50% savings off listed rates on lengthy multi-stop trips.

APEX TRAVEL, INC.
230 Park Avenue
New York, NY 10169
(phone 212/661-1606, or toll free
* 800/428-8848)*

Wide range of sharply discounted air fares to Asia: Jakarta, Bangkok, Singapore, Taipei, Tokyo, Hong Kong. Also, cheap China tours from Hong Kong.

PAN EXPRESS TRAVEL, INC.
25 West 39th Street
New York, NY 10018
(phone 212/719-9292)

Has remarkable discounted air fares to islands of the Caribbean, and to South America, in addition to the standard European destinations. Also offers "around-the-world specials" for as little as $1,299.

Eleven Reliable "Distress Merchants" of Travel (Offering Last-Minute Discounts)

From time immemorial, travel suppliers have sold off their last-minute remaining space at distress prices. As departure dates have neared, panic has set in. Employees of cruise ships and charter operators, of tour companies and hotel chains, have leaped to the phone to call relatives and friends, offering them the chance to purchase unsold cabins or seats at drastically reduced levels. At that late stage in the travel process, any sum received for a remaining cabin or seat is better than none. It is "found money."

Some tour operators even maintained lists of people who could travel on short notice. The bulletin board in a large urban hospital would periodically blossom with notices of last-minute travel bargains for nurses and doctors. Certain preferred unions would be alerted to phone their retired members with offers of seats at such low prices as to be irresistible.

Against such a well-known practice, it is not at all surprising that commercial entrepreneurs would finally attempt to organize what had earlier been random and unplanned. What is surprising is that it took them so long. Only within the past five years have "distress merchants" or "distress travel clubs" fully caught the public's attention with bargain offers for travel departures scheduled for the very next week, or even short days ahead.

With some exceptions, the clubs charge a yearly membership fee, which enables their members to use a toll-free line to listen to recorded messages of that week's bargains. Or they receive a periodic newsletter of bargains. Provided they have flexible work schedules and can literally leave "on a moment's notice," the members can cut their travel costs by as much as 60%.

There is nothing mysterious or arcane about it. Most travel products are totally "perishable" in nature, and must be sold for a particular date or departure, or else their value for that departure is lost forever for the producer of the product. Hence it behooves them to work with the "distress merchants" in disposing of their unsold product.

Here are 11 reliable sources of "distress travel products." My own recommendation as to which you should join: the club nearest your own city. I have the impression (and may be wrong) that each excels at departures from its own immediate vicinity.

MOMENT'S NOTICE, INC.
40 East 49th Street
New York, NY 10017
(phone 212/486-0500)

Perhaps the oldest of the lot, Moment's Notice is a recent subsidiary of the longer-established Matterhorn Club, which for 20 years has been offering sale-priced cabins, airline seats, and tour places to its members. Its departures are mainly from the East Coast, split almost evenly between New York and Florida. Members receive access to a "hotline phone number" to hear recorded messages of what's available in the days ahead, as well as a quarterly written update, all for a yearly membership fee of $45 (valid for the member and any number of that member's travel companions). Gil Zalman is the experienced founder of the club.

THE SHORT NOTICE PROGRAM
4501 Forbes Boulevard
Lanham, MD 20706
(phone toll free 800/638-8976)

An activity of American Leisure Industries' Encore Travel Club, but entirely separate from that group, and requiring an independent membership fee: $36 per year, for single travellers and travelling families alike. Upon joining, you're told a number to call for tapes updated daily (actually, on weekdays only) of travel products offered at discounts of as much as 65%—but last minute in nature. The "hotline" is a Maryland area code (301); for reservations, you're permitted to use a toll-free "800" number. Credit cards are used to book, and tickets and tour documents are either mailed or waiting for you at the airport counter or dock. A generous offer is the right to cancel with full refund within a full year of joining if services should seem unsatisfactory.

SPUR-OF-THE-MOMENT CRUISES, INC.
10780 Jefferson Boulevard
Culver City, CA 90230
(phone toll free 800/343-1991)

The chief West Coast "distress merchant," it deals only with cruises, but charges no membership fee for the right to use its services. Rather, you simply dial its "hotline" number—which is 213/838-9329—and hear a six-minute tape recording of all the distinguished ships sailing from ports all over the world that have sharply discounted cabins for sale in the two to three weeks ahead; your saving can be as much as 50%. "We're America's clearinghouse for unsold cruises," says operations manager Linda Sumolang. A recent example of their values was a departure from a Brazilian port of a ship that first stopped at Bahia and Rio, then crossed the South Atlantic to Dakar and Casablanca, and eventually went to both Barcelona and Genoa. Normal price, including air fare from Miami to Brazil, and from Genoa back to the U.S.: $2,800 (for the entire 18-day sailing). Spur-of-the-Moment's price (including air fare): a remarkable $1,689, less than $100 a day.

STAND-BUYS, LTD.
311 West Superior Street, Suite 404
Chicago, IL 60610
(phone 312/943-5737)

In business for eight years, and therefore one of the founders of this segment of the travel industry, Stand-Buys charges $45 per household per year for access to its hotline number, announcing discounts for the purchase of unfilled space on charter flights, cruises, and tours. You also receive a quarterly newsletter, and an "International Travel Card" granting you the "second night free" at nearly 1,400 hotels. In some of its literature the organization promises a complete refund of the membership fee if you find its services unsatisfactory within 30 days of joining.

LAST MINUTE TRAVEL CLUB,
INC.
132 Brookline Avenue
Boston, MA 02215
(phone 617/267-9800)

Though some of its products depart from New York, the overwhelming number leave from Boston, and its members are heavily New England based. The $35 a year covers you, your family, and a travel companion, and results in your receiving a monthly newsletter and access to a 24-hour hotline. David Fialkow and Joel Benard are the founders, the latter the son of a prominent tour operator. Individual memberships are available for $30.

WORLDWIDE DISCOUNT
TRAVEL CLUB, INC.
1674 Meridian Avenue
Miami Beach, FL 33139
(phone 305/534-2082)

Every third week (that's 17 times a year), it mails you a closely typed letter, front and back, listing imminent departures of tours and/or cruises leaving from Atlanta, Boston, Chicago, Los Angeles, Miami, and New York, on which seats or cabins have been radically discounted in price. You then phone a toll-free number to book the trip you desire. Membership is $35 a year for a single traveller, $50 for a family. The club has been in business for several years.

ADVENTURES ON CALL, INC.
P.O. Box 18592
BWI Airport, MD 21240
(phone 301/356-4080)

Offers last-minute availabilities on air tickets and air-plus-land packages principally from this Baltimore airport at discounts as high as 50%. Membership fee is $49 per year per household (includes two adults and children under 18 years of age). Upon joining, you receive a 24-hour hotline phone number permitting you to keep abreast of all such travel opportunities, plus a confirmed-reservation phone number to call for making bookings. Finally, at least six times a year, members are contacted to enjoy first call on special travel opportunities, again principally from BWI Airport/Baltimore.

ENTERTAINMENT HOT LINE
TRAVEL CLUB
1400 North Woodward Avenue
Birmingham, MI 48011
(phone 313/642-1406 for information
or 313/642-5253 for reservations
from Michigan or Canada, or toll
free 800/828-0826 from all other
areas)

A subsidiary of the large, publicly owned company that publishes the famous "Entertainment" discount coupons (74 volumes dealing with the 74 largest cities of the U.S.). It purports to operate nationwide (recent departures from New York, Los Angeles, Detroit, Chicago, Philadelphia) and to bring members savings of up to 65% on last-minute travel merchandise. Membership fee is $25 per year, which includes spouse, dependent children, or a travelling companion, and the fee will be refunded in full within 30 days of joining if you are not satisfied with the club's initial services.

DISCOUNT TRAVEL
INTERNATIONAL, INC.
Ives Building, Suite 205
Narberth, PA 19072
(phone 215/668-2182, or toll free
800/824-4000)

Claiming to be the nation's largest "distress merchant," it charges $45 a year for membership (applying to anyone living in the same household), for which members receive a toll-free, short-notice hotline phone number. By dialing, one receives word of imminent departures from one's own area, on which discounts of 35% to 70% are given. Additional benefits of membership: a small discount coupon book (for hotels, cars, movies), a second hotline service for condos around the world, a 5% cash bonus on any domestic air fare purchased through the club, a 7% discount on any standard nondistress charters, tour packages, or cruises.

VACATIONS TO GO, INC.
2411 Fountain View, Suite 201
Houston, TX 77057
(phone 713/974-2121, or for general
information, toll free 800/624-7338,
800/833-8047 in Texas).

Headquartered in Houston, it maintains telephone numbers (but not offices) in 76 cities for imparting "regionalized" information of imminent departures; usually these are departures from another major city, for which "add-on" fares for connecting flights are added to the price. Yearly membership is $29.95 (which covers the entire family and one guest), which brings you the special number to call from your city. You hear a hotline announcement changed two to three times a week.

VACATION HOTLINE
1501 West Fullerton Avenue
Chicago, IL 60614
(phone 312/880-0030)

Confines itself strictly to charter flights or to vacation packages based on the use of charter transportation. Is also heavily oriented to Midwest departures, and to such prominent Midwest charter-tour operators as Thomson Vacations, Carefree Vacations, MTI, Hudson Holidays, and Club Med. As President Michael Dorman explains the system: "If you have the flexibility to wait until a week or two prior to departure to make reservations, we will book you with these charter operators at reduced rates. There is some risk in doing this, as not all destinations on all dates are reduced, but those people who are willing to do so can pick up remarkable savings. Whenever the charter companies do not sell all their seats and hotel rooms, they put them on sale for as much as 30% to 50% off the regular rates. . . . We advise clients to call us seven to ten days prior to planned departure dates." From the Midwest, last-minute sales are possible.

Six Leading "Rebators" (Discounting Every Trip)

Unlike the airline bucket shops and cruise discounters that reduce the price of certain fares or certain cruises, "rebators" reduce the price of *every* travel product, but by a smaller percentage than the other companies. They perform this feat by simply "kicking back" their commission, or a portion of it, to their clients. Some pay out the entire commission—selling the trip at their net cost to their clients—but then assess a small service charge. Others pass on a part of their commission.

Either way, travellers save a substantial amount by dealing with the rebators, but only if they are willing to forego the advice and consultation they would normally have received from a standard travel agent. The rebators limit their customers to people who have already made up their minds as to where they want to go and how. If you are firm in your plans and do not need expert travel advice—if you are willing simply to "phone in" your request in a short call—then you spare the rebators' time and support their ability to work for less income per transaction.

Once again, bear in mind that you save far less dealing with a rebator than with an air-fare bucket shop or cruise discounter, but the latter firms offer discounts only on selected cruise sailings or air fares, whereas the rebators offer a reduction on every travel product sold: any departure, any date, to anywhere.

Though some rebators have fallen by the wayside, six "pioneers" have survived handsomely, and do a major business:

CASHBACK
342 Madison Avenue, Suite 400
New York, NY 10173
(phone 212/490-0080, or toll free
800/458-CASH)

Like all the other rebators, Cashback is able to "kick back" a portion of their commission to you by dealing only with people who know exactly what they want and will not consume Cashback's time with inquiries or requests for advice—as happens in dealings with standard travel agents. In their literature they explain the point with refreshing candor: "Most travellers have relatively simple needs: go from Point A to B and back. Due to modern, sophisticated computer systems, this is a relatively quick and easy transaction. We will book what you—and you alone—want. We're not biased. We won't try to sell you any particular airline or service. We will simply get you what you want. . . ." On extremely cheap tickets—like a $49 air fare—Cashback will give you back a dollar. On higher-priced tickets it will refund 5%. Obviously, it pays to deal with them only on the costlier transactions, and you can do so either through their New York branch office, or at their headquarters at 1780 South Bellaire, Denver, CO 80222 (phone 303/757-1000).

McTRAVEL SERVICES, INC.
130 South Jefferson Road
Chicago, IL 60606
(phone 312/876-1116, or toll free
800/331-2941)

McTravel—an obvious takeoff on the name of the burger chain—rebates the entire commission to their customers (usually 10% of the amount spent), but then charges a flat $10 for writing domestic tickets and $20 for writing international tickets. Let's say that you have made reservations for a trip that will cost $480. You save $48, less $10, for a net saving of $38. On higher-priced tour packages or cruises, you again receive the entire 10% commission back, less a service fee of $25 to $50, depending on the price of the package or cruise. If two people book a cabin costing a total of $4,000, they'll save $400, less a $50 fee, for a net saving of $350, which isn't bad.

PENNSYLVANIA TRAVEL, INC.
23 Paoli Pike
Paoli, PA 19301
(phone 215/251-9944, or toll free
800/331-0947 outside
Pennsylvania)

They permit you to buy at *their* cost (in effect passing on the entire commission to you), but then charge a booking fee (per transaction, not per person) of $50 if the booking is under $1,500, $100 for bookings of $1,500 to $5,000, $150 for a purchase of $5,000 to $10,000. Assume that two persons purchase a cruise for $2,200 per person, a total of $4,400. Pennsylvania Travel passes on its 10% commission ($440), and proceeds to bill you for only $3,960, plus a $100 service charge, for a total of $4,060. You save $340.

21st CENTURY TRAVEL, INC.
6950 France Avenue South
Edina, MN 55435
(phone 612/929-6695)

Any trip, anytime, anywhere: 21st Century Travel will sell you the trip at their cost, but then add on a small service charge. On charter flights, for instance, you save 10% of your ticket price but pay a service fee of $10 (for domestic charters) or $15 (international charters). On cruises, tours, packages, and scheduled air fares, you again save 10%, but pay $30 per transaction (not per person) for purchasing up to $700, $50 for tickets or fares totaling up to $1,500, $100 up to $5,000, $150 for any sum over $5,000. Edina, Minnesota, is a suburb of Minneapolis/St. Paul.

THE $MART TRAVELLER, INC.
3111 S.W. 27th Avenue
Miami, FL 33133
(phone 305/662-6677)

Rebates the entire commission, but then assesses a service charge of $30 for transactions up to $750, a fee of $50 for bookings totaling between $751 and $2,000, a fee of $100 for bookings of from $2,001 to $4,000, and $150 for bookings of from $4,001 to $6,000. Even on a transaction of only $750, you save $45—and much more, of course, on the higher-priced transactions.

TRAVEL BROKER$
393 Broadway
New York, NY 10013
(phone 212/219-0612)

Travel Broker$ charges no fee, but only rebates a part of the commission —the exact amount varying according to a complex formula. They guarantee the following *savings:* up to $15 on a purchase of up to $400; from $20 to $50 on a purchase of $401 to $800; from $40 to $60 on a purchase of $801 to $1,000; from $50 to $100 on a purchase of $1,001 to $1,500; from $80 to $130 on a purchase of $1,501 to $2,000; from $100 to $250 on a purchase of $2,001 to $3,500; and so on. "Our program," they explain, "is based on the concept that if you furnish us with the information necessary to book your trip, we save time and money, and can pass the savings on to you."

Nineteen of the Nation's Leading Discount Cruise Agencies

These are companies that cut the cost of a cruise to almost anywhere—and not simply on imminent departures; their reductions apply to sailings many months ahead. Enjoying a special relationship with major cruise-ship lines, they have been known to sell berths and cabins for as much as 40% off published rates. Although other cruise-ship specialists may, quietly, offer the same savings —and therefore I don't mean to imply that "the 20" are your only source of discounted tickets—the firms listed below are open and unabashed about their willingness to cut the cruise-ship rates: some of them send massive mailings to potential cruise-ship passengers, while others even advertise in public periodicals that they offer cruise-ship savings.

WHITE TRAVEL SERVICE, INC.
342 North Main Street
West Hartford, CT 06117
(phone 203/233-2648)

A source of remarkable savings and discounts on cruises throughout the year, it is headed by the ebullient Edie White and her son, Rick, who have themselves personally sailed on most of the major ships in service today.

CRUISES OF DISTINCTION, INC.
188 East Post Road
White Plains, NY 10601
(phone 914/682-9414)

Headed by a former cruise-ship executive, Michael Grossman (former marketing vice-president of Norwegian American Cruises), who left the industry to concentrate on discounting fares in retail sales to the public.

CRUISES INTERNATIONAL, INC.
1056 South Roselle Road
Schaumburg, IL 60193
(phone 312/893-8820)

The Chicago-area powerhouse of the cruise-ship market, selling its space at considerable reductions, in many cases, off published fares.

SEA & SAIL, INC.
2630 Fountainview, Suite 118
Houston, TX 77057
(phone 713/784-6006)

Owned by prominent longtime Houston travel agent Edna Leah Frosch, it offers major discounts on numerous sailings each month, and advertises their availability via a jaunty, periodic newsletter sent to a large mailing list. Write to have your name added.

ESTHER GROSSBERG TRAVEL, INC.
6300 West Loop South, Suite 360
Bellair, TX 77401
(phone 713/666-1761)

Another major Sunbelt retailer, it appears to have the same broad inventory of heavily discounted departures on nearly all the major lines.

BLITZ WORLD CRUISE CENTER, INC.
8918 Manchester
St. Louis, MO 63144
(phone 314/961-2700)

Big in the Midwest; throws in free travel insurance, in addition to discounts ranging from 10% to 33%.

CAPTAIN'S TABLE
(A Division of Stowaway Travel)
703 Market Street
San Francisco, CA 94103
(phone toll free 800/247-6071,
800/527-7447 in California)

Claims to provide discounts up to 50% on sailings of at least 12 major and prestigious lines.

CRUISE RESERVATIONS, INC.
8975 N.E. Sixth Avenue
Miami, FL 33138
(phone 305/759-8922, or toll free
800/892-9929 outside Florida)

Because of its location in the "cruise capital of the world," it claims to enjoy particularly close relationships with numerous lines, resulting in discounts of "hundreds of dollars" on air/sea programs.

CRUISEMASTERS, INC.
3415 Sepulveda Boulevard, Suite 645
Los Angeles, CA 90034
(phone toll free 800/242-9444,
800/242-9000 in California)

Cites discounts of up to 35% on up to 500 cruise departures yearly; will provide informative brochures to people calling.

THE TRAVEL COMPANY
333 West El Camino Real, Suite 250
Sunnyvale, CA 94087
(phone toll free 800/344-3444,
800/858-5888 in California)

In business for 20 years, and quite substantial, it publishes a "1988 Discount Cruise Catalog" available free for the asking. Promises discounts "up to 30% and more" on numerous sailings.

THE CRUISE MARKET PLACE, INC.
119 Sacramento Street
San Francisco, CA 94111
(phone toll free 800/826-4333,
800/826-4343 in California)

Will mail information, or advise over the phone, on discount opportunities as high as 50% on a broad range of cruise sailings. A long-established firm.

CRUISE PRO, INC.
2900 Townsgate Road
Westlake Village, CA 91361
(phone toll free 800/222-SHIP,
800/258-SHIP in California)

Represents 18 cruise-ship companies, and has built a considerable reputation from its policy of major discounts on their sailings.

THE SHIP SHOP
18675 East 39th Street, Suite P
Independence, MO 64057
(phone 816/795-0570, or toll free
800/922-5510 outside Missouri)

A discount-granting cruise club charging membership of $29.95; once a member, you enjoy expert counseling and considerable discounts.

CRUISES, INC.
2711 James Street
Syracuse, NY 13206
(phone 315/463-9695, or toll free
800/854-0500 outside New York
State)

"Certified and bonded," it publishes a free newsletter detailing its special offers and discounts on cruises throughout the world.

LANDRY & KLING, INC.
232 Madison Avenue
New York, NY 10016
(phone 212/686-6200)

Josephine Kling and Joyce Landry are the two former cruise-ship officials making up this cruise-only travel agency, a rather elegant firm servicing an affluent clientele. Because of their heavy volume of cruise sales, they claim to obtain group space and group rates on numerous sailings, and pass on the savings to their clients. Literature is sent to their clients on a near-quarterly basis.

BEE KALT TRAVEL, INC.
4628 North Woodward Avenue
Royal Oak, MI 48072
(phone 313/549-6733)

A reputable, old-line travel agency (at least 50 years old) that is nevertheless one of the largest cruise discounters in the metropolitan Detroit area. Its discounts are substantial ones.

EMBASSY TRAVEL BUREAU
240 South County Road
Palm Beach, FL 33480
(phone 305/655-7870 or 655-7890)

Another deluxe firm, with affluent clientele, it offers a great many cruise opportunities at discounted prices.

SEGALE TRAVEL SERVICE
2321 West March Lane
Stockton, CA 95207
(phone 209/943-0911)

The local American Express affiliate in its area, it enjoys major sales of cruises, and often offers its cruise products at substantial discounts off published levels.

GOLDEN BEAR TRAVEL, INC.
2171 Francisco Boulevard
San Rafael, CA 94901
(phone 415/258-9800)

A standard travel agency, but one that maintains a busy "discounted cruises department"; the latter not only sells reduced-price cruises to the public, but also wholesales them to other travel agencies.

The Four Leading "Hospitality Exchanges" Available to Americans

A "hospitality exchange": in theory it's simplicity incarnate. You accommodate members of the "exchange organization" as they pass through your home city; they accommodate you when you at some time pass through their home city. Each person or couple stays free, and enjoys the pleasures and contentments of true hospitality.

In practice the activity involves a considerable amount of administration—circulation of directories, change-of-addresses, etc. Those burdens caused a number of hospitality-exchange organizations to go out of business in the 1970s; consequently, the most recent attempts at hospitality exchange are by people who (in all but one instance) charge a small sum for their services and require that you reimburse the slight out-of-pocket expenses of your host. Nevertheless, while no longer free, the hospitality exchange has probably been placed on a firmer base and has greater prospects for survival.

Please note that a hospitality exchange differs from a "vacation exchange" in that there is no simultaneous swapping of accommodations. You use the service, or provide lodgings, only when you choose, and without having to coordinate your travel plans with the simultaneous travels of someone else.

Four leading groups:

EVERGREEN BED AND BREAKFAST CLUB
P.O. Box 44094
Washington, DC 20026

Offshoot and brainchild of the powerful American Bed and Breakfast Association, which limits membership in Evergreen to persons 50 and over. You pay $35 a year for single membership, $40 a year for a couple, to receive a directory of Evergreen hosts (who must also be over 50), and are then entitled to enjoy the hospitality of another member, at $10 a night for a single, $15 a night for a twin. Considering that this includes a full American breakfast, these are among the lowest bed-and-breakfast rates in all the world. Why the fee at all? Club officials think that the $10 and $15 charges, in addition to offsetting out-of-pocket costs, add a businesslike quality to normal attitudes of hospitality.

When you apply for membership, you are asked to list your own accommodations (namely, a spare room) for use by other members. But no one requires that you accept all or even most of the bookings phoned in to you. You have complete discretion in that regard. When applying for membership, or further information, send a self-addressed, stamped envelope to the above address.

INNTER LODGING CO-OP
P.O. Box 7044
Tacoma, WA 98407
(phone 206/756-0343)

With several hundred members scattered across the country (most concentrated on the two coasts), INNter Lodging can provide you with instant friends (and accommodations) for an initial fee of $45, plus $4 to $5 per person per night paid to your actual hosts for the cost of fresh linen, towels, and other usables. No minimum age for guests; children with their own sleeping bags pay only 25¢. Founder Bob Ehrenheim publishes a directory of members in May or June of each year, and requires that members agree to make their own homes available for guests at least three months a year.

VISITING FRIENDS, INC.
P.O. Box 231
Lake Jackson, TX 77566
(phone 409/297-7367)

Laura and Tom LaGess began this service as a hospitality organization for genealogists; genealogists themselves, frequently traveling, they found private homes far more pleasant than motels for overnight lodgings. The organization, a so-called guestroom exchange network, now has more than 200 members, in all but eight states, including a few in Hawaii and Alaska. The initial charge is $15 for a "lifetime membership," then a total of $20 for your stay of up to six nights at a member's home. Mr. and Mrs. LaGess centralize the reservations process, keep all addresses in their own files (not in a published directory), and thus preserve both your privacy and occasional desire to receive no inquiries at all for a number of months. Write or phone Laura or Tom at the above address.

U.S. SERVAS COMMITTEE
11 John Street, Suite 706
New York, NY 10038
(phone 212/267-0252)

Not really a travel organization per se—but by carrying out its avowed purpose of promoting peace by bringing together people of different backgrounds, it manages both to extend hospitality in large measure and to make travelling meaningful for its members. Members (now numbering over 12,000 in nearly 100 countries) pay a fee of $45, and are interviewed by a Servas representative in their area; they are then free to receive lists of hosts at their travel destinations, who will put them up free of charge—even to the extent of letting them share the family table at meals.

The normal stay with a Servas host is three days and two nights, which may be extended at the discretion of the host and the traveller. All arrangements are made by members, and no money is ever exchanged between them. The only requirement is that members are willing to talk, to exchange ideas, to become closely involved in the life of the host family. Servas, to me, is the most exalted travel organization on earth; it not only permits you to live free as you travel throughout the world—but to realize the oneness of all mankind.

Five Major "Vacation Exchange Clubs"

"Vacation exchanges" are organizations that enable you to swap your home or apartment for the home or apartment of a foreign resident (or one in another part of the country) during the periods of your respective vacations.

The swap is a simultaneous one, for a period of time that the two of you have selected. Having made the arrangements through an exchange of correspondence (usually), you settle upon the date and advise the other of where the doorkey (and sometimes the car keys) can be found. On that date, you pass in mid-air, so to speak. You fly to Edinburgh, let's say, or to the south of France, and they fly to your home in Albuquerque. Each of you receives the lodging element of your vacation absolutely free. And each enjoys a unique vacation abroad, as a resident of a new state or foreign country and not as a mere tourist.

I've listed below five major agencies that can help you make home exchanges, either for short- or long-term stays. In each case, you're the person who handles the details: you study the directories issued by each organization, find a suitable prospect, then send letters and pictures and work out a mutually satisfactory agreement. I've also listed one agency that will do the work for you, charging a fee for the service. Specific details follow under each listing:

VACATION EXCHANGE CLUB
12006 111th Avenue
Youngtown, AZ 85363
(phone 602/972-2186)

Granddaddy of all the U.S. exchange services, begun in 1960 and operating continuously ever since (something of a record in a business that is notoriously short-lived). Two directories are published yearly, the first on February 15, the second on April 15; they include some 6,000 listings in the United States and 40 countries that span the globe. A fee of $24.70 entitles you to receive both directories and be listed in one of them.

INTERSERVICE HOME EXCHANGE, INC.
P.O. Box 387
Glen Echo, MD 20812
(phone 301/229-7567)

Ted Kobrin, a foreign service officer, founded this organization nine years ago; he has since become the East Coast representative of the Europe-based Intervac International, a federation of home-exchange companies. Together they publish three catalogues—in February, March, and May —listing 5,000 homes or apartments in 30 countries, four-fifths of them outside the United States, mainly in Europe. For a single payment of $29, you receive all three catalogues and are listed; without a listing the price is $23. An exceptional feature is Kbrin's willingness to refund the fee to anyone who doesn't find what they're looking for in his catalogue.

WORLDWIDE EXCHANGE
P.O. Box 1563
San Leandro, CA 94577
(phone 415/521-7890)

Their directory lists not only 1,000 homes in the U.S. and Europe available for exchange, but also several hundred bed-and-breakfast accommodations available for rental. A subscription to the *1988 Vacation Home Directory* is $9.95, for which you receive four copies a year. The cost for listing a home is $19.95, $6 more if you wish to include a photograph. As with all the firms thus far described, you do all the matchmaking yourself, utilizing the leads set forth in the directory.

LOAN-A-HOME
2 Park Lane, Apt. 6-E
Mount Vernon, NY 10552

This is for long-term stays, suitable primarily for retired Americans. Ms. Muriel Gould of Loan-a-Home publishes the only directories that specialize in such extended stays, either as exchanges or as rentals at both ends if an exchange is not feasible (some of her clients are academics on sabbatical, or business people being transferred elsewhere for a year or two). A good portion of her listings are of second homes purchased for investment purposes, and therefore presumably available even on an open-ended basis. She also has a section on vacation housing, since many of the long-term rentals are available for short periods as well.

Loan-a-Home's directory is unique in that there is no charge for a listing; but if you want your own copy of the directory and its supplements (directories are published in June and December, supplements in March and September), you pay $25 for one directory and supplement, $35 for two directories and two supplements. Ms. Gould earns her income from sales of the directory, and charges no commission on the arrangements made; the latter are your concern, in any event.

HOME EXCHANGE INTERNATIONAL
185 Park Row, Box 878
New York, NY 10038
(phone 212/349-5340)
or
22458 Ventura Boulevard
Woodland Hills, CA 91364
(phone 818/992-8990)

These are the people to contact if you crave a home exchange but don't wish to make the arrangements yourself. The organization will send you questionnaires, ask for interior and exterior photos of your home, then try to match you up with someone whose lifestyle and surroundings are compatible with yours. There's a one-time registration fee of $40, then a closing fee of $150 to $525, depending on duration of the exchange and whether it is for foreign or domestic locations. Considering that this service saves you the phone calls, letters, wires, and sheer amount of time that may be involved in arranging an exchange, it's not a bad investment. Exchanges are usually for summer or holiday periods, but the group can also handle sabbaticals.

Five "Homestay" Organizations for Americans Travelling Abroad

Foreign "homestays" are radically different from bed-and-breakfast stays, mainly because the latter activity is too often just that: you occupy a bed, have breakfast, and "split."

On a homestay, you stay around. You share the daily life of your host family. You socialize and converse with them, eat at their table, perhaps accompany them on their daily rounds. That kind of sojourn, when properly arranged, is one of the great pleasures of life, introducing you to another variety of the family of mankind.

Earlier in this book I've written about several organizations that offer rather elegant homestays in Britain. Here I add several less expensive alternatives, all for areas where English is well spoken by your hosts.

Denmark

PEOPLE TO PEOPLE
DENMARK
9 Romersgade
DK-1362 Copenhagen K
Denmark
(phone 01-14-10-35)

What is so remarkable about the Danish homestay program is that it is absolutely free of charge. You receive room and all three meals daily, but you enjoy those gifts as a relative would, making no payment whatever to your Danish host family. They have invited you into their homes simply for the mutual benefit of an across-the-seas friendship, without expecting anything in return (such as a reciprocal stay in your home). Why else do they do this? Because they are Danes—a remarkable people, a lesson for all of us.

Of course, as a "member of the family," it would be the gracious thing to offer to help with family chores. You ought also to adapt yourself quietly and unobtrusively to the daily patterns of the family. Since some family members will have jobs to which they must attend each day, you should also take care of your own needs and entertainment when they are away. And finally, a gesture such as a postcard or letter of thanks when you return home would be much appreciated—and a great help to the homestay idea afterward.

Some 27 people-to-people homestay committees are maintained in Denmark, all of them outside the city of Copenhagen, usually in small to middle-sized towns, most on the peninsula of Jutland. Ms. Lise Heineke is one of the administrators of the organization, and a letter to her at the Copenhagen address listed above will set the process in motion. Give her plenty of advance notice, and indicate the exact dates when you expect to be in Denmark.

Great Britain

FAMILIES IN BRITAIN
Martins Cottage, Martins Lane
Birdham, Chichester
West Sussex PO20 7AU, England
(phone Birdham 0243-512-222)

This time you spend part or all of your British holiday as a paying guest with a British family, in locations scattered all over the British Isles. Though the organization's title refers to "families," they are more than happy to accept single persons traveling alone or couples.

In their literature the company makes a great point of the fact that they specialize in introducing overseas visitors of all ages to carefully selected private families by matching ages, interests, hobbies, and backgrounds. Once placed, visitors are looked after as one of the family and are encouraged to participate in the family's cultural, social, and sporting activities. Some of the participating families have private tennis courts, swimming pools, stables, even sailing boats.

Visitors can stay with a family at any time of the year, taking either three meals a day ("full pension") or two meals a day ("half pension"). Older visitors and family groups generally prefer the latter.

Charges are remarkably low. Half pension (room and two meals) ranges from £90 ($149) to £110 ($182) per person per *week*. Full pension is £100 ($165) to £150 ($215) per person per week. An agency fee (a one-time charge of £60 to £70) is assessed for matching you up and making the arrangements.

If you're interested, write far in advance of your arrival in Britain for a brochure and registration form (a small questionnaire), and then send it, with a registration payment of $16, to the address set forth above.

FRIENDS IN BRITAIN
c/o Kathleen J. Johnson
Marazion
Cornwall TR17 0A2, England
(phone 0736-710-400)

A similar organization, but this time offering hospitality for only two or three nights at a time in a wide range of private homes all over the country. Ms. Johnson also offers ten-day tours of England, Scotland, and Wales, in which she provides you with a self-drive car and a prearranged itinerary of two-night and three-night stays at the homes of her clients.

Some of the hosts are professionals —archaeologists, architects, accountants, doctors, teachers, and lecturers —prescreened by Ms. Johnson and chosen for their warmth toward visitors, and their ability to represent the best of Britain.

Charges, which include Ms. Johnson's fee, differ according to the standard of the home (luxury, standard, or simple), but usually average around £32 (around $50) per person for room, full English breakfast, and a full-scale three-course dinner (with cheese for dessert, and coffee) each night, in a medium-category home; the same charge goes down to £25 in a simpler accommodation.

For a descriptive brochure and application form, write to Ms. Johnson at the address set forth above.

Western Australia

HOMESTAY OF W.A.
40 Union Road
Carmel, West Australia 6076
(phone 09-293-5347)

Though they specialize in their own area, Jean and Mark Smiley of Homestay of W.A. can arrange homestays in continental Australia, as well as in New Zealand and Tasmania. Tariffs range from $18 Australian ($12.60 U.S.) a night, including breakfast, and evening meals are by arrangement with the families in many homes. You should probably plan to rent a car, as public transport hereabouts is not highly developed.

They also provide farmstays, and a good combination might be a two-night homestay in Perth, followed by three nights or more on a farm or ranch. If you haven't time for the country portion, Jean and Mark can arrange to have you invited for an afternoon ranch stay followed by an Aussie barbecue.

Write with complete details of your visit (flight numbers, exact dates, all else) to the address set forth above.

Continental Europe

EXPERIMENT IN
  INTERNATIONAL LIVING

Kipling Road
Brattleboro, VT 05301
(phone toll free 800/345-2929)

For young people aged 14 to 22, the classic summer homestay program is that of the distinguished organization named above. Write for a copy of their "Summer Abroad" catalogue detailing dozens of one-month to three-month homestays with families in most European countries, and in Brazil, Kenya, Ecuador, Mexico, Martinique, Australia, New Zealand, the USSR, Turkey, Morocco, China, and Japan.

Forty Student Travel Agencies at Home and Abroad

The closest thing we have to an "official" student travel agency in the United States is the Council on International Educational Exchange (C.I.E.E.). An activity funded by several hundred U.S. colleges and universities, the council is our nation's representative to the International Student Travel Conference. It issues the vitally important International Student Identity Card, which entitles students to stay and eat at student hotels and restaurants around the world, and to receive important discounts—or even free admissions—at theatres, museums, and other like facilities. It offers working vacations for American students in Britain, Ireland, France, Germany, New Zealand, and Costa Rica; operates cheap, transatlantic charter flights; and provides cheap intra-European air or rail transportation. And finally, it provides longer-term study opportunities for Americans: semester-long and full-year stints at famous universities around the world.

Usually, you secure these services simply by visiting the "student exchange" office or "travel office" on your own campus, which frequently turns out to be a representative of C.I.E.E. But a better course is to visit—if you can manage to do so—a full-scale Council Travel Office, of which there are two dozen:

COUNCIL TRAVEL OFFICES

CALIFORNIA

Berkeley

2511 Channing Way
Berkeley, CA 94704
(phone 415/848-8604)

La Jolla

UCSD Student Center B-023
La Jolla, CA 92093
(phone 619/452-0630)

Long Beach

5500 Atherton Street, Suite 212
Long Beach, CA 90815
(phone 213/598-3338)

Los Angeles

1093 Broxton Avenue, Suite 220
Los Angeles, CA 90024
(phone 213/208-3551)

Los Angeles Valley

5445 Balboa Boulevard, Suite 109
Encino, CA 91316
(phone 818/905-5777)

San Diego

4429 Cass Street
San Diego, CA 92109
(phone 619/270-6401)

San Francisco

312 Sutter Street
San Francisco, CA 94108
(phone 415/421-3473)

919 Irving Street
San Francisco, CA 94122
(phone 415/566-6222)

GEORGIA

Atlanta

12 Park Place South
Atlanta, GA 30303
(phone 404/577-1678)

ILLINOIS

Chicago

29 East Delaware Place
Chicago, IL 60611
(phone 312/951-0585)

MASSACHUSETTS

Amherst

79 South Pleasant Street
Amherst, MA 01002
(phone 413/256-1261)

Boston

729 Boylston Street
Boston, MA 02116
(phone 617/266-1926)

Cambridge

1384 Massachusetts Avenue
Cambridge, MA 02138
(phone 617/497-1497)

MINNESOTA

Minneapolis

1501 University Avenue SE, Room 300
Minneapolis, MN 55414
(phone 612/379-2323)

NEW YORK

New York City

205 East 42nd Street
New York, NY 10017
(phone 212/661-1450)

New York Student Center
356 West 34th Street
New York, NY 10001
(phone 212/661-1450)

35 West 8th Street
New York, NY 10011
(phone 212/254-2525)

OREGON

Portland

715 S.W. Morrison, Suite 1020
Portland, OR 97205
(phone 503/228-1900)

RHODE ISLAND

Providence

171 Angell Street
Providence, RI 02906
(phone 401/331-5810)

TEXAS

Austin
1904 Guadalupe Street
Austin, TX 78705
(phone 512/472-4931)

Dallas

Executive Tower Office Center
3300 West Mockingbird Lane
Dallas, TX 75235
(phone 214/350-6166)

WASHINGTON

Seattle

1314 N.E. 43rd Street, Suite 210
Seattle, WA 98105
(phone 206/632-2448)

OVERSEAS

GERMANY

Bonn

Thomas Mann Strasse 33
5300 Bonn 2
(phone 0228-659-746)

FRANCE

Paris

31 rue St-Augustin
75002 Paris
(phone 42-66-34-73)

51 rue Dauphine
75006 Paris
(phone 42-26-79-65)

16 rue de Vaugirard
75006 Paris
(phone 46-34-02-90)

Nice

10 rue de Belgique
06000 Nice
(phone 93-87-34-96)

Bordeaux

9 Place Charles-Gruet
33000 Bordeaux
(phone 56-44-68-73)

Lyon

9 Rue des Remparts D'Ainay
69002 Lyon
(phone 16-78-42-99-94)

JAPAN

Tokyo

Sanno Grand Building
14-2 Nagata-Cho, 2-Chome
Chiyoda-ku
Tokyo 100
(phone 03-581-7581)

STUDENT TRAVEL NETWORK

Still another source of student travel services is the Student Travel Network operated in the U.S. by the Australian-owned STA Travel Group —probably the world's largest student travel organization. Although it issues student cards and organizes student tours and exchange programs, its particular specialty is the sale of low-cost, cut-rate international air tickets on scheduled flights. Like a giant student-oriented "bucket shop," it negotiates with the world's most prestigious carriers to permit students to occupy their seats at stunning rates: as little as $489 round trip between Los Angeles and London, $549 round trip to Tokyo. And it provides these prices to people up to the age of 35.

Student Travel Network offices in the U.S. (others are in Europe, Asia, and the South Pacific) include:

CALIFORNIA

Los Angeles

2500 Wilshire Boulevard
Los Angeles, CA 90057
(phone 213/380-2184)

7204 Melrose Avenue
Los Angeles, CA 90046
(phone 213/934-8722)

Northridge

8949 Reseda Boulevard
Northridge, CA 91324
(phone 818/886-0804)

San Francisco

166 Geary Street, Suite 702
San Francisco, CA 94108
(phone 415/391-8407)

San Diego

6447 El Cajon Boulevard
San Diego, CA 92115
(phone 619/286-1322)

TEXAS

Dallas

6609 Hillcrest Avenue
Dallas, TX 75205
(phone 214/360-0097)

HAWAII

Honolulu

1831 South King Street, Suite 202
Honolulu, HI 96826
(phone 808/942-7755)

ILLINOIS

Chicago

3249 North Broadway
Chicago, IL 60657
(phone 312/525-9227)

MASSACHUSETTS

Boston

273 Newbury Street
Boston, MA 02116
(phone 617/266-6014)

NEW YORK

New York City

c/o Whole World Travel
17 East 45th Street
New York, NY 10017
(phone 212/986-9470)

Forty-two of America's Foremost Bed-and-Breakfast Reservations Organizations

Originally, when the movement started, each bed-and-breakfast house advertised itself—in local media—or simply hung out a "B&B" shingle on the white picket fence. That proved increasingly unsatisfactory to the out-of-state travelers seeking B&B accommodations. Most found themselves unable to use these fine, cheap, and unpretentious lodgings because they were unable to ascertain names and addresses, and were also apprehensive about staying in a home about which they knew nothing.

Enter the bed-and-breakfast reservations organization. Regional in scope, each representing about 100 homes, these firms perform the function of prescreening, inspecting each lodging to ensure its suitability for transient visitors. They also have the wherewithal to advertise (a bit), and to maintain extensive phone lines and reservations personnel.

Of the 200-or-so bed-and-breakfast reservations organizations in the U.S., the following seem to be to be effective sources, based either on a perusal of their literature or on actual phone conversations with nearly three-quarters of their owners.

In booking a B&B, be sure to make a sharp distinction between "bed-and-breakfast homes" and "bed-and-breakfast inns". The first is simply a private home or apartment occupied by a family that supplements its normal income by occasionally renting out a spare room or two to overnight visitors. The second—the "inn"—is a little hotel whose proprietors rent out multiple rooms each night and earn their living from doing so; they also specialize in touches like quiche for breakfast, or cinnamon toast, fresh flowers daily in a bedroom vase— you get the picture. The bed-and-breakfast inns can often be more cost-

ly than a hotel, whereas a bed-and-breakfast house is supposed to charge half the level of prevailing hotel rates in its area.

It's unfortunate that this semantic overlap occurred in the bed-and-breakfast field; a different name should really be found for the bed-and-breakfast inns. When I refer to a B&B, I mean a low-priced room in a private home—the term's initial meaning.

Alaska

ALASKA BED AND BREAKFAST
3/6500, Suite 169
Juneau, AK 99802
(phone 907/586-2959)

Owner Steve Hamilton represents 20 Alaskan homes, including interesting "cove" houses with panoramic views. The structures tend to be large, and often the bedrooms have their own fireplaces; locations are convenient to fishing, boating, and sightseeing. And rooms range in price from $40 to $65 nightly, which is cheap for Alaska. (Incidentally, the address of "3/6500" set forth above, is correct; that's all you need place on the envelope!)

Arizona

BED AND BREAKFAST IN ARIZONA
P.O. Box 8628
Scottsdale, AZ 85252
(phone 602/995-2831)

Has 200 houses throughout the state, charging an average of $50 a night in high season. Owners Tom Thomas and Trisha Wills stress the advantages of the locations, the comforts, hospitality, and cleanliness of the houses they offer.

California

BED AND BREAKFAST

INTERNATIONAL (SAN FRANCISCO)
151 Ardmore Road
Kensington, CA 94707
(phone 415/525-4569)

Jean Brown claims that her agency is the oldest bed-and-breakfast reservations service, offering over 300 homes in the Bay Area and throughout all other parts of California. Double rooms in homes (not inns) range from $40 to $70 a night. Homes are found in Los Angeles, Santa Barbara, the Wine Country, even in Sausalito (houseboats).

AMERICA'S CO-HOST BED AND BREAKFAST
P.O. Box 9302
Whittier, CA 90608
(phone 213/699-8427)

Coleen Davis heads this dynamic organization, and prepares fascinating write-ups of the houses and proprietors she represents. Example: "California bachelor who loves to cook will prepare mouthwatering breakfasts. His interest in fishing and hunting as well as his expertise with horses will allow you to feel you've had some time away from the daily grind. $50 per night, double." Houses are found in all parts of the state, and rooms range from $40 to $55.

Colorado

BED AND BREAKFAST ROCKY MOUNTAINS
P.O. Box 804
Colorado Springs, CO 80901
(phone 303/630-3433)

Coordinator Kate Peterson Winters handles over 100 homes and inns in Colorado, Montana, Wyoming, Utah, and New Mexico. Accommodations range from budget to luxury mansions, with a heavy concentration in the ski areas. Rates range from $35 to $75 per room. Hours are 9 a.m. to 5 p.m. daily from May 16 to September 14; and noon to 5 p.m. weekdays from September 15 to May 15.

Connecticut

NUTMEG BED & BREAKFAST
222 Girard Avenue
Hartford, CT 06105
(phone 203/236-6698 weekdays from
9 a.m. to 5 p.m.)

Nutmeg is now five years old and represents about 130 host homes ranging from simple rooms in apartments to luxurious suites in mansions. Though owner Maxine Kates is heavily involved in corporate relocation of employees (for whom she obtains temporary accommodation), she stresses her continued loyalty to the classic tourist. Her rooms are classified as "C-Conventional" (modest homes in nice neighborhoods, nonadjoining or adjoining baths, with room charges of $35 to $45 a night); "Q-Quality" (lovely homes in excellent neighborhoods, adjoining or nonadjoining baths—usually private—with room rates of $45 to $55 a night); and "D-Deluxe" (deluxe to estate homes, private baths and other private entry, some with kitchenettes, all renting for $60 to $75 per room per night).

Delaware

BED AND BREAKFAST OF
DELAWARE
P.O. Box 177
Wilmington, DE 19803
(phone 302/479-9500)

Bette Reese handles period homes in the "quaint old town" of New Castle, as well as comfortable, modern homes outside Wilmington. Two of her properties are on the National Historic Registry, several are near museums, and others are near or on the beach.

Rooms average $50 a night for singles, $55 for couples or families.

District of Columbia

BED AND BREAKFAST LTD.
OF D.C.
P.O. Box 12011
Washington, DC 20005
(phone 202/328-3510)

An assortment of about 60 homes in every major area of the city; some of the houses are rambling Victorian mansions featured on local house tours. Rates range, in this high-priced city, from $30 to $65 a night for singles, $10 more for each additional person.

Florida

B & B SUNCOAST
ACCOMMODATIONS
8690 Gulf Boulevard
St. Petersburg Beach, FL 33706
(phone 813/360-1753)

Though owner Danie Bernard specializes in Florida's west coast beach towns on the Gulf of Mexico, she also has registered host homes in and near Orlando, Delray Beach, Sarasota, Bonita Springs, Venice, Naples, Tampa, St. Petersburg, Winter Park, Clearwater, and Tarpon Springs. Standard B&B runs $40 to $50 double; better amenities, $45 to $55; "exceptional homes," $60 to $80.

B & B OF THE FLORIDA KEYS,
INC.
P.O. Box 1373
Marathon, FL 33050
(phone 305/743-4118)

Features 30 homes throughout the Keys. All are on the water, are air-conditioned, and come with a complete breakfast. Rooms range from $40 to $45 a night.

Georgia

ATLANTA HOSPITALITY
2472 Lauderdale Drive N.E.
Atlanta, GA 30345
(phone 404/493-1930)

Lists 60 homes all over the Atlanta area, most on routes of public transportation. Homes are mostly modern, yet double-occupancy rooms start at only $35 a night.

DIVISION OF TOURISM
Georgia Department of Industry
and Trade
230 Peachtree Street N.W.
Atlanta, GA 30301
(phone 404/656-3590)

By writing to this address you can obtain a free pamphlet listing 78 excellent bed-and-breakfast homes in all parts of the state. Ask for the "Georgia Bed and Breakfast" brochure.

Hawaii

BED AND BREAKFAST HAWAII
P.O. Box 449
Kapaa, HI 96746
(phone 808/822-7771)

This firm pioneered in developing a broad network of bed-and-breakfast accommodations in Hawaii, at considerably lower nightly costs than are offered by hotels.

Illinois

BED AND BREAKFAST OF
CHICAGO, INC.
P.O. Box 14088
Chicago, IL 60614
(phone 312/951-0085)

Mary Shaw disposes of 60 properties, half of which are unhosted apartments with breakfast left in the refrigerator. Apartments overlook key neighborhood attractions, often with views of the Chicago skyline and lake. Double-occupancy rooms range from $50 to $65.

Indiana

AMISH ACRES
1600 Market Street West
Nappanee, IN 46550
(phone 219/773-4188)

Richard Plecther represents about 25 homes in the Nappanee area. Most are family homes in the Amish community, and houses tend to be large and comfortable; some are working farms. Rooms average $40 a night for two.

Iowa

BED AND BREAKFAST OF
IOWA
P.O. Box 430
Preston, IA 52069
(phone 319/689-4222)

Maintains an inventory of more than 40 private homes, most in rural locations. Some overlook the Mississippi River; others are old mansions filled with antiques. Travellers, it is claimed, are treated like members of the family. As owner Wilma Bloom likes to say, "You're not buying a room, you're buying a memory." Double rooms range from $35 to $65 nightly.

Kentucky

OHIO VALLEY BED AND
BREAKFAST
6816 Taylor Mill Road
Independence, KY 41051
(phone 606/356-7865)

Sallie Parker Lotz and Nancy Cully represent 35 rooms in Victorian mansions, rural retreats, town houses, and urban condos. Homes are located in southwestern Ohio, northern Kentucky, and southeastern Indiana. Rooms range from $35 to $95 a night, and all are carefully inspected before being listed by the organization.

Louisiana

SOUTHERN COMFORT B & B
RESERVATIONS
2856 Hundred Oaks Avenue
Baton Rouge, LA 70808
(phone 504/346-1928 or 928-9815)

Operated by Susan Morris and Helen Heath. Their rates range from $37.50 for a single, $40 for a double, to a usual top of $80. While reservations services are free to you upon simply phoning the firm, they'll also send you a descriptive directory of all their homes for $3.

Maine

BED & BREAKFAST
DOWNEAST, LTD.
Box 547, Macomber Mill Road
Eastbrook, ME 04634
(phone 207/565-3517)

Represents 150 homes in rural or town locations statewide, including nine working farms. Homes are situated by the ocean, on islands, mountains, and "everywhere," boasts owner Sally Godfrey. A free brochure and a $3 directory are provided on request. Doubles range from $45 to $70 a night. Belongs to the six-state consortium of New England bed-and-breakfast reservations organizations referred to elsewhere in this book.

Maryland

TRAVELLER IN MARYLAND,
INC.
P.O. Box 2277
Annapolis, MD 21404
(phone 301/269-6232, or in the
Washington metropolitan area,
261-2233)

Disposes of more than 150 accommodations all over the state, many on or close to the water. "We shine in Annapolis, Baltimore, and the Eastern Shore," says owner Cecily Sharp-

Whitehill. Rates are $45 to $65 and up per room per night; each guest is the only guest taken at a time; and all hosts are extensively interviewed before being listed. Reservations should be made by phone and are always confirmed promptly by a friendly staff. Hours are Monday through Thursday from 9 a.m. to 5 p.m., on Friday from 9 a.m. to noon.

Massachusetts

BED AND BREAKFAST
CAMBRIDGE & GREATER
BOSTON
P.O. Box 665
Cambridge, MA 02140
(phone 617/576-1492)

Fifty homes in locations claimed to be the best in the area: Back Bay and Beacon Hill, the Waterfront and Harvard Square, M.I.T., Tufts, and Boston College, Brookline and Lexington. Rates are rather high, perhaps because of that: $42 to $69 for singles, $52 to $79 double.

BED AND BREAKFAST
ASSOCIATES BAY COLONY,
LTD.
P.O. Box 166
Babson Park
Boston, MA 02157
(phone 617/449-5302)

Has 100 homes, both downtown and suburban, Victorian and Federalist, modern as well. Owner Arline Kardasis emphasizes the firm's "concerned matching" of client to host and location. Double rooms range from $50 to $75.

NEW ENGLAND BED AND
BREAKFAST
1045 Centre Street
Newton Centre, MA 02159
(phone 617/498-9819 or 244-2112)

Fifty generally less-expensive homes,

charging $40 to $60 double, $30 to $40 single. All are within 15 and 20 minutes of downtown Boston via public transportation, and always within walking distance of a subway or bus stop, Handles properties throughout the rest of the state, too.

Minnesota

BED AND BREAKFAST, LTD.
P.O. Box 8174
St. Paul, MN 55108
(phone 612/646-4238)

A nationwide reservations service headed by Gary Winget. Offerings in Minnesota include homes in the Twin Cities near public transportation and downtown. Houses outside the city are in scenic locations worth visiting. Motto of the organization: "Because you're someone special, you deserve special treatment." Most rooms range from $30 to $55 a night for two persons.

Mississippi

SOUTHERN COMFORT BED AND BREAKFAST
2856 Hundred Oaks Avenue
Baton Rouge, LA 70808
(phone 504/346-1928 or 928-9815)

This organization headquartered in Louisiana is your best source of bed-and-breakfast reservations, at pre-inspected homes, in neighboring Mississippi.

Montana

BED AND BREAKFAST ROCKY MOUNTAINS
P.O. Box 804
Colorado Springs, CO 80901
(phone 303/630-3433)

Though it is primarily concerned with Colorado, the Rocky Mountain agency represents seven widely scattered homes in Montana, ranging from

Bozeman to Helena to Missoula (but also including Glacier National Park, the Big Mountain area, Bitterroot Valley, and Kalispell). Rates range from $35 to $65.

New Hampshire

NEW HAMPSHIRE BED AND BREAKFAST
RFD #3, Box 53
Laconia, NH 03246
(phone 603/279-8346)

Owner Martha Dorais says she "can offer just about anything to guests." She has 50 to 60 urban and country homes located statewide; some are on the ocean, lakes, or in the mountains. A few have swimming pools, or offer cross-country skiing out the backdoor. Rates range from $35 to $75 a night, including a full breakfast, and only personally inspected homes are taken on for representation.

New Jersey

BED AND BREAKFAST OF NEW JERSEY, INC.
103 Godwin Avenue, Suite 132
Midland Park, NJ 07432
(phone 201/444-7409)

Features over 500 rooms in homes ranging from modest bungalows to large country estates. Manager Aster Mould claims to have interesting accommodations scattered all over the state, including converted grist mills, stately country homes, and an artist's studio. Doubles range from $30 to $80 a night.

New Mexico

BED AND BREAKFAST ROCKY MOUNTAINS
P.O. Box 804
Colorado Springs, CO 80901
(phone 303/630-3433)

They represent around 20 properties

which are concentrated in four cities—Albuquerque, Taos, Santa Fe, and Las Vegas. Rooms cost $39 to $79 for a double.

New York

BED AND BREAKFAST USA LTD.
P.O. Box 606
Croton-on-Hudson, NY 10520
(phone 914/271-6228)

For accommodations outside New York City, in every major area of the state, this organization is unbeatable. Its 28-page directory listing hundreds of homes is a superb introduction to the world of B&B. Most rooms rent for $35 and $40 (again, outside of New York City), plus a $7.50 booking charge to Bed and Breakfast USA.

NEW WORLD BED & BREAKFAST, LTD.
150 Fifth Avenue, Suite 711
New York, NY 10011
(phone 212/675-5600, or toll free 800/443-3800 outside New York State)

One of the largest of the New York City firms, representing 100 to 150 fully inspected Manhattan homes and apartments. The aim is to offer rates 50% less than exorbitantly high New York City hotel charges. Thus B&B prices range from $40 to $80 single occupancy, $50 to $100 for double occupancy. If those seem high, wait until you inquire about rates at a hotel! Laura Tilden is president of New World.

North Carolina

CHARLOTTE BED AND BREAKFAST, INC.
1700 Delane Avenue
Charlotte, NC 28211
(phone 704/366-0979)

Ruth Hill's organization handles nearly 20 homes and ten inns in both of the Carolinas, some of them restored, historic homes and quite remarkable. Yet double rooms rent for only $25 to $40 a night, up to $65 on the coast.

North Dakota

THE OLD WEST
BED-AND-BREAKFAST
P.O. Box 211
Regent, ND 58650
(phone 701/563-4542)

A limited selection of large, rural homes, including one with a swimming pool, another with a Jacuzzi. Owner Marlys Prince boasts that his hosts are hospitable and themselves well traveled, and tend to serve large ranch breakfasts. Homes are located near the scenic Badlands, good hiking, horseback riding, and fishing. Rooms average only $25 a night.

Oregon

BED AND BREAKFAST OF
OREGON
5733 S.W. Dickinson Street
Portland, OR 97219
(phone 503/245-0642)

Marcelle Tebo offers over 115 homes all over the state, and is proud that 15% of her hosts speak foreign languages. Some are near local wineries, others near skiing or windsurfing possibilities. Rooms average between $40 and $50 a night.

NW BED AND BREAKFAST
TRAVEL UNLIMITED
610 S.W. Broadway
Portland, OR 97205
(phone 503/243-7616)

Represents bed-and-breakfast properties in 100 communities of Oregon, including Portland and Eugene, and in California, Washington, Hawaii, and British Columbia. Most charge $35 to $55 for a double room.

Pennsylvania

BED AND BREAKFAST OF
PHILADELPHIA
P.O. Box 630
Chester Springs, PA 19425
(phone 215/827-9650)

Betsy Augustine and Louise Mullen offer 100 homes in the metro area and surrounding suburbs, including a dozen renovated 18th-century homes. Locations are within walking distance of Independence Hall in the city. Both partners are concerned about placing their clients in a congenial and compatible setting. Double rooms range from $35 to $75 a night.

PITTSBURGH BED AND
BREAKFAST, INC.
2190 Ben Franklin Drive
Pittsburgh, PA 15237
(phone 412/367-8080)

Judy Antico offers 34 private homes in the city and within a 65-mile radius of it. Clients can select from casual country homes, preserved historic landmarks, working farms, or city homes near Pittsburgh nightlife. Homes in the Laurel Highland area feature mountain climbing and simple skiing. Nightly room rates for double rooms range from $34 to $65.

BED AND BREAKFAST OF
SOUTHEAST PENNSYLVANIA
RD 1, Box 278
Barto, PA 19504
(phone 215/845-3526)

Joyce Stevenson handles over 30 "charming getaways" in southeast Pennsylvania. Highlights of the locations chosen include local folk festivals, antique emporiums, flea market "extravaganzas," and birdwatching. Double rooms range from $35 to $70 a night.

Rhode Island

BED AND BREAKFAST OF
RHODE ISLAND
P.O. Box 3291
Newport, RI 02840
(phone 401/849-1298)

Lists over 80 homes throughout Rhode Island and nearby Massachusetts. Many are historic structures from the 1700s, and a few are on the waterfront. "Of course, you're never far from the water in Rhode Island," remarks president Joy Meiser. Her hosts are mostly professionals, including oceanographers, psychologists, and antique dealers. Rooms range from $50 to $80 for a double. Belongs to Bed and Breakfast Reservation Services of New England, an association of bed-and-breakfast reservations organizations in all six New England states, enabling any member to book a continuous itinerary through Connecticut, Rhode Island, Massachusetts, New Hampshire, Vermont, and Maine.

South Carolina

PALMETTO BED AND
BREAKFAST, INC.
1460 Cherokee Road
Florence, SC 29501
(phone 803/667-8956)

Mrs. Frank Yates manages this select group of half a dozen homes in Florence, near Charleston. One is a grand, plantation-style structure, near Revolutionary War forts. Nightly rates average $40 for a single and $50 for a double.

Tennessee

BED AND BREAKFAST HOST
HOMES OF TENNESSEE, INC.
P.O. Box 110227
Nashville, TN 37222

(phone 615/331-5244, or toll free 800/528-8433 ext. 270)

Fredda Odom, of the firm above named, takes reservations for 85 homes well scattered around the state. Houses are located in every sort of region, urban and rural. Many are on the National Historic Register; and although the latter rent for as much as $100 a night, the normal bed-and-breakfast homes (not inns) start as low as $40 a night for two persons.

Texas

BED & BREAKFAST TEXAS STYLE, INC.
4224 West Red Bird Lane
Dallas, TX 75237
(phone 214/298-5433 or 298-8586)

Offers bed-and-breakfast homes in 51 Texas cities, from Aledo to Wimberley, from Dallas to Waxahachie, in every important location. Ruth and Don Wilson are the owner/directors, and place the biblical adage, "In this place will I give peace . . ." at the bottom of their letterhead stationery. Their rates rarely go higher than $40 to $45 for a double room, and are often lower. A top operation.

Utah

BED AND BREAKFAST ROCKY MOUNTAINS
P.O. Box 804
Colorado Springs, CO 80901
(phone 303/630-3433)

Represents 20 properties in the state, including three in Salt Lake City. Two in that city charge as little as $35 and $40 for a double room.

Virginia

BENSONHOUSE OF RICHMOND, INC.

2036 Monument Avenue
Richmond, VA 23220
(phone 804/648-7560)

Offers 40 homes in Richmond, Williamsburg, Petersburg, Bowling Green, Fredericksberg, Orange, and the North Neck of Virginia, many in historic districts. Owner Lyn M. Benson takes special care to select enthusiastic hosts who will take special pains to entertain their guests. The agency's emphasis is on older homes, and rates average $48 to $84, but with occasional "inns" going as high as $100.

Washington

PACIFIC BED AND BREAKFAST
701 N.W. 60th Street
Seattle, WA 98107
(phone 206/784-0539)

Features a wide variety of private rooms averaging $40 to $80 a night. "People are usually amazed at what I offer," says founder Irmgard Castleberry, who handles waterfront cabins, private apartments, and full-scale houses located throughout the state, and in Victoria and Vancouver, British Columbia.

NW BED AND BREAKFAST TRAVEL UNLIMITED
610 S.W. Broadway, Suite 606
Portland, OR 97205
(phone 503/243-7616)

Represents 300 to 400 properties up and down the state, and several in neighboring British Columbia, Canada, as well as Washington, California, and Hawaii. Numerous houses charge only $35 to $45 for a double room, to which you'll need to add a one-time usage charge of $5 to the organization. For a one-year membership, including receipt of their comprehensive directory, families pay $20; only

$7.50 (including postage and handling) for the directory alone.

Wyoming

BED AND BREAKFAST ROCKY MOUNTAINS
P.O. Box 804
Colorado Springs, CO 80901
(phone 303/630-3433)

They represent about 20 properties throughout the state, including increasingly popular "bunk 'n' biscuits," homes that ranchers have opened up to augment their incomes. Price range is $25 to $70 per night for a double.

Seven Major Transatlantic Charter Operators

The transatlantic charter is alive and well. Though the number of "players" is sharply diminished, and the period of their operation (May through September) greatly reduced, the survivors are stronger than ever —better financed, more responsible and reliable. And their peak-season product is often your best means of travelling to Europe at a time when the "bucket shops" and "distress merchants" have far fewer scheduled seats to sell at reduced rates (their greatest values are had in the off- and shoulder seasons of the year).

As remarkable as it may seem, some of the charter operators are today government owned, or subsidiaries of large scheduled air carriers. I've selected seven as the most enduring, best operated of the lot:

JET VACATIONS, INC.
888 Seventh Avenue
New York, NY 10106
(phone 212/247-0999, 617/267-0202 in Boston, or toll free 800/JET-0999)

A subsidiary of Air France, it operates Boeing 747 charters between New York and Paris year round ($215 to $269 each way); between New York and Nice, nonstop, from June through September ($269 to $289 each way); between Boston and Paris from June through October ($229 to $269 each way); and between Washington, D.C., and Paris from June through October ($249 to $289 each way).

LTU INTERNATIONAL AIRWAYS
6033 West Century Boulevard, Suite 1000
Los Angeles, CA 90045
(phone toll free 800/888-0200)

It flies from New York to Düsseldorf or Munich ($379 round trip); from Miami to Düsseldorf, Frankfurt, or Munich ($449 round trip); and from Los Angeles and San Francisco to Düsseldorf, Frankfurt, or Munich ($569 round trip). These prices are guaranteed through late Spring of 1988, do not include tax, but do include complimentary movies, beer, and German wine. No advance bookings needed, no minimum stay. Weekly departures or better.

MARTINAIR HOLLAND
1165 Northern Boulevard
Manhasset, NY 11030
(phone 516/627-8711, or toll free 800/847-6677)

A subsidiary of KLM Royal Dutch Airlines. Operates weekly charters to Amsterdam from 13 North American cities, at the following round-trip rates: Baltimore, $388; Boston, $368; Chicago, $538; Cleveland, $498; Detroit, $498; JFK, $378; Los Angeles, $568; Miami, $518; Minneapolis, $538; Newark, $418; San Francisco, $568; Seattle, $548; and Toronto, $519 Canadian. Note that these are minimum round-trip prices, excluding taxes, and subject to high-season surcharges.

CONDOR
875 North Michigan Avenue
Chicago, IL 60611
(phone 312/951-0005)

A subsidiary of Lufthansa, it operates weekly charters to Frankfurt from Chicago, Cleveland, Denver, Detroit, Los Angeles, New York/JFK, Newark, Orlando, San Francisco, Seattle, Tampa, Washington/Baltimore. For reservations, phone DER Tours, Inc., toll free, at 800/782-2424.

DOLLAR STRETCHER
11990 San Vincente Boulevard
Los Angeles, CA 90049
(phone 213/820-3535, or toll free 800/826-6547 in the western states)
or
5750 Major Boulevard
Orlando, FL 32819
(phone 305/345-0064, or toll free 800/223-5430 in Florida)

A British Airways company operating weekly charters from Los Angeles and Orlando to either London or Manchester, at round-trip rates starting at $399 (plus $13 tax).

HOMERIC TOURS
595 Fifth Avenue
New York, NY 10017
(phone 212/753-1100, or toll free 800/223-5570)

A long-established, reputable company operating weekly Boeing 747 charters from New York to Athens, at rates starting at $249 one way, $449 to $499 round trip. Charters generally operate during every month of the year.

COUNCIL CHARTERS
205 East 42nd Street
New York, NY 10017
(phone 212/661-0311, or toll free 800/223-7402)

A subsidiary of the Council on International Educational Exchange, it claims to be America's oldest charter company.

The Ten Best Travel Values of 1988

Venezuela

The collapse of oil prices in 1983 caused a collapse of its currency. Result: what was once among the most expensive countries on earth is now one of the cheapest. In Caracas, and in the two chief seaside resorts—the offshore island of Margarita and the beach-lined Puerto la Cruz–high-quality hotel rooms go for $50 a night, good meals for $5.

Turkey

Always an inexpensive nation for tourism, Turkey is today bursting with new resort hotels and other visitor facilities priced at remarkably low levels; a reversal of formerly hostile government attitudes towards international tourism has lowered a number of barriers and set off a surge of European charter flights to its key areas. Americans should follow their lead.

Quebec City

The most underrated destination in North America, it is a San Francisco-style city of hills and glorious views, perched on a high cliff overlooking the broad St. Lawrence River. In its "old city": period buildings converted to inexpensive tourist-class hotels. Downstairs in most hotels: remarkable restaurants of gourmet level but moderate price.

Belize

The former British Honduras, at the southeast tip of the Yucatan peninsula, it is peaceful, secure, and English-speaking, and yet shunned by most tourists because of its dreaded location: Central America. Visitors who have overcome that mis-impression find superb snorkeling and scuba, Mayan ruins, wildlife, beaches—an undiscovered travel treasure.

"Around South America"

The greatest of air fare bargains is Aeroperu's $745 fare to as many as ten South American capitals in 45 days (they include Rio and Buenos Aires), always via Lima, supplying the basis for a remarkable, multi-city tour of that continent, where "land prices" (hotels, meals) are also unusually low.

Lafayette, Louisiana

The capital of the Cajun country is currently bursting forth into tourist consciousness. Here, Cajun cuisine, music, hospitality, are all available at rock-bottom levels (in an economy depressed by the drop in oil exploration), attracting an increasing number of visitors.

RV Rentals

At current market rates of $90-or-so per day for recreational vehicles sleeping up to six persons, the "rv" now provides the basis for a value-filled vacation, but by rental only, without the need for a substantial purchase commitment.

Cruises, to Anywhere

Provided you buy them at discounted prices from specialist travel agencies—a feat increasingly easy in today's glutted cruiseship market—today's cruise fares for all-inclusive holidays are among the greatest of travel values. Often, a cruise can be had from discount sources for $130 to $150 a day per person, including round-trip air transportation to the embarkation point.

The Republic of Vietnam

Re-opened to American tourism only within the last year, Vietnam's all-inclusive tour prices are substantial ones, but a value nevertheless, considering the extraordinary touring and sightseeing opportunities they offer and the distances covered (Ho Chi Minh City, Hanoi, Danang, Hue, others). Consult the brochures recently issued by Travcoa, Orient Flexi-Pax, Lindblad.

Irish Shopping Weekends

Travelling trans-Atlantic via Aer Lingus to three Irish cities, enjoying two meals daily, quality accommodations for three nights, and all transportation within the country, Irish Shopping Weekends for $499 are now in their third year of operation, and available through most of the fall, winter and spring. See your travel agent.

Photo Credits

Arizona Office of Tourism, *p. 266, 267*
Arizona Historical Society, *p. 180 (bottom)*
Atlanta Convention of Visitors Bureau, *p. 188–189 (center), 189 (right)*
Belgian National Tourist Office, *p. 255, 276, 277, 278, 279*
Mary Bloom, *p. 88, 89, 90, 91*
Margaret Bourke-White, Life Magazine, copyright 1937, 1965, Time Inc., *p. 10–11*
British Tourist Authority, *p. 95, 96, 247, 248*
The Cosanti Foundation, *p. 272–273, 274, 275*
Elderhostel, Inc., *p. 199, 200, 201, 215 (collage center), 218*
Exploration Cruise Lines photos: by Tim Thompson, ECL 184, *p. 154 (top)* by John Mann, #C-125, *p. 154 (bottom)*
Farm and Ranch Vacations, Inc., *p. 31 (right)*

Jess Fuller, *p. 56, 59*
Georgia Dept. of Industry and Trade, Tourist Division, *p. 188 (left center)*
Grace/SYGMA, *p. 60*
The Handbook of Early Advertising Art by Clarence Hornung, Dover Publications Inc., *p. 54, 64–69, 101, 176 (top), 179, 180 (top), 181 (bottom right), 184–186, 187 (bottom), 250, 251, 302, 303, 328, 329*
Jack Hollingsworth Prods., *p. 30, 31 (left)*
Lynn Johnson, *p. 32*
Journeys International: by Dick Salisbury, *p. 48;* by Will Weber, *p. 50, 51*
Wolfgang Kaehler/Society Expeditions, *p. 111, 112–113*
Kripalu Center, Lenox, MA, *p. 74 (bottom), 75 (bottom center), 76 (top right), 77*
Kripalu Center, Sumneytown, PA, *p. 75 (right), 76 (bottom right)*

Joyce Rogers Lyke, *p. 84, 85, 86–87*
Massachusetts Division of Tourism, *p. 187*
Denise Mitten, *p. 57, 58*
Jo-Ann Moss, *p. 3, 41, 43*
Mt. Mansfield at Stowe, VT, *p. 317*
The Newark Star Ledger, *p. 136*
Nova Scotia Tourism, *p. 165*
Ray Pfortner/Peter Arnold Inc., *p. 23, 24*
Marc Rosenthal, *p. 2, 12, 121, 135, 149, 172, 293, 327*
Senior Vacation Hotels of Florida, *p. 202, 222, 223*
Society Expeditions, *p. 110, 111*
Jose Venturelli, *p. 7*
Vermont Bicycle Touring: by B. Burgess, *p. 52 (left);* by J. Freidin, *p. 52–53 (center)*

Acknowledgments

My thanks to the following individuals and organizations for their kind assistance:
Academy International Travel Service Inc.
Adirondack Balloon Flights
Adventure Tours (Cambridge, MA)
Aero Tours International
Air France
American-Canadian Lines
American Leisure Industries Inc.
American Heritage
American President Lines Ltd.
American Youth Hostels Inc.
Amity Tours
Ananda Yoga Retreat
BBC Enterprises
Bed and Breakfast Reservation Services World Wide
Bonaire Government Information Office
Borrobol Birding
Brazilian Government Trade Bureau
Camp Alaska Tours
Centre For Alternative Technology
Center For Responsible Tourism
Clipper Cruise Lines
China Passage
Columbus Line Freighter Cruises (Ruth Benson Assoc. Inc.)
Contours Magazine
Copthorne Hotels
Costa Rica National Tourist Bureau
Costa Rica Expeditions
Country Cycling Tours
The Cuckoo Clock Manufacturing Co.
Danish Tourist Board
Earthwatch
East/West Foundation
Entertainment Publications Inc.
Esalen Institute
Escuela Salmantina de Estudios

EXPRINTER
Foundation For Feedback Learning
Franzus Co.
Free Spirit Magazine
Freighter World Cruises
The Friendship Force
German National Tourist Office
Goushā
Grand Circle Travel Inc.
Grand Hyatt New York
Greater Boston Convention & Visitors Bureau
Greater New Orleans Tourist and Convention Commission Inc.
Habitat For Humanity
Harper's Monthly
Hell's Gate Raft Trips
Himalayan Travel Inc.
Holiday Inns Inc.-Hotel Group
Holland America Lines
International Bicycle Tours
In-Tourist
The Italian Cultural Institute
Kimura Industries U.S.A.
Jacqueline Lebenthal
Living Springs of Putnam Valley, NY
Maho Bay Camps
Mallory Factor
Mary Mac's, Ltd.
Mexico Study Groups
Mid-Lakes Navigation Co., Ltd.
Migration Today Magazine
Nashville Tourist Development
Ms. Elizabeth Nebehay
New Experimental College
New Internationalist Magazine
New Orleans Tourist and Convention Commission Inc.
New York Public Library Picture Collection

Organisation Fur Internationale Kontakte
Overseas Adventure Tours
Passages Unlimited Inc.
Passenger Stop Travel Accessories
Pritikin Center
Products Finishing Corp.
Saga Holidays
Salen Lindblad Cruising
Sante International
Barbara Scott
Servas
Singleworld Cruises & Tours
Sivananda
The Smithsonian Museum
SPA-FINDERS
Specialty Travel Index
Sri Lanka Tourist Board
Swan Helennic Organization
Swedish Tourist Board
Tower Air
TRANET (Rangely, ME)
Travel and Leisure World Club, Inc.
The Travel Store
Traveller's Society
Trek America/Trek Europa
Vega Study Center
Turtle Tours
Vermont Country Cyclers
The Village Voice
Volunteers For Israel
Wilderness Travel (Berkeley, CA)
Wildwood
Womantrek
Womanship
Woodswoman
World Council of Churches
World Fellowship Center
Yugotours
Zelco Industries Inc.
Anna Zuckerman

NOTE: Portions of this book have appeared before in syndicated form.

Index

A-1 International Courier, 137
AARP (American Association of Retired Persons) Travel Service, 195, 198, 199, 204
Abano spa, 73
Above the Clouds Trekking, 38
Access International, Ltd., 120, 336
Adapters and converters, 309
Advance-purchase fares, 125
Adventists: see Seventh Day Adventists vacations
Adventure Center, 21
Adventure Guides, Inc., 301
Adventures for Women, 59
Adventures on Call, Inc., 339
Adventure travel, 21, 217
Advisory List of International Educational Travel and Exchange Programs, 286
Aegis, 89
AeroTours International, 196–7
Aihara, Herman, 78
Air Facilities couriers, 137
Air fares: advance purchase, 125; "back-haul" transatlantic, 133; bargain, 116–37; bucket shops, 116–23, 131–2; charter flights, 131; cheap airlines, 128, 130; cheapest, 129; courier, 134–7; domestic, 124–9; "free," 134–7, 326–33; MaxSaver, 128; senior citizen discounts, 220–1; Super-Savers, 221; transatlantic, 130–3; tricks, 128–9; Ultra Savers, 128
Air Malta, 261
Airport food, 14
Alarm clock, travel, 307
Alaska Bed and Breakfast, 353
Alaska camping, 302–3
Alaska Women of the Wilderness, 59
Albuquerque, New Mexico, 180
Alive Polarity, 77
All Advertising, Inc., 291
Alliance Française de Paris, 24, 102–3, 239
Allied Tours tour escorts, 326–7
All Unique Travel, 337
Alternative bus companies, 33
Alternative communities: see Utopian communities
Alternative medicine: see European spas
M/S *Ambassador*, 315
American Adventures, Inc., 51
American Association of Retired Persons: see AARP Travel Service
American Bed & Breakfast Association, 288
American-Canadian Line, Inc., 153
American Express tour escorts, 326, 332
American Field Service, 286
American Gypsy bus company, 33
American President freighter line,

146
American Society of Travel Agents (A.S.T.A.), 5, 117, 119
American Tour Management Institute, 328, 332
American vacation time, 2–5
American Youth Hostels, Inc., 55, 218–19, 226–7
America's Co-host Bed and Breakfast, 353
Amish Acres, 355
Ananda Ashram, 76
Ananda World Brotherhood Village, 77
Ananda Yoga Retreat, 76
Angel Fire, New Mexico, 181
Anniversary Tours, 26, 46–7
Antigua Tourist Office, 159
Apex Travel, Inc., 337
Appletree commune, 68
Archeological expeditions: see Earthwatch
Arcosanti, Arizona, 272–5
Arizona, 266–7
Arizona Office of Tourism, 267
Around the World in 80 Tapes, 303
Arrow to the Sun, 55
Ashrams, 74–7
Aslan, Ana, 72
Aslavital, 72
Association for World Education, 25
A.T. ("Appropriate Technology" or "Alternative Technology"), 295–6
At Home Country Holidays, 243–5
At Home in England and Scotland, Inc., 245
Atlanta historic sites, 187–9
Atlanta Hospitality, 354
Austin House, 307–8
Austrian Institute, 239
Auto rental: see Car-rental companies
Avia Travel, 158
Away to Discover, 19
Azerbaidzhan, 302

B & B Hawaii, 271
B & B of the Florida Keys, Inc., 354
B & B Suncoast Accommodations, 354
Bachelor Party Tours, 300
"Back-haul" transatlantic fares, 133
Backroads, 28
Backroads Bicycle Tours, 55
Balneotherapy, 71
Bargain air fares, 116–37
Bartered reservations, 291
Bateson, Gregory, 84
Battle Creek (Michigan) Sanatorium, 233
Baxamed Institute for Revitalization, 71–2
Beachfront travel, 22–3
Beau Rivage hotel (Lausanne)

budget rooms, 312
Beckham Travel, 330
Bed and Breakfast Associates Bay Colony, Ltd., 355
Bed and Breakfast Cambridge & Greater Boston, 355
Bed and Breakfast Downeast, Ltd., 355
Bed-and-breakfast facilities (U.S.), 178–9, 353–8
Bed and Breakfast Hawaii, 354
Bed and Breakfast Host Homes of Tennessee, Inc., 357–8
Bed and Breakfast in Arizona, 353
Bed and Breakfast International (San Francisco), 353
Bed and Breakfast, Ltd., 356
Bed and Breakfast Ltd. of D.C., 354
Bed and Breakfast of Chicago, Inc., 354
Bed and Breakfast of Delaware, 354
Bed and Breakfast of Iowa, 355
Bed and Breakfast of New Jersey, Inc., 356
Bed and Breakfast of Oregon, 357
Bed and Breakfast of Philadelphia, 357
Bed and Breakfast of Rhode Island, 357
Bed and Breakfast of Southeast Pennsylvania, 357
Bed-and-breakfast reservations organizations, 353–8
Bed and Breakfast Rocky Mountains, 353–4, 356, 358
Bed and Breakfast Texas Style, Inc., 358
Bed and Breakfast U.S.A., Ltd., 356
Bee Kalt Travel, Inc., 344
Belgian National Tourist Office, 262
Belgium, 261–2
M/V *Belorussiya*, 302
Bensonhouse of Richmond, Inc., 358
Bicycle tours, 26, 28, 52–5
Bidwells, 249
Billings, Montana historic sites, 189–90
Biological and wilderness travel, 23–4, 37–8
Biological Journeys, 23
Biotonus Bon Port Clinic, 71, 72
Blaustein, Miriam, 226
Blitz World Cruise Center, Inc., 343
Bonaire, 258–9
Bonaire Government Information Office, 259
Book light, 308
Bordas, Bonnie, 58
Boston, Massachusetts, historic sites, 186–7
Boston subway ride, 160
Branson, Missouri, 182
Breitenbush community, 69

Briar Rabbit bus company, 33
Britain's Production Engineering Research Association (PERA), 249
Britain's Robotics Center, 249
British Clothing Industry Association, 251
British Council, 239
British Isles: homestays, 242–5; industrial tours, 246–51
British Leyland Cars, Ltd., 249
British summer courses, 97
British Textile Confederation, 251
British Tourist Authority, 251
Bruges, Belgium, 276–9
Bucket shops: see Discount travel agencies
Budget motels (U.S.), 176
Buenos Aires, as cheap destination, 164
Bulgarian Youth Folk Dance Tour, 47
Bureau Internationale du Tourisme Sociale, 10
Bus travel, foam rubber, 33
Butterfield & Robinson, 54

Calculator (travel), 310
California Gold Rush historic site, 191
Call, Jan, 79
Cambridge Science Park, 248–9
Cambridge University study vacation, 94–7
CampAlaska Tours, 303
Camp Lenox, 89
Canaling in America, 301
Cancellation of flights, 14–15
"Capacity controls," 126
Cape Canaveral, Florida, 185
Caporale, Antonio, 72
Captain's Table, 343
Careers in travel, 321–33
Cargo liners: see Freighter cruises
Carnival Cruise Lines, 140
Car-rental companies (U.S.), 177
Carter, Jimmy, 19, 60–1
Car travel: see Motoring through the U.S.A.
Casa Nicaragüense de Español, 26, 283
Cashback, 341
Casio World Timer Alarm, 307
Cassettes, tape, 178
Cast freighter line, 144
Center for Responsible Tourism, 8
Centre for Alternative Technology (Britain), 80–3, 263
Centro Culturale per Stranieri, 103, 104
CET (China Educational Tours), 26
Challenge Air, 128, 298
Charlotte Bed and Breakfast, Inc., 356–7
Charter flights for transatlantic fares, 131, 359
"Cheap airlines," 128, 130
Cheap destinations, 162–5, 314

Cheapest of everything, 157–73; air fares, 128; all-you-can-eat cafeteria, 160–1; cruise, 160, 300; destinations, 162–5; discount books, 166–7; good-quality major-city hotels, 160; gourmet feast, 159–60; high-fashion clothing, 159; hotel bargains, 170–3; major sightseeing attractions, 158; one-way air fare, 158; opera, 160; poor man's spa, 168–9; public transportation, 160; round-the-world air fare, 158; second night free, 167–8; shoe store, 160; sit-down restaurant, 161; subway, 160; transatlantic ocean crossing, 159; travel secrets, 166–9
Children's theme parks, 178
Chimayo, New Mexico, 181
China Passage/Asia Passage, 28, 55
China Travel Service, 160
China travel specialists, 26
C.I.E.E., 351
Cimarron, New Mexico, 181
Cinnamon Bay Campgrounds, 23
Cities, American vs. European, 252–5
Citizen Exchange Council, 61
City in the Image of Man, 274
Civil Aeronautics Board, 124
Clearwater Beach, Florida, 185
Climatotherapy, 73
Clinic La Prairie, 71, 72
Clinic Lemana, 71, 72
Clinique Nicolo, 72
Clipper Cruise Line, 154–5
"Club Med" for Seniors, 221–2
"Club Meditation," 75
Coast Consolidators, Inc., 337
Cocoa Beach, Florida, 185
Code of ethics for tourists, 9
Coffee immersion heater, 309
Colegio de España, 105
Collette Tours tour escorts, 326, 332
Colonial Explorer, 154
Columbus freighter line, 144–5
Commander's Palace, 159–60
Communications Development Corp., 291
Communities: *see* Utopian communities
Communities Magazine, 67
Community Travel Service, 337
Comparative Economics Tour, 47
Condor, 359
Congress on Strengthening the Family and the Community, 25
Congress travel, 25
U.S.S. *Constitution*, 186
Continental Airlines, 130–1
Contours (concern for tourism), 6, 9
Converters and adapters, 309
Co-op America, 21
Cooperative camping, 29, 48–51

Cordillera Blanca, as trekking destination, 37
Cosanti Foundation, 275
Cost Less Travel, Inc., 337
Council Charters, 359
Council on International Educational Exchange (C.I.E.E.), 351
Council on Standards for International Educational Travel, 286
Council Travel Offices, 351–2
Country Cycling Tours, 28, 53–4
Country Homes and Castles, 244–5
Courier air fares, 134–7
Cowboy vacations, 300
Credit cards, as conducive to motoring holidays, 178
Crowds, avoiding while motoring, 180–5
Cruise agencies (discount) listing, 343–4
Cruise Market Place, Inc., 343
Cruisemasters, Inc., 343
Cruise Pro, Inc., 142, 343
Cruise Reservations, Inc., 142, 343
Cruise ships: choosing, 148–51; discount, 140–3, 300, 343–4; freighters, 144–7; Soviet, 302; tiny cruise ships, 152–5; Yugoslavia, 153, 314–15
Cruises, Inc., 344
Cruises International, Inc., 343
Cruises of Distinction, Inc., 141–2, 343
Cruises, world's finest value, 302
CSIET, 286
Cultural Center for Foreigners of Florence, 103
Cunard Lines, 155
Custer's Last Stand historic site, 189–90

Danish folk high schools, 98–101
Danish Institute (Det danske Selskab), 239, 240
Dante Alighieri Society, 104
Days Inn organization, 160
Dead Sea resorts, 71, 73
Den Internationale Højshole (International People's College), 99–100
Department of Transportation, 14, 117, 131
Deregulation of air travel, 124–5
Destinations: cheap, 162–5; cities of Central Mexico, 163–4; new, 257–79; Nova Scotia, 165; Orlando, Florida, 162, 185; Portugal, 164; Rio de Janeiro and Buenos Aires, 164; Soviet Union, 164–5
Detergents (travelling), 311
Dickerman, Patricia, 31, 300
Dillard, Elsie, 290–1
Dinorwic Power Station, 250
Discount cruises, 140–3, 300, 343–4
Discount entertainment books,

166–7
Discount travel agencies, 116–23, 131–2, 292; listing, 336–7
Discount Travel International, Inc., 339
"Distress merchants," 120–1, 132–3; listing, 338–40
Division of Tourism, Georgia Department of Industry and Trade, 354
Dollar Stretcher, 359
Domestic air fares, 124–9
Doppelmayr Company (ski lifts), 317
Duff's Famous Smorgasbords, 160
Duluth, Minnesota, 182
Dungeness "A" Nuclear Power Station, 249

Earthwatch, 24, 217
Earthwise, 59
Eastern Europe: as cheap destination, 314; travel specialists in, 26
East Wind Community, 65–6
"Economic" flight cancellations, 14–15
Ecumenical Coalition on Third World Tourism (ECTWT), 6, 9
Educational and study travel, 24–5
Educational trips, 93–112
Education Foundation for Foreign Study, 286
Ehrenheim, Bob, 297
Ein Bokek, 73
Eisenhower, Dwight D., 46
Elderhostel, 25, 198, 200, 201, 204, 216–17, 226–7, 296
"Elsie from England," 290–1
Ely, Minnesota, 184
Embassy Travel Bureau, 344
Encore Travel Club, 167–8
Encounter therapy, 84
English gentry accommodations: *see* British Isles homestays
Entertainment discount books, 166–7
Entertainment Hot Line Travel Club, 339
Entertainment Publications, Inc., 167
Esalen Institute, 84–7
Esplanade Tours, 111
Esther Eder's At Home in England and Scotland, Inc., 242–3, 245
Esther Grossberg Travel, Inc., 142, 343
Ethics in tourism, 6–9
Euro-Asia, Inc., 337
Euro-Bike Tours, 54
Europe: champagne tastes on a beer budget, 312–15
European spas, 70–3
European vs. American cities, 252–5
Europeds, 28
Europe off-season, 312–13

Evergreen Bed & Breakfast Club, 288, 345
Expanding Light, 77
Expedition cruising, 110–13
Experiment in International Living, 20, 286, 350
Exploration Cruise Lines, 153–4
Explorer Starship, 154
Express Discount Travel, 120, 337
Express Fun Travel, Inc., 337
Extended-stay vacations, 194–7

Fairsea, 150
Fairsky, 150
Fairwind, 150
Families in Britain, 349
S/V *Fantome*, 153
Farm & Country Vacations, 300–1
Farm and ranch travel, 30–1
Farm & Ranch Vacations, 31
Far West Tours, International, 54
Feathered Pipe Ranch, 90
Feminist tour operators, 56–9, 217
Findhorn Community, 66
Flight cancellations, 14–15
Flora Hotel (Bucharest), 72
Florida coasts, as uncrowded destination, 184–5
"Florida's Club Med," 221
Florida's Panhandle Coast, 269
Fly/drive U.S. holidays, 177
S/V *Flying Cloud*, 153
Flying for free, 134–7, 326–33
Foam-rubber bus travel, 33
Folk high school (Danish), 24; 98–101
Food: airport, 14; budget sharing, 315; highway access, 179
Forest Farm, Maine, 285
Fort Bragg-Mendocino Coast Chamber of Commerce, 270
Fort Meyers, Florida, 185
Fort Union, New Mexico, 181
Forum Travel International, 55
Foster, Jerry, 202
Foundation for Feedback Learning, 69
Fourth World Movement, 285
Four Winds tour escorts, 326
Franzus Company, Inc., 309
Free air fare: as courier, 134–7; as tour escort, 326–33
Freighter cruises, 144–7
"Freighter Space Advisory," 146–7
Freighter Travel Club of America, 147
Freighter World Cruises, Inc., 146–7
Friendly Force, 19, 60
Friendship May Day Tour, 47
Friendship Tours, 46
Friends in Britain, 349–50
Frommer's favorite destinations, 258–63; Belgium, 261–2; Isle of Bonaire, 258–9; Malta, 260–1; resorts of Silicon Valley, 259–60; Wales, 262–3

Fuller, Millard, 61

Galei Zohar, 73
GATE (Global Awareness Through Experience), 20–1, 45–6, 61
Georgia Department of Industry and Trade, 354
Georgia's "Golden Isles," 268–9
Gerhard's Bicycle Odysseys, 54–5
Gerovital, 72
Getaway Travel, Inc., 337
Giglio, Nick, 67
Glacier Bay Explorer, 154
The Globe, 294, 295
Globetrotters Club, 294–5
Globetrotter's Directory, 294
Globus Gateway/Cosmos tour escorts, 326, 330, 332–3
Goethe House, 105
Goethe Institute, 24, 104, 105, 239
Golden Bear Travel, Inc., 344
Golden Door spa, 73
Golden Gate Youth Hostels, 226
"Golden Travellers Club," 220
Gourmet restaurant, nation's cheapest, 159–60, 303
Graf Airfreight, 137
Grand Circle Travel Club, 215
Grand Circle Travel, Inc., 195, 198, 199–200, 203, 215
Grand Rapids, Minnesota, 184
Greater Fort Walton Beach Chamber of Commerce, 269
Green Pastures Estates, 69
Green Tortoise bus trips, 33
Grey Panthers, 226
Grossman, Michael, 141
Group study tour, 106–9
Guidebooks, motoring, 178

Habitat for Humanity, 60–1
Hadsell, Virginia T., 8
Halbart Express couriers, 137
Handicapped travel facilities, 178
Hannibal, Missouri, 182
Hanson, Steen, 325
Hartland Institute of Health Education, 234
Haulot, Arthur, 10
Hawaii, 271
Hawaii Visitors Bureau, 271
HBF Resorts, 71, 72, 73
Health & Pleasure Tours, 72
Henck, George, 146
Henry Davis trade show, 292–3
Herman, Missouri, 182
Hibbing, Minnesota, 184
Highland Express, 130
Himalayan Travel, Inc., 37, 51
Historic sites: Atlanta, Georgia, 187–9; Billings, Montana, 189–90; Boston, Massachusetts, 186–7; by car, 186–91
Hoffritz Cutlery, Inc., 307
Hojsbro-Holm, Eric, 100
Holland America Cruise Line, 150
Hollyhock Farm, 91
Holmes, Laurie, 245

Holm Woollen Mills, 250–1
Home Exchange International, 347–8
Homeric Tours, 359
Homestay of West Australia, 350
Homestays travel, 32–3; in British Isles, 242–5; organizations for Americans travelling abroad, 349–50; *see also* individual organizations
Homesteading tours, 285
Hospitality exchanges, 288, 297; listing, 345–6
Hostels, 224–7
Host Farms Association, 31
Hotel & Travel Index, 292
Hotel bargains, 170–3; affording luxury, 312–13
Hotel discounts to seniors, 220–2
Hôtel du Cap, 312
Hotel Lot, 73
Hotel representatives, 292

Iberoamerican Cultural Exchange Program, 286
IBIS (Institute for British and Irish Studies), 97
Icelandair, 158
Industrial visits to Britain, 246–52; British Leyland, 249; Cambridge Science Park, 248–9; Dinorwic "Stored Energy" Station, 250; James Pringle Ltd., Holm Woollen Mills, 250; Nuclear Power Stations, 249–50; Robotics Centre, 249; Welsh Plant Breeding Station, 250
INNter Lodging Co-Op, 211, 297, 345
Insta Heat immersion heater, 309
Integrated tourism, 8, 19–21
Intentional communities: *see* Utopian communities
Inter Cultural Travel Services, 32
Interhostel, 296
International Association for Medical Assistance to Travellers (IAMAT), 208
International Association of Physicians for Age Retardation, 72
International Bicycle Tours, 54
International Congress on Educational Facilities, 25
International Congress on Human Resources in Community Development, 25
International congress travel, 25
International Cruise Center, Inc., 302
International Executive Service Corps, 61
International Peoples' College, 99–100
International Student Identity Card, 351
International Student Travel Conference, 351
International Tour Management Institute, 328

International Visitors Information Service, 18
Interservice Home Exchange, Inc., 347
Interstate highway system (U.S.), 176–8
Iron (travel), 308–9
Ischia spa, 73
Island Princess, 149
Israeli Army tour, 288–9
Italian Cultural Institute, 104
"Itty-Bitty-Book Light," 308

James Pringle Ltd., 250
Japan Budget Travel, 336
Jax Fax, 290
Jericho Spa Tours Co., 73
Jet Vacations, Inc., 359
Johnson, Robert, 226
Journal of the Association for World Education, 25
Journeys, 38
Journeys, international, 21
Jurgen, Jens, 216
Just Cruises and Tours, Inc., 142

Kanga tote, 309
Kansas City, Missouri, 181
Kaplan, Fredric, 28
Kellogg breakfast food, 232–3
Kennedy Space Center, 185
Ker and Downey, 40
Kimberley Explorer, 112
Kimura Industries, Inc., 311
Kirk, Ed, 147
Kripalu Center, 75
Kripalu Yoga Ashram, 75
Kushi Foundation, 79
Kushi Institute Summer Camp, 79
Kushi, Michio, 78

L.L. Bean, 307
Lady Diane's, 79
Landry & Kling, Inc., 344
Language schools abroad, 102–5
Last-minute discounts: *see* Distress merchants
Last Minute Travel Club, Inc., 339
Las Vegas, New Mexico, 181
"Le Hol$ter," 307
Leonid Brezhnev, 302
Lewis, Alan E., 203
Liberation Theology movement, 45–6
Life Travel Service, Co. Ltd., 32
Lincoln as a Lawyer historic site, 190–1
Litoral Travel, 72
Live-cell therapy, 71–2
Living Springs Retreat, 233, 234
Loan-a-Home, 347
Loews Reservations, Inc., 292
Loners on Wheels, Inc., 216
Los Gatos, California, 259
Los Guerrilleros shoe store, 160
Love Holidays, 153
LTU International Airways, 359
Luggage cart, 307

Luxurious facilities, affording, 312–13
Lykes freighter line, 145

Machynlleth, Wales, 80–3, 263
McNally, Patricia, 46
Macrobiotic Center of Baltimore, 79
Macrobiotic centers, 78–9
Macrobiotic Summer Conference, 79
McTravel Services, Inc., 341
Magic Petit Towel, 311
Maharajah Travels, 336
Maho Bay Camps, 22–3
Majestic Explorer, 154
Malta, 260–1
Marazul Tours, 282
Marco Polo, 153
Mariah Wilderness Expeditions, 59
Martinair Holland, 359
Marxist Scholar Tour, 47
Mary Mac's, Ltd., 303
Maslow, Abraham, 84
Mature travellers, 193–235: address book, 211; avoiding crowds, 213; discount airfare, 220–1; discount hotels, 220–2; eating, 204; extended-stay vacations, 194–7; hostels, 224–7; jet lag, 206; medical references, 208; packing, 207–8; preparation, 206–7; purchase prices, 208–9; staying calm, 212; tips, 206–13; tour companies for, 198–205; tourist offices, 211–12; travel insurance, 212–13; travelling alone, 214–19; travel options, 220–2; travel products 210–11; *see also* Elderhostel
Maupintour, 326
Maurer, Willy, 71
MaxSaver fares, 128, 221
May, Rollo, 84
Mayflower II, 187
Mayflower tour escorts, 326, 330, 332
MCV, Inc., 303
Medical alternatives: *see* European spas
Mellow, Leatha, 234
Mendocino, California, 270
Meng, Gerhard, 54–5
Mermoz, 149
Mettanokit community, 68–9
Mexican cities as cheap destinations, 163–4
Mexico City metro, 160
Mexico Study Groups, 301
Miami, Florida, 184–5
Mid-Atlantic Summer Camp, 79
Mid-Lakes Navigation Co., 301
Mighty Mini Luggage Cart, 307
Mineral Shipping freighter line, 144
Minneapolis/St. Paul, Minnesota, 182, 264
Minnesota, as uncrowded destina-

tion, 181–2
Minnesota Office of Tourism, 264
Missouri, as uncrowded destina-
    tion, 181–2
Modern Maturity, 204
Moment's Notice, Inc., 338
Money belt, 307–8; can, 308
Money Exchange/Metric Convert-
    er, 310
Montecatini spa, 73
Monterey Peninsula, 260
Moriah Dead Sea Spa, 73
Moriah Gardens, 73
Moscow Marathon Tour, 47
Motels, U.S. budget, 176
Motoring guidebooks, 178
Motoring itineraries away from
    tourists: Florida coasts, 184–5;
    Minnesota, 182–4; Missouri,
    181–2; New Mexico, 180–1
Motoring through the U.S.A.,
    175–91
Mountain Travel, 38
Mount Madonna Center, 283–4
Muktananda Center, 77
Muller, Joachim, 108
Murphy, Michael, 84

Nantucket Clipper, 154
Naples, Florida, 185
Naropa Institute, 90
NASA/Kennedy Space Center, 185
Nashville Convention & Visitor's
    Bureau, 266
Nashville, Tennessee, 265–6
National Industrial Recreation As-
    sociation, 13
Navaran cargo line, 145
Nearing, Scott, 285
Nebehay, Elizabeth, 105
"Neck$afe," 308
Negresco hotel (Nice) budget
    rooms, 312
Nepal: specialists in, 21; as trek-
    king destination 36–7
New Age communities: *see* Utopi-
    an communities
New destinations, 257–79;
    Arcosanti, 272–5; Bruges,
    276–9; Frommer's Favorites,
    258–63; U.S. winter vacations,
    264–71
New Down Adventurers, 59
New England Bed and Breakfast,
    355–6
New Experimental College
    (NEC), 24, 100–1
New Hampshire Bed and Break-
    fast, 356
New Mexico, as uncrowded desti-
    nation, 180–1
New Orleans, 268
Newport Clipper, 154
New Routes, Inc., 59
New World Bed & Breakfast,
    Ltd., 356
NICA (Nuevo Instituto de
    Centroamerica), 282
Nicaragua Network, 26, 283
Nicaragua tour operators, 26,

282–3
Niehans, Paul, 71
Nieuw Amsterdam, 150
Noordam, 150
Nordic Prince, 150
Nova Scotia, as cheap destination,
    165
Now Voyager Freelance Courier,
    137
Nuclear power stations, 249–50
Nutmeg Bed & Breakfast, 354
NW Bed and Breakfast Travel
    Unlimited, 357, 358

Ocean Cruise Lines, 153
Ocean Islander, 153
M/V *Odessa*, 302
Official Travel Video Company,
    303
Off-season in Europe, 312–13
Ohio Valley Bed and Breakfast,
    355
Ohsawa, George, 78
Ojai Foundation, 91
Older Americans: *see* Mature trav-
    ellers
Old West Bed-and-Breakfast, 357
Olson Travelworld, 204, 326, 330
Omega Institute, 87, 88
Open-air beachfront travel, 22–3
Organization for International
    Contacts (Organisation für In-
    ternationale Kontakte) O.I.K.,
    31, 106, 108, 109
Organized walking: *see* Trekking
Orlando, Florida, as cheap desti-
    nation, 162–3, 185
M.T.S. *Orpheus*, 110
Osage Beach, Missouri, 182
Otopeni Sanatorium, 72
Outdoor Vacations for Women
    Over 40, 58–9
Overseas Adventure Travel, 21,
    40, 42–3, 217
Oxford University study vaca-
    tions, 94–7

Pace freighter line, 144
Pacific Bed and Breakfast, 358
Pacific Delight Tours tour escorts,
    326, 330
Pacific Northwest Explorer, 154
Pacific Princess, 149
Palace hotel (Madrid) budget
    rooms, 312
Palm Beach, Florida, 185
Palmetto Bed and Breakfast, Inc.,
    357
Pan Express Travel, Inc., 337
Paquet cruise lines, 149
Paradise Peddalers, 55
Paragon Tours tour escorts, 326
Parents & Children's Tour to the
    German Democratic Republic,
    47
Parker, Jane, 221
Participatory travel: *see* Coopera-
    tive camping
Partners-in-Travel, 215–16, 296–7
Passages, Unlimited, Inc., 198,
    200, 204–5, 216

Passenger Stop, 308, 309, 310, 311
Pearl's Travel Tips, 147
Pennsylvania Travel, Inc., 341
Pen Pal, 203
People's Air Tours, Inc., 120
People to People Denmark, 349
People to People International, 46
People-to-People travel, 18–19
PERA (Production Engineering
    Research Association), 249
Perls, Fritz, 84
Personal growth centers, 84–91
Peru; specialists in, 21; as trek-
    king destination, 37
Pittsburgh Bed and Breakfast,
    Inc., 357
Pogell, Suzanne, 59
Poland Spring Health Institute,
    235
Polish Ocean freighter line, 146
Political travel, 19, 217
Political travel agents, 44–7
S/V *Polynesia*, 153
Poor man's spa, 168
Poor people, vacations for: *see* So-
    cial tourism
Portugal, as cheap destination,
    164, 313
Poverty tours, 284–5
Price wars, 128
Pritikin centers, 228–31
Pritikin Longevity Center, 231
Procaine-based therapies, 71, 72
Products Finishing Cooperation,
    307
Psoriasis treatment, 71, 73
Psychology tours, 283–4
Public affairs travel agent, 44–7

Queen Elizabeth 2 (*QE2*), 148, 151

Rainbow Buses, 33
Raincoat (travel), 310
Rain Dance Rain Boots, 310
Ranch vacations, 30–1
"Rapid lifts" ski resorts, 316–19
Reading light (travel), 308
Rebaters, 341–2
Red River, New Mexico, 181
Regency Cruises, 298, 300
Regent Sea, 300
Regent Star, 300
Reno, Nevada, 271
Reservations: bartered, 291; bed-
    and-breakfast, 353–8
Restaurant, America's cheapest
    high-quality, 303
Restaurant Casa Miguel, 161
Retirement bargains, 194–7
Retirement Explorations, 221
Revolutionary War sites, 186–7
Rio de Janeiro, as cheap destina-
    tion, 164
Ritz Hotel (Lisbon and Paris) bud-
    get rooms, 312
Robert F. Reid and Associates,
    292
Robert Noble Ltd., 251
Robot Development Centre (Brit-
    ain), 249

Rockresorts, 23
Rolf, Ida, 84
Rolla, Missouri, 182
Rosendal-Nielsen, Aage, 101
Rotterdam, 150
Rouveix, André, 72
Royal Agricultural Society of En-
    gland, 251
Royal Caribbean cruise lines, 150
Royal Opera of Stockholm, 160
Royal Princess, 149
Royal Viking Sky, 148
Royal Viking Star, 148
Rue Alésia, 159
Rural Route Tours tour escorts,
    326, 330, 332
Rush Couriers, Inc., 137
RV club, 216

Safaris, 40–3
Safer motoring, 177
Sagafjord, 148
Saga Holidays Club, 215
Saga International Holidays, Ltd.,
    198, 200, 202–3, 215
St. James, Missouri, 182
St. Louis, Missouri, 182
St. Petersburg Beach, Florida,
    185
St. Petersburg, Florida, 185
Salamanca (Spain), 105
Salen-Lindblad Crusing, Inc., 112
Salminter, 105
San Diego, 269–70
Santa Clara County, California,
    259
Santa Cruz, California, 260
Santa Fe, New Mexico, 180–1
Santé International, 70, 72, 73
Satir, Virginia, 84
Savelsberg, Jim and Gayle, 301
Schilling Travel Service, Inc., 19,
    44–5, 217
Schumacher, E.F., 81
Sea & Sail, Inc., 343
Sea Goddess, 155
Second night free, 167
Segale Travel Service, 344
Senior citizens: *see* Mature travel-
    lers
"Senior SAAvers Club," 220
Senior Vacation Hotels of Florida,
    222
September Days Club, 220
Serengheti Plains: *see* Safaris
Servas, 19, 211, 218, 345–6
Seventh Day Adventists vaca-
    tions, 232–5
Sherman's march to the sea his-
    toric site, 187–9
The Ship Shop, 344
The Short Notice Program, 338
Shutz, Will, 84
Silicon Valley resorts, 259–60
"Silver Wings Plus," 220
Singleworld Cruises & Tours, Inc.,
    216, 300
Sirius community, 66–7
Sisters of Charity, 45, 61
Sitmar Cruises, 150

Sivanada Ashrama Vrindavan Yoga Farm, 76
Sivananda Ashram Yoga Ranch, 175–6
Sivananda Ashram Yoga Retreat, 75
Sizewell "A" Nuclear Power Station, 249
Ski resorts, modern facilities, 316–19
"Small Is Beautiful," 80–3
$mart Travellers, Inc., 342
Smithsonian Institution, 159
Smith, Wayne, 60
Sobek Expeditions, Inc., 21, 40, 42, 217
Social Science Institute, 285
Social tourism, 10–13
Società Dante Alighieri, 104
Society Expeditions, 111–12, 140
Society Explorer, 111
Society of British Aerospace Companies, Ltd., 251
Society of Emissaries, 67
Society of Motor Manufacturers, 251
Soleri, Paolo, 272–5
Solidarity travel, 26
Song of America, 150
Song of Norway, 150
Southern Comfort B & B Reservations, 355, 356
Soviet Union: as cheap destination, 164–5, 314; cruise ships, 302; gourmet meals on a budget, 314; travel specialists in, 26
"Spa Finders," 168–9
Spas: European, 70–3; poor man's, 168
Special-interest travel, 31–2
Specialty Travel Index, 324–5
Springer, New Mexico, 181
Springfield, Illinois historic sites, 190
Spur-of-the-Moment Cruises, Inc., 338
Stand-Buys, Ltd., 339
Standby transatlantic fares, 132
STA Travel Group, 352
Steamers, travel, 309
Stelle planned village, 67
Stephens, Peter, 72
Stoddart, Marian, 58
Streamline Steamer, 309
Student Ambassador Programs, 46
Student exchanges, 286–9
Student travel agencies at home and abroad, 351–2
Student Travel Network, 352
Study Abroad Programs Division, Institute of International Education, 97
Study travel, 24–5, 94–7, 106–9, 216–17
Subsidized tourism: *see* Social tourism
Sudo Tours, 336
Summer camp for adults, 289
Summer courses in Britain, 94–7

Sun Holidays, 194–5, 205
Sun International Travel, 336
Sunline Express Holidays, 337
Sun Princess, 149
Sunrise Ranch community, 67
Sun Viking, 150
"Super-Saver" fares, 221
Swami Vishnu Devananda, 76
Swan-Hellenic cruises, 110–11, 140
Sweden's futuristic society, 238–41
Swedish Institute (Svenska Institutet), 239, 240
Swiss Alps, as trekking destination, 37
Swiss Army Knife, 306–7

Tailwind Outfitters, 28
"Taking the waters," 71
Talmage Tours, 328
Tampa, Florida, 185
Tanzania specialists, 21
Taos, New Mexico, 181
Tapes, travel, 303
Tauck Tours, 326, 332
TECHNICA, 283
Theme parks, children's, 178
Thermal cures, 71
"Tiny" cruise ships, 152–5
"Tiny Touch Up" iron, 308
TNT Skypak courier, 136–7
Tobolowsky, Miriam, 216, 219
Toll-free reservations numbers, 178
Top-priced domestic fares, 125
Tortoise Trails, 33
Totebag, extra for travel, 309
Toucan Adventure Tours, Inc., 49, 51
Tour escorts, 326–33
Tour operators, one-person, 324–5
Tours, bicycle, 26, 28, 52–5
Towel, expanding, 311
Tower Air, 131
Tracks, 51
Trafalgar Tours, 205
Trafford Carpets, 251
TRANET (Transnational Network for Appropriate Technologies), 295–6
Trans-am Travel, 336
Transatlantic air fares, 130–3
Transatlantic charter operators, 359
Transoceanic Travel, 337
Transportation to airport, 15
Transvital Center, 71, 72
Travel Agent, 117, 327
Travel agents: choosing, 129; part-time, 322–3; *see also* individual interests
Travel alarm clock, 307
Travel America at Half Price, 167
Travel Broker$, 342
Travel careers, 321–33
Travel Companion Exchange, 216
Travel Company, 343
Travel firms for older Americans, 198–205
Travel iron, 308
Travel jargon, 290–3

Traveller in Maryland, Inc., 355
Travel opportunities for older Americans, 193–235
Travel organizations, largely unknown, 281–303
Travelow International, 336–7
Travel products, 306–11
Travel rain coat, 310
Travel secrets, 166–9; discount entertainment books, 166–7; poor man's spa, 168; second night free, 167
Travel Service, Inc., 336
Travel Store, 309, 310
Travel tips, 305–19
Travel Trade, 327
Travel Weekly, 327
Travel World Leisure Club, 291
Trav L Tips, 147
TravLtips, 147
Trawsfynydd Power Station, 250
Trek America, 29, 49
Trekking, 34–8, 49
Trinse Packets, 311
Truckee, California historic sites, 191
Tully, Gerrie, 70, 72
Turtle, Irma, 324–5
Turtle Tours, 324
21st Century Travel, Inc., 314
Twin Oaks community, 64–5

Uchee Pines, 234–5
Uda, Susan, 244, 245
"Ultimate SuperSavers" airfare, 128
Ultimate Travel Club, 294
"Ultra Savers" airfare, 128
Unitravel, 292
Universita Italiana per Stranieri, 103–4
University for Foreigners of Perugia, 103
University of Salamanca, 105
Unrestricted discount fares, 126
U.S.A., motoring through, 175–91
U.S. Servas Committee: *see* Servas
U.S. winter vacations, 264–71
Utell, Inc., 292
Utility bag, 310
Utopian communities, 64–9

Vacation Exchange Club, 20, 347
Vacation exchange clubs listing, 347–8
Vacation Hotline, 340
Vacation outlet, 336
Vacations to Go, Inc., 339–40
Vacations with a Difference, 33, 218
Vacation time: amount of, 2–5; for low-income people, 12
Vega Study Centers, 78–9
Vermont Bicycle Touring, 28, 53
Vermont Country Cyclers, 53
VFP International Workcamps, 28, 217
Videotapes, 303
Virgin Atlantic, 130

Visiting Friends, Inc., 211, 297, 345
Vistafjord, 148
Volunteers for Israel, 288–9
Von Manteuffel, Britta, 108

Wagon Mound, New Mexico, 181
Wainwright House, 89–90
"Waist$afe," 308
Walden Two, 65
Wales, 80–3, 262–3
Walt Disney World, Florida, 185
Washington, D.C., 267
Water cures, 73
Watrous, New Mexico, 181
Weimar Institute, 234–5
Welcome Strangers Ltd., 245
Welsh Plant Breeding Station, 250
West Tours tour escorts, 326
White Travel Service, Inc., 142, 343
Whole-grain resorts: *see* Macrobiotic centers
Wilderness Expeditions, 23
Wilderness travel, 23–4; *see also* Trekking
Wilderness Travel, 37–8
Wildwood Lifestyle Center and Hospital, 234
Wiles, Peter, 301
Windjammer Barefoot Cruises, 152–3
Wind Over Mountain, 24
Wind Song, 155
Windstar, 155
Windstar Sail Cruises, Ltd., 155
Wineland, Judy, 42
Winter vacations in U.S., 264–71
Wolsey Lodges, 244, 245
Womanship, Inc., 59
Womantrek, 58–9
Women travellers: *see* Feminist tour operators
Woodswoman News, 57, 58
Woodswoman tour operator, 57–8
Workcamp travel, 28, 217, 288–9
World Congress on the Year of Peace, 25
World Courier, 137
World Discoverer, 111
World Fellowship Center, 289
World poverty tours, 284–5
Worldwide Discount Travel Club, Inc., 339
Worldwide Exchange, 347
Wresinski, Josef, 285
Wylfa Nuclear Power Station, 250

M/S *Yankee Trader*, 153
Yoga Farm, 76
Yoga Ranch, 75–6
Yoga Retreat, 75
Yoga retreats, 74–7
Youth for Understanding, 286
Youth hostels: *see* Hostels
Yugoslavia cruises, 153, 314–15
Yugotours, 195–6

Zelco Industries, Inc., 308

About the Author

Arthur Frommer is a graduate of the Yale University Law School, where he was an editor of the Yale Law Journal, and he is a member of the New York Bar. After service with U.S. Army Intelligence at the time of the Korean War, he practiced law in New York City with the firm of the late Adlai Stevenson until the growing demands of travel writing and tour operating required his full attention. He is the author of *Europe on $5 a Day* (now in its 31st yearly edition as *Europe on $30 a Day*, and largest selling travel guide in the United States), guidebooks to Belgium, New York, and Amsterdam, and two books dealing with legal and political subjects. In New York, he is an active trustee of the Community Service Society, the nation's largest and oldest anti-poverty organization. He writes a weekly, nationally syndicated newspaper column on travel and hosts "Arthur Frommer's Almanac of Travel" on the national cable television network, The Travel Channel. He is also the founder of Arthur Frommer Holidays, Inc., one of the nation's leading international tour operators, and lectures widely on travel subjects.

Date_____

FROMMER BOOKS
PRENTICE HALL PRESS
ONE GULF + WESTERN PLAZA
NEW YORK, NY 10023

Friends:

Please send me the books checked below:

FROMMER'S $-A-DAY GUIDES™

(In-depth guides to sightseeing and low-cost tourist accommodations and facilities.)

☐ Europe on $30 a Day $13.95	☐ Ireland on $30 a Day $10.95	☐ South America on $30 a Day $10.95
☐ Australia on $25 a Day $10.95	☐ Israel on $30 & $35 a Day $11.95	☐ Spain and Morocco (plus the Canary
☐ Eastern Europe on $25 a Day $10.95	☐ Mexico on $20 a Day $10.95	Is.) on $40 a Day $10.95
☐ England on $40 a Day $11.95	☐ New Zealand on $40 a Day $10.95	☐ Turkey on $25 a Day $10.95
☐ Greece on $30 a Day $11.95	☐ New York on $50 a Day $10.95	☐ Washington, D.C., & Historic Va. on
☐ Hawaii on $50 a Day $11.95	☐ Scandinavia on $50 a Day $10.95	$40 a Day $11.95
☐ India on $25 a Day $10.95	☐ Scotland and Wales on $40 a Day . . . $11.95	

FROMMER'S DOLLARWISE GUIDES™

(Guides to sightseeing and tourist accommodations and facilities from budget to deluxe, with emphasis on the medium-priced.)

☐ Alaska $12.95	☐ South Pacific $12.95	☐ New England $12.95
☐ Austria & Hungary $11.95	☐ Switzerland & Liechtenstein $12.95	☐ New York State $12.95
☐ Belgium, Holland, Luxembourg $11.95	☐ Bermuda & The Bahamas $11.95	☐ Northwest $11.95
☐ Egypt $11.95	☐ Canada $12.95	☐ Skiing in Europe $12.95
☐ England & Scotland $11.95	☐ Caribbean $13.95	☐ Skiing USA—East $11.95
☐ France $11.95	☐ Cruises (incl. Alaska, Carib, Mex,	☐ Skiing USA—West $11.95
☐ Germany $12.95	Hawaii, Panama, Canada, & US) $12.95	☐ Southeast & New Orleans $11.95
☐ Italy $11.95	☐ California & Las Vegas $11.95	☐ Southwest $11.95
☐ Japan & Hong Kong $12.95	☐ Florida $11.95	☐ Texas $11.95
☐ Portugal (incl. Madeira & the	☐ Mid-Atlantic States $12.95	
Azores) $12.95		

THE ARTHUR FROMMER GUIDES™

(Pocket-size guides to sightseeing and tourist accommodations and facilities in all price ranges.)

☐ Amsterdam/Holland $5.95	☐ Lisbon/Madrid/Costa del Sol $5.95	☐ Orlando/Disney World/EPCOT $5.95
☐ Athens $5.95	☐ London $5.95	☐ Paris $5.95
☐ Atlantic City/Cape May $5.95	☐ Los Angeles $5.95	☐ Philadelphia $5.95
☐ Boston $5.95	☐ Mexico City/Acapulco $5.95	☐ Rome $5.95
☐ Cancún/Cozumel/Yucatán $5.95	☐ Minneapolis/St. Paul $5.95	☐ San Francisco $5.95
☐ Dublin/Ireland $5.95	☐ Montreal/Quebec City $5.95	☐ Washington, D.C. $5.95
☐ Hawaii $5.95	☐ New Orleans $5.95	
☐ Las Vegas $5.95	☐ New York $5.95	

FROMMER'S TOURING GUIDES™

(Color illustrated guides that include walking tours, cultural & historic sites, and other vital travel information.)

☐ Egypt $8.95	☐ London $8.95	☐ Venice $8.95
☐ Florence $8.95	☐ Paris $8.95	

SPECIAL EDITIONS

☐ Arthur Frommer's New World	☐ Marilyn Wood's Wonderful Weekends
of Travel 1988 . . . . $12.95	(NY, Conn, Mass, RI, Vt, NH, NJ, Del,
☐ A Shopper's Guide to the Caribbean . . $12.95	Pa) $11.95
☐ Bed & Breakfast—N. America $8.85	☐ Motorist's Phrase Book (Fr/Ger/Sp) . . $4.95
☐ Guide to Honeymoons (US, Canada,	☐ Swap and Go (Home Exchanging) . . . $10.95
Mexico, & Carib) $12.95	☐ The Candy Apple (NY for Kids) $11.95
☐ How to Beat the High Cost of Travel . . $4.95	☐ Travel Diary and Record Book $5.95
	☐ Where to Stay USA (Lodging from $3
	to $30 a night) $9.95

ORDER NOW!

In U.S. include $1.50 shipping UPS for 1st book; 50¢ ea. add'l book. Outside U.S. $2 and 50¢, respectively.

Enclosed is my check or money order for $_____

NAME _____

ADDRESS _____

CITY _____ STATE _____ ZIP _____